THE MEASUREMENT OF VALUES

THE MEASUREMENT

OF VALUES

By *L. L. THURSTONE*

HE UNIVERSITY OF CHICAGO PRESS

CHICAGO & LONDON

The University of Chicago Press, Chicago 60637
The University of Chicago Press, Ltd., London

© 1959 by The University of Chicago. All rights reserved
Published 1959. Midway Reprint 1974
Printed in the United States of America

International Standard Book Number: 0-226-80114-4
Library of Congress Catalog Card Number: 58-11960

PREFACE

In the spring of 1952 a group of my husband's former graduate students at the University of Chicago proposed to publish a collection of his papers. There were probably two motives behind their plan: first, to honor him by bringing a collection of his papers together in book form and, second, to make available a number of papers which were no longer obtainable except in libraries. Mr. Thurstone was deeply moved by their plans. At almost the same time, the University of Chicago Press spoke to Mr. Thurstone of their interest in publishing such a volume of papers, and the two plans became merged into one.

A selection of papers was made, largely by Mr. Thurstone himself, for inclusion in the volume. They were divided into five sections covering the general topics of learning, test theory, factor analysis, psychophysics, and applications in the behavioral sciences. Plans went along quite smoothly, and the project was announced at a dinner in Mr. Thurstone's honor given in Washington, D.C., in September, 1952, at the time of the meetings of the American Psychological Association.

After coming to the University of North Carolina, Mr. Thurstone prepared informal introductory statements which were to precede each of the five sections of the volume. These have not been altered. The publication of the book was delayed because of numerous technical difficulties and decisions which had to be made about the format of the book. There was, for example, the question whether it should be a lithoprinted volume or whether the papers should be reset in type. To prepare the lithoprinted volume was, of course, a much less expensive solution, but the papers had appeared in journals of such varying typography and page size that it was difficult to plan a satisfactory book.

The principle reason for delay in getting out the volume was, of course, Mr. Thurstone's interest in the new projects in psychological measurement with which he was concerned in the psychometric laboratory at the University of North Carolina. His work habits were always to publish new material as soon as he could, but the collection of papers did not seem to compete with his interest in new experimentation and publication.

In the fall of 1953 the Ford Foundation, through its Committee on the Behavioral Sciences, made a very generous grant to carry out research on psychological measurement and its applications under Mr. Thurstone's direction. This work was going along very smoothly, and one large objective of the study was to prepare a volume of papers on the subjective metric, with studies of its applications in the behavioral sciences. The title of this book, "The Measurement of Value—with Applications in the Behavioral Sciences," was in Mr. Thurstone's notes as the title of the book which he was to prepare under the auspices of the Ford Foundation.

A number of experimental studies were under way in the laboratory at the time of Mr. Thurstone's death, but very little had been written for the new book. There had been an interruption in the work during Mr. Thurstone's visit to the Swedish universities in the spring of 1954. During the academic year 1954–55 he was as active as his health would permit, but work on the volume of the papers was delayed. At the time of his death the Ford Foundation arranged to subsidize the volume of papers in this book. It is of course recognized that the content is not what the book which was planned might have been, but it is the nearest that we can come to it under the circumstances.

The most obvious fault of a book of papers of this sort is that there is overlapping among the papers, a fault which would not have been so serious in a volume written at one time and for one audience. I have not been able to correct this fault.

The reader will also notice that the drawings are reproduced from the original journals. It would have been better if we had had all of Mr. Thurstone's original drawings, because he himself was an excellent draftsman and was very particular about the quality of the drawings and charts in his publications. But these had not been saved, and the decision was made to reproduce the drawings with plates made from the pages of the various journals.

At the same time that I acknowledge the faults of the present volume which I have not been able to correct, I must express my appreciation for the opportunity to publish these papers in collected form and hope that some of my husband's former students and other readers will find the volume useful.

In preparing the papers for publication I have had the assistance of various people in the psychometric laboratory at the University of North Carolina; the University of Chicago Press has been most co-operative and efficient in the publication of the book; and my very sincere thanks are due to the Ford Foundation for making it possible to publish this volume of papers.

THELMA GWINN THURSTONE

CONTENTS

PART I. QUANTITATIVE SCIENCE

1. PSYCHOLOGY AS A QUANTITATIVE RATIONAL SCIENCE 3

PART II. SUBJECTIVE MEASUREMENT

INTRODUCTION 15

2. PSYCHOPHYSICAL ANALYSIS 19

3. A LAW OF COMPARATIVE JUDGMENT 39

4. A MENTAL UNIT OF MEASUREMENT 50

5. EQUALLY OFTEN NOTICED DIFFERENCES 57

6. THREE PSYCHOPHYSICAL LAWS 61

7. THE METHOD OF PAIRED COMPARISONS FOR SOCIAL VALUES . . . 67

8. THE PHI-GAMMA HYPOTHESIS 82

9. FECHNER'S LAW AND THE METHOD OF EQUAL-APPEARING INTERVALS . 92

10. RANK ORDER AS A PSYCHOPHYSICAL METHOD 100

11. STIMULUS DISPERSIONS IN THE METHOD OF CONSTANT STIMULI . . 112

12. THE INDIFFERENCE FUNCTION 123

13. THE PREDICTION OF CHOICE 145

14. AN EXPERIMENT IN THE PREDICTION OF CHOICE 161

15. METHODS OF FOOD-TASTING EXPERIMENTS 170

16. SOME NEW PSYCHOPHYSICAL METHODS 178

17. THE MEASUREMENT OF VALUES 182

18. THE RATIONAL ORIGIN FOR MEASURING SUBJECTIVE VALUES, by L. L. Thurstone and Lyle V. Jones 195

PART III. ATTITUDE MEASUREMENT

INTRODUCTION 213

19. ATTITUDES CAN BE MEASURED 215

20. THE MEASUREMENT OF OPINION 234

21. An Experimental Study of Nationality Preferences 248

22. Theory of Attitude Measurement 266

23. A Scale for Measuring Attitude toward the Movies 282

24. The Measurement of Social Attitudes 287

25. The Measurement of Change in Social Attitude 304

26. Influence of Motion Pictures on Children's Attitudes . . . 309

27. Comment 320

PART 1   QUANTITATIVE SCIENCE

1 PSYCHOLOGY AS A QUANTITATIVE RATIONAL SCIENCE

The purposes of this society are not new, but they represent an emphasis and direction which have not hitherto received major consideration in psychological science. It seems proper that we should devote some share of our first program meeting to a consideration of our main objectives.[1]

Our main purpose is briefly stated in the subtitle of the new journal, *Psychometrika*, namely, to encourage the development of psychology as a quantitative rational science. More briefly, this may be called mathematical psychology. We should justify our emphasis upon quantification and upon rationalization in science, as well as our conception of the fundamental nature of science.

I assume that we are in complete agreement that we cannot suddenly quantify our comprehension of psychological phenomena over their entire range. As psychologists, we are as interested as ever in making exploratory studies of new psychological effects and in discovering hitherto unknown effects. At present, the range of psychological phenomena that can be profitably reduced to mathematical formulation is limited, and it is likely that every man who works on a problem of mathematical psychology will also concern himself with exploratory studies of other problems that are as yet too new for detailed rationalization.

After the discovery of a psychological effect, we naturally turn to the second phase of scientific inquiry, namely, to relate the new effect in a simple descriptive manner to what is already known. In this stage, theories are devised to explain the experimentally known effects, and we try, of course, to make psychological theories less complicated than the effects that are to be explained. In this phase the descriptions of psychological effects are quantified but seldom rationalized. Rough indexes of covariation are in general sufficient. It is not often crucial that certain particular quantities are observed; it is enough to know that one sort of thing is larger than some other, or that one sort of thing tends to be directly or inversely related to something else.

A later phase is that in which theories in a given field are unified in terms of a relatively small number of postulates whose consequences can be de-

[1] Abstract of address by the retiring president of the Psychometric Society at Hanover, N.H., September 4, 1936. Reprinted from *Science*, LXXXV (March 5, 1937), 228–32.

duced by logical considerations. The resulting formulations are submitted to experimental test with the requirement that the functions and the parameters produce meaningful results. This phase of inquiry is much more demanding than the generally descriptive type of work, and consequently many more failures of experimental verification are to be expected.

The mathematical and rigorous treatment of a psychological problem is in no sense a substitute for the exploratory and descriptive types of experimentation. In general, mathematical formulation of a problem can only follow upon the exploratory and descriptive studies by which we first become familiar with the phenomena that call for reduction in more rigorous analysis. The history of science shows exceptions where analytical formulation far preceded experimental knowledge, but these exceptions are not a safe guide for most of us. Most of us will be the more useful by staying close to experimental check. The flights of analytical genius are attended with a risk of error that is proportionate to separation from the laboratory.

Let us mark, then, three differentiable stages of scientific inquiry—exploration, descriptive relation, and rationalization. It is to be noted that every science has problems in each stage of development. No science can be characterized as entirely of one type. In a young science like ours, it is to be expected that most of our work is in the first two phases, but it is encouraging to find that some of our problems can be pushed toward more rigorous treatment.

For the past twelve years I have been trying to introduce quantitative rational theory into psychology. Instead of merely discussing this subject in general terms, I shall describe some attempts to put these ideas into practice.

In building a unifying rational structure for psychophysics, I began by considering a simple table showing the frequency with which each of several stimuli is judged to be stronger than each other stimulus. The first question was, then, to ascertain whether such a table reveals some underlying order or law. I found a few simple postulates that would lock the whole table of experimentally determined proportions. These included a new concept in psychophysics, namely, the discriminal error. The result was the law of comparative judgment. Armed with this law, we can investigate the relations of the several psychophysical methods. For example, the simple method of rank order can be theoretically related to the constant method so that one set of experimental results can be predicted from the other.

An interesting result is that we can ask new questions which we had not thought of before. If the discriminal error is an attribute of each stimulus, what should be the consequences when this value is larger than in the conventional limen determinations? If the analysis is sound, then the so-called psychometric curve should be positively skewed for coarse discrimination. Experimental results on brightness discrimination of rats verified the theory. The new psychophysical concepts are applicable to the measurement of affective values, such as in aesthetics, and to many other forms of cognitive and affective discrimination. These concepts and laws are quantitatively formulated, and they can be tested experimentally. Psychophysical experimentation is no longer limited to those stimuli whose physical magnitudes can be objectively measured.

One of the best possibilities for the development of rational theory in psychology seems to be in the study of learning. It is a matter of very general observation that in certain forms of rote learning the errors are gradually eliminated until a perfect performance is attained. In the descriptive theories of learning occurs the idea that the making of an error has the effect of reducing the probability of its recurrence, and that a successful act tends somehow to augment the probability of its recurrence. In a first approximation to the rationalization of this problem, I assumed that the extent to which we profit by our mistakes is equal to the extent to which we profit by our successes. When these relatively simple psychological ideas are stated symbolically, they take the form of a differential equation whose solution gives a rational equation for the rote-learning function.

Instead of merely fitting a hyperbola with arbitrary parameters to experimentally determined learning records, as I did when I was a student, we are now dealing with an equation whose parameters have meaning in terms of the psychological postulates that the equation represents. The logical manipulation of these postulates leads to some interesting conclusions which must be tested experimentally. Some of these inferences are that the curve for a long rote-learning task should first be positively accelerated and later negatively accelerated. When the task is heterogeneous, the inflection point of the curve should be lower than when the task is homogeneous as to the dispersion of difficulty of its elements. A list of about fifteen such inferences can be drawn from the postulates, and each of them can be tested experimentally. Mr. Gulliksen became interested in this problem, and he has investigated logically the consequences of assuming differential rates at which we profit from success and from error. These hypotheses lead to a different set of inferences which are also subject to experimental check.

When we set down a few psychological postulates in the form of a differential equation, the equation is sometimes looked upon as something mathematical and therefore non-psychological. The equation does not represent a postulate in mathematics. It states a psychological postulate in the concise and universal language of science, namely, mathematics. If the reader does not understand it, he has the same handicap as if the postulate were stated in Russian or in some other language which he can not read. The equation is the statement of a psychological idea.

Every rational formulation of a scientific problem is a challenge to extend its range of application. It should be examined to see what happens when the parameters take limiting values. If the formulation does not make sense at the limiting values, our faith in it must be restricted. By making approximations and adaptations, I arrived at the conclusion that there should be a relatively simple relation between the length of learning time for rote material and the number of items in the lists to be memorized. In fact, the learning time should vary approximately as the 3/2 power of the number of items in the list, irrespective of whether the items are numbers or nonsense syllables. This was an intriguing possibility, and, before setting up separate experiments, I searched for available published data. I found nine experimental studies with data for this problem, including the very complete study by Lyons. In all nine of these studies the 3/2 power law was verified. Some of the subjects learned faster than others, and some of the material was intrinsically more difficult than other material, but all the experiments on rote learning verified the 3/2 power law. This is a psychological uniformity that transcends the particular numerical results in each experiment.

A study has recently come to my attention which is encouraging in the application of quantitative rational theory in the field of animal learning. Mr. and Mrs. L. E. Wiley have applied a rational learning function to the learning records of rats, with the special problem of ascertaining whether each animal can be described in terms of a learning constant for a certain type of maze. The mazes are represented in the experiments in five degrees of difficulty. The experiments were done under the general supervision of Professor Lashley. I have examined the preliminary results, and I find them to be surprisingly close to the rational learning function.

There is one field of psychology in which quantification has been the rule for many years and which should therefore have some appraisal in an outline of the objectives of this society. I am referring to the field of psychological and educational tests in which quantitative and statistical procedures have been taken for granted for several decades. No student of psychology can make even a superficial review of the literature in this field without some elementary knowledge of statistical theory. If we take stock of mental testing in relation to the psychological profession as a whole, I believe we must admit that mental testing does not have so much prestige as some other types of psychological work. There is probably good reason for this circumstance. The majority of students in this field are not expected to master the analytical theory of their subject. Too frequently they learn merely the routine of giving various tests, and college credit is given for memorizing this routine. Perhaps it is significant that there is not a single textbook on the theory of psychological tests, although the book market is full of manuals that limit themselves to the description of tests, the routine for giving them, and verbalized interpretations. With increasing attention to the quantitative logic of psychological measurement, it is quite likely that mental testing will be more favorably regarded among psychologists.

One of the old psychological measurement problems is the quantitative description of mental growth. To draw a physical growth curve for stature or for weight is a relatively simple matter when compared with the difficulties of drawing a mental growth curve. In the physical measurement, we have a unit of measurement in the centimeter scale. The application of calipers and tape to each individual is little more than careful routine. But in the measurement of mental growth there was no yardstick previously available, and there was no mental unit of measurement. The mental age, or the score in an intelligence test, is logically no more than a tag by which the individuals in a group can be arranged in an ordered series, but that is not measurement. To say that A, B, and C have scores or mental ages of five, six, and seven, respectively, does not say anything about the relation between the increment A-B and the increment B-C. To say that a person's score on a mental test is zero does not justify the conclusion that he is of zero intellect. Before the mental growth curve could be drawn, the problem of measuring intellect had to be solved.

An ordered series can be transformed into measurement if the frequency function is known. It has been customary to make this transformation on the assumption that a random sample of children has a Gaussian distribution of intellect at point age, but this assumption has often been questioned because it has not been critically tested until recently. By making this assumption and by allowing only two parameters for each age, to represent mean and dispersion, it was found that there was a linear relation between the absolute variability and the mean test performance for successive age groups. The appearance of this relation led naturally to the definition of an absolute zero of intellect as the value of the mean test performance when variability vanishes. In the nature of the case, variability can not be negative. With these developments and other critical studies of the underlying logic of mental measurement, it is now possible to draw legitimate mental growth functions for the various tests in current use.

Since most available data on psychological tests refer to children of ages five or six and older, there was necessarily a long extrapolation to locate an absolute zero. I have studied similar data for a group of children who were examined monthly or quarterly from birth during the first three years of life. The absolute scaling of these data shows internal consistency. It is of interest to note that the mental growth curve for infants is positively accelerated and that similar studies on older children show the same effect until about eight or nine years of age, after which the mental growth curve is negatively accelerated toward an adult asymptote. One of the most interesting findings concerns the age at which the mental growth curve starts at absolute zero. If we assume that the mental growth curve is continuous below the first month, as it is after that age, then the growth curve starts at absolute zero about four or five months before birth. I have been assured that such a psychological finding is consistent with the normal neurological development of the fetus.

The analytical work of discovering the nature of the abilities involved in psychological tests has been done by Cattell, Thorndike, Spearman, Kelley, and by many others who are turning their interests to these problems. The

recent extension of Spearman's single factor analysis into any number of
dimensions has given a new leverage on this problem, and within a few years
we shall have a much better knowledge about the nature of the abilities that
can be appraised by means of psychological tests.

Factor analysis is a method of scientific exploration that is not limited to
the psychological problem of finding primary abilities. The factorial methods are general, and they can be applied to many different problems that are
logically similar. We start with a population of entities that may be individuals, geographic areas, occasions in time, or anything else that can constitute the members of a population in the sense of this term in statistical
theory. Let each member be known in terms of n attributes. These attributes
may be complex and conventional, and they may be overlapping to an unknown extent. It is assumed that we can ascertain the degree of covariation
of these attributes. By this we mean that those members who have one attribute to a marked extent may tend to have a certain other attribute also,
or the relation may be inverse so that those who have one attribute tend to
be noticeably deficient in another attribute. The intercorrelations of the
attributes constitute the experimental record of the degree of relation between the attributes.

Given a system of more or less related attributes, the factor problem is to
ascertain whether there is some underlying order among them whereby we
may be able to comprehend all the n attributes in terms of a smaller number
of more fundamental or basic attributes. If such an order can be discovered,
and if it can be shown to be unique, then we shall have a very special interest
in ascertaining the nature of the smaller number of primary or basic char-
acters which combine to form the larger number of attributes of the system
as it is known directly in experience. As scientists, we have the faith that the
abilities and personalities of people are not so complex as the total enumera-
tion of attributes that can be listed. We believe that these traits are made up
of a smaller number of primary factors or elements that combine in various
ways to make a long list of traits. It is our ambition to find some of these
elementary abilities and traits. In the mathematical analysis of the problem,
it can be shown that the number of basic factors is the minimum rank of the
correlational matrix with unknown self-correlations.

All scientific work has this in common, that we try to comprehend nature
in the most parsimonious manner. An explanation of a set of phenomena or
of a set of experimental observations gains acceptance only in so far as it
gives us intellectual control or comprehension of a relatively wide variety of
phenomena in terms of a limited number of concepts. The principle of
parsimony is intuitive for anyone who has even slight aptitude for science.
The fundamental motivation of science is the craving for the simplest possible comprehension of nature, and it finds satisfaction in the discovery of the
simplifying uniformities that we call scientific laws.

Mathematics is sometimes regarded as a tool or method that can be applied to psychological problems. It is regarded somehow as co-ordinate with other methods, such as the experimental method and the comparative method. This is just as sensible as it would be to say that theoretical or systematic psychology is a method. The mathematical statement of psychological postulates and the symbolic representation of fundamental concepts in our science is the natural development of systematic or theoretical psychology which concerns itself with the foundations of our science. In testing psychological theories, stated in quantitative form, we may resort to various experimental methods. But it is hardly correct to say that the invention and development of the theories themselves constitute a psychological method. We shall probably have in our field, as in physics, those who find their talent principally in the analytical study of fundamental concepts and theories, and others who find their best talent in the invention of ingenious experiments for testing psychological theory. The development of our science will probably follow the pattern of all science in becoming more and more mathematical as fundamental ideas become more rigorously formulated.

One of the most fruitful ideas that we can give students is that most of the functional relations in nature are continuous. There are exceptions here and there in which critical values appear with sudden discontinuities, but these are exceptions. Lack of faith in the continuity of natural phenomena is one of the principal handicaps of the student who has not acquired the intuitions of science. Our teaching methods are perhaps largely responsible. Instead of teaching students to compare the first, the second, and the third trial of a performance, and the A-group and the B-group in some experiment, we should set up some of our teaching experiments so that the student learns to look for functions rather than discrete comparisons. I shall give a specific example. In studying color vision, the student learns that the maximum saturation of an induced color is produced when the gray value of the background is the same as the gray value of the inducing color. Let this be the object of an experiment with a fixed inducing color. Let the gray value of the background be varied systematically, and let the experimental result be plotted as a continuous curve. It then appears that the maximum saturation of the induced color occurs at the gray value which is equal to that of the inducing color. The student gets the idea that his experiment deals with a functional relation.

We should clarify the distinction between statistics and mathematical psychology. A study can be quantitative without being mathematical. Merely to count noses or the answers in a test or seconds of reaction time or volume of secretion does not make a study either mathematical or scientific. This is not unlike the confusion by which arithmetical labor is sometimes called mathematical. Statistical theory is a branch of logic, and as such it is applicable in all science. If the scientific rationalization of a problem demands a certain relation between parameters or that a certain function should be parabolic or that a certain parameter should have a predetermined value, and if the experimental data have been obtained for testing the hypothesis, then the statistical methods are useful in comparing the agreement between theory and experiment. This is, in fact, the principal usefulness of statistical theory. Hence, a knowledge of statistical theory should be part of the stock in trade of every experimental psychologist.

A crucial matter in the development of a psychological science is the training program for the students who are to build this science. The first requisite is some familiarity with basic science, both physical and biological. Without this familiarity the student can hardly be expected to help in building a new science. If he expects to participate in making psychology a quantitative and a rational science, he must know something about the language of science, namely, mathematics. The most profitable study of mathematics is probably done after it has become motivated by a realization that it does function not merely as an aid or tool that a psychologist can use but as the very language in which he thinks. It has been my experience that some students who are themselves unable to develop a mathematical idea are nevertheless well able to comprehend an essentially mathematical formulation of a psychological problem with its implications and experimental possibilities. Such a student may be more fertile with ideas than one who possesses considerable mathematical skill without the flexibility of mind that is essential in creative scientific work. More fortunate is the student who has all these aptitudes.

We turn now to what I regard as one of the most fundamental issues in psychological science because it concerns the possibility of such a science. We have considered the desirability of advancing as rapidly as possible, and over an increasing range, to the rationalization of mental phenomena. A rational structure for a psychological science will rest on postulates concerning fundamental psychological concepts. But what shall be the nature of these postulates? Are we willing to build a science on psychological postulates, or shall we demand that psychology develop as a branch of each one of several neighboring disciplines?

In searching for basic concepts for psychology, we must be careful lest we borrow terminology that has prestige and forget to pick up also the ideas that belong with it. This leads to a confident glibness with important-sounding words that is not backed by the understanding which the language is intended to convey. It is not unusual to hear the conversationally minded carry on fluently about relativity and the indeterminacy principle in relation to social and psychological matters even when they know nothing about these words in their technical setting. When we use a physiological or neurological manner of talking about psychological phenomena, it is well also to take note whether we really have any physiological ideas that are relevant to our problem. We may be convinced that a phenomenon is mediated by a physiological mechanism, but unless we have some physiological hypothesis concerning it, we might as well use the more direct and less pretentious psychological language.

Some rationalizations are regarded as more basic than others. We should like to have a precise physiological description of just what happens when we recall a nonsense syllable in a learning experiment. We should like it even better if the chemical equations could be written that cover the essential effects of recalling the nonsense syllable. Better still would be a detailed account, in terms of mathematical physics, of the molecular and atomic forces that characterize the recall of the nonsense syllable. In this hierarchy, we should gladly supplement a psychological explanation with one that is more basic. It would be unfortunate if the development of any psychological idea should be restricted because of a compulsion to make it look like physiology or to make it look like sociology.

Psychological theory can be rigorous. There is an erroneous impression among psychologists, as well as among our academic neighbors, that psychological ideas are necessarily loose, verbal, subjective, and unfit for the quantitative analytical treatment of science. This impression is not justified. It is not necessary for us to abandon psychological concepts if we introduce analytical rigor in dealing with these concepts.

In rationalizing several psychological problems, I have been content to build with psychological concepts and postulates, even though I believe that some of them will be rephrased eventually in terms of physiology or chemistry or physics. But it is my conviction that we shall progress better by frankly building in terms of psychological concepts than by merely adopting a terminology and a manner of work which are premature for many psychological problems. It is better to formulate the laws of learning in terms of psychological ideas, and to find them experimentally verified, than to wait until the phenomena of learning can be rationalized in neurological terms. It may be a long time before that happens, even though we have faith that it will happen eventually. It is better to formulate the law of comparative judgment in terms of the discriminal error, which is a psychological concept, than to wait until we shall understand, physiologically, what happens when we say that one vase is more beautiful than another or that one synonym is better than another or even that one gray is darker than another. Even the simplest sensory comparisons are far from rationalized in physiological terms. If we isolate the primary abilities at first psychologically, perhaps we shall aid in their ultimate identification in physiological terms. I should make the plea that we develop psychological science frankly with psychological concepts, except in those cases where physical, chemical, or physiological formulations are available.

In encouraging students to help us build an integrated interpretation of mental phenomena on an experimental foundation, let us remember that a psychological theory is not good simply because it is cleverly mathematical, that an experiment is not good just because it involves ingenious apparatus, and that statistics are merely the means for checking theory with experiment. In the long run we shall be judged in terms of the significance, the fruitfulness, and the self-consistency of the psychological principles that we discover.

PART II   SUBJECTIVE MEASUREMENT

INTRODUCTION

"Psychophysical Analysis" was my first paper in the field of psychophysics, or psychological measurement proper. In my judgment, this is my best contribution to psychology. It probably has more implications for psychological science than any other paper that I have written. The next four papers develop the theme of psychological measurement further without introducing any applications. Perhaps the principal characteristic of the law of comparative judgment is that it is entirely independent of any physical measurement. Its unit of measurement is frankly subjective, and yet it provides formal checks of internal consistency.

For many years it has puzzled me that the methods of subjective measurement have not been popular in psychology in comparison with factor analysis, for example, which has attracted so much interest that no one man even attempts to read the many hundreds of papers that are being written every year in that field. This circumstance seems all the more strange, since the methods of subjective measurement are mathematically simple at the high school level, whereas multiple factor analysis requires some degree of mathematical sophistication at the senior college level for physical science students.

Some friends have suggested that we should call this subject "Psychological Measurement" instead of psychophysics. I should be willing and, in fact, I would prefer this title for what we have been doing in this field, but I have been afraid that such a title would be interpreted to mean mental tests, mental ages, intelligence quotients, test norms, and the prediction of school grades. We ordinarily refer to this subject as test theory. The title "psychophysics" has been unfortunate because it denotes the dead subject of lifted weights and limen determinations and arguments about the best way to compute somebody's limen for lifted weights to many decimals. Graduate students are right when they agree with William James that the psychophysics of his day was, and still is, the dullest part of psychology.

In recent years I have referred to this field as "modern psychophysics" because in teaching it we always start with the classical psychophysical methods, which are then altered to fit the subjective measurement of stimuli which do not have any physically measurable attributes of interest. To make the transformation from the classical limen determination methods to the measurement of social, moral, aesthetic, and other psychological values has required the rewriting of psychophysical logic. More recently I have referred to this subject frankly as "subjective measurement" because we deal with a subjective unit of measurement and with stimuli that are generally acknowledged to have no ordinary physical dimensions.

My own introduction to the interesting problems of the subjective metric came in teaching the classical psychophysical methods when I went to the University of Chicago. Instead of asking students to decide which of two weights seemed to be the heavier, it was more interesting to ask, for example, which of two nationalities they would generally prefer to associate with, or which they would prefer to have their sister marry, or which of two offenses seemed to them to be the more serious. After obtaining the data for such a problem, we tabulated the proportion of subjects who preferred stimulus j to stimulus k. With a complete table of this kind I asked myself if we could write some rational theory that would fit all of the observed proportions. If such a rational theory could be found, and if some of the experimentally observed proportions were erased from the table, we ought to be able to reconstruct the missing proportions by means of the theory.

In dealing with a problem of this kind, the first impulse is to obtain the correlation between a pair of columns and to use a regression equation to fill in the most likely missing entries, but this is an unimaginative thing to do. It leaves us no wiser as to the underlying phenomena because the regression is only an empirical equation. I worked for many months on this problem, longer than I should admit, and finally found the equation of comparative judgment. It is a rational equation that represents a theoretical formulation of the problem. It worked. This solution introduced the concept of the discriminal dispersion which has since been found useful in describing the subjective ambiguity or stability of each stimulus.

The sixth paper deals with the application of the law of comparative judgment to the measurement of social values, namely, the relative seriousness of offenses. There is wide range of application of the new psychophysical theory in the social sciences. The complete freedom from physical measurement in a subjective metric should enable us to deal quantitatively with a wide range of social phenomena that can be studied as science. I did not then anticipate that the subject could be extended even further to the obverse psychophysical problem in the prediction of choice which did not occur to me until about twenty years later.

In teaching the classical psychophysical methods, there was trouble with several current methods. For example, the phi-gamma hypothesis was found to be entirely inconsistent with Weber's law or with any other law in which the limen increases with the stimulus magnitude. Analysis of this inconsistency led to the paper on the phi-gamma hypothesis which was modified so as to be consistent with Weber's law. The discrepancy of phi-gamma was conspicuous with coarse discrimination, and this characteristic has been experimentally verified.

The paper on the indifference function was the outgrowth partly of my sincere belief that economics could and should be an experimental science. I have found that my colleagues in this field are divided on this question. Some of them deny emphatically that economics could be an experimental science, while others welcome the idea. Around 1930 I had many discussions with my friend Henry Schultz, who was a mathematical economist. I was curious as to why he read my psychophysical papers. In our discussions it became apparent that we were interested in different aspects of the same problem. Our discussions were clarified when we considered a three-dimensional model. The two co-ordinates for the base of this model were the amounts of two commodities that were owned by the imaginary subject. The ordinates for the model were measures of utility. If horizontal sections are taken in this model, we have a family of indifference curves, and when vertical sections are taken parallel to the base co-ordinates, we should have Fechner's law. I set up an experiment with one subject to determine whether these relations could be experimentally verified, and the results were quite encouraging. In a current experiment in our laboratory in Chapel Hill we have made an experimental determination of the zero point in a scale of utility with a demonstration that subjective values are additive. I am pretty sure that much economic theory could be experimentally studied in captive populations.

In the next two papers I tried to develop an obverse psychophysical problem. Most of the methods concerned with the subjective metric have for their purpose the allocation of each psychological object to a point in a subjective space which may be unidimensional or multidimensional. When this has been accomplished, we might ask whether it is possible to predict what the subjects will do. This is in a sense an obverse psychophysical problem. I have called it the prediction of choice. As far as the theory is concerned, it matters little whether the objects are people who are candidates for elective office or different brands of canned goods. Even a superficial examination of this problem leads to some curious theorems. It may be assumed that practical politicians have intuitive awareness of some of these results, but it seems equally certain that they would never think of their problems in terms of psychophysical theorems. I doubt whether the pollsters have used these methods so far. It would be an interesting problem for someone to investigate the different systems of preferential balloting as a psychophysical problem.

In the fifteenth paper of this section we have a short summary of new problems in the subjective metric that was presented at a Chicago conference in October, 1953. The main ideas of that report are in improved methods of scaling which are now being investigated in our new psychometric laboratory. In the equation of comparative judgment for a group of subjects, it is assumed that the subjective distribution is normal for each stimulus. For many types of stimuli this assumption is defensible, but for others the assumption is almost certainly not valid. For example, if food preferences are being studied, one can hardly assume that the distribution of subjective values will be normal for artichokes, oysters, or corn bread. The distribution will depend on the selection of the experimental group. The new scaling method assumes merely that when a person repeats his judgments, they will show a normal error distribution on the subjective continuum. When the scaling has been accomplished by this assumption, it becomes a question of fact whether the distribution of subjective values for the experimental population and for each stimulus is normal or skewed or even bimodal. This scaling principle is less restrictive than the usual form of the equation of comparative judgments except in Case 1, which is not ordinarily feasible for practical situations. The equation of comparative judgment will still be used, but it will be applied to individual consistency records.

The sixteenth paper of this section is a general summary of the measurement of values in which I tried to show the diverse implications for research of this fascinating field.

2 PSYCHOPHYSICAL ANALYSIS

The purpose of this paper[1] is to present a new point of view in psychophysics and to trace some of its implications. In the determination of a difference limen, the psychophysical judgment, no matter which of the classical methods is followed, is traditionally considered to be a function of *two* factors, namely, (1) the separation or difference between the two physical stimulus magnitudes, and (2) a discriminatory power measured in terms of sense distances or just noticeable differences. The psychological continuum, no matter what it may be called, is supposedly determined by these just noticeable differences or equal appearing intervals, which are by definition assumed to be equal. The stimulus magnitudes are laid out on this continuum as landmarks, and the psychological separation between them is stated in terms of just noticeable differences or equal appearing intervals.

It will lead to a rather more flexible and illuminating analysis if we start out a little differently. I shall suppose that every psychophysical judgment is mainly conditioned by four factors, namely, the two stimulus magnitudes or the separation between them, the dispersion or variability of the process which identifies the standard stimulus, and the dispersion or variability of the process which identifies the variable stimulus. The present analysis will concern these variables and finally the experimental procedures by which they may be isolated.

At the outset it may be well to make clear some things that will *not* be assumed. I shall not assume that the process by which an organism differentiates between two stimuli is either psychic or physiological. I suppose it must really be either, or perhaps both, but it is indifferent for the present argument whether the processes by which we identify or discriminate grays and loudnesses and handwriting specimens are mental or physiological. Hence this analysis has nothing really to do with any psychological system. I shall try not to disturb the main argument with systematic irrelevances or with my personal notions regarding the psychic or physiological nature of the psychophysical judgment.

Further, I shall not assume that sensations, or whatever the identifying and discriminating functions may be called, are magnitudes. It is not even necessary for the present argument to assume that sensations have intensity.

[1] Reprinted from *American Journal of Psychology*, XXXVIII (1927), 368–89.

They may be as qualitative as you like, without intensity or magnitude, but I shall assume that sensations differ. In other words, the identifying process for red is assumed to be different from that by which we identify or discriminate blue.

A term is needed for that process by which the organism identifies, distinguishes, discriminates, or reacts to stimuli, a term which is innocuous and as noncommittal as possible, because we are not now interested in the nature of the process. "Sensations," or more generally, "subjective conditions," would be good terms, but "physiological states" or "intraorganic conditions" would also be satisfactory. In order to avoid any implications, I shall call the psychological values of psychophysics *discriminal processes*. *The psycho-*

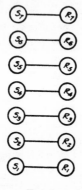

Fig. 1

physical problem concerns, then, the association between a stimulus series and the discriminal processes with which the organism differentiates the stimuli.

In Figure 1 let the circles R_1, R_2, R_3, R_n represent a series of stimuli which constitutes a continuum with regard to any prescribed stimulus attribute. It is not necessary to limit psychophysical analysis to stimuli which have intensity or magnitude as their principal attribute. For example, a series of handwriting specimens may be arranged in a continuum on the basis of general excellence. They would of course arrange themselves in a different continuum if some other attribute were specified, such as size of letters, legibility, coarseness of pen, or what not. Similarly, a series of spectral colors may be arranged in a continuum for discrimination of brightness, chroma, saturation, apparent remoteness from red, or what not. Psychologically, some of these attributes can be measured, while physically the measurement may even be impossible. We are assuming, then, that a series of stimuli has been arranged in a continuum according to any attribute about which one can say "more" or "less" and that psychophysics need not be limited to stimuli which have magnitude or size, such as lifted weights and the brightnesses of grays.

Referring again to Figure 1, suppose that each stimulus in the series has a discriminal process which is a psychic or physiological function of the organism. Thus the stimulus R_5 has a discriminal process S_5 with which the discrimination of the stimulus takes place. These discriminal processes, whatever be their nature, can be labeled only in terms of their corresponding stimuli, so that the discriminal process S_5 is labeled by the stimulus R_5 with which it is associated. In the same manner the other discriminal processes in the series may be labeled by the stimuli which produce them. Naturally the discriminal processes would arrange themselves in a totally different order by changing the attribute of the stimuli by which they are arranged in a continuum. We have then two continua, one for the stimuli and one for the discriminal processes of these stimuli. The stimulus continuum must, of course, be defined in terms of some definite stimulus attribute. The discriminal continuum is a qualitative one which does not necessarily have either magnitude or intensity.

There is, of course, no possibility of recording experimentally in any direct way these discriminal processes that correspond to a series of stimuli. It is possible, however, to make some interesting inferences about the psychological continuum indirectly. The stimuli may be used to designate locations in the psychological scale just as though the stimuli, or their names, were used as tags or landmarks in a continuum which has otherwise no identifying marks or mileposts. It is the relative separations between these landmarks on the qualitative psychological continuum which it is the central problem of psychophysics to survey. In the figure there is no attempt to indicate quantitatively the relative separations between the stimuli or between their psychological correlates. The diagram indicates only that for each of the stimuli in the stimulus continuum one may postulate a discriminal correlate and that these psychological correlates also form a continuum of some kind. Nothing more is known, for the purposes of measurement, about the psychological continuum except that a discrete series of discriminal processes of unknown nature can be used as landmarks along its course and that these processes or landmarks are experimentally controllable or identifiable only in terms of the physical stimuli that produce them.

So far the argument has proceeded as though there were a fixed one-to-one relation between the stimuli and their respective psychological correlates. It may be assumed that this relation is not so fixed as might be indicated by Figure 1. It undoubtedly happens that stimulus R_5, for example, does not always produce the same discriminal process S_5. The present method of psychophysical analysis rests on the assumption that constant and repeated stimuli are not always associated with exactly the same discriminal process but that there is some qualitative fluctuation from one occasion to the next in this process for a given stimulus. This raises an interesting possibility. It might happen, for example, that stimulus R_5 has ordinarily S_5 as its discriminal process but that sometimes the qualitative fluctuations would spread to S_4 or to S_6. It might even happen, although rather seldom, that the stimulus R_5 would have as its process S_3 or S_7. It should be recalled that each of these processes or qualities is identified by that stimulus which most frequently produces it, so that S_4, for example, is habitually associated with R_4 and so on. This is the fundamental idea of the psychophysical analysis of the present paper.

The variability of this connection between the stimulus and its discriminal process works both ways. A given process S_5 would be associated most frequently with R_5 but occasionally also with adjacent and closely similar stimuli in the stimulus continuum, such as R_3, R_4, R_6, R_7. Similarly, the stimulus R_5 can be thought of as most frequently associated with the process or quality S_5 but occasionally with the adjacent qualities, such as S_3, S_4, S_6, S_7. Since the discrimination between stimuli is made in the processes of the psychological continuum, we shall be concerned with the latter of these two regressions, namely, the qualitative fluctuations in the discriminal processes that are associated with a constant and repeated stimulus.

The psychophysical relations may be summarized, so far, in the following propositions.

(1) A series of stimuli R_1, R_2, R_3 ... R_n can be arranged in a continuum, with reference to any prescribed quantitative or qualitative stimulus attribute.

(2) These stimuli are differentiated by processes of the organism of unknown nature, and they are designated S_1, S_2, S_3 ... S_n, respectively. Every stimulus R_k is identified by the organism with the process S_k. These processes may be either psychic or physiological or both. In this discussion they are referred to as the discriminal processes or qualities.

(3) When the discriminal processes S_1 ... S_n are considered in the same serial order as the corresponding stimulus series, they constitute what may be called the discriminal continuum or the psychological continuum. This continuum is the correlate of the already postulated stimulus continuum.

(4) It is assumed that the correspondence $R_n - S_n$ is subject to noticeable fluctuation, so that R_n does not always produce the exact process S_n but sometimes nearly similar processes S_{n+1} or S_{n-1} and sometimes even S_{n+2} or S_{n-2}. It goes without saying that the numerical subscripts are here used to denote qualitative similarity and that no quantitative attributes are thereby necessarily injected into the discriminal processes. This fluctuation among the discriminal processes for a uniform repeated stimulus will be designated the *discriminal dispersion*.

In Figure 2 are represented the two continua, one for the stimulus series and one for the corresponding discriminal processes. Let R_5 be one of the stimuli in the stimulus series. It is assumed that some discriminal process S_5 occurs more frequently with this stimulus than any of the other processes. Hence it is designated the *modal discriminal process* for that stimulus. In this sense S_5 is the modal discriminal process for the stimulus R_5, and so on.

The relative frequencies of the different processes are represented for stimulus R_5 in a rough diagrammatic way. Thus there are three lines connecting R_5 with S_5 to indicate the relation between the stimulus and its modal discriminal process. There are only two lines connecting the adjacent processes with the same stimulus R_5, and this represents the relatively lower frequency of this association. The processes S_3 and S_7 are connected with the same stimulus with only one line to represent relatively infrequent association. Finally, the dotted lines represent in the same manner very infrequent association between the processes so marked and the stimulus R_5. The extreme processes without connection with R_5 represent, then, those processes which are so different from the modal process for R_5 that they never

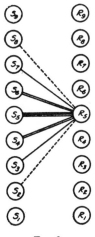

Fig. 2

occur in association with the given stimulus or that such association would take place only under unusual conditions as affected by practice, fatigue, sensory adaptation, successive or simultaneous contrast, and so on.

The simplest and perhaps the most obvious plan for scaling would be to assign linear values to the discriminal processes, with reference to a given stimulus, inversely proportional to the frequencies with which these processes occur with the given stimulus. With R_5 as the given stimulus in Figure 2 the reckoning would start with the corresponding modal process S_5 as an origin or datum. For this stimulus the other processes could be assigned distance values from S_5 inversely proportional to their frequencies of occurrence with the given stimulus. Any plan that might be adopted is subject to experimental test in that the separations between the processes can be scaled with reference to each of the various stimuli. Naturally these scale distances between the processes should remain practically constant, no matter what the stimulus may be, in order to have a valid measuring method. Experimental test shows that the plan just suggested of assigning distance values on the

psychological continuum breaks down. It is found that the separations between the processes do not retain stable values when they are determined for
different stimuli. Therefore some other plan must be adopted.

The normal probability curve has been so generally abused in psychological and educational measurement that one has reason to be fearful of
criticism from the very start in even mentioning it. The only valid justification for bringing in the probability curve in this connection is that its
presence can be experimentally tested. The writer has found experimentally
that the normal probability curve was not applicable for certain stimuli. In
most of the experiments the distributions are reasonably close to normal.

Since the assumption of a normal distribution for the discriminal dispersion can be experimentally verified and limited to those stimulus series
where its reality can be tested, it will be reasonable to make this assumption
subject to verification in every case. The hypothesis can be stated as follows:
*The discriminal dispersion which any given repeated stimulus produces on the
psychological continuum is usually normal. The frequencies with which the
discriminal processes occur for a given stimulus ordinarily describe a normal
distribution when plotted on the psychological continuum as a base.* In experimental practice the procedure is the reverse of this hypothesis because the
frequencies are known first experimentally, and from these frequencies we
construct the psychological continuum. The writer has found in several
studies that the separation between any pair of processes remains practically
constant no matter which of the neighboring stimuli is used as a base for the
calculation. Such is not the case, however, when the separation of any pair of
processes is assigned values directly or inversely proportional to their frequency of occurrence.

In Figure 2, where R_5 is chosen as the stimulus, we should therefore, according to this hypothesis, assign scale values to the various processes as
distances from S_5 as an origin. These distances would be assigned in terms of
the standard deviation of the distribution of process frequencies. There is, of
course, no further unit in terms of which this standard deviation can be expressed. It is itself a unit of measurement because all that we can do with the
psychological continuum is to lay off linear separations between the processes
proportional to their true value, since, so far as we know, there is in the
nature of the case no further absolute unit of measurement for the psychological continuum. But we shall see that it is possible to compare the discriminal dispersions for two stimuli and to determine experimentally the
ratio of any two of these dispersions. *Psychological measurement depends,
then, on the adoption of one of these dispersions as a base and the use of its
standard deviation as a unit of measurement for the psychological continuum
under investigation.*

In Figure 3 let the column of thirteen circles represent so many discriminal
processes, each of them being a modal discriminal process for a stimulus
with the same numerical designation. Two of these thirteen stimuli are indi-

cated in the figure, namely, R_5 and R_7. Suppose that these stimuli are arranged in a continuum according to any prescribed stimulus attribute, and let R_7 be more ambiguous, or less sharply defined, than R_5. An example would be two specimens of handwriting, one of which would be a beautiful but unusual handwriting, or perhaps it might be written in a foreign language, or it might be in German script, which would possibly call forth judgments influenced by prejudice from factors other than those of the handwriting characteristics. If the experiment involves the comparison of loud-

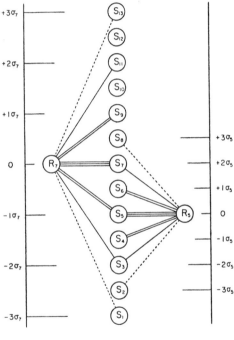

FIG. 3

nesses, a variation of the certainty or ambiguity of judgment for a particular stimulus might be caused by variations in timbre or pitch. Ordinarily, psychophysical experiments are so set up as to avoid, as completely as possible, the introduction of extraneous factors to influence the ambiguity of judgment, and the stimuli are made into as homogeneous a series as may be experimentally possible.

In Figure 3 the two stimuli are represented as differing in the certainty with which they can be judged as to the prescribed attribute for the stimulus continuum, and R_7 is indicated as the more variable or uncertain of the two. The modal discriminal process for R_7 is S_7 as before, and the discriminal processes S_5, S_3, S_1 might be assigned deviation values of 1σ, 2σ, 3σ, respectively, from S_7 as a datum. These deviation values would be assigned on the basis of the frequency with which each of these processes occurs with R_7 as a stimulus. With the same diagrammatic representation let the other processes be assigned their deviation values from S_7 as a base, and let the same processes be assigned frequency-deviation values from S_5 as a base for stimulus R_5. In Figure 3 these hypothetical deviations are given numerical values. Note from the figure that the discriminal process S_5 which is modal for stimulus R_5 has a deviation value of $-1\sigma_7$ for stimulus R_7. Similarly, the discriminal process S_4 has a deviation value of $-1.5\sigma_7$ for stimulus R_7, while it has a deviation value of $-1\sigma_5$ for stimulus R_5. If this analysis is correct, it should happen not infrequently that the stimuli which constitute a continuum according to any prescribed stimulus attribute are subject to varying degrees of dispersion when they are perceived or judged. Some stimuli are probably placed with reference to the prescribed attribute more accurately and consequently with a smaller discriminal or subjective dispersion than other stimuli. It is probably true that this variability of the discriminal dispersion on the psychological continuum is of relatively less serious importance in dealing with strictly homogeneous stimulus series, but it becomes a serious factor in dealing with less conspicuous attributes or with less homogeneous stimulus series, such as handwriting specimens, English compositions, sewing samples, oriental rugs. In measurements of the type known as judgment scales the discriminal dispersion on the psychological continuum becomes one of the unknowns to be determined as well as the scale value of the specimen. Every specimen in such a series presents two unknown values to be determined, namely, the scale value of its modal discriminal process on the psychological continuum and its discriminal dispersion.

Instead of the diagrammatic representation of Figure 3, two normal probability curves may be substituted, subject of course to subsequent experimental verification. This has been done in Figure 4. Here the psychological continuum has been constructed on the hypothesis that the discriminal processes describe a normal distribution when plotted on that continuum. When R_7 and R_5 are presented for a comparative judgment, each of the stimuli produces a discriminal process of some kind, and the certainty of the discrimination may be assumed to be mainly a function of the difference between these two processes. If R_7 happens to be associated with one of the processes at the upper range of its discriminal dispersion and if R_5 happens to be associated with one of the processes at the lower end of its discriminal dispersion, then the discrimination is made with ease and the judgment is correct. If these conditions are reversed so that R_7 has a process slightly below its modal process while R_5 happens to have a process slightly above its modal process, then the two stimuli may even have the same discriminal process, and there would be no possibility of a confident discrimination. Finally, if on some occasion R_7 happens to have a process unusually low in its scale, while R_5 has a process higher in the psychological scale, then the judgment would be made, perhaps even with confidence, that R_5 is greater than R_7, and the judgment would be recorded as incorrect. The discrimination is considered, then, as a function of the *discriminal difference* between the two processes that happen to be associated in the same judgment. By the discriminal difference is meant the linear separation on the psychological continuum between the two processes involved in any particular judgment. It may be designated $S_{7.5}$ or more generally S_{ka}. The discriminal difference is the same as the *sense distance* if we allow that the sense distance for two stimuli fluctuates from one occasion to the next.

If in a long series of experimental judgments it were possible to isolate the two discriminal processes for every judgment and if the separation between

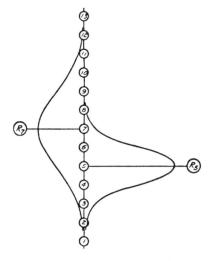

Fig. 4

these two processes for every judgment were recorded, one could tabulate them in the form of a frequency table of discriminal differences. These differences would of course be expressed in terms of some unit of measurement on the psychological continuum. Let the standard stimulus be A and the variable stimulus K. The mean of the distribution of discriminal differences would be the mean or true difference $(S_k - S_a)$, and its standard deviation would be

$$\sigma_{ka} = \sqrt{\sigma_k^2 + \sigma_a^2}$$

on the assumption that deviations from the modal processes for the two stimuli are not correlated. This distribution is represented in Figure 5. The base line of this distribution represents discriminal differences in terms of any desired unit of measurement on the psychological continuum. The mean is $(S_k - S_a)$ because that is the difference between the two modal processes. The origin represents a difference of zero. This would occur when the two stimuli happen to be associated with the same discriminal process, in which case there is no discrimination possible. The points to the right of the origin on the base line represent positive values for the differences S_{k-a} in which R_k has a process higher in the scale than R_a. Similarly, the points to the left of the origin represent negative values for the discriminal difference S_{k-a} in which R_k happens to have a process lower in the psychological scale than R_a. It should be recalled that S_{k-a} or S_{ka} represents the sense distance between two stimuli on any particular occasion, whereas $S_k - S_a$ represents the mean sense distance for several hundred judgments, and it is in scale construction called the "true" sense distance or scale distance between the two stimuli.

For the present it will simplify analysis to assume that any discriminal difference, no matter how small, is directly reflected in the judgment. A correction may be inserted for this approximation by which a *discriminal differ-*

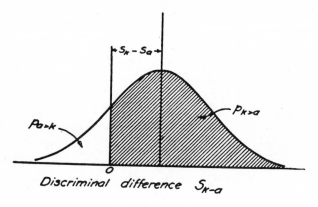

$$S_k - S_a$$

$P_{a>k}$

$P_{k>a}$

0

Discriminal difference S_{k-a}

FIG. 5

ence limen can be calculated, but this correction will not seriously alter the results. It may be assumed for the present that all positive discriminal differences, S_{k-a}, result in the judgment "R_k greater than R_a" and that all negative discriminal differences result in the judgment "R_a greater than R_k." If the two paired stimuli are presented N times, there will of course be observed N discriminal differences, and their expected distribution is represented in Figure 5. The shaded portion of that figure represents the expected proportion of judgments "R_k greater than R_a," and these judgments would be correct if K is higher than A. The unshaded portion of the surface represents the expected proportion of judgments "R_a greater than R_k." The proportion of correct judgments will of course increase if the two stimuli are chosen farther apart. Also, the proportion of correct judgments will increase if stimuli are chosen with smaller discriminal dispersions. If the shaded area is greater than $N/2$, it represents correct judgments. If it is less than $N/2$, it represents the proportion of incorrect judgments.

A discriminal difference, S_{k-a}, is not necessarily a magnitude. It is a pair of processes, a pair of qualities. The only way in which numerical value is assigned to it is by placing each of these processes on a measured continuum by means of the frequency with which each of them is associated with the same stimulus. The difference between these two assigned linear values is the discriminal difference, S_{k-a}. The scale distance, $S_k - S_a$, can be defined as the most common discriminal difference, S_{k-a}.

At this point we have arrived at a measure which can be experimentally verified. By the method of constant stimuli it is readily possible to ascertain the actual proportion of judgments "R_7 greater than R_5" for the two stimuli. This proportion is a function of four variables, namely, S_7, S_5, σ_7, σ_5. If there are n stimuli in the stimulus series, there will be $2n$ unknowns to be evaluated, namely, n scale values for the modal discriminal processes and n scale values for the discriminal dispersions. If every stimulus is used in turn as a standard, the number of possible pairs of stimuli will be

$$T = \frac{n\,(n-1)}{2}. \tag{1}$$

Since there is an experimental proportion "a greater than b" for every possible pair of stimuli, it follows that there will be $n(n-1)/2$ observation equations and $2n$ unknowns. One of the modal discriminal processes can be

TABLE 1

Number of Stimuli in the Series, n	Total Number of Unknowns, $2(n-1)$	Number of Observation Equations, $T = n(n-1)/2$
1.........	0	0
2.........	2	1
3.........	4	3
4.........	6	6
5.........	8	10
6.........	10	15
7.........	12	21
8.........	14	28
9.........	16	36
10.........	18	45

chosen as a datum or origin for the psychological scale, and one of the discriminal dispersions can be chosen as a unit of measurement for the construction of a psychological scale. This reduces the number of unknowns to $(2n - 2)$ or $2(n - 1)$.

Table 1 shows, for stimulus series of varying length from 1 to 10, the number of available observation equations and the total number of unknowns. When the stimulus series has less than four stimuli, the number of unknowns is greater than the number of observation equations, and the problem therefore cannot be solved. When there are four stimuli in the series, the number of observation equations exactly equals the total number of unknowns, and the problem can then be solved by simultaneous equations. When the stimulus series has more than four stimuli, there are more observation equations than there are unknowns, and the problem must then be solved by the method of least squares or by some other method of balancing errors of observation.

The fundamental psychophysical equation can then be stated in the following form:

$$S_k - S_a = X_{ka} \sqrt{\sigma_k^2 + \sigma_a^2}, \tag{2}$$

in which S_k and S_a are the two modal scale values on the psychological continuum for the two stimuli R_k and R_a.

X_{ka} is the sigma value for the experimentally observed proportion of judgments "R_k greater than R_a." When these proportions are greater than .50, the stimulus R_k is higher in the psychological continuum than R_a.

σ_k = the discriminal dispersion of R_k on the psychological continuum.

σ_a = the discriminal dispersion of R_a on the psychological continuum.

The assumptions underlying this psychological equation are as follows:

(1) That every stimulus in the stimulus series is associated with a modal discriminal process with which the organism identifies the stimulus for a prescribed attribute.

(2) That the modal discriminal process for any given stimulus retains at least some of its identity even when the stimulus is combined with other stimuli into a single perceptual judgment.

(3) That the modal processes may be arranged in a linear psychological continuum in the same serial or rank order as the corresponding stimulus series.

(4) In addition to arranging the discriminal processes in rank or serial order, *linear separations* between them are assigned on the assumption that the discriminal dispersion for any stimulus is normal on the psychological continuum. This assumption is subject to experimental verification.

(5) That the discriminal deviations for the different stimuli are uncorrelated. This is a fairly safe assumption, but if they are correlated, the psychophysical equation (2) becomes

$$S_k - S_a = X_{ka} \sqrt{\sigma_k^2 + \sigma_a^2 - 2 \cdot r_{ka} \cdot \sigma_k \cdot \sigma_a},$$

in which case the numerical solution becomes unwieldy.

(6) That all positive discriminal differences S_{k-a} give the judgment "$k > a$," that all negative discriminal differences S_{k-a} give the judgment "$k < a$," and that discriminal differences of zero, $S_{k-a} = 0$, are equally distributed between "higher" and "lower" if only two judgments are allowed. This is a close approximation to truth, but a correction can be introduced in terms of a discriminal difference limen for judgments "equal" and "doubtful." This correction is left for a separate paper.

Experimental Procedure for Verifying
Assumed Normality of Discriminal Dispersion

Assumption (4), that the discriminal dispersion for any stimulus is normal on the psychological continuum, may be experimentally tested by ascertaining whether the separation between any two modal processes (sense distance) remains constant no matter which of the stimuli is used as a base. Consider R_k as the base or standard for equation (2). Then the proportion of judgments $k > a$ will be controlled by the relation

$$S_k - S_a = X_{ka} \sqrt{\sigma_k^2 + \sigma_a^2}. \tag{2}$$

Similarly for the proportion of judgments $k > b$,

$$S_k - S_b = X_{kb} \sqrt{\sigma_k^2 + \sigma_b^2}.$$

Subtracting,

$$S_b - S_a = X_{ka} \sqrt{\sigma_k^2 + \sigma_a^2} - X_{kb} \sqrt{\sigma_k^2 + \sigma_b^2}. \tag{3}$$

If the same equation is written with R_l, R_m, R_n as standards, we have

$$S_b - S_a = X_{la} \sqrt{\sigma_l^2 + \sigma_a^2} - X_{lb} \sqrt{\sigma_l^2 + \sigma_b^2}$$

$$= X_{ma} \sqrt{\sigma_m^2 + \sigma_a^2} - X_{mb} \sqrt{\sigma_m^2 + \sigma_b^2}$$

$$= X_{na} \sqrt{\sigma_n^2 + \sigma_a^2} - X_{nb} \sqrt{\sigma_n^2 + \sigma_b^2}.$$

If every separation, such as $S_b - S_a$, remains constant when determined by different stimuli, suc. s R_k, R_l, R_m, R_n, as standards, then internal consistency for the meası ements has been demonstrated, and the validity of assumption (4) is there 𝑜y established. Such internal consistency depends on the nature of the assumed distribution of discriminal processes by which the psychological continuum is constructed.

The point of view that I am describing has many implications bearing on well-known psychophysical principles. One of the conclusions to which the present analysis leads is that Fechner's law and Weber's law are really independent and that it is consequently incorrect to speak of these two laws jointly as "the Weber-Fechner law." Another important conclusion relates to the well-known hypothesis that equally often noticed differences are equal. The present analysis shows that hypothesis is incorrect because it is possible for two differences to *seem unequal* on the average and yet be equally often discriminated. Other implications concern the limitations of the phi-gamma hypothesis in psychophysical experimentation and the distribution of judgments of equality. A few applications of the concept of discriminal dispersion are described below.

Fechner's Law

Fechner's law is usually phrased as follows:

$$S = K \log R,$$

in which S represents sensation intensity, which we have here called scale value. The notation R refers to stimulus intensity or magnitude. It will be noticed that in writing our psychophysical equation nothing has been said about stimulus magnitudes or intensities because of the fact that many stimulus series that are subjected to psychological measurement are not capable of quantitative measurement on their objective side. For example, the relative excellence of a series of handwriting specimens may be measured on a psychological continuum, but the corresponding physical "magnitudes" probably do not exist as a single variable. The physical handwriting specimens cannot be readily measured as to the stimulus variable "excellence."

Fechner's law can be applicable only to those stimulus series in which the attribute which is being judged can also be physically isolated. Then, if the discriminal separations of the psychological continuum are plotted against the physical stimulus attribute and if this plot is logarithmic, Fechner's law is verified.

In many cases there is no possibility of making sure that the physical variable really corresponds to the psychological one. For example, a series of circles can be arranged in a stimulus series in accordance with their diameters. The discriminal experiments may then be carried out with instructions to indicate which of two exposed circles is the larger without specifying further what is meant by larger. The circles would no doubt arrange themselves in the same serial order in the psychological continuum as in the stimulus continuum, so that the two series would have exactly the same rank orders. Now, if we want to verify Fechner's law, we should plot the separations between the modal processes for the circles along the psychological continuum against the corresponding physical stimulus variable. Shall we plot diameters on the base line, or shall we plot areas? These two plans would arrange the stimulus series in the same rank order, but the relation between diameter and area is not linear. Both diameter and area would be physical variables covariant with the apparent bigness of the circles. Now, if Fechner's law is verified for one of these physical variables, it could not possibly be verified for the other because of the non-linear relation of diameter and area. If we should find experimentally that Fechner's law is satisfied by plotting the psychological continuum against the diameters, for example, that would not justify the conclusion that Fechner's law applies. We could artificially force Fechner's law everywhere by merely selecting that particular stimulus variable which does give a logarithmic relation with the psychological continuum. Fortunately, the law has been shown to hold true for many stimulus series in which there is hardly any possibility of an ambiguous stimulus variable, and its universality therefore commands our respect.

Weber's Law as Independent of Fechner's Law

In the present discussion Weber's law is interpreted broadly for the frequently observed relation between the stimulus magnitudes and the scale distances on the psychological continuum. I am not here limiting myself to those particular applications of the law by which it is restricted to sensory intensities. The law is not always verified for sensation intensities, but, on the other hand, I have found it applicable to some other stimulus series that are not sensory intensity magnitudes. The present discussion of Weber's law concerns the functional relation between stimulus magnitudes and psychological scale distances without implying that the law is limited to sensory stimulus intensities.

Weber's law and Fechner's law are often described together, and they are frequently called jointly "the Weber-Fechner law." The two laws are independent, so that either one of them may be applicable without the other being verified for a particular set of data. The two laws must be separately verified for any given set of data.

Weber's law is usually stated as follows: The just noticeable increase of a stimulus is a constant fraction of the stimulus. The term "just noticeable" is ambiguous, so that it is necessary to specify how often a stimulus increase must be correctly noted in order for the stimulus increase to be called "noticeable." This frequency is often placed arbitrarily at 75 per cent of the judgments when two judgments are allowed. Restating Weber's law with this provision so as to remove the ambiguity of the term "just noticeable," we have the following statement of the law: The stimulus increase which is correctly discriminated in 75 per cent of the attempts, when only two judgments "higher "and "lower," or their equivalents, are allowed, is a constant fraction of the stimulus magnitude. With reference to Fechner's law there are two cases under which Weber's law may be verified. In Case 1 Fechner's law is postulated, and in Case 2 it is not postulated.

Case 1.—Let the stimulus magnitude be designated R_a, and let it be increased to the magnitude, R_b, at which separation the two stimuli are correctly discriminated in 75 per cent of the attempts by the constant method and with two judgments allowed. At this separation between the two stimuli our psychophysical equation (2) takes the following form:

$$S_b - S_a = X_{ab} \sqrt{\sigma_a^2 + \sigma_b^2},$$

which, when stated explicitly for the required proportion of 75 per cent judgments "b greater than a," becomes

$$\frac{S_b - S_a}{\sqrt{\sigma_b^2 + \sigma_a^2}} = X_{ab} = 0.674. \tag{4}$$

Weber's law states that any pair of stimuli, R_a and its increased magnitude R_b, corresponding to the two modal processes S_a and S_b in the above equation, are such that the fraction R_b/R_a remains a constant no matter what the absolute magnitudes of the stimuli may be. It is clear from the above equation that the separation between the two stimuli which gives a result of 75 per cent correct judgments is a function not only of the two stimulus magnitudes and their corresponding modal processes but also of the discriminal dispersions for the two stimuli. Weber's law may be verified under Case 1 if an additional condition is satisfied, namely, that the discriminal dispersions are the same for all the stimuli. If the discriminal dispersions are not constant, then it is possible for Fechner's law to be applicable when Weber's is not. If the discriminal dispersions are equal for all the stimuli, then equation (4) may be written as follows:

$$\frac{S_b - S_a}{\sigma \sqrt{2}} = X_{ab} = 0.674 , \qquad (5)$$

and since the discriminal dispersion which is here assumed to be constant may be taken as a unit of measurement on the psychological continuum, we have

$$\frac{S_b - S_a}{\sqrt{2}} = 0.674$$

or

$$S_b - S_a = \sqrt{2} \cdot 0.674 . \qquad (6)$$

This relation is obtained by condition (2) above. But Weber's law states a constant relation in terms of the stimuli. This transformation can be made by Fechner's law as follows:

$$S_a = K \log R_a ,$$

$$S_b = K \log R_b ,$$

$$S_b - S_a = K \left[\log R_b - \log R_a \right] ,$$

$$S_b - S_a = K \log \frac{R_b}{R_a} . \qquad (7)$$

From equations (6) and (7) we have

$$S_b - S_a = \sqrt{2} \cdot 0.674 = K \log \frac{R_b}{R_a}$$

or simply

$$\log \frac{R_b}{R_a} = \text{constant} ,$$

and hence

$$\frac{R_b}{R_a} = \text{constant} ,$$

thus verifying Weber's law. But in order to verify Weber's law under Case 1, it was necessary to make two assumptions, namely, that Fechner's law applies and also that the discriminal dispersions are constant. If stimuli were used of varying degrees of homogeneity or ambiguity, the discriminal dispersions would not be constant, and it would then be possible to discover that Fechner's law is applicable when Weber's law is not.

Case 2.—It is possible for Weber's law to be applicable when Fechner's law is not verified and when the discriminal dispersions are not all equal. This is best illustrated by a short list of stimuli with hypothetical discriminal dispersions. For the purpose of this illustration we can assume any relation between S and R except the logarithmic relation of Fechner's law. Let us tabulate some paired values for S and R such that $S = R^2$. This is clearly, then, a case in which Fechner's law does not apply. In Table 2 the first column identifies the six stimuli in the hypothetical series. Column R designates the stimulus magnitudes. Column S shows the scale values of the corresponding modal processes (sensation intensities). Column σ shows a hypothetical series of discriminal dispersions. By means of the fundamental psychophysical equation (2) it can then be shown that the stimuli 1 and 2

TABLE 2

Stimulus Series	R	$S = R^2$	σ	$P_{(R+1) > R}$
1.........	10.00	100.	20.00	.75
2.........	11.00	121.	23.94	.75
3.........	12.10	146.	29.16	.75
4.........	13.31	177.	35.40	.75
5.........	14.64	215.	43.40	.75
6.........	16.11	259.	51.90	.75

are correctly discriminated in 75 per cent of the judgments, that stimuli 2 and 3 are correctly discriminated in 75 per cent of the judgments, and so on. Since the ratio of each stimulus magnitude to the next lower stimulus magnitude is always 1.10 in this table and since these successive pairs of stimuli are correctly differentiated in 75 per cent of the observations, we conclude that Weber's law has been verified by these hypothetical data. The only new factor that we have introduced is the plausible assumption that the discriminal dispersion may not be constant throughout the whole stimulus range. With an assumed variation in the discriminal dispersion we find that it is logically possible to have a set of data in which Weber's law is verified but in which Fechner's law is not verified. All that is necessary for the discriminal dispersion to vary from one stimulus to another is that the stimuli be unequal in the ambiguity or difficulty with which they are judged, and this surely must happen much more often than we suspect when the stimuli consists in such qualitative values as handwriting specimens or specimens of English composition. It is quite probable that the variation in discriminal dispersion is rather slight and perhaps negligible when the stimulus series is rather homogeneous. A good example of a homogeneous stimulus series is a set of cylinders for the lifted weight experiment in which size, color, texture, shape, and even temperature are ruled out of the experiment by keeping them constant. In such experiments it is probable that the discriminal dispersion stays constant.

Finally, if the discriminal dispersions can be assumed to be equal throughout the whole stimulus range, then Fechner's law and Weber's law become identical. The frequent association of these two laws as though they were always identical depends on the constancy of the discriminal dispersion. It may be expected, in psychophysical experiments with stimuli that are not experimentally kept constant in all but one stimulus variable, that one or two stimuli in the series are more difficult to judge than the rest. In such a case these one or two stimuli will have larger discriminal dispersions than the other stimuli, and the consistency of the psychological continuum is thereby disturbed if these variations are not accounted for in the derivation of the scale values.

Equally Often Noticed Differences Are Not Necessarily Equal

It is usually assumed that equally often noticed differences are equal on the psychological continuum. They are rarely assumed to be equal on the stimulus continuum. It is, however, incorrect to assume that pairs of stimuli are equally distant on the psychological scale even though all the pairs are equally often discriminated. It is not even correct to say that stimulus differences *seem* equal, or that they are subjectively equal, just because the differences are equally often noticed. Two pairs of stimuli may be equally often discriminated, while one of the separations may on the average actually *seem* greater than the other.

Referring again to the psychophysical equation (2), the psychological or *apparent* separation between two stimuli R_a and R_b is expressed by the difference $(S_b - S_a)$, measured on the psychological scale, which is a scale of appearances or impressions. The frequency with which the two stimuli can be discriminated is, however, a function of their respective discriminal dispersions as well as their modal discriminal processes. The separation between the modal processes can also be called the mean sense distance. Here again, if we can assume that the discriminal dispersions are constant, then it is correct to say that equally often noticed differences are psychologically equal, but that assumption should be tested before constructing a psychological continuum or scale by means of this assumption.

A Possible Effect of Practice

It is probable that practice has the effect of reducing the discriminal dispersions and that this may account for the shifts in the proportions of correct judgments in psychophysical experiments. If two stimuli are presented to an unpracticed subject for whom these stimuli have relatively large discriminal dispersions, the denominator of equation (4) will be relatively large while the numerator remains constant. Graphically, the situation can be represented in Figure 5 by increasing the standard deviation of that probability curve while the separation $(S_k - S_a)$ remains constant. This produces a low proportion of correct judgments. With practice, the subject reduces the discriminal dispersions, and this might be represented in Figure 5 by reducing the standard deviation of that curve while the separation between the two modal processes remains constant. The effect is to increase the proportion of correct judgments. Naturally, stable results for the construction of a psychological scale depend on reaching such a practice level that the discriminal dispersions will remain practically constant throughout the experiments. The interpretation of the psychophysical equation in connection with the effect of practice would be that two lights, for example, seem just about as bright to the practiced laboratory subject as to an unpracticed subject. Practice in psychophysical experimentation does not make one of the lights seem brighter or the other one weaker. The two lights retain their same general level of brightness except for sensory adaptation and contrast, which are momentary effects. But there is a practice effect in the capacity to discriminate between the two lights. This is determined by the discriminal dispersion or subjective observational error. Here again, equally often noticed differences are not necessarily equal subjectively or psychologically.

Experimental Test

The simplest experimental procedure for verifying the assumption that the discriminal dispersions are constant for any particular stimulus series is probably to arrange a table showing the proportion of judgments, $P_{a>b}$, for all the possible pairs of stimuli. If there are N stimuli, such a table will contain $N(N-1)$ entries if identical stimuli are not experimentally compared. From such a table the stimuli can readily be arranged in rank order. From the table of proportions of judgments, a corresponding table of sigma values can be prepared. One can then plot a graph for X_{ka} against X_{kb} in which a and b are standards. If the discriminal dispersions are equal through the stimulus series, the graph should give a linear plot with a slope of unity. This may be demonstrated as follows:

If in the psychophysical equation

$$S_k - S_a = X_{ka} \sqrt{\sigma_k^2 + \sigma_a^2} \qquad (2)$$

we assume that the discriminal dispersions are equal, the equation becomes

$$S_k - S_a = X_{ka} \sqrt{2\sigma^2}$$
$$= X_{ka} \cdot \sigma \cdot \sqrt{2} , \qquad (5)$$

and if we use the discriminal dispersion as a unit of measurement on the psychological scale, we have

$$S_k - S_a = X_{ka} \cdot \sqrt{2} . \qquad (6)$$

By symmetry it follows that

$$S_k - S_b = X_{kb} \cdot \sqrt{2} \ . \tag{7}$$

Subtracting and transposing,

$$X_{ka} = X_{kb} + \frac{S_b - S_a}{\sqrt{2}} \ . \tag{8}$$

This equation is in linear form, and if X_{ka} is plotted against X_{kb}, we should have a linear plot. The slope should be unity and

$$Y\text{-intercept} = \frac{S_b - S_a}{\sqrt{2}} \ . \tag{9}$$

If the plot is linear, it proves that the assumed normal distribution of discriminal processes is correct. If the slope is unity, it proves that the discriminal dispersions are equal. It is left for a separate paper to apply this method to educational judgment scale data.

3 A LAW OF COMPARATIVE JUDGMENT

The object of this paper[1] is to describe a new psychophysical law which may be called the *law of comparative judgment* and to show some of its special applications in the measurement of psychological values. The law of comparative judgment is implied in Weber's law and in Fechner's law. The law of comparative judgment is applicable not only to the comparison of physical stimulus intensities but also to qualitative comparative judgments such as those of excellence of specimens in an educational scale, and it has been applied in the measurement of such psychological values as a series of opinions on disputed public issues. The latter application of the law will be illustrated in a forthcoming study. It should be possible also to verify it on comparative judgments which involve simultaneous and successive contrast.

The law has been derived in a previous article, and the present study is mainly a description of some of its applications. Since several new concepts are involved in the formulation of the law, it has been necessary to invent several terms to describe them, and these will be repeated here.

Let us suppose that we are confronted with a series of stimuli or specimens such as a series of gray values, cylindrical weights, handwriting specimens, children's drawings, or any other series of stimuli that are subject to comparison. The first requirement is, of course, a specification as to what it is that we are to judge or compare. It may be gray values or weights or excellence or any other quantitative or qualitative attribute about which we can think "more" or "less" for each specimen. This attribute which may be assigned, as it were, in differing amounts to each specimen defines what we shall call the *psychological continuum* for that particular project in measurement.

As we inspect two or more specimens for the task of comparison, there must be some kind of process in us by which we react differently to the several specimens, by which we identify the several degrees of excellence or weight or gray value in the specimens. You may suit your own predilections in calling this process psychical, neural, chemical, or electrical, but it will be called here in a noncommittal way *the discriminal process* because its ulti-

[1] This is one of a series of articles by members of the Behavior Research Staff of the Illinois Institute for Juvenile Research, Chicago, Herman M. Adler, Director. Series B, No. 107. Reprinted from *Psychological Review*, XXXIV (1927), 273–86.

mate nature does not concern the formulation of the law of comparative judgment. If, then, one handwriting specimen *seems* to be more excellent than a second specimen, then the two discriminal processes of the observer are different, at least on this occasion.

The so-called just noticeable difference is contingent on the fact that an observer is not consistent in his comparative judgments from one occasion to the next. He gives different comparative judgments on successive occasions about the same pair of stimuli. Hence we conclude that the discriminal process corresponding to a given stimulus is not fixed. It fluctuates. For any handwriting specimen, for example, there is one discriminal process that is experienced more often with that specimen than other processes which correspond to higher or lower degrees of excellence. This most common process is called here *the modal discriminal process for the given stimulus*.

The psychological continuum or scale is so constructed or defined that the frequencies of the respective discriminal processes for any given stimulus form a normal distribution on the psychological scale. This involves no assumption of a normal distribution or of anything else. The psychological scale is at best an artificial construct. If it has any physical reality, we certainly have not the remotest idea what it may be like. We do not assume, therefore, that the distribution of discriminal processes is normal on the scale because that would imply that the scale is there already. We *define* the scale in terms of the frequencies of the discriminal processes for any stimulus. This artificial construct, the psychological scale, is so spaced off that the frequencies of the discriminal processes for any given stimulus form a normal distribution on the scale. The separation on the scale between the discriminal process for a given stimulus on any particular occasion and the modal discriminal process for that stimulus we shall call *the discriminal deviation* on that occasion. If on a particular occasion the observer perceives more than the usual degree of excellence or weight in the specimen in question, the discriminal deviation is at that instant positive. In a similar manner the discriminal deviation at another moment will be negative.

The standard deviation of the distribution of discriminal processes on the scale for a particular specimen will be called its *discriminal dispersion*.

This is the central concept in the present analysis. An ambiguous stimulus which is observed at widely different degrees of excellence or weight or gray value on different occasions will have, of course, a large discriminal dispersion. Some other stimulus or specimen which is provocative of relatively slight fluctuations in discriminal processes will have, similarly, a small discriminal dispersion.

The scale difference between the discriminal processes of two specimens which are involved in the same judgment will be called *the discriminal difference* on that occasion. If the two stimuli be denoted *A* and *B* and if the discriminal processes corresponding to them be denoted *a* and *b* on any one occasion, then the discriminal difference will be the scale distance $(a - b)$, which varies, of course, on different occasions. If in one of the comparative judgments A seems to be better than B, then on that occasion the discriminal difference $(a - b)$ is positive. If on another occasion the stimulus B seems to be the better, then on that occasion the discriminal difference $(a - b)$ is negative.

Finally, the scale distance between the modal discriminal processes for any two specimens is the separation which is assigned to the two specimens on the psychological scale. The two specimens are so allocated on the scale that their separation is equal to the separation between their respective modal discriminal processes.

We can now state the law of comparative judgment as follows:

$$S_1 - S_2 = x_{12} \cdot \sqrt{\sigma_1^2 + \sigma_2^2 - 2\,r\,\sigma_1\sigma_2}, \qquad (1)$$

in which

S_1 and S_2 are the psychological scale values of the two compared stimuli.

x_{12} = the sigma value corresponding to the proportion of judgments $p_{1>2}$. When $p_{1>2}$ is greater than .50, the numerical value of x_{12} is positive. When $p_{1>2}$ is less than .50, the numerical value of x_{12} is negative.

σ_1 = discriminal dispersion of stimulus R_1.

σ_2 = discriminal dispersion of stimulus R_2.

r = correlation between the discriminal deviations of R_1 and R_2 in the same judgment.

This law of comparative judgment is basic for all experimental work on Weber's law, Fechner's law, and for all educational and psychological scales in which comparative judgments are involved. Its derivation will not be repeated here because it has been described in a previous article.[2] It applies fundamentally to the judgments of *a single observer* who compares a series of stimuli by the method of paired comparison when no "equal" judgments are allowed. It is a rational equation for the method of constant stimuli. It is assumed that the single observer compares each pair of stimuli a sufficient number of times so that a proportion, $p_{a>b}$, may be determined for each pair of stimuli.

For the practical application of the law of comparative judgment we shall consider five cases which differ in assumptions, approximations, and degree of simplification. The more assumptions we care to make, the simpler will be the observation equations. These five cases are as follows:

Case 1.—The equation can be used in its complete form for paired comparison data obtained from a single subject when only two judgments are allowed for each observation, such as "heavier" or "lighter," "better" or

---

[2] See chap. ii.

"worse," etc. There will be one observation equation for every observed proportion of judgments. It would be written, in its complete form, thus:

$$S_1 - S_2 - x_{12} \cdot \sqrt{\sigma_1^2 + \sigma_2^2 - 2\, r\, \sigma_1 \sigma_2} = 0 \, . \tag{1}$$

According to this equation, every pair of stimuli presents the possibility of a different correlation between the discriminal deviations. If this degree of freedom is allowed, the problem of psychological scaling would be insoluble because every observation equation would introduce a new unknown, and the number of unknowns would then always be greater than the number of observation equations. In order to make the problem soluble, it is necessary to make at least one assumption, namely, that the correlation between discriminal deviations is practically constant throughout the stimulus series and for the single observer. Then, if we have n stimuli or specimens in the scale, we shall have $\frac{1}{2} \cdot n(n - 1)$ observation equations when each specimen is compared with every other specimen. Each specimen has a scale value, S_1, and a discriminal dispersion, σ_1, to be determined. There are therefore $2n$ unknowns. The scale value of one of the specimens is chosen as an origin and its discriminal dispersion as a unit of measurement, while r is an unknown which is assumed to be constant for the whole series. Hence, for a scale of n specimens there will be $(2n - 1)$ unknowns. The smallest number of specimens for which the problem is soluble is five. For such a scale there will be nine unknowns, four scale values, four discriminal dispersions, and r. For a scale of five specimens there will be ten observation equations.

The statement of the law of comparative judgment in the form of equation (1) involves one theoretical assumption which is probably of minor importance. It assumes that all positive discriminal differences $(a - b)$ are judged $A > B$ and that all negative discriminal differences $(a - b)$ are judged $A < B$. This is probably not absolutely correct when the discriminal differences of either sign are very small. The assumption would not affect the experimentally observed proportion $p_{A>B}$ if the small positive discriminal differences occurred as often as the small negative ones. As a matter of fact, when $p_{A>B}$ is greater than .50, the small positive discriminal differences $(a - b)$ are slightly more frequent than the negative perceived differences $(a - b)$. It is probable that rather refined experimental procedures are necessary to isolate this effect. The effect is ignored in our present analysis.

Case 2.—The law of comparative judgment as described under Case 1 refers fundamentally to a series of judgments *of a single observer*. It does not constitute an assumption to say that the discriminal processes for a single observer give a normal frequency distribution on the psychological continuum. That is a part of the definition of the psychological scale. But it does constitute an assumption to take for granted that the various degrees of an attribute of a specimen perceived in it by *a group* of subjects is a normal distribution. For example, if a weight cylinder is lifted by an observer several hundred times in comparison with other cylinders, it is possible to define or construct the psychological scale so that the distribution of the apparent weights of the cylinder for the single observer is normal. It is probably safe to assume that the distribution of apparent weights for *a group* of subjects, each subject perceiving the weight only once, is also normal on the same scale. To transfer the reasoning in the same way from a single observer to a group of observers for specimens such as handwriting or English composition is not so certain. For practical purposes it may be assumed that when *a group* of observers perceives a specimen of handwriting, the distribution of excellence that they read into the specimen is normal on the psychological continuum of perceived excellence. At least this is a safe assumption if the group is not split in some curious way with prejudices for or against particular elements of the specimen.

With the assumption just described, the law of comparative judgment, derived for the method of constant stimuli with two responses, can be extended to data collected from a group of judges in which each judge compares each stimulus with every other stimulus only once. The other assumptions of Case 1 apply also to Case 2.

Case 3.—Equation (1) is awkward to handle as an observation equation for a scale with a large number of specimens. In fact, the arithmetical labor of constructing an educational or psychological scale with it is almost prohibitive. The equation can be simplified if the correlation r can be assumed to be either zero or unity. It is a safe assumption that when the stimulus series is very homogeneous with no distracting attributes, the correlation between discriminal deviations is low and possibly even zero unless we encounter the effect of simultaneous or successive contrast. If we accept the correlation as zero, we are really assuming that the degree of excellence which an observer perceives in one of the specimens has no influence on the degree of excellence that he perceives in the comparison specimen. There are two effects that may be operative here and which are antagonistic to each other.

(1) If you look at two handwriting specimens in a mood slightly more generous and tolerant than ordinarily, you may perceive a degree of excellence in specimen A a little higher than its mean excellence. But at the same moment specimen B is also judged a little higher than its average or mean excellence for the same reason. To the extent that such a factor is at work, the discriminal deviations will tend to vary together, and the correlation r will be high and positive.

(2) The opposite effect is seen in *simultaneous contrast*. When the correlation between the discriminal deviations is negative, the law of comparative judgment gives an exaggerated psychological difference $(S_1 - S_2)$ which we know as simultaneous or successive contrast. In this type of comparative judgment the discriminal deviations are negatively associated. It is probable that this effect tends to be a minimum when the specimens have other per-

ceivable attributes and that it is a maximum when other distracting stimulus differences are removed. If this statement should be experimentally verified, it would constitute an interesting generalization in perception.

If our last generalization is correct, it should be a safe assumption to
write $r = 0$ for those scales in which the specimens are rather complex, such
as handwriting specimens and children's drawings. If we look at two handwriting specimens and perceive one of them as unusually fine, it probably
tends to depress somewhat the degree of excellence we would ordinarily perceive in the comparison specimen, but this effect is slight compared with the
simultaneous contrast perceived in lifted weights and in gray values. Furthermore, the simultaneous contrast is slight with small stimulus differences,
and it must be recalled that psychological scales are based on comparisons in
the subliminal or barely supraliminal range.

The correlation between discriminal deviations is probably high when the
two stimuli give simultaneous contrast and are quite far apart on the scale.
When the range for the correlation is reduced to a scale distance comparable
with the difference limen, the correlation probably is reduced nearly to zero.
At any rate, in order to simplify equation (1) we shall assume that it is zero.
This represents the comparative judgment in which the evaluation of one of
the specimens has no influence on the evaluation of the other specimen in the
paired judgment. The law then takes the following form:

$$S_1 - S_2 = x_{12} \cdot \sqrt{\sigma_1^2 + \sigma_2^2}. \tag{2}$$

Case 4.—If we can make the additional assumption that the discriminal
dispersions are not subject to gross variation, we can considerably simplify
the equation so that it becomes linear and therefore much easier to handle.
In equation (2) we let

$$\sigma_2 = \sigma_1 + d ,$$

in which d is assumed to be at least smaller than σ_1 and preferably a fraction
of σ_1 such as .1 to .5. Then equation (2) becomes

$$S_1 - S_2 = x_{12} \cdot \sqrt{\sigma_1^2 + \sigma_2^2}$$

$$= x_{12} \cdot \sqrt{\sigma_1^2 + (\sigma_1 + d)^2}$$

$$= x_{12} \cdot \sqrt{\sigma_1^2 + \sigma_1^2 + 2\sigma_1 d + d^2}.$$

If d is small, the term d^2 may be dropped. Hence

$$S_1 - S_2 = x_{12} \cdot \sqrt{2\sigma_1^2 + 2\sigma_1 d}$$

$$= x_{12} \cdot \sqrt{2\sigma_1}\,(\sigma_1 + d)^{1/2}.$$

Expanding $(\sigma_1 + d)^{1/2}$, we have

$$(\sigma_1 + d)^{1/2} = \sigma_1^{1/2} + \tfrac{1}{2}\sigma_1^{-(1/2)}d$$

$$= \sqrt{\sigma_1} + \frac{d}{2\sqrt{\sigma_1}}.$$

The third term may be dropped when d^2 is small. Hence

$$(\sigma_1 + d)^{1/2} = \sqrt{\sigma_1} + \frac{d}{2\sqrt{\sigma_1}}.$$

Substituting,

$$S_1 - S_2 = x_{12} \cdot \sqrt{2\sigma_1}\left[\sqrt{\sigma_1} + \frac{d}{2\sqrt{\sigma_1}}\right]$$

$$= x_{12}\left[\sigma_1\sqrt{2} + \frac{d}{\sqrt{2}}\right].$$

But $d = \sigma_2 - \sigma_1$;

$$\therefore\ S_1 - S_2 = x_{12}\frac{\sigma_2}{\sqrt{2}} + x_{12}\frac{\sigma_1}{\sqrt{2}}$$

or

$$S_1 - S_2 = .707\,x_{12}\sigma_2 + .707\,x_{12}\sigma_1. \qquad (3)$$

Equation (3) is linear and very easily handled. If $\sigma_2 - \sigma_1$ is small compared with σ_1, equation (3) gives a close approximation to the true values of S and σ for each specimen.

If there are n stimuli in the scale, there will be $(2n - 2)$ unknowns, namely, a scale value S and a discriminal dispersion σ for each specimen. The scale value for one of the specimens may be chosen as the origin or zero since the origin of the psychological scale is arbitrary. The discriminal dispersion of the same specimen may be chosen as a unit of measurement for the scale. With n specimens in the series there will be $\tfrac{1}{2}n(n - 1)$ observation equations. The minimum number of specimens for which the scaling problem can be solved is then four, at which number we have six observation equations and six unknowns.

Case 5.—The simplest case involves the assumption that all the discriminal dispersions are equal. This may be legitimate for rough measurement, such as Thorndike's handwriting scale or the Hillegas scale of English composition. Equation (2) then becomes

$$S_1 - S_2 = x_{12} \cdot \sqrt{2\sigma^2}$$

$$= x_{12}\sigma \cdot \sqrt{2}.$$

But since the assumed constant discriminal dispersion is the unit of measurement, we have

$$S_1 - S_2 = 1.4142\,x_{12}. \qquad (4)$$

This is a simple observation equation which may be used for rather coarse scaling. It measures the scale distance between two specimens as directly proportional to the sigma value of the observed proportion of judgments $p_{1>2}$.

This is the equation that is basic for Thorndike's procedure in scaling handwriting and children's drawings, although he has not shown the theory underlying his scaling procedure. His unit of measurement was the standard deviation of the discriminal differences, which is $.707\sigma$ when the discriminal dispersions are constant. In future scaling problems equation (3) will probably be found to be the most useful.

Weighting the Observation Equations

The observation equations obtained under any of the five cases are not of the same reliability, and hence they should not all be equally weighted. Two observed proportions of judgments such as $p_{1>2} = .99$ and $p_{1>3} = .55$ are not equally reliable. The proportion of judgments $p_{1>2}$ is one of the observations that determine the scale separation between S_1 and S_2. It measures the scale distance $(S_1 - S_2)$ in terms of the standard deviation, σ_{1-2}, of the distribution of discriminal differences for the two stimuli R_1 and R_2. This distribution is necessarily normal by the definition of the psychological scale.

The standard error of a proportion of a normal frequency distribution is[3]

$$\sigma_p = \frac{\sigma}{Z} \cdot \sqrt{\frac{pq}{N}},$$

in which σ is the standard deviation of the distribution, Z is the ordinate corresponding to p, and $q = 1 - p$ while N is the number of cases on which the proportion is ascertained. The term σ in the present case is the standard deviation σ_{1-2} of the distribution of discriminal differences. Hence the standard error of $p_{1>2}$ is

$$\sigma_{p_{1>2}} = \frac{\sigma_{1-2}}{Z} \cdot \sqrt{\frac{pq}{N}}. \tag{5}$$

But since, by equation (2),

$$\sigma_{1-2} = \sqrt{\sigma_1^2 + \sigma_2^2} \tag{6}$$

and since this may be written approximately, by equation (3), as

$$\sigma_{1-2} = .707 \, (\sigma_1 + \sigma_2), \tag{7}$$

we have

$$\sigma_{p_{1>2}} = \frac{.707 \, (\sigma_1 + \sigma_2)}{Z} \cdot \sqrt{\frac{pq}{N}}. \tag{8}$$

The weight, w_{1-2}, that should be assigned to observation equation (2) is the reciprocal of the square of its standard error. Hence

$$w_{1-2} = \frac{1}{\sigma_{p_{1>2}}^2} = \frac{Z^2 N}{.5 \, (\sigma_1 + \sigma_2)^2 p \cdot q}. \tag{9}$$

[3] See T. L. Kelley, *Statistical Method* (New York: Macmillan Co., 1924), p. 90, equation (43).

It will not repay the trouble to attempt to carry the factor $(\sigma_1 + \sigma_2)^2$ in the formula, because this factor contains two of the unknowns and because it destroys the linearity of the observation equation (3), while the only advantage gained would be a refinement in the weighting of the observation equations. Since only the weighting is here at stake, it may be approximated by eliminating this factor. The factor .5 is a constant. It has no effect, and the weighting then becomes

$$w_{1-2} = \frac{Z^2 N}{pq} . \tag{10}$$

By arranging the experiments in such a way that all the observed proportions are based on the same number of judgments, the factor N becomes a constant and therefore has no effect on the weighting. Hence

$$w_{1-2} = \frac{Z^2}{pq} . \tag{11}$$

This weighting factor is entirely determined by the proportion $p_{1>2}$ of judgments "1 is better than 2," and it can therefore be readily ascertained by the Kelley-Wood tables. The weighted form of observation equation (3) therefore becomes

$$wS_1 - wS_2 - .707wx_{12}\sigma_2 - .707wx_{12}\sigma_1 = 0 . \tag{12}$$

This equation is linear and can therefore be easily handled. The coefficient $.707wx_{12}$ is entirely determined by the observed value of p for each equation, and therefore a facilitating table can be prepared to reduce the labor of setting up the normal equations. The same weighting would be used for any of the observation equations in the five cases since the weight is solely a function of p when the factor σ_{1-2} is ignored for the weighting formula.

Summary

A law of comparative judgment has been formulated which is expressed in its complete form as equation (1). This law defines the psychological scale or continuum. It allocates the compared stimuli on the continuum. It expresses the experimentally observed proportion $p_{1>2}$ of judgments "1 is stronger (better, lighter, more excellent) than 2" as a function of the scale values of the stimuli, their respective discriminal dispersions, and the correlation between the paired discriminal deviations.

The formulation of the law of comparative judgment involves the use of a new psychophysical concept, namely, the *discriminal dispersion*. Closely related to this concept are those of the *discriminal process*, the *modal discriminal process*, the *discriminal deviation*, the *discriminal difference*. All of these psychophysical concepts concern the ambiguity or qualitative variation with which one stimulus is perceived by the same observer on different occasions.

The psychological scale has been defined as the particular linear spacing of the confused stimuli which yields a normal distribution of the discriminal processes for any one of the stimuli. The validity of this definition of the psychological continuum can be experimentally and objectively tested. If the stimuli are so spaced out on the scale that the distribution of discriminal processes for one of the stimuli is normal, then these scale allocations should remain the same when they are defined by the distribution of discriminal processes of any other stimulus within the confusing range. It is physically impossible for this condition to obtain for several psychological scales defined by different types of distribution of the discriminal processes. Consistency can be found only for one form of distribution of discriminal processes as a basis for defining the scale. If, for example, the scale is defined on the basis of a rectangular distribution of the discriminal processes, it is easily shown by experimental data that there will be gross discrepancies between experimental and theoretical proportions, $p_{1>2}$. The residuals should be investigated to ascertain whether they are a minimum when the normal or Gaussian distribution of discriminal processes is used as a basis for defining the psychological scale. Triangular and other forms of distribution might be tried. Such an experimental demonstration would constitute perhaps the most fundamental discovery that has been made in the field of psychological measurement. Lacking such proof, and since the Gaussian distribution of discriminal processes yields scale values that agree very closely with the experimental data, I have defined the psychological continuum that is implied in Weber's law, in Fechner's law, and in educational quality scales as that particular linear spacing of the stimuli which gives a Gaussian distribution of discriminal processes.

The law of comparative judgment has been considered in this paper under five cases which involve different assumptions and degrees of simplification for practical use. These may be summarized as follows.

Case 1.—The law is stated in complete form by equation (1). It is a rational equation for the method of paired comparison. It is applicable to all problems involving the method of constant stimuli for the measurement of both quantitative and qualitative stimulus differences. It concerns the repeated judgments of a single observer.

Case 2.—The same equation (1) is here used for *a group* of observers, each observer making only one judgment for each pair of stimuli, or one serial ranking of all the stimuli. It assumes that the distribution of the perceived relative values of each stimulus is normal for the group of observers.

Case 3.—The assumptions of Cases 1 and 2 are involved here also, and in addition it is assumed that the correlation between the discriminal deviations of the same judgment are uncorrelated. This leads to the simpler form of the law in equation (2).

Case 4.—Besides the preceding assumptions, the still simpler form of the law in equation (3) assumes that the discriminal deviations are not grossly different, so that in general one may write

$$\sigma_2 - \sigma_1 < \sigma_1$$

and that preferably

$$\sigma_2 - \sigma_1 = d \ ,$$

in which d is a small fraction of σ_1.

Case 5.—This is the simplest formulation of the law, and it involves, in addition to previous assumptions, the assumption that all the discriminal dispersions are equal. This assumption should not be made without experimental test. Case 5 is identical with Thorndike's method of constructing quality scales for handwriting and for children's drawings. His unit of measurement is the standard deviation of the distribution of discriminal differences when the discriminal dispersions are assumed to be equal.

Since the standard error of the observed proportion of judgments, $p_{1>2}$, is not uniform, it is advisable to weight each of the observation equations by a factor shown in equation (11) which is applicable to the observation equations in any of the five cases considered. Its application to equation (3) leads to the weighted observation equation (12).

4 A MENTAL UNIT OF MEASUREMENT

The measurement scale of primary interest in psychophysics is the S-scale, which may be called the psychological continuum in contrast with the physical or stimulus-continuum, the R-scale. In the original formulation of Fechner's law the S-scale was described as sensation intensity, but this interpretation of the psychological continuum is now pretty much out of date. We now speak of the S-scale as though it measured so-called sense distances in relation to the corresponding differences or distances on the scale of stimulus magnitude. It is my present purpose to offer a revision of the sense-distance interpretation of the S-scale so that it will be independent of the j.n.d. and the difference limen and to propose a mental unit for mental measurement instead of the ambiguous physical unit, the j.n.d. I shall also try to show that this revised interpretation of the S-value makes it a *continuous* function of the stimulus magnitude because Fechner's paradox does not exist.[1]

This continuum which is designated S in Fechner's law, $S = k \log R$, represents, first of all, *a gradation of qualitative processes*. These processes may be described as subjective or physiological to suit individual and temperamental preferences. That distinction does not affect the psychophysical problem. The continuum implies qualitative variation, and it may or may not also possess quantitative aspects. It may be unidimensional or multidimensional.

A point on this continuum may be designated only by a corresponding stimulus. The stimulus may in turn be designated (1) by a quantitative stimulus attribute such as intensity or magnitude or (2) by a qualitatively varying stimulus attribute such as excellence of handwriting or the beauty of rug patterns or the degree of pacifism expressed in statements about peace and war. Any perceptual quality which may be allocated to a point on the psychological continuum is not itself a magnitude. It is not divisible into parts. It is not a sum of any mental or physical units. It is not twice, three times, or four times as strong, high, beautiful, or good as some other process on the same continuum. It is not a number. It is not a quantity. These are

[1] This is one of a series of articles by members of the staff of the Behavior Research Fund, Illinois Institute for Juvenile Research, Chicago. Series B, No. 109. Reprinted from *Psychological Review*, XXXIV (1927), 415–23.

statements about the psychological continuum on which at least fair agreement among psychologists is to be expected.

But furthermore, the j.n.d. is not a reliable unit of measurement along the S-scale. Any point on the scale represents a unified indivisible experience. Any two such points represent two such experiences which may be qualitatively entirely different and in every way incommensurate, so that they may represent by their own immediate attributes perhaps no similarity by which any "distance" between them could be measured.

With these negations granted, just how do these qualitative entities or processes become a measurable continuum? *They acquire conceptual linearity and measurability in the probability with which each of them may be expected to associate with any prescribed stimulus.* This is the crucial characteristic of the psychological continuum in terms of which psychological measurement is possible. The S-continuum is constructed or defined in such a manner that the frequency distribution of the S-experiences for any given stimulus R is normal. Each modal S_k experience is that particular S-experience which is most frequently associated with the stimulus R_k. Hence if measurement begins with the stimulus R_a for which S_a is the most common or modal S-experience, then some other S-experience, S_b, will be spaced far away, along the imaginary continuum, if the probability is low that S_b will be experienced with the stimulus R_a. It will be spaced close to S_a if the probability is relatively high that S_b will be experienced with R_a. Fortunately, it is possible to verify experimentally the validity of this definition or construction of the S-scale because the continuum may be constructed separately for each stimulus, and the attainment of internal consistency of the scale will indicate whether the correct form of frequency distribution has been used. Therefore the normal frequency distribution is not blindly assumed. It is tested for. If found incorrect, other forms of distribution may be tried in a similar manner. There is one assumption underlying this construction of the psychological continuum, namely, that all the stimuli in a series project the same *form* of frequency distribution on the S-scale, but it is not assumed that their dispersions are equal.

Since the dispersions which the several stimuli project on the S-continuum are not assumed to be equal, the natural unit for psychological measurement becomes the dispersion of one of these stimuli *measured on the psychological scale.* This is what I have called the discriminal dispersion or, more specifically, the discriminal error of each stimulus, and it should not be confused with the customary error of observation. There are two fundamental differences, namely, (1) the discriminal dispersion or error is measured on the S-scale, whereas errors of observation are naturally measured on the R-scale; and (2) the discriminal dispersion is the dispersion projected on the S-scale by a *single stimulus*, whereas an observational error is naturally the pooled effect of *two stimuli.* The two stimuli are the two terms in the psychophysical judgment by the method of constant stimuli, or they are the presented and the reproduced stimuli in the method of reproduction.

It should be noted that an observational error can itself be objectively produced, and it can be directly measured on the R-scale. The discriminal dispersion, though more elemental in character than the observational error, cannot by itself be objectively produced. It can be measured only indirectly since it concerns the S-scale. Every judgment when objectively produced constitutes a single observational error which is loaded with *at least two* discriminal dispersions or errors. A single discriminal dispersion or discriminal deviation cannot by itself ever become an objective record, and consequently its measurement must necessarily be indirect.

I have attempted to state briefly a definition of the psychological continuum and to show that a truly psychological unit of measurement may be established for the psychological scale. The psychological S-scale becomes, then, in effect a frequency scale as far as its experimental identification is concerned. It is an imaginary scale on which we allocate and space out the psychological counterparts of the several stimuli in the stimulus series. Since the stimulus series is regarded as strictly continuous, we define the corresponding psychological scale similarly, so that any stimulus magnitude or quality may be allocated to a point on the continuous S-scale. Similarly, since the psychological continuum is not directly or physically accessible or controllable, we identify any point on the S-scale by a stimulus magnitude.

The customary definition of the S-scale as the measurement of so-called sense distance is not here entirely rejected, but it is made more definite. As long as we define the S-scale as the measurement of sense distance and still deny that it measures sensation intensity or any other quantitative characteristic of sensation, there remains an unsatisfactory vagueness about the nature of the psychological continuum. If we insist that the sense quality is not itself an intensity or magnitude of any sort, how does it happen that we get quantitative measurement in the form of measured distances between these sense qualities which are themselves denied measurable and quantitative attributes? *What constitutes the sense distance that is measured between two qualitative entities?* That is a question concerning the very nature of the psychological continuum which, as far as I am aware, has not hitherto been answered. It is the answer to just this question that I have attempted in formulating a revised definition of the S-scale so that it may also fit the experimental facts.

Let the S-scale consist in a gradation of qualities by means of which we perceive any specified stimulus continuum. Allow that a given stimulus is not always perceived by the same process on the S-continuum. Let the quality most commonly perceived in the given stimulus be designated the modal quality or process for that stimulus. Then we can assign numerical values to other qualities in the S-scale in accordance with the *frequency* with which they are perceived in the given stimulus. It does not matter whether the S-qualities or processes are in any real sense actually spaced out in a continuum so long as they behave as though they were so spaced out. Mental measurement depends according to the present interpretation on the frequency with which each of the processes constitutes the response to a given stimulus. It is reasonable to assume that two perceptual sense qualities or processes which are close together on the psychological continuum are qualitatively similar and that therefore either one of them may more or less readily be perceived in the same stimulus. *To the extent that two perceptual processes are qualitatively similar, to that extent will their probabilities of association with the same stimulus be nearly the same, and to that extent will they tend to be adjacently spaced on the imaginary psychological continuum.* It is sufficient for the purposes of mental measurement that the qualitative perceptual processes behave as though their respective probabilities of association with a given stimulus were a normal frequency distribution. The natural psychological unit of measurement becomes, then, the standard deviation of the frequency distribution for a specified stimulus. This unit of mental measurement I have called the standard discriminal error for the specified stimulus, and it is, of course, measured directly on the psychological continuum. It is entirely independent of stimulus measurement. It is independent of the validity of Fechner's law. It is also independent of the validity of Weber's law. It is a valid unit of measurement even when the objective stimulus cannot itself be quantitatively measured.

It should be noted that the unit of mental measurement that I have proposed is not in any sense a j.n.d. The just noticeable difference is in every case a stimulus measurement. It is measured on the R-scale. Hence it is in reality a *physical unit* which in some situations can serve indirectly the purposes of mental measurement. The discriminal error is a *mental unit* of measurement since it is defined on the psychological continuum. Its physical equivalent will vary from one situation to another, depending primarily on the validity of Fechner's law or some other S–R relation for the particular perceptual function under consideration. *This proposed mental unit for mental measurement may be defined as the standard deviation of the frequency distribution projected by a standard stimulus on the psychological continuum.* I propose to call this mental unit of measurement *the standard discriminal error.* The assumption, the correctness of which will determine the validity of this unit of measurement, is that an S-scale with internal consistency will be obtained by spacing the perceptual qualities on it so that their probabilities of association with any given stimulus will be Gaussian. *With the psychological continuum so defined, the standard discriminal error, as a mental unit of measurement, will be the standard deviation of the perceptual qualities perceived in a standard stimulus.*

The Continuity of the S-Scale

We have so far taken for granted the continuity of the S-scale, but the descriptions of the psychophysical S–R relation so frequently give the idea of a discrete series of steps or jerks that the error of such a notion needs clearly to be corrected. The typical description of the psychophysical S–R relation starts with stimuli R_1, R_2, R_3, so nearly similar that they differ successively by one "j.n.d." Corresponding to these stimulus magnitudes are postulated S-values S_1, S_2, S_3. Then the implication is that any stimulus difference less than $(R_1 - R_2)$ cannot be discriminated at all and that as soon as the stimulus difference becomes as large as $(R_1 - R_2)$, then suddenly the difference jumps into perceptibility, and it is designated "a least perceptible difference," a sense minimum, the unit of mental measurement, the j.n.d. Even so clear a writer as Keyser[2] describes the S–R relation essentially in this way as an example of the data on which we built our conceptual continuities. Even Titchener does not seem to avoid this possible misinterpretation. The following quotations from Titchener illustrate the experimental discreteness which is apparently read into the S-continuum.[3] "Suppose that a brightness or a noise is given, and that we seek to determine the just noticeably brighter brightness, or the just noticeably louder noise. The experiment is identical with one of our 'friction' experiments; and its result is the ascertainment of a just noticeable sense-distance. Let us perform it at various points of the sense scale. . . . Now these are all least distances, minima of sensible distance." And similarly on page xxxvii we read: "The facts that a stimulus must attain a certain magnitude in order to arouse a sensation at all, and that it must attain a certain magnitude in order to effect a noticeable change in sensation, are facts of the same order."

Another description of the S–R relation which is just as misleading as the quotations from Titchener begins with what is known as Fechner's paradox. This description runs usually as follows: let R_1, R_2, R_3 be three stimuli of decreasing order of magnitude. Let the difference $(R_1 - R_2)$ be so slight that it cannot be noticed, i.e., less than the difference limen. Let the difference $(R_2 - R_3)$ also be less than the difference limen. Then it might still happen that the difference $(R_1 - R_3)$ would be a little larger than the difference limen so that it would be noticed. Then, so the argument goes, it would be possible to have the following psychological equalities:

$$R_1 = R_2 ,$$
$$R_2 = R_3 ,$$

which would be inconsistent with the fact that
$$R_1 \neq R_3 .$$

[2] C. J. Keyser, *Mathematical Philosophy* (1922), chap. xviii.

[3] E. B. Titchener, *Experimental Psychology*, Student's Quant. Manual, p. xxxiv.

This is known as Fechner's paradox. The truth is that no one has yet found a just noticeable difference. The least sense distance has never been experimentally demonstrated, and Fechner's paradox does not exist.

Now as a matter of fact, everyone who works at all seriously in psychophysics knows that just noticeable differences have never been found, that is necessary to specify quite arbitrarily a stipulated frequency of discrimination in order to put any sense in the j.n.d., that the phi-gamma hypothesis or its variants assume continuity of the psychometric function, and that experiments such as those of Brown[4] on very small stimulus differences indicate experimentally that sense minima in any genuine sense have not been found. It would seem best therefore to avoid these entirely misleading descriptions of the functional relation between the stimulus magnitude R and the psychological value S. These ambiguities of description disappear entirely if description of the $S-R$ relation be kept true to the experimental facts so that the psychological magnitude, or sense distance, between two stimuli be expressed *in terms of the observed frequency, or the probability, of its discrimination.* As the stimulus difference increases by gradations ever so slight, at least as far as they are experimentally controllable, the probability becomes higher and higher that the stimulus difference will be discriminated. In this sense, then, we may arbitrarily define the difference limen or the j.n.d. as that stimulus difference which has a probability of .75 of being correctly discriminated. This is the manner in which we actually do determine the limen, and it is consequently inaccurate to allow the description of the $S-R$ relation to remain as though it consisted in a series of jerks with a constant friction load for every jerk. The description of Fechner's paradox may still stand as a curious and intriguing distortion of truth. The argument that the two perceptual qualities are psychologically equal because they are equal in a single perceptual judgment simply ignores the fact that the quality perceived in the stimulus is fluctuating or varying. True, they are equal in the judgment in which they are perceived to be equal, but the S-value of a stimulus is the mean perceptual value of many repeated perceptions of the same stimulus. My point here concerning the continuity of the S-scale is nothing new. It is merely a plea for consistency so that throughout the description of psychophysical effects the continuity of the S-scale may be insured, since it is everywhere experimentally indicated.

This consistency is readily obtained if we will recognize that there is a difference between the S-value perceived in a stimulus on any particular occasion and the mean of the S-values perceived in the stimulus on many occasions. It is in the dispersion which a constant stimulus projects on the S-scale that we have the opportunity to establish a truly mental unit of measurement. It might seem that the average S-separation projected by

[4] W. Brown, "The Judgment of Difference, etc.," *University of California Publications in Psychology*, Vol. I (1910), No. 1.

a pair of stimuli would be a better unit of measurement, but such a unit would suffer from the logical disadvantage that the mental unit, so defined, would be loaded with two discriminal dispersions which would in any event have to be solved for. Since the dispersion projected by a single stimulus is more elemental than the pooled effect of two stimuli, it seems more natural to adopt the projected dispersion of a standard stimulus as the basis for a unit of measurement for the psychological continuum. This unit I propose to call the standard discriminal error. Its numerical treatment consists merely in assigning the value of unity to one of the two discriminal errors, σ_1 and σ_2, in the law of comparative judgment.

5 EQUALLY OFTEN NOTICED DIFFERENCES

Quality scales such as Thorndike's scales for handwriting and for children's drawings are constructed on the principle that equally often noticed differences are equal. It is the object of this paper to examine this principle of scale construction and to show that the principle is valid only when the stimuli or specimens are uniform in the degree of ambiguity or dispersion of excellence that is perceived in them.[1]

The principle that equally often noticed differences are equal is a psychological commonplace. Of course the principle does not say anything whatever about the physical differences between the stimuli. That is a totally different matter. Some stimuli are of such a character that a physical scale can be postulated, parallel to the psychological scale. An example is the lifted weight series. The weights may be allocated on a physical scale in grams, and the same weights may be allocated on a psychological scale in accordance with the principle that equally often noticed differences are equal. The construction of an educational quality scale is not ordinarily concerned with the physical scale.

For some kinds of stimuli there exists no physical scale that can be at all readily defined or measured. The excellence of handwriting or of freehand drawing is an example in which the specimens may be allocated on a psychological scale of excellence, as perceived, but for which it is at least difficult to define a parallel physical scale. However, it is possible to construct a quality scale without giving any consideration to the possibility of a parallel physical scale. It is an interesting inquiry to search for the physical measurements that may parallel the psychological measurements, but the present analysis is concerned only with the psychological scale which is constructed on the basis of relative frequency of discrimination between the specimens.

When we say that equally often noticed differences are psychologically equal, it sounds so obvious that we are tempted to regard the assertion as a psychological axiom. But the matter is far from being so simple. In fact, *equally often noticed differences are not always equal, not even psychologically.* The matter can be made clear by considering a simple case.

[1] This is one of a series of articles prepared by members of the staff of Illinois Institute for Juvenile Research, Chicago. Series B105. Reprinted from *Journal of Educational Psychology*, XVIII (1927), 289–93.

In Figure 6 let the vertical dimension represent a psychological continuum such as Thorndike's handwriting scale. Let a represent the scale value of one of the handwriting specimens A. The small probability curve may represent the fluctuation in scale value as perceived by several hundred judges. Let the spread or dispersion of this distribution be designated σ_a. Let b and c represent the scale values of two other handwriting specimens B and C. Suppose that specimen C is more ambiguous to judge for degree of excellence than B, and that B is more ambiguous than A. This means, merely, that the several

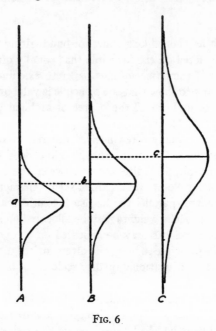

FIG. 6

hundred judges differ considerably in the degree of excellence that they see in specimen C and that they agree more closely as to the excellence they perceive in B, while specimen A shows the best agreement with the smallest dispersion in perceived excellence. In Figure 6 the three distributions are so drawn that

$$\sigma_a = \tfrac{2}{3}\,\sigma_b$$

and

$$\sigma_b = \tfrac{2}{3}\,\sigma_c .$$

The scale value b is the mean degree of perceived excellence in specimen B, and it is represented at the level $+1\sigma$ on the distribution for specimen A. In exactly the same proportional arrangement, the mean perceived excellence of C, its scale value, is located at the level of $+1\sigma$ on the distribution for specimen B.

It is readily seen in Figure 6 that the overlapping or confusion between A and B is the same as that between B and C. Hence we should expect the same proportion of judgments "*B* better than *A*" as of judgments "*C* better than *B*." By the application of the law of comparative judgment[2] to the present case, the proportion

$$p_{B>A} = p_{C>A} = .71 .$$

We have here a situation in which the two scale differences $(B - A)$ and $(C - B)$ which are clearly unequal on the psychological scale are nevertheless equally often noticed. In fact,

$$(C - B) = \tfrac{3}{2}(B - A) .$$

Without considering the validity of the fundamental psychophysical equation by which the exact proportion .71 is determined, it is clear from

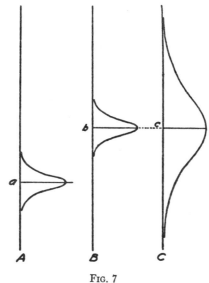

Fɪɢ. 7

inspection of Figure 6 that the proportion of judgments "*C* better than *B*" must be equal to the proportion "*B* better than *A*" because the relations between *A* and *B* are duplicated in the relations between *B* and *C*.

We conclude, therefore, that equally often noticed differences are equal only when the discriminal dispersions of the specimens are equal.[3]

Figure 7 has been drawn to show the converse statement, namely, that equal psychological separations are not necessarily equally often noticed. Let Figure 7 represent three specimens, *A*, *B*, *C*. Let the specimens *A* and *B* be easily perceived with very little ambiguity, while specimen *C* is difficult to evaluate. Specimen *C* is therefore shown with a large dispersion as compared with the dispersions of *A* and *B*.

[2] See chap. iii.

[3] For a further statement of the concept of discriminal dispersion, see chap. ii.

Since B and C have the same scale value, it follows of course that

$$(B - A) = (C - A).$$

Now consider what will happen when the judges are asked to compare specimens A and B. Since the lowest excellence that any judge sees in B is approximately equal to the highest excellence that any judge sees in A, we should expect a very high proportion of judgments "B better than A," perhaps 90 or 95 per cent.

The judges are then asked to compare B and C. Half of them see specimen B as more excellent than the scale value b, and half of them see specimen C as more excellent than the scale value c. If we assume for the sake of simplicity that the variations in perceived excellence of specimens A, B, C are uncorrelated, it is evident that the percentage of judgments "B better than C" will be .50. Hence these two specimens B and C are declared to have the same scale value, and they are so indicated in Figure 7.

Now let the judges compare specimens A and C. Notice that there is considerable overlapping in judgments of excellence for A and C. For example, a considerable proportion of the degrees of perceived excellence for C is below the average judgment for A. Hence we shall expect to find a proportion of judgments "C better than A" about 70 or 80 per cent but certainly not 90 or 95 per cent.

Since $B = C$, it follows that

$$B - A = C - A$$

and that the difference $(B - A)$ should be as often discriminated as $(C - A)$, but we have seen in Figure 7 that if the stimuli or specimens are unequal in relative degree of ambiguity, the two equal differences $(B - A)$ and $(C - A)$ will not be equally often noticed. We conclude therefore that *equal psychological differences are equally often noticed only when the discriminal dispersions of the specimens are equal.*

If the discriminal dispersions can be assumed to be constant for all of the specimens in a series or scale, then the principle that equally often noticed differences are equal is valid, but it is hardly likely that the assumption is always justified. In psychophysical experimentation with lifted weights, for example, it is probably safe to assume that the ambiguity is constant because the weight cylinders are all alike, in appearance, and they are even kept at the same temperature by careful experimenters so as to avoid thermal cues caused by having the subject handle the standard weight cylinder more frequently than the comparison cylinders. But it is hardly likely that specimens of English composition, for example, are sufficiently homogeneous in ambiguity of excellence to justify the assumption that equally often noticed differences are equal. Certainly this is an assumption to be experimentally verified in each case. Equally often noticed differences are not necessarily equal, not even subjectively or psychologically.

6 THREE PSYCHOPHYSICAL LAWS

In a previous article[1] I have shown that Weber's law and Fechner's law are separate laws, so that it is logically possible to have a set of data in which either one of these laws is verified and the other one not verified. This distinction comes about primarily by what I have called the discriminal dispersion of the stimulus. It is a vital factor in verifying Weber's law, but it is not logically a necessary factor in the verification of Fechner's law. If the discriminal dispersions of all the stimuli are equal, then the two laws can be verified by the same set of data, although even then they constitute statements about different aspects of the data.[2] In the same article I have developed the logic by which a psychological scale or continuum becomes a possibility. In that connection I formulated a third psychophysical law which I called the law of comparative judgment. It is my present purpose to explain the differences and the similarities among these three psychophysical laws.[3]

Before making comparisons it may be well briefly to review the statement of each of these three laws.

Weber's law is sometimes carelessly stated as follows: The just noticeable increase in a stimulus is a constant fraction of the stimulus. When the ambiguity of the term "just noticeable" is removed, the law takes the following form: The stimulus increase which is correctly discriminated in any specified proportion of the attempts (except 0 and 100 per cent) is a constant fraction of the stimulus magnitude. Since the experimental verification of the law practically always refers to the comparison of two stimuli as to relative magnitude, it is more accurate and satisfactory to state the law so that it really refers to this comparative situation involving differentiation of *two* compared stimuli rather than the perception of an increase in a *single* stimulus magnitude. Weber's law would then take the following form: Within the

---

[1] See chap. ii.

[2] In the previous article cited I made the statement (p. 36) that the two laws become identical when the discriminal dispersions are equal. That was not quite accurate. The two laws are then verified by the same set of data, but they describe different aspects of the data.

[3] This is one of a series of articles by members of the staff of the Behavior Research Fund, Illinois Institute for Juvenile Research, Chicago. Series B, No. 108. Reprinted from *Psychological Review*, XXXIV (1927), 424–32.

same modality and with constant experimental conditions, the ratio between two stimulus magnitudes which are correctly discriminated in any specified proportion of the attempts, excepting 0 and 100 per cent, is a constant. Restating the law in more convenient form, we have

$$\frac{R_2}{R_1} = K \qquad \text{or} \qquad R_2 = KR_1, \tag{1}$$

in which K is a constant and R_1 and R_2 are defined by the relation

$$P_{R_1 > R_2} = C. \tag{2}$$

From (1) we have

$$P_{R_1 > KR_1} = C,$$

in which C is any arbitrarily assigned constant between zero and unity. This may be generalized into a complete algebraic statement of Weber's law, as follows:

$$P_{R > KR} = C \qquad \qquad \text{(Weber's law)}. \tag{3}$$

Here the notation R refers to any stimulus magnitude, P is a proportion, $P_{R > KR}$ is therefore the proportion of judgments "R is greater than KR," while K and C are constants. The constant C may be arbitrarily assigned. It is customary to specify .75 as the arbitrary value for C, while the constancy of K remains to be experimentally verified.

Another frequent but erroneous statement of the law is as follows: Sensations increase in arithmetical progression as the stimuli increase in geometrical progression. This is actually a statement of Fechner's law and not of Weber's law. It will be noticed that Weber's law says absolutely nothing about sensation intensities. These do not occur in the above statement of the law, and it is brought into the discussion of Weber's law only when this law is confused with that of Fechner. None of the variables in equation (3) above say anything directly about sensation intensities. The principal variables are the stimulus magnitude and the factor K, the constancy of which is subject to experimental verification.

Fechner's law is usually and correctly stated in the form

$$S = K \log R \qquad \qquad \text{(Fechner's law)}, \tag{4}$$

in which R again refers to the stimulus magnitude and S refers to the so-called sensation intensity. The factor K is a constant. The universality as well as the psychological acceptability of this law will probably be greatly increased if, instead of interpreting S to mean the intensity of a sensation, we interpret it to mean a linear measurement along an abstract psychological continuum from the sensory process of a specified stimulus magnitude as an origin. The term S then refers to a measurement along a psychological continuum from an arbitrary but specified origin. These measurements can of course be objectively identified experimentally only in terms of their respective stimuli. But in either the literal interpretation of the term S as an actually measured intensity of sensation or the more liberal interpretation of it as a measurement along an abstract psychological continuum, we have two variables, S and R, which are related by a simple logarithmic function.

Notice that Fechner's law says absolutely nothing about any proportion of correct discriminatory judgments which constitutes an integral part of Weber's law. In fact, Fechner's law is not at all concerned with the phenomenon of confusion of stimulus magnitudes, a phenomenon the description of which Weber's law is essentially aimed at. It is possible to test Fechner's law by using exclusively supraliminal stimulus differences, whereas the testing of Weber's law requires obviously the use of liminal and infraliminal stimulus differences because Weber's law is primarily concerned with the phenomenon of confusion of stimuli. Fechner's law is a statement concerning the rather common functional relation between the stimulus magnitude and the corresponding psychological continuum.

The law of comparative judgment[4] can be stated without approximations in the following form:

$$S_1 - S_2 = x_{12} \sqrt{\sigma_1^2 + \sigma_2^2 - 2\,r\,\sigma_1\sigma_2} \qquad (5)$$

(Law of comparative judgment),

in which the two terms S_1 and S_2 define a linear distance on the psychological continuum, x_{12} is the sigma value of the observed proportion, $p_{R_1 > R_2}$, of judgments "R_1 is greater than R_2," σ_1 and σ_2 refer to the relative ambiguities or discriminal dispersions of the two stimuli, while r is the coefficient of correlation for the two discriminal deviations involved in each of the comparative judgments.

Note that this law is entirely independent of the stimulus magnitudes. Hence it is directly applicable for measuring the psychological continuum corresponding to any qualitative series, to any psychological values which are perceived as a continuum, even though the objective counterparts of these values may not be themselves measurable. Since this law deals with the discriminatory process independently of the objective stimulus magnitudes, there can be no objective criterion for the "correctness" of each discriminatory judgment. The proportions which enter into the law of comparative judgment are not proportions of "*correct*" judgments. They are merely proportions of *similar* judgments, preferably when each judgment is a choice between only two stimuli, omitting the alternatives of "equal" and "doubtful," and when the procedure follows otherwise the method of constant stimuli. It does not depend on the phi-gamma hypothesis, because the stimulus magnitudes do not enter into this law.

In order to summarize the similarities and the differences between these three psychophysical laws, the following tabular statement may be useful.

[4] For a more complete statement of this law with different degrees of approximation for its experimental verification, see chap. iii.

In the first column are listed the variables that are involved in these laws. The plus sign refers to the fact that the law in question does include this variable, while the minus sign indicates that the law does not say anything regarding it. The variables are as follows:

S = a linear measurement on the abstract psychological continuum.

R = stimulus magnitude.

p = proportion of judgments "R_1 greater than R_2."

ΔR = $(R_1 - R_2)$ corresponding to the proportion of judgments, $p_{R_1 > R_2}$.

σ = discriminal dispersion.

Variables	Weber	Fechner	Comparative Judgment
S............	−	+	+
R............	+	+	−
p............	+	−	+
ΔR.........	+	−	−
σ............	−	−	+

The first row of comparison shows that measurement along a truly psychological continuum is not involved in Weber's law but that it is involved in Fechner's law and in the law of comparative judgment. This may be seen by direct reference to the explicit statements of the three laws. The second row of comparison shows that the stimulus magnitude is involved in both Weber's law and Fechner's law but that stimulus measurement is not involved in the law of comparative judgment. The psychological continuum is defined according to this law in terms of the proportion of similar discriminatory judgments, and the validity of the continuum can be established only in terms of experimental consistency of all the observed proportions.

With the factor P goes also the phenomenon of confusion of stimuli, which is not involved in Fechner's law while it is involved in the other two. Still another way of describing the same difference is to point out that Fechner's law might be experimentally verified by *a single* set of observations of the stimuli selected so that they appear equally distant from each other. When the physical stimulus magnitudes are plotted against a scale of equal-appearing intervals, the logarithmic law should be at least roughly verified. Such a demonstration is not possible for either of the other two laws. For them it is necessary to have a rather long series of separate judgments with a *proportion* of judgments for each pair of stimuli. This is but another way of showing that Fechner's law is, strictly speaking, not explicitly concerned with errors of observation, whereas the other two laws deal *primarily* with the magnitudes of errors of judgment.

The stimulus increase $(R_1 - R_2)$ which yields a prescribed proportion of similar discriminatory judgments is involved in Weber's law, but it is not involved in either of the other two laws. The stimulus increase is involved in the proportion which is a principal factor in Weber's law, but the proportion involved in the law of comparative judgment defines the psychological continuum without reference to the stimulus magnitudes. Hence the stimulus increase becomes a part of Weber's law but not of the law of comparative judgment.

The last row of the comparative table shows that the discriminal dispersion, the relative ambiguity with which each stimulus is perceived, is a part of the law of comparative judgment but that it is not explicit either in Weber's law or in Fechner's law. It is in the possibility of variation in the discriminal dispersions of the stimuli that the separation between Weber's law and Fechner's law appears. I have previously shown that when the discriminal dispersions can be assumed or shown to be constant for all the stimuli in an experiment, then the same set of data will be found to verify both Weber's and Fechner's laws, but that if the discriminal dispersions are not constant, then one of these laws may be verified when the other one is not.

In brief, Fechner's law deals with the *apparent* interval in relation to the stimulus interval, while Weber's law deals with the *frequency of correct discrimination* of an interval in relation to the stimulus interval. Since apparently equal intervals are not necessarily equally often discriminated, the two laws become logically separated.[5] Fechner's law concerns the nature of the S–R function, while Weber's law concerns the frequency with which adjacent stimuli are confused. It would be logically possible for Fechner's law to be applicable to a set of data even if errors of observation or confusion should never occur, but in such a state of discriminatory perfection Weber's law could not exist.

Cattell's Formulation of Weber's Law

Cattell's formulation of Weber's law, or a substitute for it, makes it a relation between (1) the magnitude of the stimulus and (2) the magnitude of the standard observational error, *expressed also in terms of the stimulus scale.* His literal statement is as follows:[6] "The error of observation tends to increase as the square root of the magnitude, the increase being subject to variation. . . ." Whether the exact relation is that of the square root function is not for the moment our primary concern. We are noting here primarily the variables involved in these laws. Cattell's formulation may be restated explicitly as follows:

$$E_1 = M \sqrt{R_1} \, ,$$

in which E_1 is the standard observational error for the stimulus magnitude R_1, while M is a constant. Restating it more generally without committing ourselves to the square root function, we have

$$E_1 = M \cdot f(R_1)$$

[5] See chap. v.

[6] G. S. Fullerton and J. McK. Cattell, "On the Perception of Small Differences," University of Pennsylvania Philosophical Series (1892), p. 25.

which brings out clearly the two variables, E_1 and R_1, in terms of which
Cattell has cast Weber's law. This is consistent with our tabular analysis in
that the law involves the stimulus magnitude R explicitly. It involves ΔR,
which is synonymous with the observational error E, and it involves the proportion, p, in the definition of the observational error. The standard error, E,
can be defined as follows:

$$E = \sqrt{\frac{(\Delta R)^2}{n}}$$

for the method of reproduction so that p is about $\frac{2}{3}$, or in some other equivalent manner. No matter how the observational error, E, may be defined, it
automatically locks the proportion, p, of the reproduced stimuli which are
counted within the range $(R + \Delta R)$ or $(R + E)$. Conversely, a prescribed
proportion, p, for the method of reproduction automatically determines the
error of observation, E. According to Cattell, Weber's law does not involve
the sensory or psychological continuum, S. Speaking of Weber's law, he says
(p. 23): "All the experiments made by the first three methods which we have
described seem to us to determine the error of observation under varying
circumstances, and not to measure at all the quantity of sensation." Nor does
Weber's law recognize the subjective standard error of observation, σ_1, of
single stimuli.

If Fechner's law, or a substitute for it which involves the S–R relation, can
be assumed, it is possible to express Cattell's objective observational error,
E, in terms of our discriminal dispersion, σ, for single stimuli. The objective
observational error, E, is measured on the stimulus continuum, whereas the
discriminal dispersion, σ, is measured on the psychological continuum.

In attempting to make an algebraic statement of Weber's law, Cattell
writes (p. 21)

$$N = C \cdot \frac{\Delta S}{S},$$

in which he defines S as his stimulus, ΔS is the increase in the stimulus S
which can be just noticed, while N is also defined as a least difference, with
insistence that it be a physical quantity also. I fail to see any meaning in it,
since there are three physical quantities, N, S, and ΔS, and it seems that N
and ΔS are the same thing. This equation is not a statement of Weber's law.
His verbal formulation is clearer. The main point we get from Cattell in the
present analysis is that Weber's law does not directly concern the measurement of sensation intensity or the psychological continuum.

These three psychophysical laws have been stated algebraically in equations (3), (4), and (5), respectively. The principal variables are (1) the stimulus magnitude, (2) the psychological S-value, and (3) the degree of confusion
of stimuli. It has been shown that each of the three laws relates two of these
variables and ignores the third.

7 THE METHOD OF PAIRED COMPARISONS FOR SOCIAL VALUES

This is an attempt to apply the ideas of psychophysical measurement in the field of social values.[1] Some of the psychophysical methods have been applied in a crude way to the measurement of educational products such as handwriting and English composition, and it seems feasible to apply the same ideas as well to social values, although the attempt cannot readily be made without making compromises that the psychophysicist would not tolerate. The application of the principles of psychophysical measurement to educational products has been made with more or less similar logical handicaps, but these do not seem to have disturbed the popularity of these methods in the field of educational measurement. Since the final results show a rather satisfactory internal consistency, one may possibly assume that the methods, though theoretically imperfect, have some value also in social psychology.

For the present experiment the seriousness of different crimes or offenses was chosen for such measurement. The seriousness of an offense we shall assume to be the seriousness *as judged* rather than as measured in terms of objective consequences or in some normative way. It may very well be that the relative seriousness of offenses, as judged by a group of individuals, may be quite wrong when looked at from the standpoint of objective checks or standards, but we shall be concerned here with the relative seriousness as judged by a group of several hundred students. These records we shall use for the purpose of ascertaining how the offenses arrange themselves in a quantitative continuum from those that seem to be most serious to those that seem relatively least objectionable. There is no doubt but that we imply such a continuum of seriousness in speaking about offenses. In fact, we are supposed to regulate punishment more or less in accordance with the seriousness of the offense. Is it possible to reduce these qualitative judgments about relative seriousness of different offenses to a quantitative basis?

The main principle that underlies the measurements in this study may be stated very briefly. Suppose that 90 per cent of the judges say that crime *A*

[1] The writer wishes to acknowledge his obligation to Dr. Herman Adler, Director of the Institute for Juvenile Research, Chicago, for making it possible to carry out this study. Valuable assistance has been received from Mr. W. H. Cowley and Mr. C. W. Brown, research assistants at the institute. Mr. Cowley was largely responsible for collecting the data. Reprinted from *Journal of Abnormal and Social Psychology*, XXI (1927), 384–400.

is worse than crime B and that the remaining 10 per cent vote that B is the more serious. Now suppose, further, that 55 per cent, barely more than half of the judges, say that crime B is more serious than crime C. Then we should be justified in saying that the separation between the two offenses A and B on a scale of seriousness is much greater than the separation between B and C on that same scale. We might be able to talk even sensibly about "distances" on a scale of seriousness of crime. Some of these distances or separations are then to be considered greater than others. There is really nothing in common-sense judgments that would be violated in such an analysis. Common qualitative judgment would probably be to the effect that murder, for example, is very much more serious than smuggling and that there is not so much difference between smuggling and bootlegging. Some of us may individually disagree, but the above comparisons would probably be true for most people. The present experiments constitute an attempt to measure these relative differences and to indicate one possible procedure in extending at least some of the ideas of psychophysical measurement to social values.

The following is a list of the nineteen offenses that were judged in these experiments.

Abortion	Kidnapping
Adultery	Larceny
Arson	Libel
Assault and battery	Perjury
Bootlegging	Rape
Burglary	Receiving stolen goods
Counterfeiting	Seduction
Embezzlement	Smuggling
Forgery	Vagrancy
Homicide	

The offenses were arranged in pairs so that every one of them was paired with every other one. The total number of pairs of offenses presented was therefore $n(n-1)/2 = 171$.

The instructions to the subjects were as follows:

The purpose of this study is to ascertain the opinions of several groups of people about crimes. The following list of crimes has been arranged in pairs. You will please decide which of each pair you think more serious and underline it.

An example: Cheating—Murder.

You would probably decide that murder is a more serious offense than cheating; therefore you would underline Murder.

If you find a pair of crimes that seem equally serious, or equally inoffensive, be sure to underline one of them anyway, even if you have to make a sort of guess. Be sure to underline one in each pair.

Receiving stolen goods—Perjury
Kidnapping—Adultery
Abortion—Libel
Burglary—Counterfeiting
Bootlegging—Arson
The remainder of the 171 pairs of offenses were presented in the same manner.

In the preliminary experiments it was found that some of the college students were unfamiliar with some of the terms, and it was therefore necessary to supply a sheet of brief definitions. All of the subjects whose records are here reported were supplied with such a list of definitions.

The lists of pairs of offenses were given to 266 students at the University of Chicago, and the returns were practically complete. When the tabulations were made, it was found that the number of omissions did not exceed five for any pair of offenses for the 266 subjects. The exact number of subjects who checked each side of each pair was tabulated, and from these figures the proportions of Table 3 were calculated. Table 3 is to be read as follows. In any column, such as that for forgery, the records indicate the proportion of subjects who regarded forgery as more serious than the offenses listed in the left column. For example, if we compare forgery with bootlegging, we find in the table that 75.4 per cent of the students considered forgery more serious than bootlegging. If we look in the column for bootlegging, we find that the complementary proportion, 24.6 per cent, considered bootlegging more serious than forgery. Such information is available in Table 3 for all the possible pairs of offenses.

The problem to be solved now is that of constructing a scale for the measurement of the seriousness of these offenses in the minds of the 266 students who served as subjects. Our raw data consist in the original frequency tables of checks and the resulting proportions in Table 3. Assume that the base line of Figure 8 represents the scale that we are seeking to establish. Let a be any one of the offenses that we choose to use as a standard, more or less as we should choose a standard in the method of right and wrong cases. Let k be any one of the other offenses which is being compared with the standard offense a. These two offenses, k and a, are of course separated by some unknown distance on the scale.

At this point it is of some interest to note a contrast between the scaling problem and the conventional psychophysical problem. In psychophysics we take for granted that we know the stimulus intensities, and we seek the proportion of correct judgments for varying stimulus differences. On the basis of such data we determine the standard deviation of the psychometric function and the stimulus value which corresponds to the origin of that curve. In the scaling problem the situation is more or less reversed. We are seeking to determine the stimulus values themselves. It is clear that the scaling problem is

TABLE 3

TABLE OF PROPORTIONS p_{ka} OR $p_k > a$

	Abortion	Adultery	Arson	Assault and Battery	Bootlegging	Burglary	Counterfeiting	Embezzlement	Forgery	Homicide	Kidnapping	Larceny	Libel	Perjury	Rape	Receiving Stolen Goods	Seduction	Smuggling	Vagrancy
Abortion		.323	.338	.211	.128	.238	.244	.245	.212	.760	.318	.222	.191	.256	.822	.143	.419	.174	.045
Adultery	.677		.415	.242	.172	.281	.285	.253	.274	.863	.365	.207	.182	.245	.925	.143	.589	.204	.034
Arson	.662	.585		.260	.136	.226	.321	.348	.254	.017	.563	.215	.144	.349	.944	.140	.716	.170	.019
Assault and battery	.789	.757	.740		.379	.515	.556	.485	.534	.070	.743	.385	.385	.587	.947	.344	.785	.346	.072
Bootlegging	.872	.828	.864	.621		.764	.745	.738	.754	.955	.924	.678	.506	.728	.985	.527	.871	.576	.116
Burglary	.762	.719	.774	.485	.236		.593	.605	.580	.981	.856	.333	.322	.478	.981	.221	.769	.284	.027
Counterfeiting	.756	.715	.679	.444	.255	.407		.540	.488	.947	.804	.303	.284	.532	.963	.199	.756	.215	.042
Embezzlement	.755	.747	.652	.515	.262	.395	.460		.350	.958	.752	.305	.248	.474	.977	.141	.774	.251	.049
Forgery	.788	.726	.746	.466	.246	.420	.512	.650		.951	.819	.343	.320	.534	.966	.195	.820	.260	.035
Homicide	.240	.137	.083	.030	.045	.019	.053	.042	.049		.083	.030	.034	.079	.441	.027	.181	.026	.011
Kidnapping	.682	.635	.437	.257	.076	.144	.196	.248	.181	.917		.170	.106	.288	.902	.098	.595	.086	.026
Larceny	.778	.793	.785	.615	.322	.667	.697	.695	.657	.970	.830		.348	.648	.970	.268	.848	.365	.053
Libel	.809	.818	.855	.615	.494	.678	.716	.752	.680	.966	.894	.652		.702	.981	.530	.886	.456	.067
Perjury	.744	.755	.651	.413	.272	.522	.467	.526	.466	.921	.712	.352	.298		.951	.204	.767	.222	.015
Rape	.178	.075	.056	.053	.015	.015	.037	.023	.034	.559	.098	.030	.019	.049		.019	.076	.023	.015
Receiving stolen goods	.857	.857	.860	.656	.473	.779	.801	.859	.805	.973	.902	.732	.470	.796	.981		.875	.525	.061
Seduction	.581	.411	.284	.215	.129	.231	.244	.226	.180	.819	.405	.152	.114	.233	.924	.125		.121	.023
Smuggling	.826	.796	.830	.654	.424	.716	.785	.749	.740	.974	.914	.635	.544	.778	.977	.475	.879		.037
Vagrancy	.955	.966	.981	.928	.884	.973	.958	.951	.965	.989	.974	.947	.933	.985	.985	.939	.977	.963	

much the more difficult, theoretically, because on the basis of the proportions such as those of Table 3 we seek to determine the stimulus intensities and the coarseness of discrimination, whereas the psychophysical problem is concerned only with the coarseness of discrimination while the stimulus intensities are known. The constant errors occur in both problems.

Let us assume first that we are dealing with *one* subject who would repeatedly check the list of pairs of offenses according to the same instructions. The particular offense k would then on some occasions seem to him a little more serious than ordinarily, while on other occasions he would judge that particular offense more leniently. It is probable that he would never judge the offense k a whole scale above or below its average value, whereas small fluctuations in apparent seriousness would be very common. Here we shall assume that these fluctuations follow the laws of probability, but we shall not be entirely satisfied to make this common assumption without some experimental check on its approximate validity.

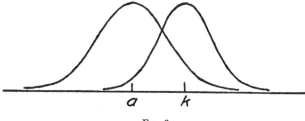

FIG. 8

We shall have then in Figure 8 a scale of seriousness of offenses with the offenses k and a hypothetically located thereon. We shall also assume that each offense is perceived with a certain standard error of observation. These standard errors of observation we shall designate σ_k and σ_a, respectively. Now it is necessary to remind oneself that every single judgment "k is greater than a" or "k is less than a" involves the perception, recognition, or cognitive placement of not one but two entities, k and a. Hence *every* psychophysical judgment is the product of *two* errors of observation, one observational error for the standard and another observational error for the comparison stimulus. This fact is not generally acknowledged in psychophysical theory, and it is usually ignored entirely in educational measurement. As we have drawn the distributions of observational errors in Figure 8, it sometimes happens that k is perceived at low values, even lower than the average for a, and similarly it happens that a is perceived sometimes even higher than the scale value of k. If we take any pair of these observations of k and a, we shall find that k is usually perceived worse or stronger than a, but the perceived difference $(k^1 - a^1)$ is sometimes negative. When k is perceived as stronger than a, the perceived difference $(k^1 - a^1)$ is positive, and when k is perceived as less serious or weaker than a, then the perceived difference $(k^1 - a^1)$ is negative.

If we were able to plot a distribution of the perceived differences we should have a distribution like that of Figure 9. The base line in this figure represents the perceived difference $(k^1 - a^1)$. To the right of the origin on the base line these differences are positive, and the corresponding ordinates of the frequency curve represent the relative expected frequencies of such perceived differences. The most common perceived difference is assumed to be the true difference $(k - a)$, and its frequency ordinate is therefore highest. To the left of the origin on the base line the differences are negative; in other words, that section of the base line represents perceived differences in which a is judged to be more severe than k. The standard deviation of this curve is a function of the two standard errors of observation for the two stimuli separately perceived and indicated in Figure 8. It is clear that the area of the probability curve in Figure 9 represents the total number of judgments. The shaded area to the right of the origin represents that portion of the judgments

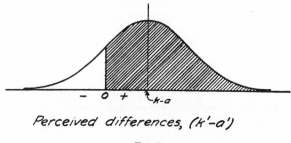

Perceived differences, $(k'-a')$

Fig. 9

in which $(k^1 - a^1)$ is positive, while the unshaded remaining area represents the portion of judgments in which a is judged worse or stronger than k.

So far we have considered the judgments as though they had been made by a single observer repeating his judgments several hundred times. But our data actually involve such judgments, one set from each observer, for 266 subjects. This is a weak point in the argument in that we shall assume that the seriousness of a particular offense has some unmeasured relative mean value for all the subjects and that the extreme judgments about its seriousness are less common than judgments at or near the unmeasured mean degree of seriousness for the whole group. That this assumption is not altogether unreasonable is indicated by two facts, namely, that the proportions in Table 3 for any two standards, i.e., any two columns in the table, do not give a linear plot, as they should do if we were dealing with rectangular distributions of judgments of seriousness. The second and more convincing fact is that the final scale values enable us to compare the theoretical with the actually observed proportions of judgments, and these two sets of proportions for any given offense as a standard do give a fairly good linear plot, as will be demonstrated later.

In Figure 9 we have, then, the theoretical distribution of perceived differences $(k^1 - a^1)$, and if the two stimuli, which are offenses in this case, are sufficiently close together, these differences will sometimes be positive and sometimes negative. The mean of this distribution represents the most commonly perceived difference, which may be assumed to be the true difference. The shaded area represents the proportion of perceived positive differences in which k is judged greater or stronger than a. That area is the theoretical or expected proportion of judgments "k worse or stronger than a." But this proportion is the one which is experimentally given for all pairs of stimuli in Table 3. Hence our problem is to determine those relative scale values a, b, $c \ldots k$ and those standard errors of observation σ_a, σ_b, $\sigma_c \ldots \sigma_k$ which will best satisfy the experimentally observed proportions in Table 3. We shall then apply certain tests to ascertain whether our results contain sufficient internal consistency to warrant acceptance of the procedure.

In Figure 9 let the shaded area be represented by p_{ka}. The area or proportion between the origin and the point $(k - a)$ is therefore $p_{ka} - .50$. The relation between the theoretical distribution and the experimentally obtained proportions is given by the following equation:

$$k - a = x_{ka} \sqrt{\sigma_k^2 + \sigma_a^2} \qquad (1)$$

$$= x_{ka} \cdot \quad \sigma_{ka} , \qquad (2)$$

in which $(k - a)$ is the distance on the base line between the origin of the curve and the mean ordinate.

x_{ka} = the deviation $(k - a)$ in terms of the standard deviation. It is ascertained from the probability tables by means of the observed proportion p_{ka}.

σ_{ka} = the standard deviation of the distribution of perceived differences for the two stimuli k and a.

Since the scale values of the offenses will be obtained by a process of summation, it may be an acceptable approximation to assume all of the standard errors of observation, σ_{ka}, as equal. This approximation is not theoretically satisfactory, but the solution of the problem without this assumption becomes prohibitive and unwieldy. It probably does not affect the scale values seriously because these are to be determined by an arithmetical summation method in which all of these standard errors of observation are involved.

Let the standard errors of observation be designated σ_{ka}, and assume that they are all equal. Then, considering a as a standard stimulus and k as the variable stimulus,

$$k - a = x_{ka} \cdot \sigma_{ka} \qquad (2)$$

$$(\Sigma k - a) - (n - 1) a = \Sigma x_{ka} \cdot \sigma_{ka}$$

$$\Sigma k - n a = \sigma_{ka} \cdot \Sigma x_{ka} , \qquad (3)$$

and, by symmetry, using stimulus b as a standard instead of a,

$$\Sigma k - n b = \sigma_{kb} \cdot \Sigma x_{kb} .$$

But, by assumption,

$$\sigma_{ka} = \sigma_{kb} .$$

Hence,

$$\Sigma k - n b = \sigma_{ka} \cdot \Sigma x_{kb} . \tag{3}$$

From the two equations (3) we get

$$n b - n a = \sigma_{ka} (\Sigma x_{ka} - \Sigma x_{kb})$$

$$b - a = \frac{\sigma_{ka} (\Sigma x_{ka} - \Sigma x_{kb})}{n} .$$

Let σ_{ka} be the unit of measurement for the scale. Then

$$b - a = \frac{\Sigma x_{ka} - \Sigma x_{kb}}{n} . \tag{4}$$

Hence it follows that the scale values, assuming that the errors of observation are identical for all of the stimuli, will be given directly by the following relations, the signs obtained from equation (4) being arbitrary.

$$a = \frac{\Sigma x_{ka}}{n}; \qquad b = \frac{\Sigma x_{kb}}{n}; \qquad c = \frac{\Sigma x_{kc}}{n}; \quad \text{etc} . \tag{5}$$

In order to obtain the scale values of the offenses by equations (5), a table was prepared showing the value of x for each proportion. This table corresponds exactly to Table 3 except that, instead of listing the proportions directly, these were translated into their equivalent deviations in terms of their respective standard errors of observation. The table was obtained directly from Kelley's probability tables, and the values Σx_{ka}, Σx_{kb}, Σx_{kc}, etc., were obtained as summations of the columns.

In order to make the scale values all positive, an arbitrary origin was located at the offense which was judged least serious, namely, vagrancy. The other offenses are scaled with that offense as a datum. The unit of measurement for the scale is the standard error of observation, σ_{ka}, which is assumed to be constant for all of the offenses. This unit of measurement is theoretically 1.42 σ_a. In other words, the standard error of observation for any pair of stimuli is always greater than the standard error of observation for either of the stimuli observed separately. The standard error of observation for any single stimulus is a subjective intensity distance which can never be directly measured by any objective means. It can, however, be indirectly determined.

In Figure 10 the scale values of the offenses are represented graphically. Numerical designations on the scale are intentionally omitted. The scale values were determined from equations (5). The small circles represent the same scale values for offenses classified in groups. It is of some interest to note that all of the four sex offenses which were included in the list were judged to be more serious than all of the property offenses. In the minds of the 266 college students none of the property offenses was considered to be as

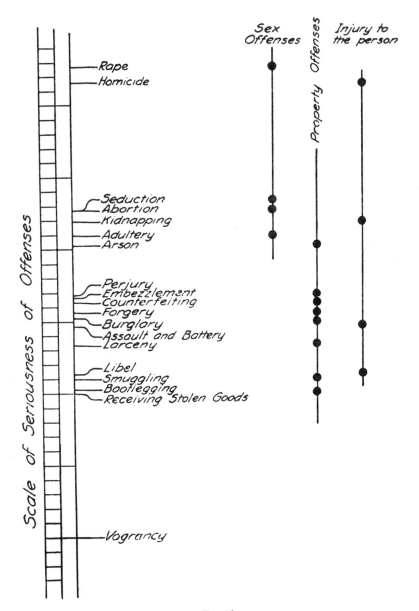

FIG. 10

serious as any of the sex offenses. There is no overlapping on the scale of sex offenses and the property offenses.

Another observation of some interest is the comparison of the two offenses which were judged to be most serious, namely, rape and homicide. In the direct comparison of these two offenses in Table 3, 56 per cent of the subjects rated homicide as the more serious. But when the scale values of these two offenses are determined by the independent comparison with the other offenses, rape comes to the top as the more serious. The latter judgment is the indirect one obtained not by comparing the scaling of the two offenses directly with each other but by comparing their respective scaling with other offenses. The variation may, of course, be due merely to unreliability of the data.

Before we can test the internal consistency of the scale values just obtained, it is necessary to calculate, at least approximately, the standard errors of observation for each of the offenses. In doing this we shall, of course, not make the assumption that they are all equal, an assumption that we found convenient in the summation procedure for determining the scale values themselves. We start again with equation (1), which can be rewritten in the form

$$\frac{(k-a)^2}{x_{ka}^2} = \sigma_k^2 + \sigma_a^2.$$

If stimulus a is the standard in this equation, we can write $(n-1)$ similar equations with the same standard, since there are n stimuli in the series. The summation of these $(n-1)$ equations takes the form

$$\Sigma\left[\frac{(k-a)^2}{x_{ka}^2}\right] = [\Sigma\sigma_k^2 - \sigma_a^2] + (n-1)\,\sigma_a^2 = m_{ka}, \qquad (6)$$

in which the notation m_{ka} is adopted for convenience.

All of the $(n-1)$ equations summed in equation (6) have stimulus a as a standard. A similar summation equation may be written for the $(n-1)$ equations which have b as a standard, and so on for each of the k stimuli. These n summation equations may be represented as follows:

$$\Sigma\left[\frac{(k-a)^2}{x_{ka}^2}\right] = \Sigma\sigma_k^2 - \sigma_a^2 + (n-1)\,\sigma_a^2 = m_{ka} \qquad (6)$$

$$\Sigma\left[\frac{(k-b)^2}{x_{kb}^2}\right] = \Sigma\sigma_k^2 - \sigma_b^2 + (n-1)\,\sigma_b^2 = m_{kb}$$

$$\Sigma\left[\frac{(k-c)^2}{x_{kc}^2}\right] = \Sigma\sigma_k^2 - \sigma_c^2 + (n-1)\,\sigma_c^2 = m_{kc}$$

$$\cdots\cdots\cdots\cdots\cdots\cdots\cdots\cdots\cdots$$

$$n\cdot\Sigma\sigma_k^2 - \Sigma\sigma_k^2 + (n-1)\,\Sigma\sigma_k^2 = \Sigma m_{kk} = M$$

$$(2n-2)\,\Sigma\sigma_k^2 = M$$

$$\Sigma \sigma_k^2 = \frac{M}{2n - 2}. \tag{7}$$

The notation M for Σm_{kk} is also used for convenience. From equation (7) we may determine the sum of the standard errors of observation for all of the nineteen offenses. This sum will be used in determining the separate standard errors of observation for each of the offenses.

In making the calculation of $\Sigma \sigma_k^2$, a tabulation is made of $(k - a)^2$ from the scale values and of x_{ka}^2 from the deviations determined from Table 3. The summation

$$\Sigma \left[\frac{(k - a)^2}{x_{ka}^2} \right] = m_{ka}$$

is then determined numerically for the eighteen values with offense a as a standard. The other eighteen summations corresponding to equation (6) are

TABLE 4

SCALE VALUES AND DISPERSIONS OF JUDGMENTS
OF THE NINETEEN OFFENSES

Offenses	Scale Value	σ_k
Abortion	2.271	.660
Adultery	2.103	.453
Arson	2.021	.333
Assault and battery	1.474	1.194
Bootlegging	1.032	1.254
Burglary	1.510	.614
Counterfeiting	1.634	.605
Embezzlement	1.658	.964
Forgery	1.562	.613
Homicide	3.156	.682
Kidnapping	2.198	.272
Larceny	1.326	.236
Libel	1.124	1.289
Perjury	1.676	.759
Rape	3.275	.630
Receiving stolen goods	0.999	.665
Seduction	2.273	.438
Smuggling	1.102	.523
Vagrancy	0.000	.688

made in a similar manner. The total sum of these nineteen numerical values gives M, which is used in equation (7) to determine $\Sigma \sigma_k^2$ for all of the nineteen offenses.

The individual standard errors of observation are obtained from equation (6) in the following manner:

$$m_{ka} = \Sigma \sigma_k^2 - \sigma_a^2 + (n - 1) \sigma_a^2 \tag{6}$$

$$= \Sigma \sigma_k^2 + (n - 2) \sigma_a^2$$

$$\frac{m_{ka} - \Sigma \sigma_k^2}{n - 2} = \sigma_a^2. \tag{8}$$

By means of equation (8) one may determine the individual standard errors of observation. These are summarized in Table 4.

TABLE 5

Comparison of the Calculated and Experimental Proportions of Judgments "Forgery Worse than K" in Which K Represents in Turn Each of the Other Nineteen Offenses

The calculated values, x^1_{ka}, are obtained from Table 4 and equation (1).
The experimental values, x_{ka}, are obtained from Table 3.

Offenses	Calculated x^1_{ka}	Experimental x_{ka}	Calculated p^1	Experimental p
Abortion	− .79	− .80	.21	.21
Adultery	− .71	− .60	.24	.27
Arson	− .66	− .66	.25	.25
Assault and battery	+ .07	+ .09	.53	.53
Bootlegging	+ .38	+ .69	.65	.75
Burglary	+ .06	+ .20	.52	.58
Counterfeiting	− .08	− .03	.42	.49
Embezzlement	− .08	− .39	.42	.35
Homicide	−1.74	−1.65	.04	.05
Kidnapping	− .95	− .91	.17	.18
Larceny	+ .36	+ .40	.64	.66
Libel	+ .31	+ .47	.62	.68
Perjury	− .12	− .09	.45	.47
Rape	−1.95	−1.83	.03	.03
Seduction	− .94	− .92	.17	.18
Receiving stolen goods	+ .62	+ .86	.73	.80
Smuggling	+ .57	+ .64	.72	.74
Vagrancy	+1.70	+1.81	.96	.96

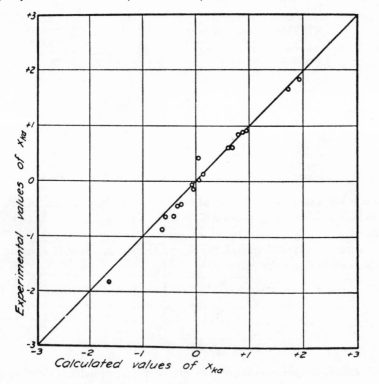

FIG. 11

The final test of internal consistency is to calculate the expected proportions of judgments "$k > a$" and to compare these calculated proportions with the actually obtained proportions. This can readily be done by means of the original equation (1), since we have assigned scale values $a, b, c \ldots k$ and the corresponding standard errors of observation, listed in Table 4.

For example, if we wish to predict from the scale values and their corresponding errors of observation in Table 4 the proportion of the subjects who would rate seduction as a more serious offense than forgery, we should use equation (1) as follows:

Offenses	Scale value	σ_k
Seduction.............	2.273	.438
Forgery...............	1.562	.613

With these data from Table 4 we determine the value of x_{ka} from equation (1), and we find it to be $+.94$. This corresponds to a proportion of 83 per cent as determined by Kelley's tables. In other words, we should expect 83 per cent of the 266 students to say that seduction is a worse offense than forgery. In the experimental results of Table 3 we find that the actual proportion was 82 per cent. In many of the comparisons between the calculated and the experimental results the correspondence is even closer, while in some of them the discrepancy is as much as 6 or 7 per cent, with an occasional discrepancy

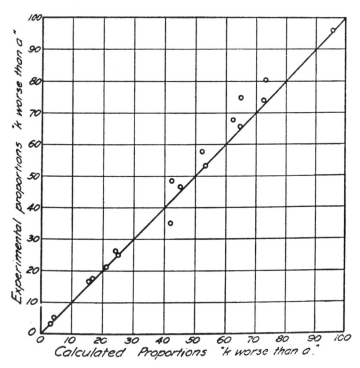

FIG. 12

of 8 or 9 per cent. This correspondence is as close as may be expected from proportions based on 266 subjects.

Such comparisons for isolated pairs of offenses in the list are not satisfactory as a check of internal consistency. It is better to compare the calculated and experimental proportions for all of the offenses with each one in succession as a standard. In Table 5 such a set of comparisons has been tabulated for forgery as a standard. These calculated data are obtained by means of equation (1). A similar table can be easily prepared for any of the other offenses as a standard. The table gives the calculated and experimental proportions of the 266 subjects who considered forgery to be worse than each of the offenses listed. It also gives the corresponding sigma values. In Figures 11 and 12 these results are represented in graphical form. Since the fit is a fairly good one, we can assume that the original equation (1) is a satisfactory statement of the discriminatory judgments of the seriousness of the offenses.

Summary of the Method

The stimuli whose magnitudes are to be measured are presented to the subject in paired comparisons. For each comparison he decides which of the two is the stronger. It is assumed that each of the stimuli has an unknown mean magnitude for the group and that there is a standard error of observation for each stimulus. Every judgment is assumed to be the result of four determinable factors, namely, the two stimulus magnitudes and the two standard errors of observation. The proportions of judgments are expressed in equation (1) as a function of these four factors. The experimental data consist in the observed proportions of judgments, and from these data the best-fitting scale values of the stimuli as well as their respective observational standard errors are determined.

A table of proportions like Table 3 is first prepared which summarizes the experimental data. A corresponding table of sigma values is then prepared, in which the experimental proportions, represented by the shaded area of Figure 9, are expressed in terms of the deviation $(k - a)$. The scale values of the stimuli are then determined by equations (5) on the assumption that the observational errors are approximately equal.

The sum of the standard errors of observation is then determined from equations (6) and equation (7). The individual standard error of observation for each stimulus is then calculated from equation (8). The internal consistency of the determinations is ascertained by comparing the experimental proportions with the calculated proportions by inspecting the goodness of fit for either of the procedures shown in Figure 11 or Figure 12.

The present study does not have for its purpose the discovery of any startling facts with regard to crime. It does show that qualitative judgments of a rather intangible sort, loaded usually with personal opinion, bias, and even strong feeling, and regarded generally as the direct antithesis of quantitative measurement, are nevertheless amenable to the type of quantitative analysis which is associated historically with psychophysics. It is of some interest to see that a set of numerical values can be established by which the 171 observed proportions of judgments about crimes and offenses can be summarized in generalized form.

8 THE PHI-GAMMA HYPOTHESIS

Some time ago I wrote a note calling attention to the fact that the phi-gamma hypothesis is at best an approximation formula and that it is theoretically incorrect. At that time I was not sure whether teachers of psychophysics generally acknowledged this limitation of the phi-gamma hypothesis since I had not seen any explicit statement of its theoretical limitations. As far as I knew, the theoretical inaccuracy of the hypothesis might have been considered obvious by psychophysicists generally. Before the note was published, I discovered that the theoretical inadequacy of the phi-gamma hypothesis is not generally acknowledged, and in consequence I have extended the note into a more complete statement which takes the form of three theorems and several corollaries concerning the psychometric curve and the phi-gamma hypothesis.[1]

The theoretical limitation of the phi-gamma hypothesis consists essentially in the fact that it requires a constant limen for all values of the stimulus. As is well known, the limen for a large stimulus is usually larger than for a small stimulus. Therefore the phi-gamma hypothesis which requires a constant limen is inconsistent with the generally observed fact that the limen is some increasing function of the stimulus. This increasing function is not necessarily that of Weber's law.

It is true that the phi-gamma curve can frequently be used as a good approximate fit for the psychometric curve; but when it is so used, it should be thought of not as a psychophysical hypothesis but rather as any other empirical equation which is used to draw a smooth curve through a set of experimental observations.

In this discussion I limit myself to psychometric experiments which are carried out with only two judgments allowed, heavier or lighter, and from which the intermediate category of judgment is barred. There is, of course, a difference of opinion as to whether the intermediate category should be used in psychophysics, but that is a different story. *The present argument concerns the phi-gamma hypothesis for psychometric data obtained with only two categories of judgment.*

My propositions concerning the phi-gamma hypothesis are as follows:

Theorem.—If the absolute limen increases as the stimulus increases, then the psychometric curve for two categories of judgment is positively skewed.

[1] Reprinted from *Journal of Experimental Psychology*, XI (1928), 293–305.

Corollary.—The only condition under which the phi-gamma curve can fit the psychometric curve is that of a constant absolute limen independent of the stimulus magnitude.

Corollary.—If the absolute limen increases as the stimulus increases, then the phi-gamma curve, which is symmetrical, cannot fit the psychometric curve, which is skewed.

Corollary.—The phi-gamma hypothesis is incompatible with Weber's law. Both cannot apply to the same set of data.

Theorem.—If the absolute limen is proportional to the stimulus magnitude (Weber's law), then the positive skewness of the psychometric curve increases with the coarseness of the perceptual process.

Corollary.—The necessary error in fitting the phi-gamma curve to psychometric data increases with the relative limen of the perceptual process. The error of the phi-gamma hypothesis is large for coarse discrimination. It becomes negligible for keen discrimination.

Theorem.—If Weber's law is satisfied by the psychometric data, i.e., if the absolute limen is proportional to the stimulus, then the psychometric curve becomes Gaussian when plotted against the logarithm of the stimulus magnitude.

For the sake of completeness we shall first define the terms used in the theorems and their corollaries. The limen has been described as the absolute amount by which a stimulus must be increased in order that the increase shall be noticeable. With the proverbial lifted weights taken as an example, the limen for a weight of one hundred grams is the number of grams by which this weight must be increased in order that the increase shall become noticeable. As is well known, the limen is larger for heavy weights than for light.

The above rough description reads as though one experimented with a single weight which is increased in magnitude until the increasing weight becomes noticeably heavier. But that is not the experimental procedure by which the limen is determined. The psychometric function refers to the constant method in which *two* stimuli, *two* weights, are presented and the subject decides which of them is the heavier. Hence the limen is described as the absolute difference between *two* weights which is noticeable.

In order to reduce the term "noticeable" to something measurable, the noticeability is defined usually as that difference between *two* stimuli which is correctly discriminated in 75 per cent of the attempts. Then *the limen is more accurately defined, with reference to the constant method, as that absolute difference between two stimuli which is correctly discriminated in 75 per cent of the attempts.*

The two terms "standard stimulus" and "variable stimulus" are not infrequently misinterpreted. When the subject is presented with two stimuli, either simultaneously or in succession, his task is to discriminate between them by deciding which is the heavier, larger, or stronger, as the case may be.

It should be carefully noted that the subject in his task of discrimination between the two stimuli has absolutely no concern with the distinction between the standard stimulus and the variable stimulus. In other words, this distinction between standard and variable is an arbitrary one introduced later by the experimenter merely for convenience in tabulating and analyzing the records. As far as the subject is concerned, the ideal situation is one in which he is faced with two stimuli and he decides which of them is the stronger.

When every stimulus has been paired with every other stimulus in the series several hundred times, it is possible to tabulate the frequency with which each pair of stimuli is correctly discriminated. The experimenter may then tabulate in a single column all the pairs in which any particular stimulus A is a member. These records are then said to have stimulus A as a standard. The same thing can of course be done for each of the other stimuli taken in turn as a standard. It is therefore clear that if the judgment "A is greater than B" is returned in (let us say) 82 per cent of the attempts, then this experimental result belongs equally well in the column where A is the standard and in the column where B is the standard. It would of course be possible to set up an experiment with a single standard initial stimulus which is itself made to increase or decrease gradually until the subject indicates that he has recognized the direction of change. Such a setup would be unusual, and it does not involve the phi-gamma hypothesis. It would be a variation of the limiting methods.

The *psychometric curve* is plotted with one of the stimuli chosen as a standard. The coordinates of this curve are as follows. The x-axis represents the variable stimulus magnitude. The y-axis represents the proportion of judgments "Variable stimulus greater than the standard stimulus." It is designated $p_{v>s}$. Note that the subject had nothing to do with the designation of any one or all of the stimuli as standards. He simply discriminated, as best he could, between pairs of stimuli.

When the variable stimulus is much smaller than the standard, then there will be very few judgments "$v > s$" because this judgment is incorrect and in the minority. Consequently, $p_{v>s}$ will be small, i.e., $p_{v>s} < .50$. When the variable stimulus is equal to the standard, the judgments of the subject will be equally divided between "$v > s$" and "$v < s$" and hence $p_{v>s} = p_{v<s} = .50$. We are assuming that space and time errors have been eliminated or counterbalanced. When the variable stimulus is much greater than the standard, there will be a majority of correct judgments "$v > s$," so that $p_{v>s} > .50$.

The *phi-gamma hypothesis* states that the psychometric curve is the function described by the integral of the normal probability curve, namely,

$$p_{v>s} = \frac{1}{\sqrt{2\pi}\,\sigma} \int_{-\infty}^{v} e^{-(v-s)^2/2\sigma^2} d\,v \qquad \text{(phi-gamma hypothesis)}. \quad (1)$$

If $p_{v>s}$ is plotted against v, we have the well-known ogive for the normal probability curve. The phi-gamma curve $\phi(\gamma)$ is symmetrical about its origin in the sense that the upper and lower quartile points of the ogive are equidistant from the mean. The phi-gamma hypothesis simply states that the psychometric curve can be fitted by the integral of the normal probability curve.

My first theorem merely asserts that if the absolute limen increases with the stimulus, then the psychometric curve for two categories of judgment is positively skewed. This theorem may be proved as follows.

Let there be n stimuli in the experimental series, and assume, for simplicity, that they are equally spaced on the stimulus continuum. Let each one of the stimuli be compared with every other stimulus in the series. Let

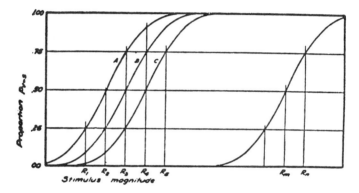

FIG. 13

each pair be presented a sufficient number of times to stabilize the proportions $p_{v>s}$.

From such an experiment it is of course possible to tabulate the proportion of judgments "A is greater than B" for every possible pair of stimuli in the series. There will be $n(n-1)$ proportions in such a table. It is obvious that, since the subject is allowed only two categories of judgment, the proportion of judgments "A is greater than B" must necessarily be the complement of the proportion of judgments "B is greater than A." In other words,

$$p_{a>b} + p_{b>a} = 1 \ . \tag{2}$$

Now let us collect all the proportions in which the stimulus R_2 is involved in order to plot the psychometric curve with that stimulus as a standard. It is represented in curve A of Figure 13. Let the experimental proportion

$$p_{1>2} = .25 \ .$$

Then the lower quartile point for the curve A is R_1, and its median is R_2. Now, by the $\phi(\gamma)$ hypothesis, the curve is symmetrical, and therefore the upper and lower quartile points are equidistant from the median. But the stimuli are also equally spaced. Therefore the upper quartile point of curve A must be R_3. In other words,

$$R_3 - R_2 = R_2 - R_1,$$
$$R_2 = \text{median of curve } A,$$
$$R_1 = \text{lower quartile of } A,$$
$$R_3 = \text{upper quartile of } A.$$

Therefore

$$p_{3>2} = .75 .$$

But then, by (2)

$$p_{2>3} = .25 ,$$

and this locates the median and the lower quartile for curve B, in which R_3 is the standard. In other words,

$$R_4 - R_3 = R_3 - R_2 ,$$
$$R_3 = \text{median of curve } B,$$
$$R_2 = \text{lower quartile of } B,$$
$$R_4 = \text{upper quartile of } B .$$

This can be continued indefinitely so that

$$R_n - R_m = R_2 - R_1 \qquad (3)$$

and

$$p_{n>m} = p_{2>1} , \qquad (4)$$

where R_n is a large stimulus and R_2 is a small one.

But we have postulated that the absolute limen increases with the stimulus magnitude. Hence the two stimulus increments $(R_n - R_m)$ and $(R_2 - R_1)$ which are equally often correctly discriminated must be such that

$$(R_n - R_m) > (R_2 - R_1) , \qquad (5)$$

and hence the psychometric curve must be positively skewed rather than symmetrical. This is the first theorem. *It does not postulate Weber's law.* It merely postulates that the limen is an increasing function of the stimulus.

The first corollary is seen in Figure 13, in which the symmetry of the psychometric curve is postulated. It leads to equations (3) and (4) as the only condition under which the psychometric curve can be symmetrical.

The second corollary makes the necessary inference that if the absolute limen is an increasing function of the stimulus, then the symmetrical phi-gamma curve cannot fit the psychometric curve which is positively skewed. This does not depend on Weber's law.

The third corollary introduces Weber's law. Weber's law states that the difficulty of discriminating between two stimuli is a function of the ratio of their magnitudes. The difficulty of discrimination is measured in terms of the relative frequency of correct discrimination. The law can be stated in algebraic notation as follows:[2]

$$p_{R>KR} = C . \qquad (6)$$

If the constant C is arbitrarily set at .75, then the constant K represents the relative limen while R is the higher of the two compared stimuli. The relative limen constant is here less than unity. The same equation may be written

$$p_{KR>R} = 1 - C . \qquad (7)$$

If it is desired to use the notation R' for the lower of the two stimuli, then the law takes the equivalent form

$$p_{R'l>R'} = C ,$$

where

$$l = 1/k > 1 ,$$

and this can of course be turned into the complementary form

$$p_{R'l<R'} = 1 - C .$$

Weber's law asserts that the limen is proportional to the stimulus, while the phi-gamma hypothesis requires that the limen be constant. Both cannot be true of the same set of data.

The second theorem is that if the absolute limen is proportional to the stimulus (Weber's law), then the positive skewness of the psychometric curve increases with the coarseness of the perceptual process. This theorem and its corollary regarding the necessary discrepancy between the symmetrical phi-gamma curve and the positively skewed psychometric curve can be shown perhaps best by several examples of different degrees of keenness of discrimination.

The psychometric curves in Figures 14, 15, and 16 are drawn with the supposition that Weber's law holds in the vicinity of the magnitude of the standard stimulus. We do not need to assume that Weber's law holds for extremely large or for extremely small stimuli in order to draw these three psychometric curves. We shall designate the magnitude of the standard stimulus arbitrarily as 100, and we shall assume that Weber's law holds in the vicinity of this magnitude in order that a comparison may be made between the phi-gamma curve and the psychometric curve.

In Figure 14 we have taken Weber's ratio as 1/3, which represents coarse discrimination, such as for loudness of sound. With the coarseness of discrimination represented by this ratio, we shall expect two stimuli of magnitudes 100 and 133 to be correctly discriminated in 75 per cent of the attempts. This is represented graphically by the fact that the psychometric curve of Figure 14 reaches the level .75 when the variable stimulus is 133 and

[2] See chap. vi.

the standard stimulus is 100. Since Weber's ratio is here assumed to be 1/3, we shall expect the same frequency of correct discrimination, namely 75 per cent, for two stimuli 75 and 100, since they have the same ratio as the two stimuli 100 and 133. The psychometric curve shows that the proportion $p_{75>100}$ has the value .25, so that $p_{100>75} = .75$. The psychometric curve has been drawn to represent the fact that it is as difficult to discriminate between two stimuli of 75 and 100 as it is to discriminate between two stimuli of 100 and 133, since these two pairs of stimuli have the same ratio. This is the condition described by Weber's law when the ratio is 1/3.

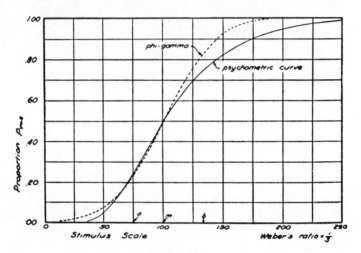

FIG. 14

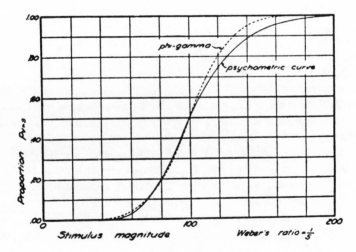

FIG. 15

But it is immediately clear that this psychometric curve cannot possibly be symmetrical because

$$133 - 100 \neq 100 - 75 \,,$$

and consequently the curve cannot be Gaussian. The dotted line of Figure 14 represents a phi-gamma curve which has been so drawn that it passes through the median and the lower quartile of the psychometric curve. If the phi-gamma curve must be fitted to the psychometric curve in this instance, it can be moved to the right or left, and its standard deviation can be altered; but it cannot possibly be made to fit the psychometric curve, which is clearly non-symmetrical.

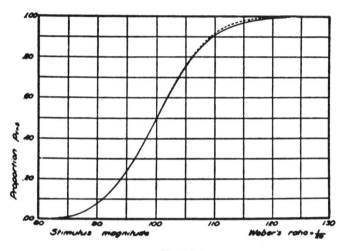

FIG. 16

In Figure 15 we have drawn two curves in the same manner as in Figure 14 except that here we have assumed Weber's ratio to be only 1/5. In other words, this figure represents a keener discriminatory function than the previous figure. Here, again, we are assuming that Weber's law holds in the vicinity of the standard stimulus value of 100. The psychometric curve is so drawn that the two stimuli of 100 and 120 are correctly discriminated in 75 per cent of the attempts and also that the two stimuli 83.3 and 100 are as often correctly discriminated. The psychometric curve is here also non-symmetrical, since

$$120 - 100 \neq 100 - 83.3 \,,$$

although the degree of asymmetry is not so pronounced. The discrepancy between the phi-gamma curve and the psychometric curve is smaller than in the preceding figure, where Weber's ratio was assumed to be larger.

In Figure 16 we have the same type of diagram for a perceptual function in which Weber's ratio is much smaller, namely, 1/20. In other words, when the difference between two stimuli is 5 per cent of the smaller one, the frequency of correct discrimination is expected to be 75 per cent. It will be seen in Figure 16 that the discrepancy between the psychometric curve and the phi-gamma curve is relatively small, since the discrepancy

$$105 - 100 \neq 100 - 95.2$$

is much smaller than in the previous examples.

Finally, when Weber's ratio is only 1 or 2 per cent, as in the perception of visual brightness, then the discrepancy is so small that the phi-gamma curve can be used to advantage in fitting the psychometric curve. It is of some interest, however, to know that the phi-gamma curve is theoretically incorrect, that it cannot possibly be the correct function for the psychometric curve, and that its usefulness is merely that of an empirical equation or curve. It serves the purposes of a scroll, as it were, in drawing a smooth curve for the psychometric data with an error that is very small, perhaps smaller than the observational errors, when the perceptual function which is being studied is keen.

The fact that the fallacious character of the phi-gamma hypothesis has not previously caused trouble is to be found in the fact that most of the perceptual functions that have been investigated have been rather keen. Examples of these are the perception of visual brightness and of line lengths. In cases of coarse discrimination, such as that of sound intensity, there has been the uncertainty of stimulus measurement which introduces another ambiguity into the handling of psychometric data. When the perceptual function is rather coarse, it is necessary to take into consideration the error of the phi-gamma hypothesis.

The third theorem is that if Weber's law is satisfied by the psychometric data, then a $\phi(\log \gamma)$ hypothesis will also be satisfied by the same data. If we want an empirical equation for the psychometric function which shall be at least not theoretically inconsistent with Weber's law, then we may propose as a substitute for the $\phi(\gamma)$ hypothesis a $\phi(\log \gamma)$ hypothesis. The integral of the normal curve would then be fitted on a psychometric function in which the proportions $p_{v>s}$ are plotted against the logarithm of the stimulus intensity.

Even if Weber's law is not exactly verified by the data, it is in the great majority of experiments more nearly true to assume that the limen is proportional to the stimulus than to say that the limen is constant and independent of the stimulus magnitude. The latter assumption of the phi-gamma hypothesis flies in the face of the simplest experimental evidence.

Let the points a and b of Figure 14 be the base line values corresponding to the ordinates .25 and .75, respectively, of the psychometric function. If the empirical equation used in fitting the psychometric function is to be sym-metrical, then

$$b - m = m - a .\qquad(8)$$

Let

$$a = \log R_a ,$$

$$b = \log R_b ,$$

$$m = \log R_m .$$

Then, by (8),

$$\log R_b - \log R_m = \log R_m - \log R_a ,$$

or

$$\log \frac{R_b}{R_m} = \log \frac{R_m}{R_a} ,$$

and hence

$$\frac{R_b}{R_m} = \frac{R_m}{R_a} ,$$

which is the condition required by Weber's law.

This manner of fitting the psychometric function is at least consistent with Weber's law, and it may be called the $\phi(\log \gamma)$ hypothesis as a substitute for $\phi(\gamma)$ hypothesis. It should be regarded merely as an empirical equation for determining the limen and the precision. It should not be taken too seriously either in the form $\phi(\gamma)$ or in the form $\phi(\log \gamma)$.

The actual fitting of the curve may be accomplished graphically to a fair degree of accuracy by means of arithmetic-probability cross-section paper, or it may be done by plotting the sigma value corresponding to the experimental proportion against the logarithm of the stimulus magnitude. The plot should be linear. A constant error will be revealed by the intercept, and the slope of the linear plot will be the precision. The function can also be fitted by the method described by Kelley,[3] with this difference: the logarithm of the stimulus should be used instead of the stimulus magnitude. The system of weighting which is ordinarily used need not be modified because the weight is a function of the observed proportions, which are retained as before. Urban's tables and Rich's checking tables are unfortunately not ordinarily applicable to this modification of the phi-gamma hypothesis because these tables pre-suppose that the stimulus magnitudes are equidistant. They would be applicable if the experiments were so set up that the logarithms of the stimulus magnitudes should constitute an arithmetical series.

It should be noted that my main criticism of the phi-gamma hypothesis is not contingent on the acceptance of Weber's law. The phi-gamma hy-pothesis is denied if the absolute limen increases with the stimulus magnitude even if Weber's law is not exactly verified.

[3] T. L. Kelley, *Statistical Method* (New York: Macmillan Co., 1924), pp. 326–28.

9 FECHNER'S LAW AND THE METHOD OF EQUAL-APPEARING INTERVALS

The purpose of the present experiment was partly to ascertain whether Fechner's law holds for a certain kind of stimulus but primarily to bring out certain limitations of the method of equal-appearing intervals and the ways in which some of them may be overcome.[1]

One of the best known examples of the method of equal-appearing intervals in the experimental verification of Fechner's law is the Sanford weight experiment.[2] The envelopes are so weighted that they present as far as possible the same appearance and that they are in all respects identical

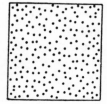 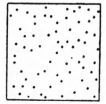

FIG. 17

except as to their weights. The subject is asked to sort out these envelopes into five piles so that the piles seem to be equally spaced as to apparent weight. Each pile of envelopes is weighed, and then it is easy to ascertain the average weight of the envelopes in each of the five piles. The five equally spaced S-values, the five successive piles, are then plotted against the average weight of the envelopes in each of the five piles. The plot is expected to be logarithmic to satisfy Fechner's law. This procedure involves a methodological error which can be avoided by the procedure to be explained.

The stimuli for the present experiment consisted of a series of 96 cards. On each card was printed a $2\frac{1}{2}$-inch square which was filled with irregularly spaced dots. The stimulus magnitude was the number of dots in the square. The lowest and the highest magnitudes are illustrated in Figure 17. They were arranged in a geometrical series of 24 steps from 68 dots to 198 dots.

[1] Reprinted from *Journal of Experimental Psychology*, XII (1929), 214–24.

[2] E. B. Titchener, *Experimental Psychology* (1905), II, Part I, 33; E. C. Sanford, *A Course in Experimental Psychology* (1898), Part I, p. 340.

Each stimulus magnitude was represented by four cards in the series. The subject was given the pile of 96 cards and asked to sort them out into ten piles which should constitute as far as possible a series evenly graduated as to the apparent density of the dots on the cards. There were 101 subjects in the experiment, so that there were 404 sortings for each stimulus magnitude.

The raw data are summarized in Table 6. The S-scale is represented by ten equal class intervals, the ten piles. The R-scale is represented by the number of dots on the card.

Fechner's law is a statement of the relation between these two variables. It is usually written in the form

$$S = K \log R , \qquad (1)$$

in which S is the allocation of the stimulus to the psychological or discriminal continuum, and R is the stimulus magnitude, the number of dots. In order to provide for any units of measurement for R and S, and in order to provide

TABLE 6

THE S-SCALE IN TEN EQUAL-APPEARING INTERVALS (PILES)

No. Dots	0–1	1–2	2–3	3–4	4–5	5–6	6–7	7–8	8–9	9–10	Total No. Sortings
68	246	85	38	27	4	3	.....	.....	1	.....	404
71	147	123	77	40	12	2	1		2	.....	404
74	169	112	66	42	12	2	1	.....		.....	404
77	72	140	103	53	20	12	3	1		.....	404
81	51	122	126	51	34	13	5	1	1	.....	404
84	55	113	120	58	40	12	3	3		.....	404
89	13	59	126	104	56	34	8	4		.....	404
93	14	54	106	92	69	39	20	7	3	.....	404
97	8	53	89	104	95	40	11	2	2	.....	404
102	1	30	59	102	119	52	32	9		.....	404
107	7	26	73	92	115	49	34	8		.....	404
112	1	21	26	73	119	75	68	16	5	.....	404
117		9	26	57	90	79	97	36	10	.....	404
123		6	11	34	84	118	89	47	15	.....	404
129		3	15	34	71	88	113	58	21	1	404
135		4	14	39	59	107	101	63	17	.....	404
142		2	4	15	28	73	122	92	64	4	404
149				6	25	58	112	122	69	12	404
156			5	8	15	36	89	117	104	30	404
164			1	3	14	27	61	127	123	48	404
172			1	6	13	21	43	108	143	69	404
180			1	2	3	14	23	76	154	131	404
189				2	1	9	14	40	116	222	404
198					1	1	6	16	83	297	404
	784	962	1087	1044	1099	964	1056	953	933	814	(9696)
Average no. dots in each pile	74.19	82.71	89.75	99.84	110.59	124.06	135.39	151.59	166.97	185.81	......

for an arbitrary origin on the S-scale, it is desirable to write the equation in the more flexible form

$$S = K \log (CR) .   \tag{2}$$

This equation is easily rectified by writing it in the form

$$S = K \log R + K \log C ,   \tag{3}$$

in which $K \log C$ is a constant. The verification of Fechner's law would be complete if the plot of S against $\log R$ should be linear. If this plot is not linear, then Fechner's law is not verified. This assumes, of course, as in any experimentation of this type, that there is sufficient curvature of the plot S against R so that its rectification by the above logarithmic plot is convincing.

The detailed interpretation of the table is as follows. There were 246 sortings in which cards containing 68 dots were placed in the first or lowest of the ten piles. The cards containing 68 dots were placed in the second of the ten piles 85 times. It is to be expected that the cards with relatively low stimulus magnitudes (number of dots) should be placed in the lowest piles, while the cards with the large number of dots should be placed in the higher numbered piles. This is seen to be the case in that there is a drift of entries in the table from the upper left-hand corner to the lower right-hand corner. Since each stimulus magnitude was sorted 404 times, the sum of the entries in each row is 404. The piles were designated as equal class intervals on the S-scale, and the origin for the scale is placed arbitrarily at the lower edge of the lowest of these ten class intervals. For this reason the entries in the first of the ten columns can be handled as class frequencies for the interval 0–1 on the S-scale. The next column represents the frequency of sortings of each stimulus magnitude for the class interval 1–2 and so on.

In order to ascertain whether Fechner's law holds, it is necessary to compare the S- and R-values, which are expected to give a logarithmic plot. In the present instance there can hardly be any ambiguity about the stimulus magnitude, which is simply the number of dots in the square. We must decide, however, on a method for determining the S-value which is to be assigned to each stimulus magnitude. At this point appears the methodological error which is involved in the well-known Sanford weight experiment, which has been quoted by Titchener and others. If we should proceed as in the Sanford weight experiment, we should merely ascertain the average number of dots in each pile. These would be considered as the adjusted R-values to be plotted against the equal intervals on the S-scale. As a matter of fact, such a procedure makes use of the wrong regression for this problem.

In many experimental problems it is necessary to ascertain which of two regressions is to be used. Whenever the object is prediction, one should use the regression "unknown on known." In the present case we are not interested in predicting S-values from known R-values, or vice versa. We are interested in the intrinsic relation between S and R. In such a situation one should minimize experimental discrepancies in the variable which is least accurately measured. In this case there can be no doubt that the S-value is far more inaccurate than the R-value, which is merely the number of dots on the card. Consequently, we should adjust the S-values against constant R-values. The regression "S on R" assumes that the R-values contain no error, and that is for all practical purposes true. Probably the only error in the present R-values is the very slight fluctuation in the diameters of the dots, by which apparent density might conceivably be affected. But this error is almost infinitesimal compared with the discrepancies in the S-values, the apparent magnitude. In a situation in which both variables are measured with equal accuracy, and in which no problem of prediction is involved, one should fit the data by a function intermediate between the two regressions.

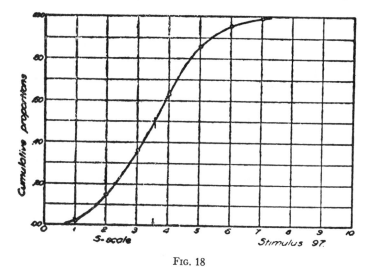

FIG. 18

For linear functions this is easily done, but non-linear functions for such experiments are sometimes troublesome.

The instructions for the Sanford weight experiment call for the regression R on S, which is a violation of good experimental practice. We shall use the correct regression in this case, which is S on R. This necessitates that we ascertain an S-value for each of the 24 stimulus magnitudes. Inspection of our table shows immediately that the distributions represented by the horizontal rows are by no means normal. They are banked toward the end piles by the "end effect." Merely to ascertain the arithmetic mean of the piles is therefore not a suitable procedure. This objection also holds against the incorrect procedure of the Sanford weight experiment, in which the student is asked merely to ascertain the average weight per envelope in each pile. We have adopted the median S-value for each stimulus magnitude as the most suitable measure of central tendency on the S-scale. For this purpose a cumulative frequency distribution was drawn for each of the horizontal rows of the table. An example of this procedure is illustrated in Figure 18 for stimulus magnitude 97. The class frequencies for the R-value of 97 have here been represented in a cumulative frequency distribution of the percentile form. The median S-value is the S-value at which the smoothed curve reaches an elevation of .50, which is 3.55 for the stimulus 97. This means merely that half of the subjects perceive this stimulus as larger than 3.55 on the S-scale, while half of them perceive it as smaller than that apparent magnitude. One cumulative frequency diagram was drawn for each stimulus, so that there were 24 diagrams for this experiment similar to Figure 18.

We now have the experimental S-values, S_e. They are listed in Table 7. We are now ready to determine whether the linearity of equation (3) is

TABLE 7

Number of Dots R	S_e	log R	$k \cdot$ log R	Median S-Value S_c
68............	0.65	1.8325	34.1248	0.7113
71............	1.40	1.8513	34.4749	1.0614
74............	1.30	1.8692	34.8082	1.3947
77............	1.90	1.8865	35.1304	1.7169
81............	2.20	1.9085	35.5401	2.1266
84............	2.30	1.9243	35.8343	2.4208
89............	3.05	1.9494	36.3017	2.8882
93............	3.30	1.9685	36.6574	3.2439
97............	3.55	1.9868	36.9982	3.5847
102............	4.10	2.0086	37.4041	3.9906
107............	4.05	2.0294	37.7915	4.3780
112............	4.70	2.0492	38.1602	4.7467
117............	5.20	2.0682	38.5140	5.1005
123............	5.50	2.0899	38.9181	5.5046
129............	5.85	2.1106	39.3036	5.8901
135............	5.85	2.1303	39.6704	6.2569
142............	6.65	2.1523	40.0801	6.6666
149............	7.00	2.1732	40.4693	7.0558
156............	7.45	2.1931	40.8399	7.4264
164............	7.75	2.2148	41.2440	7.8305
172............	8.10	2.2355	41.6295	8.2160
180............	8.60	2.2553	41.9982	8.5847
189............	9.10	2.2765	42.3930	8.9795
198............	9.45	2.2967	42.7691	9.3556

satisfied by the experimental data. The values of log R are also listed in the same table. In Figure 19 we have plotted S against log R as indicated by equation (3). The linearity of Figure 19 is immediately apparent. Its slope is the constant K in equation (3), and the S-intercept is the constant K log C. These constants may be determined by the method of least squares, but for the present problem that may hardly be necessary. The linearity of Figure 19 constitutes final proof that Fechner's law holds for the stimuli of the present experiment. If Figure 19 had been non-linear, it would have disproved Fechner's law for the present experiment. The straight line of this figure was drawn by inspection, so that approximately as many points may be found on one side of the line as on the other. The constant K is determined graphically to be 18.621, and the S-intercept is also determined graphically to be -33.4135. These two values would undoubtedly shift slightly by different methods of fitting the line of Figure 19, such as the method of least squares, the method of averages, or Reed's method of minimizing normals.[3] But for our purposes such slight fluctuations in the constants are not of importance.

The column $K \log R$ of Table 7 can then be filled in since the constant K has been determined. The last column of this table shows the calculated S-values, S_c. These are obtained again from equation (3) with the known values for K, $K \log C$, and the known stimulus magnitudes.

In order to ascertain the magnitude of the experimental discrepancies from Fechner's law, we have drawn Figure 20. The small circles represent the

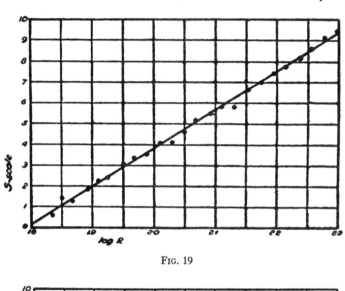

FIG. 19

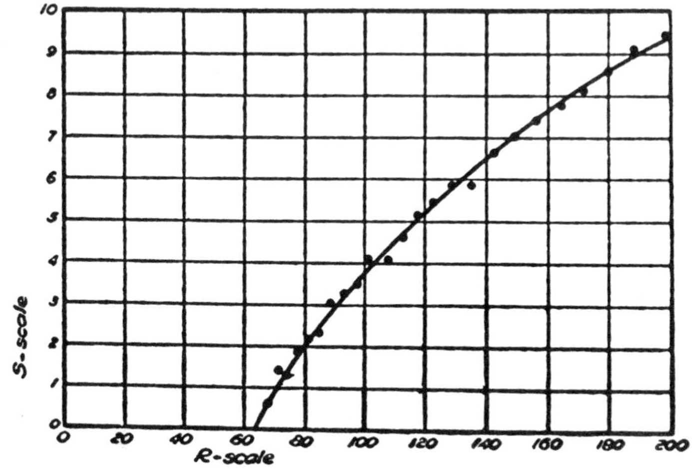

FIG. 20

[3] L. J. Reed, *Metron*, I (1921), 54–62.

experimental S-values, S_e, which have been plotted against the corresponding stimulus magnitudes. These data are obtained directly from Table 7.
The smooth curve has been drawn through the calculated S-values, S_c, of
this table. This diagram shows rather clearly that experimental deviations
from Fechner's law are very slight in the present experiment, and we are
therefore justified in concluding that the law has been verified.

There are several psychological and methodological considerations that
are fairly well illustrated in this simple experiment. The final equation of the
curve of Figure 20 is

$$S = 18.621 \log R - 33.4135 .\tag{4}$$

One might inquire about the psychological meaning of this equation when S
is zero. In that case R takes the value 62. In other words, when there are
about 62 dots on the card, the S-value according to our equation should be
zero. This is entirely sensible because the origin for the S-scale is arbitrary.
In fact, according to Fechner's law in its most general form, equation (1)
automatically prescribes an origin for the S-scale for unit stimulus magnitude. In the present case 62 dots on the card happens to be unit stimulus
magnitude for the law in its simplest form. There is no psychological ambiguity about this fact if we remember that we are dealing with an arbitrary
origin on the S-scale. Naïve interpretation might ask whether the apparent
magnitude is zero for unit stimulus magnitude. But such a question is of
course entirely irrelevant when S-measurements are made from an origin
arbitrarily assigned to unit stimulus magnitude.

The same question may appear in slightly different form by inquiring
about negative values for S. Myers[4] speaks of a "difficulty" about Fechner's
law in that it leads to negative sensations. Any value for anything can be
negative if you place the arbitrary origin high enough. And so in this case the
S-value for a stimulus would be negative if the unit stimulus magnitude
were arbitrarily assigned high enough. Consequently, negative S-values in
Fechner's equation do not mean that the apparent magnitude is less than
nothing. This alleged difficulty with Fechner's law is caused by failure to
understand the meaning of Fechner's simple equation. The issue simply does
not exist.

It is of some interest to study the dispersion that a stimulus projects on
the S-scale. This can be done by inspecting the data of Table 6. The inspection shows the end effect rather conspicuously. This effect can probably be
explained most simply in terms of the mechanical restrictions of the method
of equal-appearing intervals. The subject adopts a scale of subjective magnitudes for the ten piles, and when he sees an unusually large stimulus magnitude, he may have the impulse to place it in pile 12 or pile 15 if such piles
were available or allowable. Since he is restricted to ten piles, he sorts all of
these large apparent magnitudes in pile 10. Undoubtedly the next stimulus

[4] C. S. Myers, *A Textbook of Experimental Psychology* (1909), p. 249.

which is slightly smaller is affected by such a restriction, so that it is sorted into piles 8 or 9 instead of into 10 or 11. The same effect is seen at the lower end of the S-scale. For this reason we cannot deal with the distributions of Figure 20 as in any sense true projections of the stimuli on the S-scale. They are subject to gross distortions by the mechanical limitations of the method of equal-appearing intervals. It is of course possible that we are also dealing with an adaptation effect caused by familiarity with the experimental stimulus range and that this may itself constitute a source of distortion in addition to the mechanical limitation of the method of equal-appearing intervals. It is probably not so great as that of the restraint to a specified number of piles. There would seem to be good reason to assume that the distribution of the stimulus magnitude 198 should be approximately the same in form as the distribution for the stimulus magnitude 68. Consequently, if we want to study the dispersion that a stimulus projects on the S-scale, we must resort to other psychophysical methods than that of the method of equal-appearing intervals. In fact, this is one of the most serious limitations of that method. It is entirely absent in the method of paired comparison, which is probably the best of all the psychophysical methods.

Another serious limitation of the method of equal-appearing intervals for which I can offer no solution is that the determinations are undoubtedly affected by the distribution of stimulus values which the experimenter happens to use. In the present case we use 24 stimulus magnitudes in a geometric series from 68 to 198 dots. If we had so selected the same number of stimuli as to constitute an arithmetical series with the same range, the subject would have been compelled to make the tenth pile rather large, while the first pile would be rather small. It is almost certain that the subject would have been confused by the fact that his sortings gave gradually increasing piles from the first to the tenth. He might unwittingly disturb his scale of apparently equal intervals in an attempt to make the class frequencies in the ten piles roughly equal. On the other hand, the same question may be raised as a criticism against our procedure, in which the stimulus magnitudes constituted a geometric series. If the subject sorts the stimuli into ten successive piles with instructions to make all of the ten piles approximately equal in size and without any instructions to make the intervals between them equal, then we should automatically verify Fechner's law, provided we were to interpret the intervals to be equal even though the subject were never told to make them so. This is a serious limitation in the method of equal-appearing intervals by which our confidence in this psychophysical method should be markedly disturbed. Whenever it is at all possible, we certainly should avoid the method of equal-appearing intervals and use instead the method of paired comparison or one of its equivalents.

10 RANK ORDER AS A PSYCHOPHYSICAL METHOD

In every psychophysical experiment it is necessary for the investigator to select a psychophysical method, and in doing so he is guided by two principal types of consideration, namely, experimental convenience and theoretical propriety.[1] Other things being equal, he will choose that experimental procedure which is simplest for the subject and most convenient. He will also be constrained to select a method which is legitimate for his problem. One of the simplest of experimental procedures is to ask the subject to arrange a series of stimuli in absolute rank order according to length, weight, brightness, beauty, or whatever the psychological continuum may happen to be. This experimental procedure does not ordinarily lend itself to psychological measurement because the subjective increments represented by the successive rank orders are ordinarily entirely unknown. Occasionally it is legitimate to assume that the entire distribution of subjective values is Gaussian, and then it is possible to translate rank orders into legitimate psychological measurement. We are dealing now with the situation in which a small number of stimuli, such as ten or twenty, are to be dealt with and in which no assumption can be made legitimately regarding their distribution in subjective value.

For theoretical purposes the constant method is probably the best in most experimental problems. The ideal form of the constant method is the method of paired comparison in which not one but all of the stimuli serve as standards. But the constant method is also one of the most laborious experimental methods. If there are twenty stimuli and if the method is to be complete, there would be required 190 judgments in order to compare each stimulus with every other stimulus. This assumes that the constant method is used in complete form with every stimulus serving in turn as a standard. The method has serious limitations when only one or two of the stimuli are used as standards. We shall also assume that the intermediate category is excluded. If the reader insists on using the intermediate category of judgment in the constant method, this paper is of no interest to him.

Our present problem is to devise a plan whereby simple absolute rank order may be used as the experimental procedure with the advantages of the much more laborious constant method. Given the data for absolute rank

[1] Reprinted from *Journal of Experimental Psychology*, XIV (1931), 187–201.

order, we shall extract the proportion of judgments "*A* is greater than *B*" for every possible pair of stimuli in the given series. These derived proportions will be used instead of the proportions that are obtained directly in the constant method. From these derived proportions the subjective separations between any pair of stimuli can then be readily calculated by the equation of comparative judgment. First the method will be derived theoretically, and then we shall describe its empirical verification.

If a subject has placed four stimuli *A B C D* in the rank order *B D A C*, it is possible to tabulate his various comparisons as though he had made them separately. If each of the four stimuli were to be compared with every other one in the series, it would require six separate judgments, namely, *AB AC AD BC BD CD*. If there are *n* stimuli in the series, it would require $n(n-1)$ such judgments with counterbalanced order of presentation

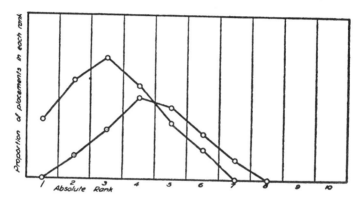

Fig. 21

or half that many if counterbalanced order is disregarded. This would give only one judgment for each of the possible pairs of stimuli. Now if the four stimuli have been placed in the rank order *B D A C* by one subject, it is clear that six judgments may be extracted from this one rank order. Evidently the above rank order series is equivalent to the judgments $B > D$, $B > A$, $B > C$, $D > A$, $D > C$, $A > C$. If a large number of subjects have arranged fifteen or twenty stimuli in rank order, it is an almost prohibitive task to tabulate the separate judgments to which the single rank order is equivalent. However, it can be done by a shorter procedure.

Let there be *n* specimens in the series to be arranged in rank order by *N* subjects. Let *A* and *B* be two of these specimens, and let a_1 = frequency with which specimen *A* is placed in rank 1 by the *N* subjects, b_1 = frequency with which specimen *B* is placed in rank 1 by the *N* subjects, p_{a1} = proportion of the *N* subjects who place specimen *A* in rank 1, p_{b1} = proportion who place specimen *B* in rank 1, and similarly for the other specimens and the other rank orders. See Figure 21.

Since these values of p may be regarded as probabilities, we have $p_{b2} + p_{b3} + p_{b4} + \ldots p_{bn} = p_{b>1} =$ probability that any subject at random (or any one judgment of a single subject) will place B in a rank higher than rank 1.

Hence $p_{a1} \cdot p_{b>1} =$ probability that any subject, chosen at random, will place A in rank 1 and B in a higher rank. Similarly, $p_{a2} \cdot p_{b>2} =$ probability that a subject will place A in rank 2 and B in a higher rank.

In general, this product may be written $p_{ak} \cdot p_{b>k} =$ probability that A will be perceived in rank k and that B will be perceived in a rank higher than k.

Summing for all of the n ranks, we have $\Sigma(p_{ak} \cdot p_{b>k}) =$ probability that B will be perceived in a rank higher than that of A.

But we must also consider the possibility that the two specimens will be perceived as of practically equal or nearly equal rank. If it were possible for two specimens to be perceived in the same rank order, then $p_{ak} \cdot p_{bk} =$ probability that both specimens A and B will be perceived in the same rank order k. But we assume that the subject is asked to place all the n specimens in absolute rank order without any duplicate or tied ranks, and hence it is experimentally impossible for the two specimens to be placed in the same rank order. We shall make the assumption that if the two specimens are perceived to be sufficiently nearly alike to warrant the same rank order, the probability $p^1_{a>b} = .50$, and the probability $p^1_{b>a} = .50$. The notation p^1 refers to a single class interval. This is not quite correct because we know that if the two stimuli are slightly different in objective measurement, then there will be a slight majority of correct judgments, while the incorrect judgments will be in the minority.

This, of course, ignores the possible time and space errors. This is legitimate in dealing with rank order as an experimental method because the subject is given a series of stimuli or specimens to sort out into a rank order by his own devices. It is therefore a matter of chance which of any pair of stimuli is perceived first and whether it happens to be held to the right or to the left of the second stimulus. The subject has the privilege of revising his results and of looking at any and all of the specimens in any order and as many times as he may choose. The problem of constant errors may therefore be ignored.

However, if the two specimens differ slightly in psychological value so that $A > B$ and if they are presented to a subject repeatedly or once to a group of subjects in counterbalanced order by the constant method, we should find that $p_{a>b} > .50$. In other words, a slight majority would favor specimen A. The departure of the judgment $p_{a>b}$ from .50 will be small if the difference between A and B is small. Since in a rank order experiment we shall assume that n is as large as ten or fifteen or twenty, the interval in value represented by one rank order is relatively small. In such situations and especially when the discriminal error is much larger than the interval represented by one rank order, our assumption is approximately correct, namely, that

$(p_{ak} \cdot p_{bk})/2 =$ probability that both A and B will be perceived in the same rank order interval and that B will be perceived higher than A.

Hence we may write the formula with this approximation as

$$p_{b>a} = \Sigma \, (p_{ak} \cdot p_{b>k}) + \tfrac{1}{2} \Sigma \, (p_{ak} \cdot p_{bk}) \, . \qquad (1)$$

In other words, we have expressed the proportion of subjects who perceive B higher than A in terms of the frequencies with which the two specimens are placed in the n rank orders. We can now use simple absolute rank order as an experimental procedure, and we can obtain the same results as with the order of merit method and practically the same results as with the constant method with counterbalanced order. It is taken for granted here that the intermediate category is not used.

The approximation involved in the last term of equation (1) is close enough for all situations in which the number of stimuli to be arranged in rank order is greater than ten or fifteen. The approximation is not satisfactory when the number of stimuli is small, such as five or six. In the present study we have used the approximation represented by equation (1), but we shall develop here a more general formula for translating rank order into the proportions of the constant method which can be used when the experiment involves only a small number of stimuli.

If the number of stimuli represented in Figure 21 is rather small, it is evident that some distortion is introduced by regarding the probability ordinates to be constant within each class interval. That is in effect the assumption in deriving the approximation equation (1). That equation is derived as though the diagrams in Figure 21 were drawn as column diagrams instead of probability polygons. Let Figure 22 represent one of these class intervals in which the probabilities show variation within the class interval. The probability that stimulus 1 will be perceived in this class interval is p_1, and the notation p_2 has a similar interpretation for the second stimulus. The horizontal dotted lines in Figure 22 represent the situation in which a stimulus would be as likely to be perceived at one part of the class interval as at any other part of it. Let the sloping straight line through p_1 represent for each value of x the probability that stimulus 1 will be perceived at x. As we have drawn Figure 22, the stimulus is more likely to be perceived in the upper part of the class interval than in the lower part of it, but our correction formula will cover the general case in which the probability is assumed to vary throughout the class interval according to any linear function.

By inspection of Figure 22 we see that the equations of the two sloping straight lines are as follows:

$$p_{1x} = m_1 x + p_1 - \frac{m_1}{2}, \qquad (2)$$

$$p_{2x} = m_2 x + p_2 - \frac{m_2}{2},\qquad\qquad(3)$$

in which

p_{1x} = the probability that stimulus 1 will be perceived at any point x within the class interval.

p_{2x} = the probability that stimulus 2 will be perceived at any point x within the class interval.

m_1 and m_2 are the slopes of the lines.

p_1 and p_2 are the probabilities that stimuli 1 and 2, respectively, will be perceived in the class interval.

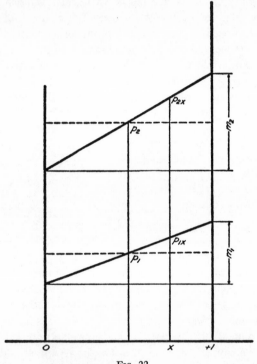

FIG. 22

The probability P_{1x} that stimulus 1 will be perceived higher than x but within the class interval is therefore

$$P_{1x} = \int_x^{+1} \left(m_1 x + p_1 - \frac{m_1}{2} \right) dx.\qquad\qquad(4)$$

The probability that stimulus 2 will be perceived at x and that stimulus 1 will be perceived higher than x but within the class interval is the product of these probabilities, namely,

$$p_{1>2}^1 = \int_0^{+1} p_{2x} \cdot P_{1x} \cdot dx$$
$$= \int_0^{+1} \left[\left(m_2 x + p_2 - \frac{m_2}{2} \right) \int_x^{+1} \left(m_1 x + p_1 - \frac{m_1}{2} \right) dx \right] dx.\qquad(5)$$

After integrating and simplifying, we have

$$p^1_{1>2} = \frac{p_1 p_2}{2} + \frac{1}{12}(m_1 p_2 - m_2 p_1). \tag{6}$$

Inspection of equation (6) makes it evident that if the two slopes m_1 and m_2 are zero, this term becomes identical with the second term of equation (1), which is what we should expect. Furthermore, if a and b are interchanged as well as p_1 and p_2, we should have

$$p^1_{1>2} + p^1_{2>1} = p_1 p_2. \tag{7}$$

In other words, the probability that both stimuli will be perceived in the same class interval is $p_1 p_2$. This probability is split into two parts, namely, the probability $p^1_{1>2}$ that 1 is perceived above 2 and the probability $p^1_{2>1}$ that 2 is perceived above 1 *in the same class interval.*

If we use equation (6) in summation form instead of the second term of equation (1), we shall have a closer approximation to the true value of $p_{1>2}$. Let the class interval of Figure 22 be designated k and let the two stimuli 1 and 2 in Figure 22 be designated b and a, respectively, so that p_2 and p_1 in that figure become, in the more general notation, p_{ak} and p_{bk}, respectively. Then the complete formula becomes

$$p_{b>a} = \Sigma(p_{ak} \cdot p_{b>k}) + \tfrac{1}{2}\Sigma(p_{ak} \cdot p_{bk}) + \tfrac{1}{12}\Sigma(m_{bk} \cdot p_{ak} - m_{ak} \cdot p_{bk}), \tag{8}$$

in which the slopes m_{ak} and m_{bk} are defined as follows:

$$m_{ak} = \frac{p_{a(k+1)} - p_{a(k-1)}}{2} \quad \text{and} \quad m_{bk} = \frac{p_{b(k+1)} - p_{b(k-1)}}{2}. \tag{9}$$

The notation in the general equation (8) may be summarized as follows:

$p_{b>a}$ = estimated proportion of subjects who judge stimulus b higher than stimulus a.

p_{ak} = proportion of subjects who place stimulus a in any particular rank order k. Similar interpretation for p_{bk}.

$p_{a>k}$ = proportion of subjects who place stimulus a higher than any specified class interval k. Similar interpretation for $p_{b>k}$.

$p_{a(k+1)}$ = proportion of subjects who place stimulus a in the rank order next higher than k. Similar interpretation for $p_{b(k+1)}$.

$p_{a(k-1)}$ = proportion of subjects who place stimulus a in the rank order next lower than k. Similar interpretation for $p_{b(k-1)}$.

It should be noted that both the equations (1) and (8) are approximation equations but that equation (8) involves the least assumptions. Thus equation (1) assumes that the probabilities in Figure 21 can be adequately represented as column diagrams. This is legitimate for most problems where the number of stimuli is as large as, say, twenty. Equation (8) assumes only that the variation in the probabilities of each class interval in Figure 22 is linear. It is represented by frequency polygons in Figure 21 instead of column diagrams. In most experimental situations formula (1) is adequate, since it shows only a very slight discrepancy with the actual count for $p_{b>a}$.

Returning to formula (1), we shall now show its application to some experimental data. The psychophysical comparisons of social stimuli are much more complex than the comparisons of simple sensory stimuli such as line lengths and weights. If our method is applicable to the complexities of social stimuli, they may safely be assumed to be applicable to the simpler case of sensory stimuli. We shall test the formula on Miss Hevner's data for judgments about handwriting specimens.[2]

In her experiment on the order of merit method she asked 370 subjects to arrange twenty specimens of handwriting in rank order. From such experimental data it was of course possible to count the number of subjects who placed each one of the twenty specimens in each one of the twenty rank orders. For example, 59 out of the 370 subjects placed specimen 4 in the fifth place from the top in excellence. In a table of this kind there must, of course, be as many rank orders as there are specimens because tied ranks were not allowed. From this table a second table was prepared showing the *proportion* of all the subjects who placed each specimen in each of the twenty rank orders. In the above example this proportion is 0.1595. This means that about 16 per cent of the entire group of 370 subjects placed specimen 4 in rank order five. This is shown in Table 8, and the rest of the table is interpreted in the same manner.

Table 9 is a summary of the calculation for estimating the proportion of subjects who perceived specimen 2 to be better than specimen 1. The first column is a list of the twenty rank orders. For each specimen a strip was prepared similar to the second and third columns. Columns four and five in Table 9 represent such a strip for the second stimulus. These strips were used in calculation so as to avoid unnecessary transcription. The sixth column shows the product $p_{1k} \cdot p_{2>k}$ for each of the rank orders. This is merely the product of columns two and five in the table. The last column shows the product $p_{1k} \cdot p_{2k}$ for each of the rank orders. It is the product of items in columns two and four. In actual calculation the entries in the last two columns were not recorded. The products were calculated on a Marchant calculating machine, and they were allowed to total without recording of the separate items in the last two columns. The entries of these two columns are here shown for completeness, although in practice it is not necessary to write them. Only the sums for the last two columns are recorded. These sums are shown at the bottom of the table. The simple calculation of the estimated proportion of all the subjects who perceived specimen 2 to be better than specimen 1 is also there indicated. It is done in accordance with equation (1).

This procedure was carried out for each of the $\frac{1}{2}n(n-1) = 190$ possible

[2] K. Hevner, "An Empirical Study of Three Psychophysical Methods," *Journal of General Psychology*, IV (1930), 191–212.

TABLE 8

PROPORTION OF 370 JUDGES WHO PLACED EACH ONE OF TWENTY HANDWRITING SPECIMENS IN EACH OF TWENTY ABSOLUTE RANK ORDERS BY THE ORDER OF MERIT METHOD. TWENTY SPECIMENS

Rank Order	1	2	3	4	5	6	7	8	9	10	11	12	13	14	15	16	17	18	19	20
1	.3108	.1081	.0676	.0838	.1973	.1595	.0676	.0027	.0027											
2	.2027	.0865	.1297	.1351	.1378	.1838	.1054	.0027	.0081		.0081	.0081								
3	.1649	.1135	.1595	.1270	.1324	.1162	.1595	.0054	.0189		.0000	.0027								
4	.0919	.1405	.1514	.1378	.1351	.1081	.1595	.0162	.0459		.0054	.0027		.0027						
5	.0784	.1135	.1135	.1595	.1027	.1432	.1784	.0135	.0649	.0027	.0081	.0270	.0054	.0000	.0027					
6	.0757	.1432	.1054	.1486	.1162	.1054	.1027	.0568	.1108	.0000	.0297	.0216	.0027	.0054	.0027					
7	.0378	.1378	.1000	.1135	.0784	.1027	.1459	.0703	.1405	.0054	.0811	.0486	.0162	.0108	.0054	.0027				
8	.0270	.0703	.0676	.0622	.0703	.0378	.0459	.1405	.2892	.0027	.1216	.1243	.0351	.0108	.0189	.0027				
9	.0054	.0243	.0486	.0189	.0162	.0189	.0243	.2378	.1973	.0054	.2486	.2243	.0676	.0568	.0324	.0000				
10	.0027	.0297	.0324	.0027	.0081	.0162	.0027	.2135	.0676	.0432	.1892	.2649	.1189	.1270	.1081	.0000	.0027	.0054		
11	.0000	.0135	.0162	.0081	.0000	.0054	.0054	.1000	.0270	.0757	.1757	.1189	.1703	.2135	.1892	.0054	.0027	.0000		
12	.0027	.0081	.0027	.0000	.0027	.0027	.0000	.0703	.0216	.1730	.0919	.0811	.2946	.3162	.1757	.0000	.0000	.0000		
13		.0027	.0054	.0027	.0000		.0027	.0405	.0000	.2622	.0270	.0486	.1973	.1297	.1838	.0081	.0135	.0135		
14		.0081			.0000			.0189	.0054	.2054	.0081	.0162	.0622	.0676	.1703	.0216	.0108	.0270	.0027	.0027
15					.0027			.0108		.1162	.0054	.0027	.0216	.0270	.0784	.0351	.1081	.1324	.0081	.0081
16										.0730		.0054	.0081	.0054	.0189	.1541	.2892	.2541	.0459	.0108
17										.0216		.0027		.0027	.0081	.2054	.3162	.2216	.0892	.0486
18										.0135					.0054	.2757	.1541	.2784	.1243	.1270
19																.1649	.0811	.0514	.4108	.2865
20																.1243	.0216	.0162	.3189	.5162

pairs of stimuli, although it should be noted that when the two specimens
are far apart in excellence, the amount of overlapping is small, so that the
calculation is then short. For example, the strip for specimen 1 covers the
first 12 rank orders as shown in the second and third columns of Table 9. The
corresponding strip for specimen 20 covers the rank orders from 14 to 20
inclusive. Since there is no overlapping, it is clear that none of the subjects
regarded specimen 20 as better than specimen 1, and consequently we can
write without further calculation that the estimated proportion of the sub-

TABLE 9

Rank Order	Strip No. 1		Strip No. 2		Products	
	p_{1k}	$p_{1>k}$	p_{2k}	$p_{2>k}$	$p_{1k} \cdot p_{2>k}$	$p_{1k} \cdot p_{2k}$
1.......	.3108	.6894	.1081	.8919	.2772	.0336
2.......	.2027	.4865	.0865	.8054	.1633	.0175
3.......	.1649	.3216	.1135	.6919	.1141	.0187
4.......	.0919	.2297	.1405	.5514	.0507	.0129
5.......	.0784	.1513	.1135	.4379	.0343	.0089
6.......	.0757	.0756	.1432	.2947	.0223	.0108
7.......	.0378	.0378	.1378	.1569	.0059	.0052
8.......	.0270	.0108	.0703	.0866	.0023	.0019
9.......	.0054	.0054	.0243	.0623	.0003	.0001
10......	.0027	.0027	.0297	.0326	.0001	.0001
11......	.0000	.0027	.0135	.0191	.0000	.0000
12......	.0027	.0000	.0081	.0110	.0000	.0000
13......			.0027	.0083		
14......			.0081	.0002		
15......						
16......						
17......						
18......						
19......						
20......						

$$\Sigma(p_{1k} \cdot p_{2>k}) = .6705$$
$$\tfrac{1}{2}\Sigma(p_{1k} \cdot p_{2k}) = .0549$$
$$p_{2>1} = .7254$$

jects who perceived specimen 1 as better than specimen 20 is unity. The
amount of calculation is a maximum when the two specimens are nearly of
the same degree of excellence, and two such specimens are shown in the
example of Table 9. Consequently, the labor of calculation is not nearly so
great as would be indicated by merely multiplying the labor of Table 9 by
190.

Miss Hevner actually tabulated the number of judges who placed each
one of the twenty specimens higher than every other specimen. This was accomplished by her records of order of merit for 370 subjects. This was an
exceedingly laborious procedure, but it was done in order to compare the
order of merit method with two other psychophysical methods, namely, the
method of equal-appearing intervals and the method of paired comparison.

In order to test our equation (1), we listed the proportions estimated by equation (1) and also the actual proportions tabulated by Miss Hevner for the order of merit method. The discrepancy for each proportion was listed in the form $(p_H - p_C)$, in which p_H refers to the actual proportion found by Miss Hevner by the order of merit method and p_C refers to the estimated proportions calculated by our present equation (1). The distribution of discrepancies is shown in Figure 23. The average discrepancy, disregarding sign, is .0078, which shows a very close agreement. The fact that the average discrepancy is less than 1 per cent constitutes practical justification for equation (1) as a method of estimating the proportions of the constant method when the experimental procedure was that of simple rank order. The close similar-

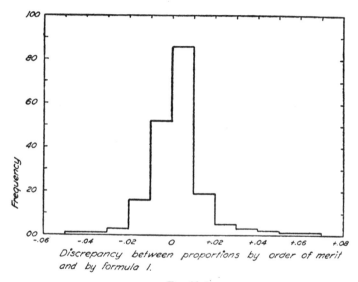

FIG. 23

ity in results from the order of merit method and the constant method was demonstrated by Miss Hevner.

It is to be expected that the scale values for the twenty specimens determined by the two sets of proportions should be practically identical, and this is shown in Figure 23. We have tabulated the scale values determined by Miss Hevner for the order of merit method and for the same raw data treated by the present formula. The agreement is practically perfect, as shown in Figure 24. Not only are the two scales comparable, but the units are identical since the proportions themselves agree, and consequently the slope of the plot in Figure 24 is unity.

An important psychophysical inference may be drawn from these experiments. In a previous paper I have assumed that the correlation between discriminal errors of two specimens that are being compared is zero. That is a fundamental assumption of the law of comparative judgment. At that

time I did not see any clear method of testing that assumption separately
from the other assumptions involved in the same study. Since the equation
of comparative judgment has been shown to fit experimental data for a wide
variety of stimuli, I have felt assured that the assumptions were justified. In the present data we find, however, a specific verification for the assumption that the correlational term of the equation of comparative judgment is zero. If it were not zero, then the probabilities involved in equation
(1) would not be independent, and consequently the product of the several

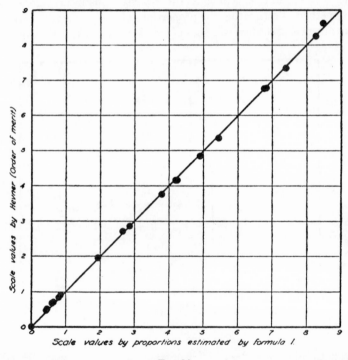

FIG. 24

probabilities would not tally with the experimentally observed proportion
of judgments that constitute a compound event. Since the equation satisfies
the experimentally observed frequencies with a degree of accuracy that is
unusual in psychological work, we are justified in concluding that the several
probabilities are truly independent and that therefore the correlational term
in the law of comparative judgment is zero, as has been previously assumed.

In Miss Hevner's study a comparison was made between the order of
merit method and the constant method in its complete form, namely,
paired comparison. These two methods were shown to be identical when
treated by the equation of comparative judgment. We have here shown that
it is not necessary in the order of merit method to tabulate separately all of

the $n(n-1)$ judgments for each subject that are implied in his arrangement of n stimuli in a single rank order. It is possible to estimate the proportions directly from a frequency table of rank orders for each specimen. This makes it possible to use simple rank order when that method is experimentally the easiest and to extract from the rank order data the proportions that would be obtained by the laborious constant method or the even more laborious paired comparison method. Miss Hevner has previously shown that the order of merit method gives results practically identical with the constant method. We have also verified our previous assumption that the discriminal errors in a comparison of two stimuli are usually uncorrelated. This assumption enters the law of comparative judgment when the correlational term is assumed to be zero.

11 | STIMULUS DISPERSIONS IN THE METHOD OF CONSTANT STIMULI

The purpose of this paper[1] is (1) to develop a method of numerically evaluating the stimulus dispersions for stimuli that have been experimentally presented by the constant method, (2) to compare two forms of approximation of the law of comparative judgment, namely, Case 3, which allows for differences in stimulus dispersion among the stimuli, and Case 5, which assumes that all of the stimulus dispersions are equal, and (3) to describe a criterion by which to decide whether Case 3 or Case 5 should be used with a set of data collected by the method of constant stimuli. Since the present study is a continuation of previous work on the law of comparative judgment, the concept of stimulus dispersion[2] and the concept of the psychological or experiential continuum will not here be repeated. For the same reason the assumptions underlying the five cases of the law will not be repeated. We are concerned here with the solution of a problem that has been found rather troublesome, namely, the numerical evaluation of the dispersion or ambiguity of each stimulus. Description of the experimental data and the two cases under which they may be treated will be preceded by a short discussion of the logic of the problem.

Psychophysics is the quantitative study of the discriminatory process. In such a study we deal with two principal continua, namely, the physical stimulus increments and the apparent or experienced increments. These two continua are designated the R-scale for stimulus increments and the S-scale for the apparent or experienced increments. Fechner's law expresses the logarithmic relation between these two variables in the form $S = k \log R$, in which k is a constant and in which the experienced increments are measured from the experience of unit stimulus as an origin.

A psychophysical problem may be stated in two essentially different ways. First, it may be the problem of describing the discriminatory process in terms of the physically measured stimuli, or, second, it may be the reverse, namely, to describe the stimuli in terms of the discriminatory process. Both of these types of psychophysical problem employ the same experimental methods and the same logic. Of these two types of problem the first is much the more common in psychophysics, but it is probable that the second type of psycho-

[1] Reprinted from *Journal of Experimental Psychology*, XV (1932), 284–97.

[2] See chap. iii.

physical problem is much the more important for psychology. Limen determinations belong to the first type, in which one aspect of the discriminatory process is described in terms of a stimulus measurement. The limen is a stimulus measurement which is used to describe the discriminatory process. It will be readily seen that this first type of psychophysical problem is much the more restricted because it can be stated only for those stimuli which can be rather unambiguously measured, physically, in the attribute by which they are discriminated. No such limitation exists for the second type of psychophysical problem, in which we pivot on the discriminatory process so that stimuli and their differences are described in terms of the discriminatory process. Thus, for example, the similarity or difference between two stimuli A and B may be described in terms of the ease with which they are differentiated even though neither stimulus can be physically measured in the attribute by which the subject differentiates between them. Of course, the same problem can also be stated for those stimuli that can be so physically measured, but physical measurement of the stimuli is in no sense a prerequisite for the description of their degree of similarity in terms of the ease with which they are actually differentiated.

Suppose that a series of brightnesses is to be studied by the two formulations here described. According to the first we should determine, experimentally, that brightness increment from any one of them as a standard which is correctly discriminated in, let us say, 75 per cent of the attempts. That stimulus measurement would be the limen. But with the same data before us, we may reverse the question and ask how many experiential units there are between two of the brightnesses. That question can be answered without even knowing the photometric values of the brightnesses and without altering the psychophysical experiment.

In both of these forms of the problem we need to have an experiential unit of measurement. It is necessary for the limen determination as well as for our second formulation of the psychophysical problem. The just noticeable difference is regarded as experiential unity, but it is of course measured physically. The writer has proposed a truly mental unit of measurement, the discriminal error,[3] as a substitute for the just noticeable difference, since the discriminal error is by definition an experiential process, and as such it is more appropriate for measuring experienced increments than the physical measurement, the j.n.d.

In the method of constant stimuli there are two stimuli presented to the subject for discrimination in a prescribed attribute. If the stimuli can be physically measured, it is of course possible to say definitely whether any judgment of the subject is correct or incorrect. The correctness of an experienced difference between the two stimuli is assigned then by pivoting on the physical measurement as relatively infallible. If the two stimuli cannot be physically measured in the attribute judged, then the judgment is handled

[3] See chap. iv.

statistically in the same way except that the judgment returned in the majority of the attempts is then called the correct order. This latter criterion of correctness agrees with the first and is applicable to stimuli that can be physically measured as well as to those stimuli that cannot be physically measured in the attribute by which they are discriminated. Hence the latter criterion is the more universal and psychologically the more significant.

The principal psychophysical problem is the measurement of the experiential increment between the two stimuli because their physical measurement presents no psychological problem when the attribute that is discriminated can be physically defined. In psychophysical problems of this type it has been assumed that equally often noticed differences are psychologically equal. This assumption is known as the Fullerton-Cattell theorem, and it is no doubt correct for many simple stimulus series, but it is not valid for stimuli that differ in what the writer has defined as stimulus ambiguity.[4] By this is meant the disperion projected by the stimulus on the experiential or psychological continuum that has been described so that it lends itself to objective experimental treatment.

The law of comparative judgment is the fundamental equation for the method of constant stimuli. It expresses the experiential increment as a function of the frequency of similar discrimination, $p_{a>b}$, and the two stimulus ambiguities or dispersions on the experiential continuum, σ_a and σ_b. The law has been discussed under five cases,[5] each of which has its own assumptions and approximations. In the simplest case the stimulus dispersions are all assumed to be equal, and the Fullerton-Cattell theorem is then valid. The customary stimuli of psychophysical experimentation, such as brightnesses, line lengths, and lifted weights, are obviously so uniform as to stimulus dispersion or ambiguity that the usefulness of the equation of comparative judgment is more clearly demonstrated on stimuli that may be assumed to vary considerably in stimulus dispersion. Such is the case with the affective values[6] of nationalities and races in response to the question, "Which would you rather associate with?"

The Experimental Data

A printed schedule of pairs of nationalities and races was submitted to 250 children in the Hyde Park High School in Chicago. The instructions were as follows:

This is an experimental study of attitudes toward races and nationalities. You are asked merely to underline the one nationality, or race, of each pair that you would rather associate with. For example, the first pair is:

ENGLISHMAN—SOUTH AMERICAN

If, in general, you prefer to associate with Englishmen rather than with South Americans, underline *Englishman*. If you prefer, in general, to associate with South

---

[4] See chap. iii.   [5] Chap. iii.   [6] See chap. xxi.

Americans, underline *South American*. If you find it difficult to decide for any pair, simply underline one of them anyway. If two nationalities are about equally well liked, they will have about the same number of underlinings in all of the papers. Be sure to underline one of each pair even if you have to make a sort of guess.

The schedule contained a list of pairs of nationalities and races so arranged that each of the nationalities listed in Table 10 was paired with every other nationality and race in the list. Since there are thirteen nationalities in the list, there were

$n(n - 1)/2 = 78$ experimentally independent judgments from each subject.

It is entirely irrelevant for the purposes of the present problem whether

TABLE 10

EXPERIMENTAL PROPORTIONS

		1 Eng.	2 Ca.	3 Fr.	4 Ir.	5 Sc.	6 Sw.	7 Ge.	8 Ho.	9 Sp.	10 Be.	11 S.A.	12 Jew	13 It.
1......	Eng.	....	.388	.218	.324	.165	.221	.227	.162	.144	.103	.065	.155	.066
2......	Ca.	.612	....	.457	.406	.280	.260	.297	.102	.201	.100	.088	.180	.073
3......	Fr.	.782	.543	....	.541	.500	.370	.380	.255	.184	.214	.149	.192	.081
4......	Ir.	.676	.594	.459	....	.361	.387	.378	.253	.273	.243	.162	.221	.128
5......	Sc.	.835	.720	.500	.639	....	.400	.409	.268	.249	.258	.262	.223	.128
6......	Sw.	.779	.740	.630	.613	.600	....	.471	.444	.377	.317	.318	.229	.228
7......	Ge.	.773	.703	.620	.622	.591	.529	....	.347	.391	.325	.345	.253	.152
8......	Ho.	.838	.898	.745	.747	.732	.556	.653	....	.471	.432	.389	.263	.310
9......	Sp.	.856	.799	.816	.727	.751	.623	.609	.529	....	.510	.422	.289	.217
10......	Be.	.897	.900	.786	.757	.742	.683	.675	.568	.490	....	.461	.360	.271
11......	S.A.	.935	.912	.851	.838	.738	.682	.655	.611	.578	.539	....	.420	.320
12......	Jew	.845	.820	.808	.779	.777	.771	.747	.737	.711	.640	.580	....	.524
13......	It.	.934	.927	.919	.872	.872	.772	.848	.690	.783	.729	.680	.476	....

the thirteen social stimuli were nationalities or races or religions in any anthropological sense. It is possible, for example, to have a prejudice against South Americans without reference to any particular South American country, and hence such a category is legitimate for a psychophysical study even though it might be entirely illegitimate in an anthropological study. We shall refer to the thirteen stimuli as nationalities without repeating this reservation.

In Table 10 we have a summary of the preferential judgments of our subjects. It shows the proportion of the subjects who preferred each nationality at the top of the table to each nationality at the side of the table. For example, the proportion of subjects who preferred Hollanders to Canadians was .102, and, since the intermediate category of judgment was not allowed, the proportion of subject who preferred Canadians to Hollanders was .898. All the other entries in Table 10 are read in the same manner.

In Table 11 we have the corresponding *x*-values which were read directly from the Kelley-Wood tables. Continuing the same example, we enter the Kelley-Wood tables with the proportion .102, and we find the *x*-value 1.27,

TABLE 11

X-VALUES

	1 Eng.	2 Ca.	3 Fr.	4 Ir.	5 Sc.	6 Sw.	7 Ge.	8 Ho.	9 Sp.	10 Be.	11 S.A.	12 Jew	13 It.
1 Eng.	.00	−.28	−.78	−.46	−.97	−.77	−.75	−.99	−1.06	−1.26	−1.51	−1.02	−1.51
2 Ca.	.28	.00	−.11	−.24	−.58	−.64	−.53	−1.27	−.84	−1.28	−1.35	−.92	−1.45
3 Fr.	.78	.11	.00	−.10	.00	−.33	−.31	−.66	−.90	−.79	−1.04	−.87	−1.40
4 Ir.	.46	.24	.10	.00	−.36	−.29	−.31	−.67	−.60	−.70	−.99	−.77	−1.14
5 Sc.	.97	.58	.00	.36	.00	−.25	−.23	−.62	−.68	−.65	−.64	−.76	−1.14
6 Sw.	.77	.64	.33	.29	.25	.00	−.07	−.14	−.31	−.48	−.47	−.74	−.75
7 Ge.	.75	.53	.31	.31	.23	.07	.00	−.39	−.28	−.45	−.40	−.67	−1.03
8 Ho.	.99	1.27	.66	.67	.62	.14	.39	.00	−.07	−.17	−.28	−.63	−.50
9 Sp.	1.06	.84	.90	.60	.68	.31	.28	.07	.00	−.03	−.20	−.56	−.78
10 Be.	1.26	1.28	.79	.70	.65	.48	.45	.17	.03	.00	−.10	−.36	−.61
11 S.A.	1.51	1.35	1.04	.99	.64	.47	.40	.28	.20	.10	.00	−.20	−.47
12 Jew	1.02	.92	.87	.77	.76	.74	.67	.63	.56	.36	.20	.00	−.06
13 It.	1.51	1.45	1.40	1.14	1.14	.75	1.03	.50	.78	.61	.47	.06	.00
Σx	11.36	8.93	5.31	5.23	3.06	.68	1.02	−3.09	−3.23	−4.68	−6.31	−7.56	−10.72
V	.4261	.5385	.5774	.4521	.5790	.4728	.4896	.5587	.6506	.5583	.5738	.3161	.4946

which has a negative sign because the proportion .102 is less than .50. When the proportion is greater than .50, the x-value has a positive sign.[7] At the foot of each column is the algebraic sum of the x-values, Σx, and the standard deviation, V, of the column of x-values.

The law of comparative judgment in Case 3 is written in the form:[8]

$$S_1 - S_2 = x_{12} \sqrt{\sigma_1^2 + \sigma_2^2}. \tag{1}$$

This equation can be written in the linear approximation form:

$$S_1 - S_2 = .707\, x_{12}\sigma_1 + .707\, x_{12}\sigma_2 , \tag{2}$$

which has been called Case 4. When the two stimulus dispersions in (1) are assumed to be equal to unity, the law takes the simplest form, namely,

$$S_1 - S_2 = x_{12} \sqrt{2} , \tag{3}$$

which we have called Case 5.

Case 5 of the Law of Comparative Judgment

The data will be evaluated first by Case 5 because it is the simplest. Let S_k be the scale value of any one of the thirteen stimuli. We then have

$$S_1 - S_k = x_{1k} \sqrt{2} . \tag{4}$$

Summing for all thirteen stimuli, we have

$$nS_1 - \Sigma S_k = \sqrt{2}\Sigma x_{1k} . \tag{5}$$

But we may allocate the origin at the mean of all the experiential values so that

$$\Sigma S_k = 0 , \tag{6}$$

and then

$$nS_1 = \sqrt{2}\Sigma x_{1k} . \tag{7}$$

Hence,

$$S_1 = \frac{\sqrt{2}}{n} \Sigma x_{1k} . \tag{8}$$

The sum of the first column of x-values is 11.36, and hence the affective or experiential value of the first stimulus is $+1.2357$. This is the affective value recorded for the English in Table 12 by Case 5. All the other affective values by Case 5 are computed in the same manner. See Table 12. The sum of the affective values in Table 12 is -0.0001 or practically zero, as postulated in equation (6).

With the thirteen scale values in Table 12 calculated by Case 5, we next ascertain how well these scale values fit the data. The thirteen scale values

[7] See chap. xxi.   [8] See chap. iii.

should lock the 78 experimentally independent proportions on Table 10. For
example, the scale values of the Canadians and the Spaniards are +.9714
and −.3514, respectively. Their difference is 1.3228, which, when substituted
in equation (1), gives an x-value of .935; and this, by the Kelley-Wood
tables, gives an expected proportion of .825 favoring the Canadians when
compared with the Spaniards. The experimentally obtained proportion was
.799, which shows a discrepancy of .026. This is a fairly satisfactory agreement. In order to ascertain the agreement over the whole table, the 78 dis-

TABLE 12

COMPARISON OF DISCREPANCIES FOR CASE 3 AND FOR CASE 5
OF THE LAW OF COMPARATIVE JUDGMENT

	CASE 5 AFFECTIVE VALUE S	CASE 5 AVER. DISCREP.	CASE 3		
			Affective Value S	Stimulus Disper. σ	Aver. Discrep.
1 English..........	1.2357	.0372	1.4050	1.3121	.0185
2 Canadian........	.9714	.0386	.8718	.8295	.0299
3 French..........	.5777	.0398	.4902	.7062	.0288
4 Irish............	.5689	.0261	.6159	1.1791	.0132
5 Scotch..........	.3329	.0445	.2828	.7015	.0364
6 Swede..........	.0740	.0248	.1029	1.0837	.0256
7 German.........	.1110	.0222	.1298	1.0122	.0222
8 Hollander.......	− .3362	.0370	− .2573	.7634	.0319
9 Spaniard........	− .3514	.0381	− .2805	.8224	.0311
10 Belgian.........	− .5091	.0262	− .4229	.7646	.0194
11 South American....	− .6865	.0296	− .5686	.7170	.0254
12 Jew.............	− .8224	.0582	−1.2540	2.1167	.0225
13 Italian..........	−1.1661	.0395	−1.1151	.9918	.0191
Summation.......	−0.0001	....	0.0000	13.0002	....
Average.........	....	.0355	....	....	.0249

crepancies were calculated as in the above example. In the fourth column of
Table 12 we have the average discrepancy between the experimental and the
calculated proportions for Case 5. Thus, in Table 12 the average discrepancy
between the twelve experimental and calculated proportions for the English
is .0372; for the Germans it is smallest, namely, .0222, while for the Jews it
is the largest, namely, .0582. The average discrepancy for the whole table is
.0355, which is here the principal value sought. This value we shall compare
with the average discrepancy for Case 3, in which the stimulus dispersions
are not assumed to be equal.

Case 3 of the Law of Comparative Judgment

If we write equation (4) for any two stimuli, such as the English, No. 1,
and the Canadians, No. 2, we have

$$S_1 - S_k = x_{1k} \sqrt{2} \, ,$$

$$S_2 - S_3 = x_{23} \sqrt{2}$$

(9)

Subtracting,

$$S_1 - S_2 = x_{1k}\sqrt{2} - x_{2k}\sqrt{2}, \tag{10}$$

in which $(S_1 - S_2)$ is constant, namely, the difference between the two scale values for the English and the Canadians, irrespective of the nationalities that are successively represented by the notation k. Equation (10) may be rewritten in the form,

$$x_{1k} = x_{2k} + \frac{S_1 - S_2}{\sqrt{2}}, \tag{11}$$

in which

$$\frac{S_1 - S_2}{\sqrt{2}} = \text{a constant}.$$

Now this is evidently the equation of a straight line with a slope of unity. It may be tested by plotting experimental values of x_{1k} against x_{2k}, and similar tests may be made for any other pair of columns in Table 11. When that is done, it is seen that the best-fitting straight lines do not have a slope of unity, and the author suspects the reason to be largely in the differences of stimulus dispersion among the thirteen stimuli. For this reason we may try Case 3, which does not make the assumption that the dispersions are all equal.

We may write the law of comparative judgment for two stimuli 1 and k in the form:

$$S_1 - S_k = .707 x_{1k}\sigma_1 + .707 x_{1k}\sigma_k, \tag{12}$$

and, similarly, for the stimuli 2 and k:

$$S_2 - S_k = .707 x_{2k}\sigma_2 + .707 x_{2k}\sigma_k. \tag{13}$$

Subtracting, we have

$$S_1 - S_2 = .707 x_{1k}(\sigma_1 + \sigma_k) - .707 x_{2k}(\sigma_2 + \sigma_k), \tag{14}$$

or

$$x_{1k} = x_{2k}\frac{\sigma_2 + \sigma_k}{\sigma_1 + \sigma_k} - \frac{S_1 - S_2}{.707(\sigma_1 + \sigma_k)}. \tag{15}$$

If x_{1k} be plotted against x_{2k}, this plot should be linear with a scatter that is due to (1) chance errors in original proportions and (2) the ignoring of variations in σ_k, which may be assumed equal to unity in the linear regression or approximation equation:

$$x_{1k} = x_{2k}\frac{1 + \sigma_2}{1 + \sigma_1} - \frac{S_1 - S_2}{.707(1 + \sigma_1)}. \tag{16}$$

It should be noted that σ_1 and σ_2 are not assumed to be equal. The slope of this linear plot should be

$$\text{Slope} = \frac{1 + \sigma_2}{1 + \sigma_1}. \tag{17}$$

But the slope can also be determined from the ratio of the dispersion of the values of x_{1k} and the dispersion of the values of x_{2k}.

Let V_1 = standard deviation of values of x_{1k} and
V_2 = standard deviation of values of x_{2k}.

Then

$$\text{Slope} = \frac{V_1}{V_2}. \tag{18}$$

But equations (17) and (18) are two measures of the same slope. Hence, approximately,

$$\frac{V_1}{V_2} = \frac{1+\sigma_2}{1+\sigma_1}. \tag{19}$$

In other words, the dispersion of the values of x_{1k} is inversely proportional to $(1 + \sigma_1)$, and similarly for each of the other stimuli, so that

$$\frac{a}{V_1} = 1 + \sigma_1,$$

$$\frac{a}{V_2} = 1 + \sigma_2, \tag{20}$$

$$\frac{a}{V_3} = 1 + \sigma_3,$$

and so on, in which a is a constant. If we sum these n equations (20) we have

$$a\Sigma\left(\frac{1}{V_k}\right) = n + \Sigma\sigma_k. \tag{21}$$

But we may define our unit of measurement as the average stimulus dispersion, so that

$$\Sigma\sigma_k = n, \tag{22}$$

and hence,

$$a\Sigma\left(\frac{1}{V_k}\right) = 2n. \tag{23}$$

The value of the constant a may be readily determined from equation (23) as

$$a = \frac{2n}{\Sigma\left(\dfrac{1}{V_k}\right)}. \tag{24}$$

With the constant a known, we calculate each of the n stimulus dispersions from the following equations, obtained directly from equation (20).

$$\sigma_1 = \frac{a}{V_1} - 1,$$

$$\sigma_2 = \frac{a}{V_2} - 1,$$

$$\sigma_3 = \frac{a}{V_3} - 1 \tag{25}$$

$$\cdots\cdots\cdots$$

$$\sigma_n = \frac{a}{V_n} - 1.$$

When the stimulus dispersions $\sigma_1, \sigma_2, \sigma_3 \ldots \sigma_n$ have been calculated, we may proceed with the calculation of the psychophysical values $S_1, S_2, S_3 \ldots S_n$. This can be done as follows:

$$S_1 - S_k = .707 x_{1k}\sigma_1 + .707 x_{1k}\sigma_k .$$

Summing, we have

$$nS_1 - \Sigma S_k = .707 \sigma_1 \Sigma x_{1k} + .707 \Sigma x_{1k} \cdot \sigma_k . \qquad (26)$$

But

$$\Sigma S_k = 0 ,$$

since we may place the origin at the arithmetical mean of the thirteen psychological values. Hence

$$nS_1 = .707 \sigma_1 \Sigma x_{1k} + .707 \Sigma \sigma_k \cdot x_{1k} , \qquad (27)$$

or

$$S_1 = .707 \sigma_1 \frac{\Sigma x_{1k}}{n} + .707 \frac{\Sigma \sigma_k \cdot x_{1k}}{n} . \qquad (28)$$

Let M_{x1} = mean of all values of x_{1k}, and similarly for each of the other stimuli. Then

$$S_1 = .707 \sigma_1 M_{x1} + \frac{.707 \Sigma \sigma_k \cdot x_{1k}}{n} , \qquad (29)$$

and a similar form can of course be written for each of the other stimuli.

The numerical work consists in calculating the standard deviations, V, of each column in Table 11. Thus the standard deviation, V, of the first column is .4261. The sum of the reciprocals of these standard deviations is 26.3915, which enables us to calculate the constant a by equation (24). It has a value of .98517. The stimulus dispersions can then be determined approximately by equation (25), and these have been recorded in column six of Table 12 for Case 3. Their sum is 13, which is postulated in equation (22). The scale values in column five of the table are then computed by equation (29). Their sum is zero, which satisfies the assumption of equations 26 and 27.

It will be seen in Table 12 that the discrepancies in scale value between Case 3 and Case 5 are in general largest for those stimuli that are found to have the largest stimulus dispersions, and this is what should be expected, partly because of the assumption in Case 5 that they are all equal and partly because of the assumption in Case 3 that they do not deviate markedly from unity.

The choice between the two cases should be made by noting which of them satisfies the experimental data with the least average discrepancy. With the thirteen scale values and approximate discrepancies calculated by Case 3 we can, of course, return to equation (2) for every pair of stimuli to calculate the proportion of the subjects who should prefer any one of the stimuli to any other. This has been done, and the results are listed in the last column of Table 12. The average discrepancy between the experimental and the calculated proportions is 0.0249, which is smaller than the corresponding value for Case 5.

Summary

The numerical evaluation of the stimulus dispersions in the method of constant stimuli has been a troublesome problem. In this paper we have developed a procedure for obtaining an approximate value for the dispersion of each stimulus. The average discrepancy between the experimental and the calculated proportions is 0.0355 by Case 5, in which the stimulus dispersions are assumed to be equal, but it is reduced to an average discrepancy of 0.0249 by Case 3, in which allowance is made for differences in stimulus dispersion. A criterion for deciding whether the simpler form of Case 5 or the more laborious Case 3 should be used for an experiment that has been conducted by the constant method is to plot pairs of columns of x-values in Table 11. If the best-fitting straight lines in these plots have a slope nearly equal to unity, then Case 5 can be used advantageously. If not, then a better agreement between experimental and calculated values will be obtained by Case 3. In any event, the stimulus dispersions that are calculated by the procedure here described are approximate values. Their probable errors are undoubtedly large, but the procedure does give a fairly good idea of the order of magnitude of the stimulus dispersions. For example, it is probably safe to assume that there is greater variation of attitude toward the Jews in our experimental population than for any of the other nationalities or races. This is found in the calculations according to which there is much greater variation in attitude toward the Jews than toward any of the other groups. It is approximately measured by the stimulus dispersion in Table 12. This observation also agrees with the fact that the discrepancies for the Jews are much larger in Case 5 than for any of the other groups. In other words, the greater the deviation of the stimulus dispersion from the average dispersion of all the stimuli, the greater will be the error caused by the principal assumption of Case 5, and the greater will be the discrepancies between experimental and calculated proportions.

12 THE INDIFFERENCE FUNCTION

The purpose of this paper[1] is to introduce a new problem in psychophysics which concerns also some fundamental economic theory. The problem in its economic setting is old, but the restatement of it in experimental form and its formulation as a psychophysical problem are probably new. The problem involves two psychological functions that we shall call the *satisfaction curve* and the *indifference curve*, respectively. The general nature of these two functions will first be described, then the mathematical development of both functions from psychological postulates, and finally their experimental verification.

The formulation of this problem is due to numerous conversations about psychophysics with my friend Professor Henry Schultz of the University of Chicago. It was at his suggestion that experimental methods were applied to this problem in economic theory. According to Professor Schultz, it has probably never before been subjected to experimental study. The writer dares not venture far into the economic theory which may be implied in this psychophysical problem, but it is clear that here is a fertile field for investigation in a very old problem that overlaps economic theory and psychophysical experimentation.

If you have a certain amount of some desirable commodity, it is not inconceivable that you would like to have some more. That is the kind of commodity we are studying here. We shall assume that your satisfaction from this commodity increases, the more you have of it, at least within the limits of plausible experimental or practical judgments. This fact we represent in Figure 25, in which s = satisfaction and x = number of items of a commodity. This rising satisfaction curve has been drawn so as to show an increase in satisfaction with increase in the amount of the commodity possessed by an individual. We are not concerned with those commodities which do not show such an increase in satisfaction, and of course we are not concerned with absurd extremes in quantity, as, for example, the immediate physical possession of a million apples, for which our satisfaction might be obscured by embarrassment as to what to do with so many apples. Furthermore, Figure 25 is not concerned with the exchange or barter value of a commodity. For example, to possess a million apples would constitute wealth that could

[1] Reprinted from *Journal of Social Psychology*, II (1931), 139–67.

be exchanged for other things that we personally might desire more than a pile of apples, but we are concerned in this problem with the satisfaction that the owner may derive from a specified number of some commodity without regard to money cost. Our main question is rather to study the satisfaction that the owner derives from a specified number of the commodity itself.

It is frequently easy enough to count the number of items of a commodity that an individual possesses so that measurement of x constitutes no serious

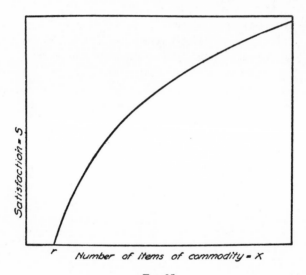

FIG. 25

theoretical problem. In the measurement of satisfaction we shall imply throughout that it is accomplished in terms of the subjective unit of measurement, the discriminal error, or some multiple of this unit.[2]

In order to write an equation for the satisfaction curve, we shall start with five fundamental psychological postulates, namely:

(1) *Satisfaction increases with increase in the amount of the commodity possessed by an individual.* This assumption has been described above.

(2) *There is a lower limit in the amount of the commodity below which the owner will not or cannot barter.* If, for example, you are accustomed to possess two new hats every year, this amount of the commodity might be so commonplace for you that it is taken for granted. You may regard it as a minimum necessity. Such a rate of consumption causes you neither noticeable pleasure nor pain. This lower limit in x is indicated in Figure 25 at r, and the cor-

[2] See chaps. ii, iv, and L. L. Thurstone, "The Measurement of Psychological Value," in *Essays in Philosophy*, ed. T. V. Smith and W. K. Wright (Chicago: Open Court Publishing Co., 1929), pp. 157–74. On this whole subject, see also Irving Fisher, *Mathematical Investigations in the Theory of Values and Prices* (New Haven, Conn.: Yale University Press, 1925).

responding satisfaction is chosen as the origin for the scale of satisfaction. This postulate is not absolutely necessary for our problem, but it simplifies one aspect of it to designate the origin for s in this manner.

(3) *Motivation is defined quantitatively as the anticipated increment in satisfaction per unit increase in the commodity.*[3] Here, as elsewhere in this problem, the satisfaction increments are expressed in terms of the discriminal error or as multiples of this unit. It is consistent with common sense that the motivation to acquire an additional unit of the commodity is smaller, the greater the amount already possessed. It is also clear that the motivation at any given value of x is the slope of the curve at that point.

Here we have defined the slope of the satisfaction curve at any particular point as motivation. It may be suggested that this definition of motivation as a quantitative psychological concept is by no means limited to the present problem. Stated more generally, motivation toward any specified goal, or toward unit accretion of any kind, may be defined as the increment in satisfaction represented by imaginal attainment and expressed in terms of the discriminal error. It is then possible to compare the motivation toward one object with the motivation of the same person toward some other object in a meaningful way and in quantitative terms.

(4) *The motivation is finite when satisfaction is zero.* This simply means that, if you possess an amount of a commodity to which you are accustomed or which you take for granted, your motivation toward an accretion cannot at that time be infinite. This assumes an origin for the continuum of satisfaction which facilitates a part of the solution, though not necessary for it, since the origin as defined can be treated as arbitrary.

(5) *The motivation is inversely proportional to the amount already possessed.* This is our most fundamental psychological postulate. It is, in fact, the turning point in our rationalization of the problem, which might proceed along several lines. This postulate is a simple one, and it will be shown that it satisfies experimental results. This psychological postulate can be written more concisely in the form

$$\frac{ds}{dx} = \frac{k}{x}, \tag{1}$$

in which s = satisfaction, x = amount of the commodity possessed, ds/dx = motivation, and k = a constant which characterizes the person and the particular commodity. Integrating, we have

$$\int ds = k \int \frac{dx}{x} \tag{2}$$

or

$$s = k \log x + c, \tag{3}$$

which is certainly no stranger in psychophysics. It is our old friend, Fechner's law.

---

[3] This is said to be equivalent to the economist's "marginal utility."

To those who are familiar with psychophysics it might seem as though the writer merely adopted Fechner's law in accordance with psychophysical habits, but such was not the case. As a matter of fact, many other psychological postulates have been tried instead of the fifth postulate above, but the one which leads to Fechner's law seems to fit the experimental data better than any of the others that were tried. To the writer it still seems as though it would be psychologically preferable to start with the postulate that motivation is inversely proportional to the amount of *satisfaction* already attained from the commodity. That would lead to a square root law instead of the logarithmic law of Fechner. But in spite of much nursing of that hypothesis, the writer was not able to make the square root law fit the data so well as the law of Fechner. Therefore we returned to Fechner's logarithmic law, which has been applied to the data in this paper. There is still a possibility that the square root law will be found to be superior when the two hypotheses are compared with the same number of parameters, so as to allow comparable degrees of freedom.

This is the equation represented in Figure 25, and it satisfies all of the psychological postulates listed above. The first postulate is satisfied by the fact that the curve of satisfaction rises with increase in amount of the commodity possessed. The second postulate is satisfied by placing the origin for satisfaction to correspond with some amount of the commodity such as r. It is clear that in the logarithmic equation the origin for satisfaction depends merely on the constant of integration, and it can therefore be regarded as essentially in the nature of an arbitrary origin. Our experimental study does not include negative values for satisfaction. It would be possible to determine experimentally whether the law as stated in equation (3) continues for negative values of S or whether it is necessary then to write a separate law for pain, as we have done here for satisfaction. If such should be the case, then the origin would no longer be arbitrary but a functionally true origin. Since our experimental study does not cover negative values of S, we shall treat only the one logarithmic law for satisfaction as though it were continuous, and we shall regard the origin as essentially arbitrary in character.

The third postulate is really only a definition of motivation by which this psychological term may be given a quantitative formulation. It is at least consistent with the usual conversational meaning of the term "motivation." The fourth postulate is satisfied by the equation in that the slope of the curve when satisfaction is zero cannot be infinite. In fact, the slope of the curve is infinite only when satisfaction is $-\infty$. The fifth postulate, which is the fundamental one, is the simple differential equation which leads directly to Fechner's law.

Before using the satisfaction curve for the construction of the indifference curve, the general nature of the latter function will be described. Referring to Figure 26, let the variables x_1 and x_2 represent the amounts of two commodities that one person possesses. The point e in this figure represents the fact that one person owns a items of the first commodity and b items of the second. We shall suppose that both commodities are of such a character that he would like to have as many as possible of each of the two commodities. He might be willing to give up one item of the first commodity in order to obtain one or more items of the second. The rate at which he is willing to make the exchange depends, of course, on the actual quantities of the two commodities that he possesses at the time of barter, and it also depends on his relative preferences for the two commodities. Let us suppose that our subject is just barely willing to reduce his supply of No. 2 from b to d provided that he is given an increment in his supply of No. 1 from a to c. The latter situation, in

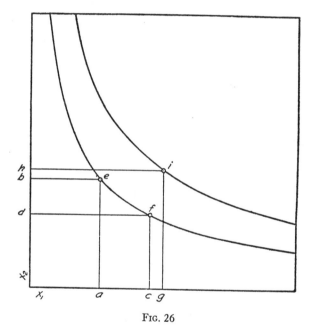

Fig. 26

which he owns c items of No. 1 and d items of No. 2, is represented by the point f in Figure 26. Here we have two situations, e and f, which are equally attractive to the owner. If we imagine a curve drawn through all of the points of equal satisfaction, we shall have an extended curve ef that we shall call an indifference curve. It may be so called because every point on such a curve represents a combination of quantities of the two commodities, and the subject is indifferent as to which of the numerous combinations he possesses.

It is to be expected that such a curve will have a negative slope when we are dealing with commodities that are in general desirable in all the quantities that are practically feasible because a reduction in one of these commodities will be associated with an increment in the other one. It is as though a reduction in one of these quantities must be paid for by an increment in the other quantity. Needless to say, we are not here dealing with the money cost of these quantities. We are concerned with the satisfaction that they would give the owner irrespective of their money cost.

It is easy to imagine an indifference curve of positive slope to represent two quantities, one of which is in general desirable while the other one is regarded as undesirable. The subject would then judge whether he would be willing to accept so many items of a disadvantage in order to possess so many items that are desirable. The supposition is that as the amount of advantage is increased, he would be willing to accept a greater amount of corresponding disadvantage. The slope of such an indifference curve would be positive, but we shall here limit ourselves to the comparison of commodities that are regarded as desirable in all of the amounts that can be ordinarily handled or imagined.

The total amount of satisfaction remains constant for all the combinations that are represented by points on the indifference curve. In moving from one point on this curve to any other point on the curve, we necessarily reduce the amount of one of the commodities and correspondingly raise the amount of the other commodity. The two simultaneous transactions constitute the barter by which satisfaction from one commodity is reduced by the same amount by which the satisfaction from the other commodity is raised. Hence we shall treat the problem as though the total amount of satisfaction were constant for all combinations represented by the indifference curve.

If we start with g items of the first commodity and h items of the second, then, by Figure 26, we shall have a greater amount of total satisfaction than at either e or f because we are starting with a larger amount of each of the two commodities. It is clear that another indifference curve may be drawn through the point i in the same manner. This makes it evident that in Figure 26 we might draw a family of indifference curves such that the total satisfaction remains constant throughout any one of the indifference curves. The several curves would differ in the total amount of satisfaction that they represent. For example, the curve through the point i represents a higher total amount of satisfaction than the curve ef. We can look upon these indifference curves as contour lines on a topographic map. If a solid model were constructed with Figure 26 as a base, the vertical dimension would represent total satisfaction, which would of course be high near the upper right corner of the diagram. The lowest point in the model would be at the lower left corner of the diagram. In the topographic analogy Figure 26 would represent a hill with its top in the upper right corner of the diagram and with the indifference curves representing points of constant elevation or total satisfaction. (See Figure 42.)

A rather simple objection might be raised in the assertion that the kind of satisfaction derived from one of these commodities might be entirely different from the kind of satisfaction derived from the second. This is true, but it is also true that all of us make decisions daily of the very kind that is implied by the indifference curves. For example, if you cannot buy a radio and a fur coat at the same time, you must decide whether to have one or the other or something else, such as a bank balance, even though the satisfactions involved in these various purchases are qualitatively quite different. We shall assume that for analytical purposes any purchase or barter means the reduction in satisfaction from one commodity and an equal increment in satisfaction from the other. In practice it is probable that the positive increment must at least slightly exceed the negative decrement in order to effect barter.

We shall now make use of the equation of satisfaction in order to write the equation of the indifference curve. We may rewrite equation (1) specifically for one of the two commodities which is indicated by the subscript:

$$\frac{d\,s_1}{d\,x_1} = \frac{k_1}{x_1}. \tag{4}$$

The same equation may be written for the second commodity as follows:

$$\frac{d\,s_2}{d\,x_2} = \frac{k_2}{x_2}. \tag{5}$$

From (5) it is clear that

$$\frac{d\,x_2}{d\,s_2} = \frac{x_2}{k_2}. \tag{6}$$

The indifference curve is drawn so that an increment in satisfaction from one of the commodities in simple barter is, in absolute magnitude, equal to the decrement in satisfaction for the other commodity, and hence

$$d\,s_1 = -\,d\,s_2. \tag{7}$$

Therefore, from equations (4), (6), and (7), we may write

$$\frac{d\,x_2}{d\,s_2} \cdot \frac{d\,s_1}{d\,x_1} = -\frac{d\,x_2}{d\,x_1} = \frac{k_1 \cdot x_2}{k_2 \cdot x_1}. \tag{8}$$

Integrating, we have

$$k_2 \int \frac{d\,x_2}{x_2} = -\,k_1 \int \frac{d\,x_1}{x_1} \tag{9}$$

or

$$k_1 \log\,x_1 + k_2 \log\,x_2 = \log\,m, \tag{10}$$

in which k_1, k_2, and $\log m$ are three constants. The two constants k_1 and k_2 represent the different rates at which satisfaction increases with increase in the amounts of the two commodities, respectively. It will be shown that the constant $\log m$ represents essentially the elevation or total amount of satisfaction represented by the indifference curve.

The above equation may be written in exponential form as follows:

$$x_1^{k_1} \cdot x_2^{k_2} = m, \tag{11}$$

and this may be regarded as the general equation of the indifference function at which we have arrived by assuming that Fechner's law is applicable to the satisfaction curve. This is synonymous with the assumption that motivation is inversely proportional to the amount of each commodity already possessed.

The constant log m of the indifference equation can be defined further as follows. If we rewrite equation (3) specifically for each of the two commodities, we have

$$s_1 = k_1 \log x_1 + c_1 , \qquad (12)$$

$$s_2 = k_2 \log x_2 + c_2 , \qquad (13)$$

and hence

$$s_1 + s_2 - c_1 - c_2 = k_1 \log x_1 + k_2 \log x_2 . \qquad (14)$$

But from equation (10) it follows that

$$s_1 + s_2 - c_1 - c_2 = \log m . \qquad (15)$$

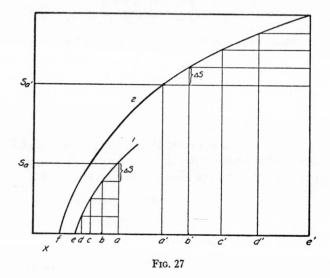

FIG. 27

From this equation it is clear that

$$s_1 + s_2 = \text{a constant} , \qquad (16)$$

which is what we should expect from our general analysis of the nature of simple barter.

The interpretation of equations (10) and (11) may be facilitated by means of Figure 27, in which two satisfaction curves are represented on the same diagram. Let the two curves, 1 and 2, be the satisfaction curves for two commodities. They are drawn so as to represent different values for the constants k_1 and k_2, and they are also so drawn that the values of r_1 and r_2 are different. Let us start with the possession of a items of the first commodity and a' items of the second commodity. The corresponding satisfactions are represented by the two ordinates S_a and $S_{a'}$, respectively. The possession of both of these quantities is assumed to give the owner a total satisfaction equal to the sum of these two ordinates, namely $(S_a + S_{a'})$, and the combination a and a' can of course be represented as a point on an indifference curve.

Suppose that the subject is indifferent about a proposal to reduce the quantity a to the quantity b at the same time that the quantity a' is augmented to the quantity b'. Then the satisfaction S_a suffers a decrement of ΔS, while the satisfaction $S_{a'}$ is augmented by the same amount, namely, ΔS. This trade is represented graphically. In this manner it will be possible to reduce S_a until it vanishes. In the diagram this is shown in four successive equal decrements, ΔS, by which the quantity a is reduced successively to the values b, c, d, and e. At the same time the satisfaction $S_{a'}$ is augmented by four successive identical increments, ΔS, by which the quantity a' is augmented successively to the values b', c', d', and e'. It is clear, therefore, that the five points aa', bb', cc', dd', and ee' all lie on the same indifference curve because the total satisfaction derived from the two commodities is constant. Every decrement in the satisfaction from one of the commodities is exactly balanced by an equal increment in the satisfaction from the second commodity.

We shall interpret Figure 27 to mean that the subject is willing to barter by reduction in the quantity a for increases in the quantity a' as long as he has any satisfaction from the first commodity to give up but that there is a lower limit below which he will not barter. This lower limit is e items of the first commodity and f items of the second commodity. In a practical situation it means that we might be willing to get along with fewer shoes in order to have a large supply of new hats but that there is a limit below which we will not barter away our shoes for any number of hats. For such commodities as hats and shoes these limits are determined partly by physical necessity and partly by the economic or social level at which the subject is living. These quantities e and f are interpreted as more or less taken for granted by the subject, so that any further reduction in either of them would be regarded with actual displeasure or pain which cannot be offset by any quantity of a different commodity.

In Figure 28 we have drawn three satisfaction curves with different x-intercepts. Curve 1 represents the type of function that we have used for the above illustrations. But it is possible, of course, to have a satisfaction curve which passes through the origin in the sense that it causes neither pleasure nor pain to be without the particular commodity. Curve 2 is so drawn, however, as to represent an increase in satisfaction from ownership of that commodity, while its absence does not result in actual pain or displeasure. It is essential to distinguish between motivation and satisfaction. By motivation we mean the strength of the urge toward an accretion. It has been defined as the amount of satisfaction that is represented by an imaginal unit accretion. The satisfaction, however, represents the summation of positive affect that has already been derived from the commodity in question. It is therefore possible to have none of a commodity and to have experienced no satisfaction from it and yet have some motivation toward acquiring it.

Curve 3 in Figure 28 represents the situation in which the subject has experienced some satisfaction from a commodity without owning any of it. This is of course possible, and it is also conceivable that the motivation or slope of the curve at the *s*-axis is therefore smaller than it would be if the same subject did not experience any satisfaction from the commodity at all.

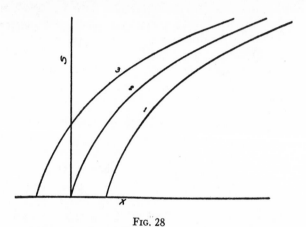

FIG. 28

Experimental Procedure

Having developed rational equations for the satisfaction curve and for the indifference curve, our next step is to ascertain whether they can be verified experimentally. In Figure 29 we have represented hats and shoes as the two commodities. Any point on this diagram represents a combination such as eight hats and eight pairs of shoes. If the curve in Figure 29 were an indifference function, then the subject would say that eight hats and eight pairs of shoes would give him as much satisfaction as six hats and ten pairs of shoes, because both of these points lie on the curve. Perhaps the simplest experimental method that comes to mind is to ask a subject to fill in the blank space in a series of choices of the following type:

> eight hats and eight pairs of shoes
> or six hats and——— pairs of shoes.

If the subject would fill in the blank space with the number of pairs of shoes which would give him as much satisfaction to own as the first combination of eight and eight, and if similar judgments were made for a series of quantities of hats, more than six as well as less than six, it would of course be possible to plot the indifference curve. This is the method of reproduction as it might be applied to this problem. In the present situation the judgments would probably be so unstable and so markedly influenced by the desire for numerical consistency that the curve so obtained would be of doubtful value. It is possible that the method of reproduction could be applied to this problem in a manner which would make it experimentally satisfactory, but in the present study we have used the constant method.

The constant method takes the following form. One of the combinations, such as eight hats and eight pairs of shoes, is chosen as a standard, and each of the other combinations is compared directly with it. Thus in Figure 29 we should expect to find that if the subject were asked to choose (eight hats and eight pairs of shoes) or (seven hats and fourteen pairs of shoes) he might

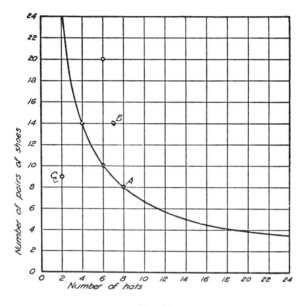

FIG. 29

be quite willing to give up one of the hats in order to possess six additional pairs of shoes, assuming of course that the money cost to him were the same. We should therefore expect to find the point B marked plus because the combination at that point is preferred to that of the standard at A. This may be judged from Figure 29 because the point B lies on an indifference curve at a higher elevation of satisfaction than the point A.

On the other hand, if the subject were asked to choose either the combination at A or the one at C, he would probably prefer A, since very likely he would not care to give up six of his eight hats in order to get only one additional pair of shoes. We should expect the point C to be marked with a minus sign to show that the subject preferred the standard at A. If all of the judgments were consistent, we should expect to find only plus signs above the indifference curve and only minus signs below the curve. In actually drawing the indifference curve, we record the preferences of the subject in the form of plus and minus signs in a diagram, and we then draw the indifference curve so that, as far as possible, there are only plus signs above the curve and only minus signs below it. Naturally, the records from only one subject who makes only one judgment for each combination cannot be expected to be free from inversions, especially in the field close to the curve, where the difference in satisfaction is at best rather slight. If our analysis of the function is correct, it should be possible to draw a curve of equation (10) so as to satisfy the above described conditions.

In order to make the test of equation (10) fairly complete, we have carried out the test with four standards for each of the three possible pairs of three commodities. The procedure was simply to present to the subject a list of alternatives of the following type:

> 8 hats and 8 shoes
> 6 hats and 9 shoes
>
> 8 hats and 8 shoes
> 4 hats and 15 shoes
>
> 8 hats and 8 shoes
> 9 hats and 3 shoes

The subject was asked to indicate for each alternative which of the two combinations would probably give him the more satisfaction on the assumption that the two alternative combinations would cost him the same and with the further assumption that the articles would be of his free selection within the general range in price and quality to which he is accustomed. If the standard was checked, the corresponding variable combination was marked with a minus sign on the diagram. If the variable was checked, that variable combination was checked with a plus sign on the diagram. Evidently it would be useless to ask a subject to choose between eight hats and eight shoes or ten hats and ten shoes because in such a presentation both of the commodities are augmented in quantity, and the obvious answer is of course to check the greater quantity of both commodities. For this reason we limited ourselves to those alternatives in which one of the commodities is reduced while the other is augmented. In this manner it required an act of judgment beyond the mere inspection of the numbers to make an intelligent choice. These judgments are sufficiently numerous to allow a fair determination of the course of the indifference curve.

The subject whose records are here analyzed was entirely naïve as regards the psychophysical problem involved and had no knowledge whatever of the nature of the curves that we expected to find. The judgments were made as indicated above in random order, and the subject did not make any tabulation or analysis of the judgments.

In Figure 31 we have a record of the actual judgments made by our subject when the standard combination was eight hats and eight pairs of shoes.

Every small black circle indicates a judgment in which the variable combination was preferred, while every small open circle represents a judgment in which the standard was preferred. For example, in Figure 31 we find that our subject would rather have six hats and fourteen pairs of shoes than to have eight of each. In a similar manner, he would rather have eight hats and eight pairs of shoes than to have twelve hats and three pairs of shoes. All of the other black circles and open circles are to be interpreted in the same manner.

If the judgments were perfectly consistent, it would be possible to draw the indifference function so that all of the black circles lie above the curve and all of the open circles lie below the curve. This would mean that all of the combinations represented by points above the curve represent greater satisfaction than the combinations represented by the points that lie on the curve. Similarly, all points below the curve would represent combinations that are less desirable than those that lie on the curve. Since every circle in these diagrams represents only one judgment by a single subject, it is to be expected that there will be inversions, especially in view of the fact that the difference in satisfaction represented by neighboring points is not very marked. Our problem is to draw the best-fitting indifference curve through the field of black and white circles, so that the black circles lie, as far as possible, above the curve, while the open circles lie below it.

It is evident that the black and white circles represent two fields such that the ideal indifference curve should really separate them. In order to locate a series of points for the purpose of curve-fitting, we proceed as follows. In Figure 31 we note that the column for four hats has twelve black circles and four white ones. We put a small cross, as shown in the figure, at such a point in this column that there are as many inversions above it as there are inversions below it. In this column it happens that there is one white circle above the cross and one black circle below it. We proceed in this manner for every column and for every row in each of our diagrams. In the column for three hats, for example, the small cross is so located that there are two white circles above it and two black circles below it. In the horizontal row for six shoes the small cross is so located that there is one black circle to the left of the cross and one white circle to the right of it. All of these crosses are located in this manner in Figure 31. Usually there are either no inversions or only one inversion. Occasionally there are two inversions.

Equation (10) is to be fitted by the values represented by the small crosses in Figure 31. We write the equation in summation form as follows:

$$k_1 \Sigma \log x_1 + k_2 \Sigma \log x_2 = n \log m \ .$$

In order to define the S-scale, we let the constant k_1 be unity. Then there are two constants to be determined, namely, k_2 and $\log m$. We determine these two constants by the simple method of averages, which need not be described in detail here. The constants for Figure 31 are $k_2 = 1.39$ and $\log m = 1.80$.

In Table 13 we have summarized the constants for each of the figures from 30 to 37, inclusive. These are the comparisons of hats with shoes and of hats with overcoats.

Inspection of Figures 30–33, inclusive, shows that Figure 30 is a curve much closer to the coordinates than the other three. It is probable that the judgments in the vicinity of the curve in Figure 30 are not so trustworthy as the judgments in the other three figures, partly because of the fact that the curve in Figure 30 is rather close to the level of satisfaction at which the subject refuses to barter away the small quantities of either commodity. For this reason we have chosen the average value of k_2 from Figures 31–33, inclusive, as the general value for this constant, namely, 1.26. In a similar manner, the average value for k_3 is 1.32. The values of the constants k_1, k_2, and k_3 are summarized at the bottom of Table 13. These values indicate that for our subject the satisfaction curve rises fastest for overcoats and slowest for hats. In other words, the increment of satisfaction per unit accretion of overcoats is larger than the satisfaction derived for each additional hat when

TABLE 13

Figure	k_2/k_1	k_3/k_1
30..............	1.39	
31..............	1.30	
32..............	1.28	
33..............	1.19	
34..............		1.57
35..............		1.25
36..............		1.34
37..............		1.37

$$k_1 = 1.00$$
$$k_2 = 1.26$$
$$k_3 = 1.32$$

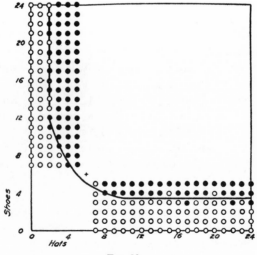

FIG. 30

these increments are measured from the same satisfaction level. This is per-haps what one might expect from the common-sense values of hats and over-coats. It is also apparent that, for our subject, additional shoes give larger increments of satisfaction than are derived from additional hats.

Having determined the best-fitting values of k_2 and k_3, we can now deter-mine the value of log m for each diagram. This is done again by the method of averages, and the values are listed in the second column of Table 14. These values would be altered slightly by different methods of calculation. The

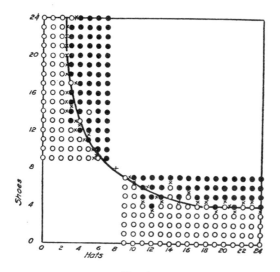

Fig. 31

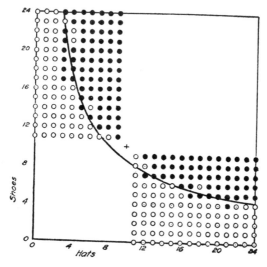

Fig. 32

satisfaction log m, which is represented by the standard combination for each curve, can be ascertained from the same equation in which x_1 and x_2 are the coordinates of the standard combination. Let this be designated log m_s, and let the corresponding constant for the equation of the best-fitting curve be designated log m_a. The difference between these two constants is the constant error of the method of right and wrong cases. It is the difference in elevation between the indifference curve that passes through the standard combination and the best-fitting indifference curve through the small crosses that were drawn in each diagram. The constant error for each figure is listed in the last

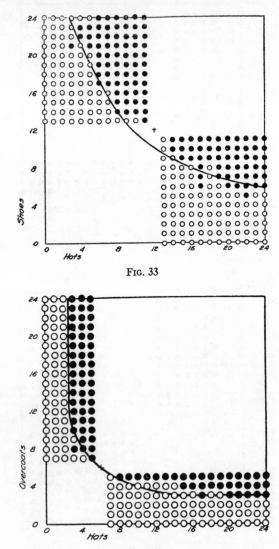

FIG. 33

FIG. 34

column of Table 14. The constant error for the method of right and wrong cases is designated E, and it is taken to be the average of the constant errors for the eight diagrams. The value of E, which is the average value of the eight values of e, is $-.066$.

Now that we know the values of k_1, k_2, and k_3, and the constant error of the psychophysical method involved, which is $-.066$, we should be able to predict the indifference curves for the comparison of shoes and overcoats. So far we have made use of only two sets of comparisons, namely, hats-shoes

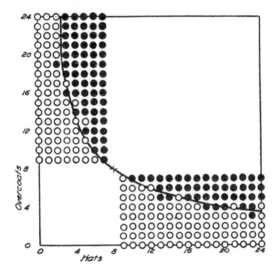

Fig. 35

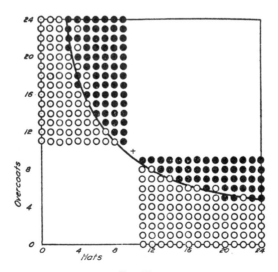

Fig. 36

and hats-overcoats. We shall now predict the equations of the indifference curves for the third comparison, namely, shoes-overcoats. Since we have the experimental data for all three sets of comparisons, we can ascertain how closely the third set of indifference curves can be predicted from the known constants, derived from the first two sets of comparisons. This constitutes the test of the fundamental psychological hypothesis that is involved, namely, that the satisfactions from several commodities are summative when all of the quantities involved are above the level which the subject regards as the level of absolute necessity.

In Table 15 we have listed the four standards for the third set of comparisons, namely, shoes-overcoats. These comparisons are shown graphically in

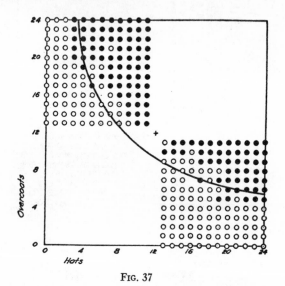

Fig. 37

TABLE 14

Figure	log m	log m_s	e
30........	1.67	1.76	−.09
31........	2.01	2.04	−.03
32........	2.14	2.26	−.12
33........	2.34	2.44	−.10
34........	1.79	1.81	−.02
35........	2.11	2.10	+.01
36........	2.28	2.32	−.04
37........	2.35	2.50	−.15

$E = $ Constant error = average $e = -.066$

TABLE 15

Figure	x_2	x_3	log m_s	log m_a
38........	6	6	2.01	1.94
39........	8	8	2.33	2.26
40........	10	10	2.58	2.51
41........	12	12	2.78	2.72

Figures 38–41, inclusive. The standard combinations are listed in the second and third columns. The value of log m_s is listed in the next column. It is calculated again by equation (10) with the known values of k. But the best-fitting curves for the first two sets of comparisons revealed a slight constant error in log m. Applying the same constant error to the predicted third set of comparisons, we have the predicted values of log m_a, which are listed in the last column of Table 15. With these values we can write the four predicted equations and plot each of them (see tabulation on p. 142).

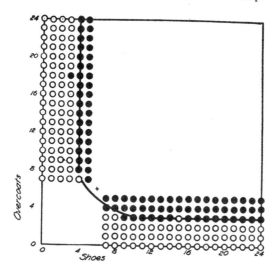

Fig. 38

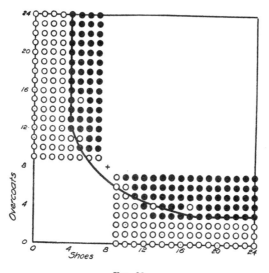

Fig. 39

Predicted Equations for the Indifference
Curves (Shoes-Overcoats) with Four   Standard   Combination
Standard Combinations   Shoes   Overcoats

Equation	Standard Shoes	Combination Overcoats
$1.26 \log x_2 + 1.32 \log x_1 = 1.94$	6	6
$1.26 \log x_2 + 1.32 \log x_3 = 2.26$	8	8
$1.26 \log x_2 + 1.32 \log x_3 = 2.51$	10	10
$1.26 \log x_2 + 1.32 \log x_1 = 2.72$	12	12

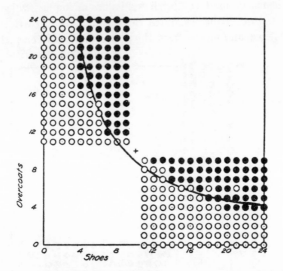

FIG. 40

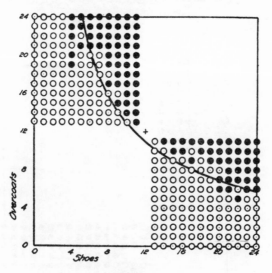

FIG. 41

Inspection of Figures 38–41, inclusive, indicates that the agreement between the predicted curves and the distributions of black and white circles is quite satisfactory. In general, the black circles lie above the predicted indifference curve, while the white circles lie below it.

In each of the indifference curves that run close to the two coordinates it is apparent that there is a lower limit for each commodity below which the subject is not willing to barter. According to equation (10), the indifference curve should be asymptotic to the two coordinates. But, as a matter of fact, the subject refuses to barter for certain minimum quantities of each commodity. When the number of hats is lower than three, the subject does not barter away any of them, no matter how many shoes or overcoats are offered in exchange. The lower limit for shoes is four pairs, and the lower limit for overcoats is three. The curves in our diagrams are drawn to these lower limits

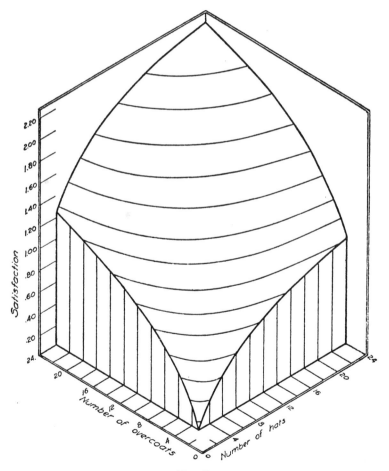

Fig. 42

but not beyond them. It is clear, therefore, that while the indifference function should be asymptotic to the coordinates according to the equation, the experimental function does not extend beyond the lower limits indicated. This fact can be interpreted to mean that the commodities have certain values for exchange purposes which depend on the quantities possessed but that all barter ceases entirely when the quantity of a commodity reaches a lower limit which the subject evidently regards as a necessity.

Conclusions

The object of this paper has been to show that it is possible to reduce the indifference function to experimental treatment and that it is possible to write a rational equation for the indifference function which is based on plausible psychological postulates. We have developed two psychological functions, namely, the curve of satisfaction and the indifference curve. The equation for the satisfaction curve which agrees with the experimental data is similar in form to Fechner's law, and it may, in fact, be regarded as an extension of that law, which has been ordinarily interpreted as limited to sensory discrimination. The rational equation for the indifference curve takes the general form $x_1^{k_1} \cdot x_2^{k_2} = m$, in which x_1 and x_2 are the quantities of the two commodities. The constants k_1 and k_2 are descriptive of the individual subject and his preferences for the two commodities, while the constant m designates the total amount of satisfaction which is represented by the indifference curve. This equation is based on the fundamental psychological postulate that motivation toward accretion in each commodity is inversely proportional to the amount of the commodity already possessed. We have also offered a quantitative definition of motivation as the amount of anticipated satisfaction per unit increase in the commodity. This definition of the concept of motivation makes it possible to treat motivation generally in a quantitative manner, and it lends itself to other psychological problems that involve motivation. Throughout this paper it has been assumed that increments in satisfaction are measured in terms of the psychological unit of measurement, the discriminal error, or multiples of that unit. We have described the experimental records for only one subject. The same procedures have been tried on several other subjects with similar results.

13 THE PREDICTION OF CHOICE

This paper[1] is concerned with a central concept in social measurement, such as opinion polls, the measurement of attitudes, the prediction of political elections, the measurement of moral values, the measurement of consumer preferences, the measurement of utility, and the measurement of aesthetic values. The concept is that of the discriminal dispersion and its interesting effects in the prediction of choice.

We shall describe first some special cases to illustrate the nature of the problem, and we shall develop several psychophysical theorems in the prediction of choice and a method of computation.

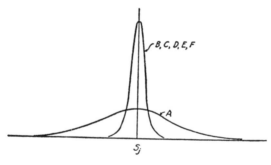

FIG. 43

As an example, let there be six psychological objects which may be as many candidates for elective office. To simplify the situation in this special case, let all of the six candidates be equally popular, on the average, so that their scale positions on the subjective continuum are all the same, namely, S_j, as shown in Figure 43. Let us assume that candidate A does or says something by which a thousand people become his enthusiastic supporters and that, at the same time, another thousand people hate him. Let this process continue in such a manner that the first candidate attains a large discriminal dispersion, whereas the other candidates, B, C, D, E, F, retain their small discriminal dispersions. It is assumed in this example that the mean subjective values S_j remain the same during the campaign.

Before considering what will happen at the election, let us suppose that

[1] Reprinted from *Psychometrika*, X (1945), 237–53.

the six names are presented to the subjects in pairs where each candidate is paired with every other candidate. Such a list contains $n(n-1)/2 = 15$ pairs of names. The voters check their preferences for each pair of names. From such returns we can make a square table of proportions of judgments, $p_{j>k}$, to show the proportion of the voters who prefer j to k for every pair of names. In the present situation we should find that all of the proportions would be exactly the same, so that $p_{j>k} = .50$. In other words, the table of proportions of preference would show all of the six candidates to be equal in average popularity, since their scale positions S_j are all the same.

Now, having the relations of Figure 43, or their numerical equivalents, the problem is to predict what the voters will do when they record their first choices for the six names. From the diagram it is evident that the first candidate will get half of the votes and that the other five candidates will divide the other half. Hence we should expect the following division of the votes: .50, .10, .10, .10, .10, .10. The first candidate would have at least a plurality. The reason for the apparent discrepancy between the table of proportions

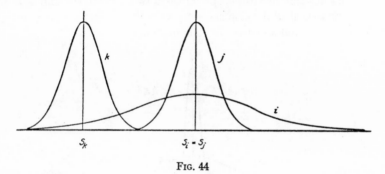

FIG. 44

for paired preferences and the prediction of first choice is in the great differences in the discriminal dispersions for the six candidates. The effect that has been described in this example can be summarized in the theorem that *if three or more psychological objects with the same average affective value and with symmetric dispersions are competing for selection as first choice, then the object which has the largest discriminal dispersion will obtain the largest number of votes.* The effect which is here stated in terms of psychophysical concepts is no doubt known to practical politicians and perhaps to advertisers and to students of consumer preference. With the development of a theoretical structure for psychological measurement from the more restricted methods of traditional psychophysics, we should have frequent contacts between theory and the intuitions of experience in practical affairs if our scientific rationalizations of social phenomena are sound.

Another example will now be described. Let Figure 44 represent the frequency distributions of two leading candidates, i and j, and let them have the same average affective value $S_i = S_j$. Assume that these distributions are Gaussian on the subjective continuum with different dispersions, so that $\sigma_i > \sigma_j$ as shown in the figure. In this situation we should expect that the two candidates would draw the same number of votes, so that it would be a matter of chance which of them actually became the winner. Now let us introduce a dark horse in the third candidate, k, whose scale value S_k is lower than that of the two leading candidates. This situation can be considered under two cases, namely, (1) the case in which the distributions of j and k do not overlap and (2) the case in which the distributions j and k do overlap. The first case is shown in Figure 44.

Before the candidate k is introduced, the expectation is a tie between candidates i and j. After the introduction of candidate k, the expectation remains unaltered because the entire distribution for j exceeds the entire distribution for k. Hence *with no overlapping of* j *and* k, *the expectation is that candidate* k *gets no votes at all.* The expected vote is then the same as if the third candidate had not been introduced.

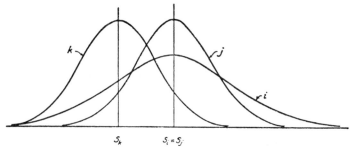

FIG. 45

Case 2 is different, as shown in Figure 45. Here there is an overlap between the less variable j of the two leading candidates and the candidate k. Most of those who perceive i in the lower half of the affective range have the preference $j > i$. If some of them shift their first choices to k, the result will be a larger decrement in the votes for j than for i. Therefore the expectation is that i will have a plurality. We can summarize this situation in several theorems. *If two candidates have equal average affective values* ($S_i = S_j$) *and different dispersions* ($\sigma_i > \sigma_j$), *and if there is a third candidate with lower scale value and overlapping dispersion, there will be a plurality for the more variable of the two leading candidates. In the case of a threatened tie between two leading candidates, the more variable of the two candidates can win the election by introducing a less popular candidate.* This is a curious result. Perhaps this effect is also known to practical politicians. A limiting case is that in which the average popularity (S_k) of the third candidate is equal to that of i and j. Then, if i is still the most variable in affective dispersion, he wins the plurality. This case is covered by the first theorem. These theorems are not intended to be exhaustive. They are presented primarily for the purpose of indicating the potentialities of the concept of discriminal dispersion in the prediction of conduct. The subject sketched by these examples can be extended analytically into one of considerable proportions.

In voting for a first choice in a set of names, physical objects, or ideas, the subject sometimes encounters one or more objects that are complete strangers to him. He may even omit such candidates from consideration. In listing the distributions for computation of first choice, we have then a reduced frequency for the active preference votes for this object. The residual frequency can be recorded at any point on the affective continuum below the active distributions of the other candidates.

Analytical Method

We turn now to a more formal consideration of the problem. A method of computation will be described which covers both of two general cases,

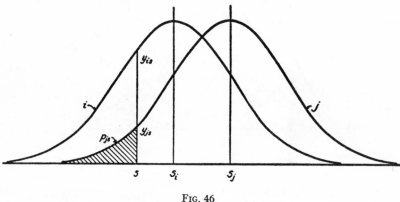

FIG. 46

namely, (1) that in which the affective dispersions are Gaussian and (2) that in which the affective dispersions take any form, including bimodality, which is characteristic of the latter phase of a political campaign. The computations will normally be based on experimental data obtained by the method of successive intervals. This psychophysical method will be described in improved form in a separate paper.

We begin the analysis with two overlapping Gaussian distributions on the affective continuum, as illustrated in Figure 46. These two distributions represent two stimuli, i and j, with scale values S_i and S_j and with discriminal dispersions σ_i and σ_j. The distributions will be assumed to be drawn with unit area so that their ordinates may be interpreted directly as probabilities with any suitable class intervals. The probability that any percipient will experience stimulus i at any specified affective value s is then the ordinate of the probability curve y_{is} at the point s. The probability that the same percipient will experience stimulus j at some value lower than s is then

$$p_{js} = \int_{-\infty}^{s} y_{js} d s ,\qquad (1)$$

which is represented by the shaded area of Figure 46. Assuming that these probabilities are independent, we have

$$P_{i>j} = \int_{-\infty}^{+\infty} y_{is} p_{js} d s ,\qquad (2)$$

where $P_{i>j}$ is the probability that i will be perceievd higher than j, irrespective of where i is perceived. The values of $P_{i>j}$ are, in fact, the experimentally given values in the method of paired comparison in which each stimulus is compared separately with every other stimulus. This method implies $n(n-1)/2$ comparisons if each stimulus is not compared with itself and if the space or time orders ij and ji are not differentiated experimentally. When that is done, we have $n(n-1)$ comparisons, and when we include the comparison of each stimulus with itself, as is possible when the stimuli are defined in such a manner that their individual identities are not recognized by the subject, then we have n^2 comparisons for the method of paired comparison in its complete form. When only one of the stimuli is chosen as a standard for comparison with each of the other stimuli, then we have the constant method with n or $(n-1)$ comparisons. The constant method of traditional psychophysics is a special case of the more fundamental paired comparison method. The analysis so far is that of the law of comparative judgment, which has been described in previous publications, but we are here concerned with the obverse problem of predicting behavior when S_j and σ_j are known.

Let us now consider a set of three overlapping affective distributions. Let the three stimuli be denoted i, j, and k, as shown in Figure 47. As before, the probability that i will be perceived at s is y_{is}. The probability that j will be perceived below s is p_{js}, which is the single crosshatched area. The probability that k will be perceived below s is p_{ks}, which is the double crosshatched area. Assuming, as before, that the probabilities are independent, we have

$$P_{i.1} = \int_{-\infty}^{+\infty} y_{is} p_{js} p_{ks} d s ,\qquad (3)$$

where $P_{i.1}$ is the probability that the stimulus i will be selected as first choice when all three stimuli are presented. If there are N individuals, we should have

$$N P_{i.1} = E_{i.1} ,\qquad (4)$$

where $E_{i.1}$ is the expected number of votes for stimulus i when all three stimuli are presented for selection of one stimulus by each subject.

Instead of dealing with continuous distributions, we can restate the same relations in summational form for a set of frequencies in successive intervals. Let the affective continuum be divided into s successive intervals $1, 2, 3 \ldots m \ldots s$, where m denotes the general interval. It should be noted explicitly that these intervals need *not* be equal, as is illustrated in Figure 48. In fact, the method of successive intervals is a psychophysical method in which the intervals are not ordinarily equal. Their magnitudes can be determined for each set of observations. However, the problem of prediction of choice can

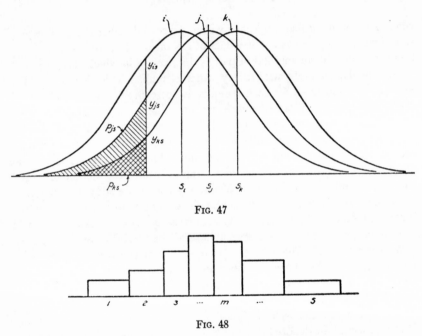

FIG. 47

FIG. 48

be solved without even knowing the relative sizes of the successive class intervals.

Let f_{im} denote the frequency with which the stimulus i is perceived in the interval m, so that

$$\sum_m f_{im} = N_i = N ,$$ (5)

where N is the number of experimental subjects who perceived and classified the stimulus i. The corresponding relative frequency is then

$$\frac{1}{N} f_{im} = y_{im}$$ (6)

in the class intervals m, so that y_{im} is the probability that the stimulus i will be perceived in the affective interval m.

Let the stimulus i be the one about which we want to predict the number of first choices. Let each of the other stimuli be denoted k. Then $P_{i.1}$ will denote the proportion of subjects who vote for the stimulus i as their first choice in comparison with the whole group k.

The probability that any one of the stimuli k will be perceived below any specified class interval m is then

$$p_{k(m-1)} = \sum_{t=1}^{m-1} y_{kt} = p_{k<m}, \tag{7}$$

where t denotes successive intervals. The summation is here over $(m-1)$ intervals, since $P_{k<m}$ denotes the probability that any stimulus k will be perceived *below* the interval m. Since we want to determine the probability that the stimulus i will be perceived higher than all of the stimuli in group k,

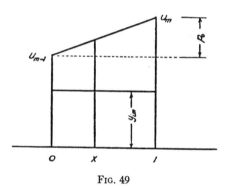

FIG. 49

we must deal with the whole group k. The probability that all of the $(n-1)$ stimuli k will be perceived below any designated class interval m is the product of the $(n-1)$ probabilities $p_{k(m-1)}$. Denoting this product $u_{(m-1)}$, we have

$$u_{m-1} \equiv p_{1(m-1)} p_{2(m-1)} \ldots p_{k(m-1)} \ldots p_{(n-1)\,(m-1)} = \prod_{k=1}^{n-1} p_{k(m-1)}. \tag{8}$$

If we take the product $y_{im}\, u(m-1)$, we have the probability that the stimulus i is perceived in the interval m and that all of the stimuli in group k are perceived below the interval m. To sum this product for all the intervals would not give the desired answer because when the stimulus i is perceived in interval m, it may exceed one or more of the stimuli k which are also perceived in the same interval. To cover this situation consider Figure 49.

In Figure 49 we have a class interval which is here given the range 0 to 1 as shown. Let y_{im} be the probability that stimulus i is perceived in the interval m. This ordinate is drawn in the figure as in a histogram, so that we are assuming a rectangular distribution within each interval. The ordinate u_m

is the probability that all of the stimuli in group k are perceived below the top of the interval m. Then

$$u_m = p_{1m} \cdot p_{2m} \cdot p_{3m} \ldots p_{km} \ldots p_{(n-1)m} = \prod_{k=1}^{n-1} p_{km} . \qquad (9)$$

The corresponding probability for the bottom of the same class interval is given by equation (8). Let x be any point in the class interval m, as in the figure. The probability that stimulus i is perceived at the point x is $(y_{im}\, dx)$; and the probability that, at the same time, all of the stimuli in group k are perceived below x is $(u_{m-1} + xp_0)$, where

$$p_0 = (u_m - u_{m-1}) . \qquad (10)$$

Hence we have

$$P_{im>k} = \int_0^1 y_{im} (u_{m-1} + xp_0)\, d x = y_{im}u_{m-1} + \tfrac{1}{2} y_{im} p_0 , \qquad (11)$$

which is the probability that i is perceived in the interval m and that all of the group k are perceived below i. The desired probability $P_{i.1}$ that i will be an individual voter's first choice is the summation of $P_{im>k}$ for all intervals m. Expressing p_0 in terms of the u's, we have

$$p_{i.1} = \frac{1}{2}\sum_{m=1}^{s} y_{im} (u_m + u_{m-1}) . \qquad (12)$$

This summation can also be written in the form

$$P_{i.1} = \frac{1}{2}\sum_{m=1}^{s} [y_{im} + y_{i(m+1)}]\, u_m = \frac{1}{2}\sum_{m=1}^{s} z_{im}u_m , \qquad (13)$$

where

$$z_{im} = y_{im} + y_{i(m+1)} . \qquad (14)$$

It should be recalled that this prediction of first choice for any given stimulus i can be made even though the class intervals remain unknown as to their relative magnitudes. Further, this computing formula has no restriction as to the shapes of the affective distributions. Several of them might be skewed, while others are bimodal. A reservation about this computing formula is that it assumes independent probabilities. In dealing with affective discrimination for a large class of psychological objects, this assumption is valid. If the affective deviations of a pair of objects are correlated, then the analysis becomes more complex. It can be made in terms of experimental data for the method of successive intervals. When the psychophysical problem is concerned with repeated judgments by the same individual, then the assumption of independence is valid except when the experimental situation introduces affective contrast or related effects. These can usually be avoided with good experimental procedures.

Numerical Examples

In Table 16 we have tabulated the distributions for three stimuli on the affective continuum as they might be found from the experimental method of successive intervals. Here we have chosen arbitrary bimodal and skewed distributions to illustrate the latitude of the method. In this problem it is not necessary to evaluate the relative sizes of these intervals. They are denoted merely as successive intervals from 1 to 9, inclusive. The number of intervals is arbitrary. The probabilities y_{1m}, y_{2m}, y_{3m} are listed as shown. Next we compute the corresponding values of p_{jm}. These summations are made from the lowest intervals, so that the value of p_{jm} for $m = 9$ is unity for each stimulus j.

TABLE 16

m	y_1	y_2	y_3	p_1	p_2	p_3	u_1	u_2	u_3	z_1	z_2	z_3
1.......	.04	.03	.00	.04	.03	.00	.0000	.0000	.0012	.20	.16	.02
2.......	.16	.13	.02	.20	.16	.02	.0032	.0040	.0320	.29	.31	.16
3.......	.13	.18	.14	.34	.34	.16	.0544	.0528	.1122	.24	.35	.48
4.......	.11	.17	.34	.44	.51	.50	.2550	.2200	.2244	.19	.32	.68
5.......	.08	.15	.34	.52	.66	.84	.5544	.4368	.3432	.14	.27	48
6.......	.06	.12	.14	.58	.78	.98	.7644	.5684	.4524	.17	.22	.16
7.......	.11	.10	.02	.69	.88	1.00	.8800	.6900	.6072	.30	.18	.02
8.......	.19	.08	.00	.88	.96	1.00	.9600	.8800	.8448	.31	.12	.00
9.......	.12	.04	.00	1.00	1.00	1.00	1.0000	1.0000	1.0000	.12	.04	.00

i	$2P$	P
1......	.9516	.47
2......	.6029	.30
3......	.4609	.23
	2.0154	1.00

The values of u_{jm} are next recorded. For example, the value for u_{1m} in the interval $m = 2$ is $p_{2m}p_{3m} = .16 \times .02 = .0032$. In the next three columns we list the values of z_m. For example, the entry z_{3m} for $m = 5$ is $(.34 + .14) = .48$.

The final step is to sum the cross products $z_{jm}u_{jm}$. The sums give values of $2P_{j.1}$. These are listed separately in the table. The result gives 47 per cent of the votes for the first stimulus, 30 per cent for the second stimulus, and 23 per cent for the third. An adjustment of less than 1 per cent is indicated in the summation. This discrepancy is due to the assumed linearity of the function u within each class interval. It is small for a large number of class intervals.

In Table 17 we have a numerical example of the theorem that when two psychological objects are tied in average popularity, as measured by the mean scale positions S_i and S_j, then the more variable of them can win election for first choice by the introduction of a third competing object of lower average popularity. Here we used 24 successive intervals. All three of these affective distributions were made Gaussian, and it is here assumed that the distributions are at least roughly symmetric. The first two candidates are the leading ones that are tied. The third candidate has a lower average popularity, as shown in the columns y_{im}, y_{jm}, y_{km}. The computations are similar to those of the previous example, and we have the following results:

Expected votes for only two
    candidates: $i = 50$ per cent; $j = 50$ per cent
Expected votes after introduc-
    ing new candidate: $i = 48$ per cent; $j = 45$ per cent;
                                  $k = 7$ per cent.

Here the more variable candidate i has obtained a plurality by introducing a new candidate with lower average popularity.

The examples have been limited to groups of two or three objects, but the theory can be extended to groups of any size. For large groups, the computational procedure can be rearranged in a more economical manner.

TABLE 17

m	y_1	y_2	y_3	p_1	p_2	p_3	u_1	u_2	u_3	z_1	z_2	z_3
1.......	.00	.00	.00	.00	.00	.00	.0000	.0000	.0000	.01	.00	.00
2.......	.01	.00	.00	.01	.00	.00	.0000	.0000	.0000	.01	.00	.00
3.......	.00	.00	.00	.01	.00	.00	.0000	.0000	.0000	.01	.00	.01
4.......	.01	.00	.01	.02	.00	.01	.0000	.0002	.0000	.03	.00	.02
5.......	.02	.00	.01	.04	.00	.02	.0000	.0008	.0000	.05	.00	.06
6.......	.03	.00	.05	.07	.00	.07	.0000	.0049	.0000	.07	.01	.14
7.......	.04	.01	.09	.11	.01	.16	.0016	.0176	.0011	.09	.02	.24
8.......	.05	.01	.15	.16	.02	.31	.0062	.0496	.0032	.12	.06	.34
9.......	.07	.05	.19	.23	.07	.50	.0350	.1150	.0161	.15	.14	.38
10.......	.08	.09	.19	.31	.16	.69	.1104	.2139	.0496	.17	.24	.34
11.......	.09	.15	.15	.40	.31	.84	.2604	.3360	.1240	.19	.34	.24
12.......	.10	.19	.09	.50	.50	.93	.4650	.4650	.2500	.20	.38	.14
13.......	.10	.19	.05	.60	.69	.98	.6762	.5880	.4140	.19	.34	.06
14.......	.09	.15	.01	.69	.84	.99	.8316	.6831	.5796	.17	.24	.02
15.......	.08	.09	.01	.77	.93	1.00	.9300	.7700	.7161	.15	.14	.01
16.......	.07	.05	.00	.84	.98	1.00	.9800	.8400	.8232	.12	.06	.00
17.......	.05	.01	.00	.89	.99	1.00	.9900	.8900	.8811	.09	.02	.00
18.......	.04	.01	.00	.93	1.00	1.00	1.0000	.9300	.9300	.07	.01	.00
19.......	.03	.00	.00	.96	1.00	1.00	1.0000	.9600	.9600	.05	.00	.00
20.......	.02	.00	.00	.98	1.00	1.00	1.0000	.9800	.9800	.03	.00	.00
21.......	.01	.00	.00	.99	1.00	1.00	1.0000	.9900	.9900	.01	.00	.00
22.......	.00	.00	.00	.99	1.00	1.00	1.0000	.9900	.9900	.01	.00	.00
23.......	.01	.00	.00	1.00	1.00	1.00	1.0000	1.0000	1.0000	.01	.00	.00
24.......	.00	.00	.00	1.00	1.00	1.00	1.0000	1.0000	1.0000	.00	.00	.00

		$2P$	P
i......	1	.9634	.48
j......	2	.9109	.45
k......	3	.1327	.07
		2.0070	1.00

Implications of Discriminal Dispersion

While the examples of this paper have referred to political elections, the psychophysical theory is applicable to the comparison and ranking of psychological objects of any kind. Since it is a major purpose of this paper to indicate some analytical and experimental implications of the concept of discriminal dispersion, it may be in order to mention briefly its relations to psychological measurement of several kinds of objects.

First, consider the formal laboratory measurement of sensory and perceptual functions. In measuring pitch discrimination, we can get along with the traditional psychophysical methods if we use stimuli that are carefully controlled so as to be quite homogeneous in all but the attribute to be discriminated. But suppose we want to study pitch discrimination under wide variations in timbre, including noises. Then the stimuli are not homogeneous in other attributes, and they will almost certainly differ widely in discriminal dispersion. It would still be possible to measure pitch discrimination under such variant conditions, and the individual differences so found might be of considerable psychological and physiological interest. The older psychophysical methods would then be inadequate. The discriminal dispersions as well as the scale values can be determined from complete paired comparison data if the stimuli cover a supraliminal range in pitch.

In the measurement of social attitudes of a group it is not only the average affective value of a proposal or idea that is of significance but also the dispersion of affective values within the group. It may even be possible to *define the morale of a group in terms of the sum of affective dispersions of all its debatable issues.* The effects of propaganda are no doubt determined in part by the heterogeneity of affective values, which are themselves to be altered by propaganda. Moral values are essentially affective in nature. The moral code of a social group can be described by its affective values, in which the highest ones are what the group considers to be sacred. Measurement of the seriousness of crimes can be made by psychophysical methods in which the dispersions are signs of heterogeneity or lack of unity in the group and its code.

Studies have been made of international attitudes by asking the subjects to rate their preferences for nationalities in pairs. If some of the subjects are given the question "Which of these two nationalities would you rather associate with?" and if others are asked the question "Which of these two nationalities would you rather have your sister marry?" the results will be essentially the same as regards rank order with a linear relation between the two sets of scale values for the nationalities. But the dispersions will be widely different, showing greater discrimination for the second question than for the first. This is what we should expect. It is another example in which social judgments are represented in part by the discriminal dispersions with effects that are not always so obvious as in this example.

International attitudes can be studied with the psychophysical methods. This was done with newspaper editorials for the period 1910 to 1930, which included the period of World War I. The analysis showed the rate of decline of editorial attitudes toward Germany and the rise of attitude toward France and the later recovery of prewar attitudes. It seems likely that if such studies were made in a manner to reveal the group dispersions as well as the scale values, the result might be a rather sensitive barometer of increasing heterogeneity in international attitudes. Rapid changes in scale values or in group dispersions would be signals of impending crises.

The measurement of consumer preferences should be done by psychophysical methods that yield central tendencies and group dispersions as two parameters for each object. The experimental methods are easily used, and they can yield predictions of relative consumption of competing commodities.

In the measurement of utility the psychologists and the economists are dealing with overlapping problems. The utility concept is essentially the same as that of mean affective value for the individual. The addition of a parameter for dispersion could lead to interesting results for psychological and economic theory. Consider, for example, a surface whose base coordinates represent amount of two commodities and whose ordinates represent the associated utility or affective value for the individual. Horizontal sections of this surface give a family of indifference curves, whereas vertical sections, parallel to either base axis, give satisfaction curves which are interpreted as Fechner's law. Now, if the dispersions in affective values among the individuals are introduced as new parameters, we have the possibility of summing the effects for the individuals to that of the group. Further, *the first derivative of the satisfaction curve at any point is the motivation of the individual* with reference to the commodity concerned.

The application of psychophysical methods in experimental aesthetics is well known. The addition of a parameter for group dispersion would be indicative of the heterogeneity of aesthetic criteria for each object. Aesthetic theory is often regarded as a subject to be settled by scholarly debate or by reference to Aristotle. It would be better to test aesthetic theory by reference to experimental methods that are available. We could then find out where Aristotle guessed right and where he guessed wrong. Here we are assuming that aesthetics is not normative. We assume that the aesthetic value of an object is determined by what goes on in the mind of the percipient. What is an aesthetic object for one percipient is prosaic to another. In a homogeneous culture, it should be possible by experimental means to describe, and even to measure, those objects attributes which have aesthetic value for most individuals in that culture.

The purpose of the psychophysical methods is to allocate each one of a set of psychological objects to the subjective continuum, which is also called the discriminal continuum. Measurement in this continuum is effected with *a subjective unit of measurement*, namely, *the discriminal error*, with criteria for internal consistency that differentiate measurement from mere rank order. The psychological objects may be any objects or ideas about which the subject can make comparative judgments in the form "A is x'er than B," where x is any designated attribute. When each psychological object j has been allocated, it is described by two parameters, namely, its mean scale position S_j and the discriminal dispersion σ_j which the stimulus projects on the subjective continuum. The purpose of this paper has been to consider the obverse problem of predicting the behavior of the subjects in terms of these parameters. In particular we wanted to predict the relative frequency with which the subjects select any designated object as their first choice.

William James said that psychophysics was the dullest part of psychology. He was right. But if we extend and adapt the psychophysical concepts to the theory of discriminatory and selective judgment, the subject takes a different color and it is no longer dull.

The Case of Prediction with Correlated Ratings

In the previous sections of this paper the writer has presented several psychophysical theorems concerning the problem of predicting how many people will select any given stimulus as their first choice when the scale values and discriminal dispersions are known for each stimulus. Those theorems were written with the explicit reservation that they assumed independent probabilities; i.e., they assumed the scale values of the stimuli to be uncorrelated. In practice it is to be expected that the scale values will be correlated for many types of preferential judgments, and it is desirable, therefore, to devise methods of prediction of choice that are free from this restrictive assumption. Here we shall describe a method of prediction of choice which is independent of the shapes of the affective distributions and also independent of their intercorrelations.

The problem is, then, to predict the proportion of voters (or buyers) who will select any particular psychological object (person, idea, or thing) as their first choice in a group of such objects. It will be assumed that there is available a random and representative sample of individuals from the population about which the prediction is to be made. It will be assumed that we want to determine the scale values and discriminal dispersions of a large *collection* of objects but that the actual presentation to the total population will be a smaller *group* of such objects. Let the large collection contain N objects or stimuli which will be referred to as the *collection*. Let the smaller group to be presented to the total population contain u objects which will be referred to as the *group* of stimuli. The reason for this formulation is that it may be desirable to select the group of stimuli for selection by the population on the basis of information concerning relative popularity and dispersions of a large collection of objects. When these are known, the smaller group can be selected with foresight as to the desired objectives. For example, the stimulus collection may consist in a set of principles, and we may want to predict which set or group of these principles can be combined into a proposal that the population will accept with a majority indorsement. This requires a labeled neutral point in the method of successive intervals. Or the stimulus group may consist of ten neckties whose patterns and colors should be so selected from a large collection as to maximize acceptance by the population. The scale values and dispersions may be examined to select the most appropriate smaller combination which shall constitute the stimulus group for general presentation.

If each individual may select one necktie, then the group of neckties should be so assembled from the available collection as to maximize the scale values *of those which are rated as first choices*. This solution is not the same as that of assembling a group of stimuli with the highest scale values. Such a group may please a number of individuals with more than one stimulus of their favorite kinds while others remain disappointed. The problems in this area are not only of theoretical interest in the adaptation of psychophysics to practical affairs. Their solutions may also bear interesting relations to problems of social theory.

The experimental procedure is to ask each subject to place each stimulus in one of seven successive categories. The procedure is superficially similar to to that of the method of equal-appearing intervals, but there is an important difference in the instructions to the subject. In the method of equal-appearing intervals, the subject is asked to place the stimuli in the several piles so that they seem to him to be about equally spaced as to the attribute in which the stimuli are being rated. It can be shown experimentally that the subject is unable to carry out such instructions and that in fact the intervals toward the ends are greater than the intervals in the middle range. In the method of successive intervals, we do not impose any such restriction. Either the successive intervals are given successive numbers, 1, 2, 3, etc., or they are given descriptive names. When the successive classes are identified by descriptive phrases, the wording should be carefully done so that the subjects accept immediately the successive nature of the categories. If the subjects object that the labels on the successive classes are out of sequence, then the experimental procedure fails. It is usually rather easy to designate the successive categories in such a way that their order is accepted by all of the subjects. They then proceed to place each stimulus in one of the classes according to the labels without any restriction that the intervals shall be in any sense equal. There is, of course, no restriction as to the shape of the distribution of judgments in this successive interval classification. Occasionally, students of psychology need to be reminded that the normal distribution of categories has nothing to do with this case.

The computational procedure is rather simple. For each subject we record the particular stimuli that he rated in the highest category which he used. In addition we record the number of stimuli in that category. This category need not be the highest in the set because a subject may leave blank one or more of the upper categories. It is the highest category in which he rated any stimuli.

From these basic data we tabulate n_{jm}, which is the number of subjects who placed stimulus j in the highest category in a group of m stimuli that were rated in the same category. The highest category is not necessarily the same for all subjects. Thus n_{j3} means the number of subjects who placed j in their highest class and who placed a total of three stimuli in that class.

In estimating the number of subjects who would rate stimulus j as their first choice, we make several plausible assumptions. First, we assume that those who rated j in their highest interval or category and who placed all other stimuli in lower classes would be expected to rate j as their first choice. Further, we assume that those who placed j and one other stimulus k in the highest interval would divide their votes for first choice between j and k with equal frequencies. Similarly, those who placed j in the highest interval together with a total of m stimuli in that interval would also divide evenly their selections for first choice among the m stimuli. This assumption is not quite correct, but it is very nearly so if the total number of categories is not too small. Theoretically, one could differentiate among the m stimuli in the highest class by the shapes of the frequency distributions, treating them as continuous frequency curves rather than as histograms, but such a correction is probably not worth the trouble in most practical work.

These assumptions lead to an estimation formula which can be written in the form

$$N_{j1} = n_{j1} + \tfrac{1}{2} n_{j2} + \tfrac{1}{3} n_{j3} + \ldots + \frac{1}{m} n_{jm} + \ldots + \frac{1}{t} n_{jt}, \qquad (15)$$

where

N_{j1} = number of subjects who give stimulus j their first choice,
t = largest number of stimuli which any subject put in his highest interval.

Summing, we have

$$N_{j1} = \sum_{m=1}^{t} \left(\frac{n_{jm}}{m} \right), \qquad (16)$$

which applies to each stimulus in turn.

The experimental procedure contemplates the sorting by each subject of a relatively large number of stimuli into a relatively small number of successive categories. This procedure is feasible, whereas it is not feasible to ask a subject to put, say, fifty or one hundred stimuli in rank order. From the data for the sortings into a rather small number of categories, say seven, one can estimate the number of subjects who would give their first choice to any particular stimulus j when this stimulus is presented with any particular combination of other stimuli in the collection.

Several psychophysical methods and concepts have been described in other papers by the author. (See chaps. ii–vi, ix–x, xii, xxi, and L. L. Thurstone, "Ability, Motivation, and Speed," *Psychometrika*, II [1937], 249–54.)

14 AN EXPERIMENT IN THE PREDICTION OF CHOICE

The purpose of this paper[1] is to describe a method of predicting the proportion of the population that will select each of a number of competing items. Each subject is asked to fill in a simple check list of preferences. These check lists are analyzed by the method of successive intervals to predict the proportion of subjects which will select each item.

In the experiment to be described, the subjects were 250 men. Each man was asked to check on a nine-point scale his relative like or dislike for each

TABLE 18

FORTY FOODS IN THE PREFERENCE SCHEDULE

Applesauce	Fresh pineapple	Wieners	Blueberry pie
Lamb chops	Peas	Broccoli	Turnips
Baked potatoes	Parsnips	Chocolate cake	Fried potatoes
Sweetbreads	Biscuits	Hamburgers	Rye bread
Cantaloupe	Vanilla ice cream	Corn bread	Liver
Asparagus	Roast beef	Rhubarb	Roquefort cheese
Whole wheat bread	Eggplant	Fried ham	Spaghetti
Fried chicken	Jello	Creamed onions	Spinach
Cauliflower	Baked beans	Mashed potatoes	Rice pudding
Sweet potatoes	Artichokes	Salmon loaf	Scalloped oysters

of forty foods. This schedule required seldom more than five minutes of the subject's time. He was also presented with a list of sixteen menus that were drawn from the longer list of forty food items. Each menu consisted of several entrees or several vegetables or several kinds of bread or several desserts. Each menu consisted of from two to five items in the same class. The menu choices were then predicted from the check list. Prediction of choice can be made for any number of menus from the same check list.

The forty foods in the preference schedule are listed in Table 18. Each subject responded with one check mark for each of these foods on a nine-point

[1] This study was financed in part by a research grant from Swift & Co. and in part by funds available under Contract No. DA 11-009 qm-598 with the Chicago Quartermaster Depot covering research on "Prediction of Consumer Choice." The examining and computing for this study were done by Thomas Jeffrey, Andrew Baggaley, and Fred Damarin of the Psychometric Laboratory. Published as "An Experiment in the Prediction of Food Preference and the Prediction of Choice," in *Proceedings of the Fourth Research Conference*, pp. 58–66. Sponsored by the Council on Research, American Meat Institute, March 20–21, 1952, at the University of Chicago.

scale. These check lists contained the data that were used for prediction. The instructions for the food preference schedule are shown in Table 19, together with an illustrative check list for four items.

In a separate folder the subjects were given the sixteen menus that are shown in Table 20. It will be seen that these menus varied from two items to five items. For each menu the items belong in the same class. For example, we did not ask a subject to choose between a vegetable and a dessert. There were four menus in which all of the items were desserts. One of these menus contained three desserts, namely, blueberry pie, chocolate cake, and pine-

TABLE 19

FOOD PREFERENCE SCHEDULE

Opposite each food below are nine boxes. Each box represents a different degree of like or dislike for the food, as indicated by the adjectives at the top. Put an X in a box opposite each food, showing your relative likes and dislikes.

| | DISLIKE | | | | NEU-TRAL | | LIKE | | |
	Extreme	Strong	Moder-ate	Mild		Mild	Moder-ate	Strong	Extreme
Waffles								X	
Grapefruit					X				
Beef stew		X							
Peaches							X		

The person who marked these foods is quite fond of waffles; he is indifferent about grapefruit; he definitely dislikes beef stew; and he likes peaches fairly well.

Indicate your own likes and dislikes in the same manner on the next page. Be sure to mark every item.

TABLE 20

SIXTEEN MENUS

1	2	3	4
Cantaloupe	Roast beef	Rye bread	Spinach
Applesauce	Fried chicken	Corn bread	Asparagus

5	6	7	8
Spaghetti	Blueberry pie	Liver	Parsnips
Baked beans	Chocolate cake	Wieners	Turnips·
Salmon loaf	Pineapple	Sweetbreads	Cauliflower

9	10	11	12
Fried potatoes	Rice pudding	Lamb chops	Rye bread
Sweet potatoes	Vanilla ice cream	Scalloped oysters	Corn bread
Baked potatoes	Jello	Roast beef	Biscuits
Mashed potatoes	Applesauce	Fried ham	Whole wheat bread

13	14	15	16
Liver	Roquefort cheese	Eggplant	Fried potatoes
Baked beans	Vanilla ice cream	Creamed onions	Rye bread
Hamburgers	Rice pudding	Broccoli	Whole wheat bread
Scalloped oysters	Rhubarb	Peas	Baked potatoes
Salmon loaf	Cantaloupe	Artichokes	Biscuits

apple. The object of the experiment was to determine whether one can predict from the simple check list the proportion of subjects that will select each one of these desserts. The proportion of first choices for any particular dessert will obviously be partly dependent on the distribution of hedonic values for that item in the experimental population. The proportion of first choices will also be a function of the popularities of the competing items in the same menu. In the check list of forty foods the subject gives his general degree of like or dislike for each of the foods considered separately. In the schedule of menus the proportion of preferences will be affected by the hedonic values of all the competing items in the same menu. Although the purpose of the experiment was to determine whether we could predict the number of first choices within each menu, the subjects were asked to rate the items in each menu in rank order.

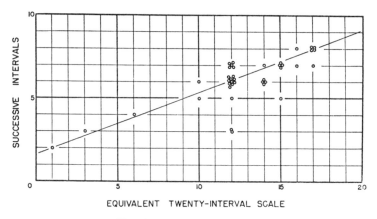

EQUIVALENT TWENTY-INTERVAL SCALE

Fig. 50.—Consistency diagram

In the same folder that contains the sixteen menus, the subjects were given also a second schedule of the forty food items. The subjects were asked to indicate their like or dislike for each food item by merely putting a check mark on a line to indicate degree of preference for the foods. This schedule was similar to the first check list except that the line was not marked off into nine boxes. In evaluating the results, the line was divided into twenty parts, and the location of the check mark was recorded. These two forms of check list were obtained from the same subjects in connection with another psychophysical problem. As far as the theoretical problem is concerned, the two check lists might have been identical, but they were altered in appearance in order to minimize the possible objections from the subjects when they were asked to do the same task twice. The use of these two check lists for reliability purposes will be considered in a separate paper.

In Figure 50 we have a consistency diagram showing the way in which one subject marked the forty food items in the nine-point scale and in the second check list, in which each line was divided into twenty sections for scoring purposes. Figure 50 represents the actual result for one of our subjects. The purpose of these consistency diagrams was to check each subject to determine whether he gave reasonably good attention to the task. If the consistency diagram shows considerable scatter with very low correlation, as determined by inspection, then the subject's record can be discarded because he evidently did not give sufficiently close attention to be reasonably consistent in expressing his food preferences. Such a consistency diagram was plotted for each of the 250 subjects, and we found only four diagrams in which there was any doubt as to whether the subject had paid careful attention to the checking. A consistency check of this kind would be generally

TABLE 21

SAMPLE SCHEDULES

SUBJECT	ITEM	DISLIKE				NEU-TRAL		LIKE		
		I	II	III	IV	V	VI	VII	VIII	IX
1	a								×	
	b						×			
	c							×		
	d					×				
	e						×			
2	a									×
	b						×			
	c							×		
	d									×
	e					×				
3	a								×	
	b						×			
	c					×				
	d								×	
	e								×	

useful in consumer preference surveys to avoid tabulating a lot of data from subjects who were quite indifferent in making their responses. For practical purposes it is not necessary to compute the correlation coefficient. Inspection of a diagram indicates sufficiently well for all practical purposes whether the subject's record shows a reasonable degree of consistency. The items in the diagram in Figure 50 would undoubtedly have a very high positive correlation. There were only two food items that were outside the positive relation in the first and third quadrants.

The prediction of menu choices from the check lists was made by equation (15) in a previous paper on the prediction of choice.[2] The principle of the calculation is represented by three short examples in Table 21. This table shows the check list for three subjects in a five-item menu. The five

[2] See chap. xiii.

TABLE 22

PREDICTION OF CHOICE

Menu No.	Food	Number		Proportions	
		Check List	Menu	Check List	Menu
1........	Cantaloupe	$171\frac{1}{2}$	178	.678	.698
	Applesauce	$81\frac{1}{2}$	77	.322	.302
	Out	4	2		
2........	Roast beef	150	130	.591	.512
	Fried chicken	104	124	.409	.488
	Out	3	3		
3........	Rye bread	$126\frac{1}{2}$	139	.508	.545
	Corn bread	$122\frac{1}{2}$	116	.492	.455
	Out	8	2		
4........	Asparagus	137	155	.581	.610
	Spinach	99	99	.419	.390
	Out	21	3		
5........	Spaghetti	$112\frac{1}{3}$	109	.444	.427
	Baked beans	$84\frac{1}{3}$	89	.333	.349
	Salmon loaf	$56\frac{1}{3}$	57	.223	.224
	Out	4	2		
6........	Blueberry pie	$81\frac{1}{6}$	86	.320	.337
	Chocolate cake	$99\frac{1}{6}$	102	.390	.400
	Pineapple.	$73\frac{2}{3}$	67	.290	.263
	Out	3	2		
7........	Liver	$95\frac{2}{3}$	106	.381	.416
	Wieners	$126\frac{1}{6}$	123	.503	.482
	Sweetbreads	$29\frac{1}{6}$	26	.116	.102
	Out	6	2		
8........	Parsnips	$37\frac{2}{3}$	33	.169	.130
	Turnips	$32\frac{1}{6}$	45	.144	.178
	Cauliflower	$153\frac{1}{6}$	175	.687	.692
	Out	34	4		
9........	Fried potatoes	$62\frac{2}{3}$	67	.264	.264
	Sweet potatoes	$57\frac{1}{2}$	58	.243	.228
	Baked potatoes	$63\frac{1}{3}$	64	.267	.252
	Mashed potatoes	$53\frac{2}{3}$	65	.226	.256
	Out	20	3		
10........	Rice pudding	$23\frac{1}{3}$	24	.096	.095
	Vanilla ice cream	$157\frac{5}{6}$	177	.650	.700
	Jello	$18\frac{1}{3}$	10	.075	.039
	Applesauce	$43\frac{1}{2}$	42	.179	.166
	Out	14	4		
11........	Lamb chops	$36\frac{1}{3}$	40	.147	.158
	Scalloped oysters	$14\frac{1}{2}$	20	.058	.079
	Roast beef	$144\frac{1}{6}$	151	.584	.597
	Fried ham	$52\frac{1}{6}$	42	.211	.166
	Out	10	4		
12........	Rye bread	$60\frac{1}{3}$	64	.246	.252
	Corn bread	$51\frac{5}{8}$	45	.212	.177
	Biscuits	$98\frac{1}{3}$	105	.401	.413
	Whole wheat bread	$34\frac{1}{2}$	40	.141	.157
	Out	12	3		
13........	Liver	$50\frac{1}{6}$	56	.206	.220
	Baked beans	$42\frac{2}{3}$	32	.176	.126
	Hamburgers	$91\frac{2}{3}$	107	.377	.421
	Scalloped oysters	$36\frac{5}{6}$	44	.152	.173
	Salmon loaf	$21\frac{2}{3}$	15	.089	.059
	Out	14	3		

TABLE 22—*Continued*

Menu No.	Food	Number		Proportions	
		Check List	Menu	Check List	Menu
14.........	Roquefort cheese	$24\frac{1}{2}$	27	.100	.106
	Vanilla ice cream	$108\frac{5}{8}$	124	.446	.488
	Rice pudding	19	21	.078	.083
	Rhubarb	$28\frac{5}{8}$	23	.118	.091
	Cantaloupe	$62\frac{5}{8}$	59	.258	.232
	Out	13	3		
15.........	Peas	$101\frac{2}{3}$	115	.422	.455
	Eggplant	$32\frac{1}{3}$	30	.134	.119
	Artichokes	28	27	.116	.107
	Broccoli	$42\frac{5}{8}$	44	.178	.174
	Creamed onions	$36\frac{1}{8}$	37	.150	.146
	Out	16	4		
16.........	Baked potatoes	$59\frac{5}{8}$	63	.255	.248
	Whole wheat bread	$22\frac{1}{2}$	23	.096	.091
	Biscuits	64	62	.272	.244
	Fried potatoes	$51\frac{1}{2}$	67	.219	.264
	Rye bread	$37\frac{1}{4}$	39	.158	.154
	Out	22	3		

items of the menu are denoted *a, b, c, d, e.* Subject No. 1 gave only one check mark in box VIII and no check marks higher than that. One can therefore assume that this subject will make item *a* his first choice. Subject No. 2 gave a rating of IX for the items *a* and *d.* All of the other choices were lower than IX. We therefore credit items *a* and *d* with one-half vote each. Subject No. 3 gave no choices in category IX, but he gave three choices in step VIII. These choices were given to *a, d,* and *e.* These three items were given one-third vote each. For each subject the highest ratings are considered even though they are not in the top category of the rating schedule. By summing the votes assigned to the five items from all of the subjects, we obtain an estimate of the proportion of subjects that will choose each of the five items as their first choice. These calculated proportions constitute the predicted proportions of first choice for each item in each menu. These predictions can then be compared with the actually observed proportion of first choices for each item in each menu.

A comparison between the predicted and the actually obtained proportions of first choices is shown in Table 22. The first menu consisted of only two desserts, namely, cantaloupe and applesauce. The predicted proportion was .678 and .322, and the actually obtained proportion of first choices from the menus was .698 and .302. Similar comparisons were made for all the items in the sixteen menus. There are fifty-six predicted proportions which are compared with the actually obtained proportions of first choices in the menus. In Figure 51 we have a plot of the predicted proportions against the actually obtained proportions, and it will be seen that the discrepancies are rather small. Table 23 shows a frequency distribution of the discrepancies between the proportions predicted from the check lists and the proportions obtained from the menus. The two extremes in Table 23 represent a single

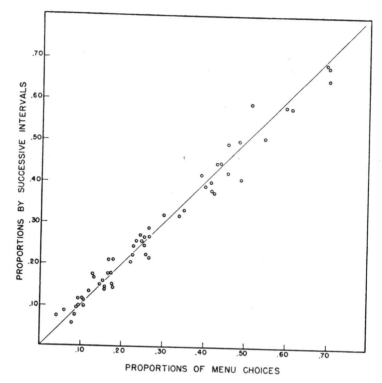

Fig. 51

TABLE 23

DISCREPANCIES BETWEEN PREDICTED
PROPORTIONS FROM CHECK LISTS
AND OBTAINED PROPORTIONS FROM
MENUS

From	To	f
+.07	+.08	1
+.06	+.07	0
+.05	+.06	1
+.04	+.05	1
+.03	+.04	5
+.02	+.03	7
+.01	+.02	6
.00	+.01	8
−.01	.00	5
−.02	−.01	8
−.03	−.02	4
−.04	−.03	5
−.05	−.04	3
−.06	−.05	1
−.07	−.06	0
−.08	−.07	1
		N = 56

pair, namely, the choice between roast beef and fried chicken. The discrepancy is nearly 8 per cent, as shown in Table 22. Inspection of the distributions in the check lists shows that both of these items were rated exceptionally high, in the top two or three categories, by practically all of the subjects. The approximation that is represented by equation (15) that we used for these predictions assumes in effect that the distributions can be treated as histograms. When the distribution of check marks is concentrated in two or three class intervals on the check list, there is probably an error of coarse grouping. The discrepancies between the predicted proportions and the actually obtained proportions in the menus are so small that for practical purposes the simple survey check list, as analyzed here, should be a generally useful device.

It should be noted that in the present experiment we were not concerned with any sampling problem. The 250 subjects in this experiment filled in both the check list and the menus, so that we are not here dealing with a problem of sampling the general population. Our interest was to determine the correspondence between the two situations, namely, a check list of preference for forty items and a first choice from competing items in a menu. In comparing these two psychophysical procedures, nothing could be gained by confusing the problem with sampling errors. In any practical application, the experimental group should, of course, be a random sample of the population that is to do the actual selection, and the ordinary statistical criteria would then apply.

In setting up this simple experiment, we intentionally avoided several complications that one would meet in practical applications. Among these it would be necessary to consider certain conventional combinations, as, for example, corned beef and cabbage. Conventional association between certain entrees and certain vegetables would not be covered by the methods described here. In preparing check lists for items involving such combinations, it will be best to include the combination itself as an item to be judged. In that way the effects of conventional combinations of items could be appraised as to hedonic value, because the combination can be treated as an item in the same way as the separate foods themselves are treated.

The present study was essentially a laboratory experiment because the menus were checked by the 250 men without reference to what they themselves actually select at lunch or dinner. The next step should be to compare a check list preference record with actual choices in a cafeteria or dining room. The check list should be submitted to a random sample of the clientele, and the results should be compared with the consumption of the separate items. The study could be carried out in a cafeteria or in a restaurant, but in the first experiments it will be preferable to have the items of comparable cost. In the present study we did not include any considerations of differential costs of the items. A field study should be carried out in a situation where the items to be considered are of comparable cost. If the prediction by these methods can be sustained in such a field study, then it should be of interest to extend these methods to choices with differential costs. Such a study would introduce several new psychophysical problems in the experimental study of utility. The present experiment does not pretend to cover choices of items of different costs. The utility or hedonic value of a purchase can be considered as the algebraic sum of the hedonic value of the item and the negative hedonic value of its cost.

The check list that has been described here is essentially an example of the method of successive intervals. In this method the procedure is the same as in the method of equal-appearing intervals, except that the intervals are not here considered to be subjectively equal. Their successive character should, however, be taken for granted by the subject. The favorable results with the present simple experiment in prediction should justify practical applications and the further study of the psychophysical problems in the prediction of choice.

15 METHODS OF FOOD-TASTING EXPERIMENTS

When I first learned about the food-tasting laboratory at the Quartermaster Corps here in Chicago, I was much interested to see it. I found in that laboratory five booths which were specially designed for experimental work in this area. I volunteered as a subject, and I was seated at a table next to a wall. On the other side of the wall were technicians who placed the food specimens on a small revolving platform. I was presented with a number of specimens of tomato juice. The instructions told me to rank the specimens according to my preferences. These specimens had been stored for different lengths of time at different temperatures in different types of containers. The practical question was to determine whether people can tell the differences and whether they will reject some of these foods. It has been found that the human subject can make discriminations to accept or reject foods with criteria that are not evident in the chemical and bacteriological analyses. In developing new foods, it is then an essential preparation to ascertain whether people will eat them. This is called food acceptance research.[1]

It is an interesting circumstance that the laboratory methods for determining sensory limens and hedonic values have here an important practical application. This is the oldest part of experimental psychology, and it is called psychophysics. Traditionally, this field has been known among students of psychology as a very theoretical and dull subject, but it has in recent years found so many applications that it is now coming to be regarded as an interesting aspect of psychological method.

One of the first problems of the food-tasting laboratory is to arrange the procedures to obtain a maximum of information from each subject in the minimum time. In testing a new food product by taste experiments, it is desirable to compare different specimens which have been kept at different temperatures for different lengths of time so that it will be known under what latitude the product remains not only edible but also desirable.

One of the controls in the food-tasting booths is the color of the illumination. By light switches the examiner can instantly change the color of the food that is being rated. A piece of butter suddenly looks like a piece of lard, and acceptability might be affected.

[1] Reprinted from *Proceedings of the Second Conference on Research*, American Meat Institute (March, 1950), pp. 85–91.

A theoretically more interesting problem is that of predicting from the ratings what proportion of the subjects will choose food A when it is offered in competition with foods B and C and D, for example. It is not possible to experiment explicitly with every possible food combination. There are too many. How should the ratings be made so as to enable us to make predictions of this kind? Such a problem is of analytical and practical interest.

Taste experiments are sometimes conducted with an especially selected panel of expert tasters. Such people are selected supposedly because they excel in the ability to make fine discriminations in tastes and sometimes because of their familiarity with the particular product. In selecting such panels, one should keep in mind that a person who can make very fine discriminations in one class of tastes is not necessarily superior in tasting different products. In general, it is probably true that a person who has keen taste discrimination tends to excel in all taste discriminations, but this is not a dependable rule for individual cases. A different policy is to select a group of tasters who represent the public that is to be pleased rather than a small group of experts. If the taste experiments are conducted for the purpose of predicting relative sale or consumption for competing flavors or brands, then it would seem best to work with an experimental population that is truly representative of the public for whom the product is manufactured. On the other hand, since it has been found that the human subject can make taste discriminations correctly even when the chemists and bacteriologists are unable to demonstrate the differences objectively, the expert taster can be used to advantage. Before a panel of expert tasters are put to work, they certainly should qualify by objective tests as to their ability to discriminate and as to the consistency with which they make taste discriminations.

Most of the experimental work in psychophysics has been done with vision and hearing. Such experiments are usually carried out more easily with visual stimuli, where the subject can see two objects simultaneously. With auditory stimuli that cannot be done. The stimuli must be perceived in succession. This is also true in experiments with taste and smell. In conducting taste experiments, one must deal with several difficulties that are specially annoying. When the subject has tasted one specimen, he cannot immediately turn to the next specimen. Preferably, he should rinse his mouth and even then several minutes should elapse before he can taste the next sample under normal conditions. He may be asked to express his preferences, or he may be asked to make comparisons as to some particular taste quality. In the cases of smells, experimental work has the additional difficulty of adaptation. For some odors continued exposure reduces the ability to discriminate because of adaptation.

Because of these difficulties in experimental work in taste and smell, it is essential in any practical problem to arrange the procedure in such a way that the maximum possible information can be obtained from each subject with the smallest possible number of separate judgments. Because of these difficulties one must make some practical compromises. In some types of psychophysical experiments one can present all of the stimuli in pairs, so that each subject makes a comparison of each pair of stimuli. For example, a set of ten specimens requires forty-five distinct paired comparisons. In practice, such a procedure is almost out of the question in dealing with taste.

Another procedure is to give the subject, say, three, four, or five samples and to ask him to arrange them in rank order of preference. If a larger number of specimens are to be tasted, they can be divided into several small groups. For each group the subject is asked to arrange the specimens in rank order of preference. It is assumed that with a small group of specimens, say four or five, the subject can keep them in mind well enough to make dependable judgments of rank order. However, even with the rank order method the subject ordinarily samples each specimen several times unless the differences are so gross that one hardly needs to conduct taste experiments to determine them.

The best procedure is probably to have a fairly large number of subjects and to ask each subject to sample each specimen only once. We might consider here two variations of this principle. If the subject is asked to sample a fairly large number of specimens by tasting each specimen only once, he may be asked to allocate the specimens to a set of, say, ten steps. These might be numbered from 1 to 10, and he might be asked to let number 1 represent the most disagreeable, while number 10 represents the most agreeable, taste. These ten steps would really represent intervals on a subjective scale of taste preference. One method that could be used for this work is called the method of equal-appearing intervals. In this procedure the subject is asked to think of the ten steps as representing subjectively equal increments in taste preference from the worst to the best. After tasting each specimen, he allocates it to one of the ten classes. In another context this experimental method has been used to advantage, but it is probably not the most appropriate method for this type of problem. It has been shown that even when the subject attempts to make the intervals subjectively equal, he rarely succeeds in doing so. This can be demonstrated by comparing the method of equal intervals with other psychophysical methods that can be checked for internal consistency.

The method of successive intervals is probably the best experimental method for this problem. In this method the subject samples each specimen only once, and he states his degree of preference in terms of one of a number of short descriptive phrases which are assigned to the successive intervals. There is no assumption that these successive intervals of the scale are in any sense equal. The descriptive words or phrases must, however, be sufficiently distinct so that the subject accepts the rank order of the descriptive phrases. In effect, then, the subject expresses his degree of preference or dislike in terms of eight or ten descriptive phrases. For convenience these descriptive phrases can be denoted by numbers or letters. Instead of having a small number of subjects do the taste experiments, it is probably better to have a fairly large number who represent the true population and to ask each of them to describe his judgment about each specimen in terms of the eight or ten successive descriptive phrases. This procedure probably enables us to get the maximum amount of information from the subject in the shortest time.

Each specimen is identified by a code number or suitable name. On the record sheet the subject has a row of eight or ten spaces. Immediately under these spaces he finds descriptive phrases, from extreme dislike, some dislike, indifference, some preference, to strong preference. When he has tasted a sample, he merely records a check mark to indicate his rating of the degree of preference. This procedure is very coarse compared with the discrimination he could give if his attention were limited to only three or four specimens. The experimental work with other types of stimuli have indicated that this simple method of successive intervals with only one judgment for each specimen from each subject gives results that are useful in prediction. It is assumed that an experimental population of at least several hundred individuals is available. They should be a random sample of the population for which the food products are intended. It is possible to get a fairly large number of specimens examined by each subject without undue fatigue. The subjects find it easier to make judgments of this kind than to make the more refined paired comparison judgments that are called for when the purpose is to determine the taste limens of the individual subjects.

This is not the occasion to discuss the psychological scaling problem except to indicate the general nature of that problem. In psychological measurement we differentiate between two types of scales, the objective physical scale and the subjective or psychological scale. The physical or objective scale is the type of scale that we all know. The unit of measurement is some physical unit such as the inch, the gram, or the liter. The subjective or psychological scale represents equal steps in apparent or perceived magnitude as contrasted with the physically measured magnitudes of the stimuli. Sometimes we refer to the physical magnitudes as real magnitudes, but one could insist that the real magnitude is that which the subject actually experiences when he does make the differentiation. Let us consider a very simple example to illustrate the difference between the physical stimulus scale and the psychological scale. Suppose that we place before the subject two standard weights which differ markedly. They might be, say, 50 grams and 500 grams. Now suppose that the subject has available a large number of intermediate weights and that we ask him to select one of these weights which seems to him to lie midway between the two standard weights. When he finds a weight that seems to him to lie midway between the two given standard weights, then we can determine the physical magnitude of this intermediate weight. It will then be found that the intermediate weight which seems to the subject to lie midway between the two standards is actually physically closer to the lower weight than to the upper one. On the psychological scale the three weights are equally spaced because the subject perceives the two intervals to be equal. On the physical scale, the three weights are not equally spaced. The lower interval is smaller than the upper one. In this case we expect to find that the psychological scale is a logarithmic function of the physical scale. When we deal with problems of discrimination that are concerned with food acceptance, or indeed with accepting and rejecting other commodities, we are dealing with the apparent magnitudes, the subjective scale, because that is a scale that actually functions when we express preferences among several competing objects. One of the central problems in psychological measurement is to determine the ratio of the successive intervals. This problem has been solved, so that we can speak of a subjective metric with a subjective unit of measurement and not merely about a set of rank orders.

There is one concept in psychological measurement to which I should like to draw your special attention because it can have far-reaching effects in many practical problems. The concept is rarely understood by those who have the responsibility for making decisions in which this concept should play a part. I am referring to the concept of discriminal dispersion. The central idea of this concept is relatively simple. I shall try to express it briefly and to indicate some of its curious practical effects. Consider two objects which might as well be food products in the present context. Let these two objects have the same average popularity. This may mean that the two products are equally popular or equally unpopular. We mean that the average scale values for these two objects are the same. Let us suppose that they differ in one important respect, namely, that object A has wide range of values in the population, so that some people are enthusiastic about it, whereas others have intense dislike for it. We say that such an object has a large discriminal dispersion. People differ very markedly in the hedonic values that they assign to this object. Let object B have a small discriminal dispersion. This means that nobody is very enthusiastic about it and no one has any violent dislike for it. The range of hedonic values for this object in the population is small. It can easily be seen that two objects can differ in this way in the range of feeling that people have for or against them in spite of the fact that the two objects have the same average popularity. We should expect food products like roast beef to have a rather small discriminal dispersion, whereas oysters would have a large discriminal dispersion.

If two objects A and B are presented to a group of subjects with instructions that each subject select only one of the pair, then if the average popularity is the same and if the discriminal dispersions are different, we should expect that half of the population would select each item. However, if we have several competing objects which have the same average popularity and one object which has a large discriminal dispersion, then we would expect a rather curious and startling result. Let us suppose that we have six objects of equal average popularity. Let the object A have large discriminal dispersion, and let the other five objects have vanishingly small discriminal dispersions, so that people are fairly well agreed about them. If these six objects are presented to the population and if each person chooses one of the objects, then we should discover that the object A gets one-half of the votes, while the other five objects get only 10 per cent each. In this example I am assuming for illustrative purposes that the preferences for these single items are uncorrelated. It is quite likely that some of the errors in the prediction of elections have been caused by the striking effects of differences in discriminal dispersions. The theory of this problem is very much the same whether we are considering the popularity and dispersions of a group of political candidates or of any other competing objects that are to be chosen.

If we have a record of preference judgments from an experimental population about each one of a large number of foods which might be listed merely by name, then it should be possible to predict the proportion of that population which will select each item as its first choice when it is presented with any given set of alternatives. For example, if we have obtained several hundred preference records with the method of successive intervals for a list of foods, then, if any arbitrary list of four, five, or six of these foods is presented for choice, it should be possible to predict the proportion of the subjects who will select each of those foods. This kind of prediction has been made on other types of material, and there should be no reason why the same principle should not be extended to the prediction of choice in foods. Here also the concept of discriminal dispersion plays an important role which market research men could make use of if they knew about it.

If we have the problem of presenting, say, five objects out of a total list of fifty objects with the purpose of maximizing the number of individuals who will select one of the five, then there is a fairly definite analysis that should be made. The first impulse is usually to select the five most popular objects from the whole list of fifty and to present these five, but that is the wrong answer. Although this is the wrong answer, I suspect that such a solution is often attempted. The number of choices from a population depends on the dispersions of hedonic values and also on the correlations among these items. It usually happens that those who prefer item A are more likely to prefer also some other item, say, B and that those who prefer item C might be those who dislike item E, and so on. Merely to select the five most popular items from the total available list of fifty usually means that many persons will find several items that please them, so that they have difficulty in making up their minds, while other people will find nothing that pleases them in the presented list of five objects. A better solution can be described briefly. We start assembling the required list of five objects by selecting the most popular single item A from the available set of fifty objects. We remove from the experimental population all those individuals who did choose this object A as their first choice. Now we ascertain the most popular object B in the remainder of the experimental population. Object B is then added to the collection. Again we remove from the survey population all those individuals who did select *B* as their first choice. Now we ascertain the most popular object *C* in the remainder of the survey population. After removing all of the members of the survey population who did select object *C* as their first choice, we might discover that most of our survey population has been accounted for. If this should happen, then not only would we have discovered which objects to present to maximize acceptance, but we could also discover the number of objects that are necessary to attain the required degree of acceptance. That required degree of acceptance is, let us say, 90 per cent of the population. This type of solution actually maximizes the proportion of acceptance. The number of rejections will be smaller with this solution than if we presented the five most popular objects from the whole available supply. I am venturing to guess that this principle has not been applied in dealing with psychophysical problems concerned with food, but I see no reason why it should not apply in this field.

The traditional psychophysical problems have been concerned with the establishment of the subjective scale, but we have considered here briefly an obverse problem, namely, to predict from such a scale what people will do. This is the problem of prediction of choice. The problem that we have called the prediction of choice is that of predicting the proportion of the population that will select each particular competing object when a sample population has expressed its preferences about each of the separate objects. There is a related problem to which I have recently given considerable thought. I am calling this problem the prediction of purchase, which is distinct from the prediction of choice. If all of the available objects are of the same price, then the theorems about the prediction of choice can be applied over the whole range of objects. If these objects differ in price, we have, of course, different degrees of inhibition on free choice. The motivation to a purchase can be thought of as the algebraic sum of the hedonic value of the object and the negative hedonic value of the price. We are working on several psychophysical theorems concerned with the prediction of purchase, which is, of course, a much more difficult problem than the prediction of the free choice among the available objects. In these psychophysical problems we are not concerned with the prediction of total volume because that is for economists to worry about. Given, however, the expected total volume, it is largely a psychophysical problem to ascertain how the total volume is divided among competing objects. It seems quite likely that psychophysical theories will find useful application in the solution of important problems of this kind. I see no reason why economics should not be developed along these lines as an experimental science.

In this paper I have tried to describe briefly the nature of some of the difficulties of experimental work on taste and smell with special reference to judgments of preferences. The conventional psychophysical methods which involve paired comparison seem to be less desirable in this field than the more general method of successive intervals, even though this method does not claim to be so refined as the traditional methods. If our purpose is to ascertain the frequency distributions of hedonic values of different foods, then it seems best to use as experimental subjects random samples from the population for whom the foods are manufactured. It seems best also to obtain in a similar manner a single judgment from each subject about each one of a large number of foods presented, either by name or by actual specimens, than to confine attention to the work of a small group of expert tasters. In the inevitable practical problems of predicting consumption among competing food items, it should be profitable to take into consideration the discriminal dispersions as well as the inter-food correlations. These correlations can also be obtained from the data that are assembled by the method of successive intervals. The expert food taster still has an important function to supplement other laboratory analyses.

A central theme in food-tasting experiments and in survey questionnaires about food preferences is that of maximizing the useful information that can be obtained with minimum effort. The practical problems can be classified in several groups. First is the problem of determining the effect of various conditions of manufacture and storage and containers on food acceptance. Another problem is the prediction of relative volume among different items as determined by experiments on food acceptance. Another problem is that of combining food items so as to maximize acceptance among competing items which differ in discriminal dispersions. It seems likely that formal experimentation is this field can produce more significant and useful results than simple frequency counts at the descriptive level.

16 SOME NEW PSYCHOPHYSICAL METHODS

The purpose of this paper[1] is to describe briefly several new psychophysical methods as regards both experimental procedure and the analysis of data. This discussion will probably be of interest primarily to those who are working on the different methods of scale construction for the appraisal of consumer preferences and problems in the measurement of values. Subsequent studies in the practical application of these new methods will probably be of more general interest in terms of the specific content of each application.

In the complete form of the equation of comparative judgment there is a correlational term which has caused some difficulty in the computational work with consumer preference data. The meaning of this correlation can be described in terms of the principal interests of this symposium. If we consider any two foods, j and k, and if the correlation r_{jk} is high, then the interpretation is that those who like food j tend to be those who also prefer k. Two methods of determining these correlations will be described. One method of determining the correlation is to examine the individual paired comparison schedule for each subject. Since each subject states his preference for all pairs of stimuli, one can determine a rank order for all of the stimuli for each subject. One can then easily tabulate the number of subjects who rate a stimulus above or below the median rank. This can be done for each stimulus and for each subject. We can then prepare a fourfold table to show the extent, for example, to which those who rate stimulus j above the median rank are also those who tend to rate stimulus k in the same manner. From this fourfold table a tetrachoric correlation coefficient can be computed.

The correlation can also be obtained by the method of successive intervals. Here we can proceed in two ways which will not give the same correlation. If the successive intervals have been scaled, we can assign a scale value to each of the stimuli, and then it is a relatively simple matter to compute the correlation between scale values for each pair of stimuli j and k. Such a correlation will almost certainly be higher than the correlation obtained from

[1] This paper was prepared as *Psychometric Laboratory Report No. 7* (October, 1953). It was presented at a symposium sponsored by the National Research Council Advisory Board on Quartermaster Research and Development at the Palmer House in Chicago on October 9, 1953. This report was later reprinted in the proceedings of the symposium by the Quartermaster Food and Container Institute (National Academy of Sciences–National Research Council) in October, 1954, pp. 100–104.

the paired comparison data. The reason for this circumstance can be explained in terms of an example. In the method of successive intervals a subject may rate all of the stimuli in the upper half of the scale. Another subject may rate all of the stimuli in the lower half of the scale. If subjects of this kind are rather numerous in the experimental population, the resulting correlation would be higher than that which is obtained by paired comparison, in which the subject merely expresses his preference for each pair without saying whether both of them are to be rated very high or very low.

Another way to proceed with successive intervals is to put all of the stimuli in rank order for each subject. A tetrachoric correlation for each pair of stimuli can then be computed, and it should agree very closely with such a correlation determined from paired comparisons. In the theoretical model that is represented by the equation of comparative judgment we are dealing with discrimination of pairs of stimuli, and it seems likely that the best determination for the correlation will be that which is obtained from the rank orders of paired comparison or from the successive interval schedules.

Recently I have formulated a new principle of scale construction that will avoid an important restrictive assumption. This assumption can have serious effects on the validity of a scale for certain types of stimuli, including foods. Let us first consider the restrictive assumption that we should like to avoid. Most of the methods of scaling make the assumption that the subjective values of a stimulus have a normal distribution for the experimental population. For many types of stimuli this is a legitimate assumption which gives very good results. If we ask a group of subjects to rate the relative excellence of handwriting specimens, for example, one would expect that almost any group of experimental subjects would show a normal distribution for each stimulus. The situation is quite different when we ask people to rate their relative likes and dislikes for food. The shape of the distribution of subjective values for a food may be positively or negatively skewed or even bimodal, depending on the manner in which the experimental group is assembled. The shape of the distribution of attitudes toward corn bread, for example, could take almost any form, depending on the geographic distribution of the experimental population. We should like to avoid the assumption that the distribution of subjective values of a stimulus is normal for the experimental population.

The new principle of scale construction makes a different assumption. We assume that if each individual were asked to give repeated ratings, his variations would show a normal error distribution for his successive attempts to rate the same stimulus. In fact, we can use this principle for measuring the successive intervals. We shall definitely not assume that this error distribution has the same dispersion for stimuli of positive or negative values or near the indifference point. We can make the assumption, however, that these error distributons for each subject are Gaussian. Indications so far are that this principle can be used to obtain an internally consistent scale. We can readily see that even though each individual has a normal distribution of errors for successive ratings, the resulting distribution of mean values for the whole population may take any form including any degree of skewness or even bimodality. The definition of a scale in such a way that the individual error distributions in perception are normal is evidently less restrictive than the more common assumption that the distribution of subjective values is normal for any experimental population.

Let us now consider alternative ways in which a scale can be constructed on the assumption that the error distribution for each subject is normal. If we use the method of successive intervals, we would ask the subjects to do the task twice. Some variation can be introduced in the appearance of the schedules so as to minimize objections from the subject in doing the task twice. We prepare a tabulation in which the first set of ratings is plotted against the second set for all stimuli. The sizes of the intervals in the vertical arrays are then adjusted so as to produce normal distributions in the vertical arrays. These discrepancies represent variations between the first and second judgment of the same things. In the same manner the horizontal arrays are adjusted as to the sizes of the intervals so that the distributions in the horizontal arrays are normal. It should be clearly understood that we are not assuming that the resulting table would be homoscedastic because the dispersions may vary from one range of the table to another. When the scaling of the vertical and the horizontal arrays has been done, we should expect a linear relation between the scale intervals for the first and second attempts, but we would not expect them to be exactly the same. The dispersions in perception would be slightly larger on the second occasion because when a subject does the same task a second time, his attention is not quite so good as on the first attempt. However, the relation should be linear between the two sets of scale values. When this task has been completed, the marginal distributions should represent the distribution of subjective values for the population, but these distributions do not need to be normal.

The same principle can be used in analyzing the data from paired comparison. With paired comparison data we might proceed in two alternative ways. The rank order of a set of stimuli can be ascertained for each subject by merely counting the number of votes that he has given to each stimulus in the comparisons. Then we can find the proportion of the subjects who show discrepancy with their own rank order for each pair of stimuli j and k. The higher this proportion, the closer are the stimuli. Again, this does not assume a normal distribution of subjective values for these stimuli for the whole population. In this manner we might avoid asking the subject to do the paired comparison schedule twice. This is a new procedure which has not yet been tried, but it is now being set up for analysis.

Another more direct way is to ask the subject to fill in a paired comparison schedule twice. For each pair of stimuli j and k we find the proportion of subjects who were inconsistent for the two trials. This determines the scale separation between the two stimuli. The larger the proportion of inconsistencies, the closer are the two stimuli on the scale. Again this does not assume a normal distribution of stimulus values for the whole population. Both of these methods should be tried to ascertain whether they give the same result.

We have data for several food preference schedules that were presented to the same group of 250 men. They gave paired comparison records as well as successive intervals records. The successive intervals method was given twice. Analyses will be made of these records to determine whether the different psychophysical methods give the same results for scale values, skewness, and dispersions. Studies of this sort will eventually answer the question whether these different psychophysical methods define the same subjective metric. Previous studies indicate that such is the case, but the new scaling principle here described has not yet been investigated with different methods of obtaining the data.

Some time ago I obtained some data in the attempt to ascertain whether we can make an experimental determination of the zero point in a scale of preferences. The zero point would be that point at which the subject is neutral as to whether he wants the object or not. Any object in the scale below the neutral point is then an object which the subject dislikes. In order to solve this problem, we prepared a schedule with pictures of various objects that the subject might choose as birthday presents. Our subjects were students at the University of Chicago and the University of North Carolina in Chapel Hill. The objects were a desk lamp, pen and pencil set, phonograph, unabridged dictionary, and brief case. Each of these objects was compared with every other. In addition we also presented the objects in pairs, so that the subject was asked whether he would rather have a phonograph or a large dictionary *and* a desk lamp. Other comparisons of the same type were included, so as to make a complete schedule of all combinations. Each of the single stimuli and the double stimuli were treated as separate entities for the purposes of scaling. Now the question is whether we can locate a zero point in such a way that the sum of the scale values for two stimuli A and B would be equal to the scale value of the combination $(A + B)$. We have made an initial analysis by the simple assumption of Case 5 of the equation of comparative judgment, and the results are very satisfactory. The same data are now being analyzed by more refined methods in which the dispersion for each stimulus will be included explicitly. This study will be completed shortly, and it does demonstrate that scale values under these conditions are additive and that a rational zero point can be located on a preference schedule.

Several of these studies are being made jointly with Dr. Lyle Jones at the University of Chicago. These problems which are concerned with the subjective metric, both in the one-dimensional form and in the multidimensional form, are of considerable theoretical interest, and they give promise of important and useful applications in the measurement of many types of social values.

17 THE MEASUREMENT OF VALUES

In this paper[1] I shall try to summarize briefly the attempts of several investigators to extend the concepts of measurement to the subjective domain. While this work is admittedly crude and exploratory, the results do look promising, so that this field should be challenging for further study. Here we shall have time only for brief statements of the fundamental ideas without details of theory or experimental procedure. Our purpose here is only to sketch the nature of this field of research.

When we propose to measure human values, colleagues in the humanities may shudder at the very idea. When I wrote a paper entitled "Attitudes Can Be Measured," some of my colleagues did shudder. They were sure that social attitudes contain some essence that could not be identified and measured. They were sure that, in making the attempt, we would measure only the trivial.

Human values are essentially subjective. They can certainly not be adequately represented by physical objects. Their intensities or magnitudes cannot be represented by physical measurement. At the very start we are faced with the problem of establishing a subjective metric. This is the central theme in modern psychophysics in its many applications to the measurement of social values, moral values, and aesthetic values. Exactly the same problem reappears in the measurement of utility in economics.

In order to establish a subjective metric, we must have a subjective unit of measurement. Before we can accept a subjective metric, it must satisfy the logical requirements of measurement as distinguished from rank order. These objectives have been approximated in the equation of comparative judgment and its variants.

Before proceeding to discuss the many applications of the subjective metric, we shall review briefly the principal psychophysical concepts by which a subjective metric can be established.

Let us consider these concepts in terms of a rather simple example, namely, the judgment of excellence of handwriting. When we look at several specimens of handwriting, it is fairly easy to select some that are considered to be excellent and others that are judged to be poor. In general, there is good agreement in such judgments. If we were asked to equate our judg-

[1] Reprinted from *Psychological Review*, LXI (1954), 47–58.

ments of excellence in a handwriting specimen to some physical measurements on the script, we would find it difficult. One of the main requirements of a truly subjective metric is that it shall be entirely independent of all physical measurement. In freeing ourselves completely from physical measurement, we are also free to experiment with aesthetic objects and with many other types of stimuli to which there does not correspond any known physical measurement.

If we present a single handwriting specimen to a subject with the request that he tell us how good he thinks it is, then he must try to convey the degree of excellence in terms of words. It is well known that people vary tremendously in their use of superlatives in appraisals of experience, and, consequently, it is preferable to avoid such a direct procedure. Next we proceed to pairs of stimuli. We can ask the subject to judge which is the better of two specimens. In so doing, the subject gives his comparative judgment for each pair, and he is not asked to give any verbal description of excellence.

The degree of excellence of a handwriting specimen is experienced by the subject in terms of some subjective process or quale. Since nothing is known about the neurological correlates of judgments of excellence of handwriting, we shall dodge all such terminology by merely referring to the discriminal processes by which the subject does, in fact, discriminate between the different specimens. These processes may be assumed to be physical or truly subjective according to the preferences of the investigator. His preference on this point has nothing to do with the subsequent development of the law of comparative judgment.

When the subject makes a judgment that one specimen seems to him to be better than another specimen, we postulate discriminal processes which differ in some manner in terms of which the percipient does make the discrimination. The more excellent specimen has some quale which differs from that of the poorer specimen. Imagine that the discriminal processes which correspond to different values are arranged in a spectrum from those discriminal processes in terms of which the percipient experiences the good specimens to the other end of the spectrum with discriminal processes in terms of which he experiences what he calls the poorer specimens.

Consider next the phenomena of dispersion. If one subject were to examine the same specimen in comparative situations on a large number of occasions it is not to be expected that he would always experience a particular specimen with the same discriminal process. It can be assumed that the same specimen will be experienced in terms of discriminal processes in the same general region of the subjective continuum that has been postulated. So far we have no metric.

At this point we recall one of the fundamental restrictions on the problem of establishing a subjective metric. The discriminal processes must be assumed to be of such a character that they do not necessarily have intensities or magnitudes which can be in any sense measured. This is an old problem that was discussed many years ago in psychophysical theory. For theoretical considerations, imagine that the discriminal processes could actually be identified on each occasion when the subject makes a comparative judgment. The repeated observations of the same specimen can be assumed to produce an error variation from one occasion to the next. If we consider the relative frequencies of these discriminal processes as responses to the same stimulus, then we can postulate a Gaussian error distribution for the responses to the repeated observations of the same stimulus. Let us now assume that the spectrum of discriminal processes is stretched or contracted in different parts in such a way that the frequency distribution of these processes is Gaussian in terms of any given stimulus. Now we have a metric, but it is so far an entirely arbitrary metric. Imagine, at least in theory, that the same procedure can be repeated for many different stimuli which cover the whole range of discriminal processes in terms of which degree of excellence is experienced. It is now a question of experimental fact whether the metrics determined for the separate stimuli will be the same when all of the stimuli are considered together. It has been found in many experiments that such is the case.

If we represent in the same model the comparative judgment of two stimuli in which the subject says for each presentation which of the pair is the better, then we can observe the proportion of attempts in which the subject judges specimen j to be better than specimen k. If we have a whole table of such proportions, it is possible to infer the spatial separations of the different distributions of discriminal processes. Each stimulus is then assumed to project a Gaussian distribution on the subjective continuum with a mean and a discriminal dispersion. An ambiguous stimulus will project a wider dispersion on the subjective continuum than a sharply defined or relatively unambiguous stimulus. Each stimulus will then be defined in the subjective continuum by its mean position, which is called a scale value, and by the standard deviation of its dispersion of discriminal processes. Each stimulus is then defined by two parameters in the subjective continuum.

Before we can put numbers into these parameters, we must define an arbitrary origin which may be taken as the mean value that one of the stimuli projects on the continuum. As a unit of measurement we may choose arbitrarily the standard deviation of the dispersion which that stimulus projects on the subjective continuum. When that has been done, similar numerical values can be assigned to all of the other specimens that have entered into the comparative judgments. Further, we can test for the internal consistency of this theoretical model.

It should be carefully noted that we have not assumed that the discriminal processes have magnitudes of any kind. They have been dealt with merely as subjective qualia, and we have assumed only that in principle their relative frequency of association with any given stimulus can be ascertained. While this cannot be done directly, these frequencies can be inferred indirectly from the observed comparative data. It should also be noted that we have not postulated the existence of any physical measures of any kind for the stimuli that have entered into the comparative judgments.

With this formulation of the law of comparative judgment, we are free to proceed with comparative studies of all kinds of stimuli which have no physical measure whatever. Hence we can turn to a wide array of interesting psychological problems involving value judgments. The freedom from any postulated physical measurement is the key that makes studies of this kind possible.

The method of comparative judgment turns out to be a rather general experimental procedure, and the well-known constant method in psychophysics is a special case in which one of the stimuli is arbitrarily taken as the standard which is compared with all of the other stimuli. Classical psychophysics was concerned with the more restricted problem of limen determinations.

We turn next to a brief review of some of the classical psychophysical methods because some of them have application in modern problems which transcend the determination of limens. In the method of equal-appearing intervals, the subject is asked to sort a large number of stimuli into a specified number of successive categories, say, six or eight or ten. He is instructed to sort them in such a way that the intervals represented by the categories seem to him to be equal. This method is useful for rough survey purposes, but it can be shown that, even when the subject attempts to do this, he actually does not succeed in making the intervals subjectively equal. The method is, however, useful for coarse scaling, such as the construction of attitude scales. The old method of equal-appearing intervals has been modified into what we call the method of successive intervals, in which the intervals are defined by descriptive phrases or by sample specimens. This method has been found to be very useful in various types of surveys to be discussed.

One of the old psychophysical methods was to ask the subject to sort a number of specimens into rank order. It has been found that rank orders can be analyzed in such a way as to obtain data approximately equivalent to those of the method of paired comparison. The method of successive intervals can even be analyzed as a variant of the method of single stimuli.

Since Weber's law and Fechner's law have figured so prominently in the history of psychophysics, we shall make a few comments about these two laws in relation to the modern setting. These two laws are frequently referred to as the Weber-Fechner law with the implication that they are the same law, but that is an error. It is possible to set up experiments with rather simple stimuli in which one of these laws will be verified when the other one is not verified. It would be useful to set up such experiments in order to show clearly the separation between the two laws. Weber's law states that the proportion of judgments $R > kR$ is a constant. R signifies here the physical magnitude of the stimulus, and k represents another constant. Weber's law is concerned solely with physical measurements. It does not explicitly refer to the subjective continuum. On the other hand, Fechner's law states frankly the relation between the subjective continuum and the physical stimulus continuum. Fechner's law states that this relation is generally logarithmic, and it should be taken as a rough approximation to the relation between the subjective and the physical continua. Further, it can be seen that Fechner's law is applicable only to those stimuli which have a physical magnitude as well as an experienced intensity. The law of comparative judgment is completely independent of any physical stimulus magnitudes. The problem of the stimulus error is not ordinarily of serious concern to our problem. It deals with the ambiguity in the mind of the subject when he is asked to judge a stimulus as to the intensity of the subjective experience. Sometimes he attempts instead to judge the physical magnitude. A good example is that of a grocery clerk who can judge the weight of a bag of sugar. If he were asked to serve as a subject in the method of mean gradation, he would probably commit what Tichener would have called the stimulus error. In the measurement of social values, we are not interested in physical measurements because in general they do not exist for such values.

A very important advance in the application of psychophysical methods was accomplished by Richardson when he devised the triad method for studying the dimensionality of a domain. Instead of asking a subject to judge whether one stimulus is x'er than some other stimulus, where x is any specified attribute, he set up the discrimination experiment in such a way that no attribute was specified. In the method of triads, the subject would be shown three patches of color, for example, and he would be asked to indicate which is the odd one, with the implication that the remaining pair are more alike than any other of the three pairs. In this way the subject can make judgments of the degree of similarity or difference without having any specified attribute. Data collected in this manner can be transformed into the equation of comparative judgment, and the dimensionality of the domain can then be ascertained by the Young-Householder theorem. Such a method can be used experimentally to determine the dimensionality of the various sensory modalities.

Perhaps the best-known application of these experimental methods for the study of values is in the measurement of social attitudes. The most sensitive experimental procedure is to present the subject with pairs about which he is asked to make certain judgments. For example, he may be presented with pairs of nationalities, and he may be asked to judge for each pair which he would rather associate with. That type of experiment has been carried out in several ways. The judgments that are made by the subject depend, of course, partly on his own preferences, which are closely related to his own nationality, and the judgments are also determined by the nationalities that are judged. If two groups of subjects are asked to make judgments of this kind, one can say on the basis of objective evidence which of the two groups is more tolerant of other nationalities. At one extreme we would have people who are completely tolerant toward all nationalities. They would then also, of course, be completely indifferent about their own. Such people would have no national loyalty or identification. At the other extreme we would have people who are said to be strongly prejudiced or biased. They would have extreme loyalties to some nationalities and extreme dislikes for others. I doubt whether we should consider either of these two extremes to be ideal.

Some years ago Professor Eggan wrote a master's thesis in psychology before he went into the field of anthropology. In that master's thesis he wanted to know the effect of different forms of question with reference to nationalities. He had five different questions representing different degrees of intimacy. All five groups of subjects were given the same lists of pairs of nationalities, but there were different questions. One group had the question, Which of each pair of nationalities would you rather associate with? Another group had the same nationality lists, but they were given the question, Which would you rather have as a fellow student? Another group had the question, Which nationality would you rather have your sister marry? The proportions were superficially quite different, but the rank orders of the nationalities were essentially the same. In this case, we would probably find that the form of the question has a tremendous effect on the discriminal dispersion but relatively little effect on the order of the nationalities. The effectiveness of comparative judgment for studies of this type should be exploited further.

In studying the measurement of social attitudes, the attempt is sometimes made to validate such experiments in terms of overt behavior, but that is an error. Professor Sam Stouffer at Harvard wrote a doctor's dissertation some years ago at the University of Chicago on this problem. He investigated social attitudes by means of statement scales in reference to the prohibition issue. He obtained data about his subjects as to their actual behavior on prohibition. He found that there was pretty fair agreement between what the subjects said on the attitude scales and how they actually behaved. I should like to point out that, while such a comparison is of considerable interest, it is not a validation of the attitude scale. A man may be entirely consistent in what he says and in what he does about a controversial issue, and yet both of these indexes may be dead wrong in reflecting his attitude. In order to determine a man's attitudes in the sense of affective disposition about a controversial issue, it will be necessary for his friends to ask him privately when he is free to speak his mind and when he is not likely to be quoted. His personal attitudes may or may not agree with what he says and what he does. Here again, attitudes are essentially subjective experiences which may or may not conform with overt action.

Another distinction in the study of social attitudes which is sometimes lost sight of is that the cognitive and the affective appraisals may be entirely independent. For example, a group of subjects may agree in their strong dislike of communism. Someone might give them an examination in order to show that the subjects actually do not know what they are talking about. That might very well be true, but the psychological fact is nevertheless inescapable that the affective attitudes may be strongly for or against a stimulus even if there is a great deal of confusion about its cognitive description.

The statement scale is not so sensitive as the paired-comparison procedure. It consists in a set of statements to which the subject responds by acceptance or rejection for each statement. In constructing such a scale, one presents a large number of statements to a group of subjects whose principal qualification is that they can read English. These subjects are asked to indicate for pairs of statements which represents the stronger attitude for or against x, where x represents the psychological object to which the attitude scale refers. For rough survey purposes the attitude scales are useful.

An interesting application of these methods of studying values is to appraise the effects of propaganda. We made a large number of experiments on the effects of motion-picture films on the social attitudes of high school children. Statement scales and paired-comparison schedules of various kinds were given before and after the showing of a motion picture. By this method we were able to ascertain whether a given picture had a significant effect and in what direction it did affect the children's social attitudes.

The method has also been applied in the study of international tensions by noting newspaper editorials. In one of those investigations a study was made with Chinese and Japanese newspaper editorials concerning each other, and it was shown, by treating key statements from the newspaper editorials, that the tensions increased at a very great rate before the two countries were at war. Professor Quincy Wright has suggested in his political science studies that such applications of psychophysical methods might be useful in studying international tensions before they become very marked.

An application of these subjective measurement methods which has not yet been made will be in the definition of the morale of a group. In general, the morale of a group is described by newspaper reporters and by others who mix their own value judgments with the characteristics of the group to be described. For scientific work we should have a definition of morale which is entirely independent of the value judgments of the observer. Such a definition could be stated in terms of the dispersions of all of the debatable issues within the group. Other applications would be in the comparison of cultural and nationality differences as to the values that are considered to be essential. It is unfortunate that most students of social psychology and political science are too descriptively minded to adapt the quantitative methods that may be available.

Let us turn next to the experimental study of moral values. We have carried out several experiments in which a group of subjects was given a list of offenses that were presented in pairs. For each pair the subjects were asked to indicate which of the pair they considered to be the more serious. On the basis of data of this kind and with the aid of the equation of comparative judgment, we ascertain the scale values and dispersions for these offenses. In one case we gave a group of high school students such a list of offenses, and we determined the scale values and dispersions for these stimuli for three occasions. The first presentation was a day or two before they saw a film that described the life of a gambler. A few days after seeing the film they were given the second similar schedule. About six months later they were given the third schedule. The film described the life of a gambler, and we wanted to know whether this film had an appreciable effect on the attitudes of the high school youngsters toward gambling. We found that they considered gambling to be a much more serious offense after seeing this film than they did before seeing the film. In a number of experiments of this type, we also found that the motion pictures had much more lasting effects than is ordinarily supposed. In many cases we found that only half of the effect of the film wore off in six months. It should be said, however, that these experiments were carried out in small towns in Illinois, where the children do not see so many movies as in the large cities. We carried out a similar experiment in the Hyde Park High School in Chicago, where the children were given free tickets to a movie at the Tower Theater, a few blocks away. There we found that the effect was very slight. Our interpretation was that one movie more or less for children in a large city high school makes very little difference in their attitudes. These methods of studying moral values could be used very effectively in the comparison of different groups in a large city. The groups might represent different nationality backgrounds and different religious backgrounds. It would be interesting to ascertain what these differences would be. Such social psychological studies would help us to understand the problems of the extremely heterogeneous populations in the large cities. In a similar manner we have investigated experimentally the summation effect in propaganda, where the effect of a single stimulus does not show a statistically significant effect.

Another interesting field of application is in experimental semantics. It would be useful, for example, to have an index of affective intensity for adjectives in a dictionary. Two adjectives may be equivalent as to cognitive meaning and yet differ widely in affective meaning. The words "famous" and "notorious" might be examples. So are the words "pleasant," "gay," and "hilarious." Such affective indexes would be useful in translating a foreign language.

We turn now to another type of psychophysical problem. In the psychophysical methods that we have considered so far, the main problem was to allocate each idea or object to a subjective continuum which may be unidimensional or multidimensional, depending on the nature of the problem. In most problems it is unidimensional. For example, if we ask subjects to judge the relative seriousness of offenses, we are dealing frankly with a unidimensional continuum, even though the discriminations may take place in a multidimensional continuum. We have here an obverse psychophysical problem. Having determined the subjective space which describes a group of subjects as to their attitudes in some field, we now inquire whether we can predict in any way what these people will do. When we turn the psychophysical problem in this manner, we find some exceedingly interesting psychophysical theorems of a new kind. I shall give a few examples.

Consider two poltical candidates for an election. Let one of them have a wide dispersion on the affective continuum. By this we mean that some people are very enthusiastic about this candidate, whereas others actually hate him. Let the other candidate have the same average popularity, but assume that he has a narrow dispersion, so that very few people are enthusiastic about him and very few people strongly dislike him. If these two candidates come to an election, we should expect them to split the vote evenly. However, the more variable of these two candidates might introduce a third candidate of approximately equal popularity and who also has a narrow dispersion. Then we would have three candidates, one with wide dispersion on the affective continuum, and two candidates of narrow dispersion, and all three of them would be equally popular on the average. In such a situation the more variable of the candidates would draw half the votes, and the other two candidates would get 25 per cent each. These proportions would be altered somewhat, depending on intercorrelations between the attitudes toward the candidates, but the principle can be illustrated in the general case for zero correlation. This principle is no doubt well known among politicians, but I doubt whether any of them have ever thought of this principle as a psychophysical theorem.

Let us turn to another simple example from the field of market research. Consider a mail-order house or a retail store which carries a limited number of neckties. They desire to please the majority of their clientele. The manufacturers offer many hundreds or thousands of necktie patterns. If you turn to market research people with this problem, they may ascertain the twenty or thirty or perhaps fifty of the most popular designs, and they may suggest that these be the designs that should be carried. But that is the wrong answer. Suppose that several hundred necktie patterns were submitted to a sample of the clientele. With such records one could rather easily determine not only which patterns should be carried but also the number of patterns that should be carried in order to satisfy a specified proportion of the clientele. We would start with the most popular design and set that aside to be included. In the sample population we would then eliminate all who chose that popular pattern. Then we would inquire about the most popular pattern in the remainder of the sample population. That pattern would be set aside as the second design to be accepted. Eliminating those who chose that pattern, we would ascertain the most popular pattern in the remainder of the sample population. Proceeding in this way, we would come to the point where an additional pattern would increase the selection by only a very small percentage of the population, and that would be the time to stop. In such a procedure we could determine the number of patterns as well as the designs which should be used in order to satisfy a specified proportion of the clientele. The ordinary solution of selecting the most popular designs would lead to a situation where some customers are confused by having many patterns which are equally acceptable, while other customers find nothing to please them. The maximum satisfaction will be derived by proceeding in some such way as I have outlined. There is nothing profound about this procedure, and yet it would probably be novel in market research. There are situations where problems of this sort can be of national importance. If it should be necessary to restrict the manufacture of civilian goods, then it might be important to encourage the manufacture of a limited number of designs for all sorts of things and to select those designs in such a manner as to please the majority of the civilian population. In this manner the psychophysical methods may be important in contributing toward national morale.

Recently we made an experiment on the prediction of choice with regard to menus. In this problem we were concerned with the simplification of psychophysical methods to the point where they would be practically useful for survey purposes. The psychophysical methods of the laboratory are often too laborious to be used in practical surveys. It was decided to adapt the method of successive intervals for this problem. We presented a list of forty foods on a successive interval schedule in which each subject was asked to indicate by a single check mark his relative degree of like or dislike for each food item. There were nine short descriptive phrases which represented degrees of like and dislike for foods. This schedule of forty items required less than five minutes for each of several hundred adult men subjects. In addition to this short survey schedule, we also presented them with sixteen menus in which they were asked to indicate what they would be likely to choose from each menu. For example, there were four lists of desserts, several lists of entrees, other lists of vegetables, and the like. For each menu the subjects were asked merely to check which they would select from a given list. Vanilla ice cream occurred in several of the desert menus. The proportion of the subjects who selected vanilla ice cream for dessert depends, of course, in part on their relative like or dislike for this dessert, but the selections would also depend on the competing items in the dessert list. By the application of the method of successive intervals and some theorems in psychophysics, we predicted the proportion of the subjects who would select each one of the items, and there were fifty-six such predictions. These predictions were based entirely on the short, five-minute schedule for the whole list of forty foods. We compared these predictions with the actual choices that the subjects made when they were confronted with the actual menus. The agreement was remarkable. The maximum discrepancy was between 3 and 4 per cent, with one conspicuous exception for a dichotomy, namely, roast beef and fried chicken. The ratings for these two items were both in the upper two categories, and the discrepancy there was 8 per cent, which was probably due to the effect of coarse grouping. The experiment demonstrated quite adequately that the prediction of choice can be effectively made with very simple survey schedules if these schedules are properly analyzed.

Some of these experiments deal with rather trivial values, while others deal with socially more important values, but our principal concern here is in the development of those scientific methods which can be adapted over a wide range of values whether they be socially important or trivial.

We turn next to the application of psychophysical theory to some experimental problems in economics. For a long time there has been considerable interest in the measurement of utility, but the measurements have generally been indirect. Psychologists have been able to measure utility experimentally for over two decades, but economists have not until very recently expressed interest in these methods. In the last few years there seems to have been a marked change in the attitude of economists to these problems. In principle, utilities can be measured for an individual subject, but it is easier experimentally to apply these methods to the measurement of utility for a group of subjects. Psychophysical theory lends itself well to a number of variations in the measurement of utility. For example, the utility of a purchase can be described as the algebraic sum of the utilities of the object and of the price. In this case, the utility of the object would presumably be positive, whereas the utility of the price would be negative. The question then arises about the location of a rational zero point for the scale of utility. An experiment is now in progress to demonstrate an experimental procedure for locating the zero point in the scale of utility. It seems reasonable that the prices of various competing objects should be checked with their utilities to ascertain for any specified population to what extent some objects are overpriced or underpriced. Survey methods are available for doing these things. In determining the zero point for the scale of utility, we are asking several hundred subjects to express their preferences among various objects that might be given to them as birthday presents. Each of these single objects will then be given a value on the scale of utility. In addition to these judgments, we also asked the subjects to make a number of different judgments. We asked them whether they would prefer to receive gifts A and B or C. In this case they must judge whether the satisfaction from A and B is greater or less than the anticipated satisfaction from the single birthday present C. By judgments of this sort we expect to be able to locate the zero point of utility, because the sum of the affective values of A and B combined should equal the utilities for these two objects taken separately. Within the range of the experiment with a small number of different objects to be selected, an additive theorem can be assumed to hold reasonably well. Diminishing returns would probably not be noticeable within the choice of four or five different objects.

In making these adaptations of psychological measurement theory to economics, one naturally wonders whether economics could be developed as an experimental science. Although I am not an economist, it has seemed to me entirely feasible that economics should be developed as an experimental science. In discussing this question with some of my friends in economics, I find that they are divided. Some of them insist emphatically that economics can never be an experimental science, while others are equally certain that this is possible. As an example we might consider the indifference function in economic theory. An indifference curve can be considered as a curve showing the combinations of two commodities X and Y which have the same utility value. If the amounts of the two commodities are considered to be the x and y axes in a three-dimensional model, then utility can be considered as the ordinates which are perpendicular to the x-y plane. An indifference curve would then be a horizontal section parallel to the x-y plane which represents constant utility. For different values of utility we would then have sections at different elevations which give a family of indifference curves. It has been shown that these indifference curves can be determined experimentally. There are many situations of controlled economies where the shapes of these functions can be studied experimentally. Such situations are in occupied countries or in prisons and in other situations with central control of prices. By altering the price of a commodity, the changes in the indifference curves can be noted experimentally.

As a final example of the adaptation of psychophysical theory in the measurement of values, we shall consider the field of aesthetics. If aesthetics were to be regarded as a purely normative science, then we should expect the aesthetic value of an object to be determined by its physical properties. Such an interpretation seems well-nigh hopeless. It seems much more fruitful to recognize that the aesthetic value of an object is determined entirely by what goes on in the mind of the percipient. In this manner of looking at the problem, we deal again with values that are subjective experiences and which may vary from one person to another and certainly from one culture to another. An esthetic object symbolizes human emotional experience and its resolution in a conceptual and abstract manner. Except in extreme cases the aesthetic experience is not itself emotional. It is essentially an abstraction. There is nothing absolute about the value of an aesthetic object. The aesthetic value is determined by the experience and the attitudes of the observer.

Some time ago I attended a series of seminars on aesthetics at the home of one of my colleagues. Most of the participants in that seminar were from the humanities and the arts. The seminars were devoted to discussions about the theory of aesthetics. In some of those discussions it occurred to me that the question at issue could be treated as a question of experimental fact, and I ventured to suggest how the psychophysical methods could be adapted to obtain an empirical answer to the question at issue. It was an illuminating experience to discover that some of my friends in the humanities were hostile to the very idea of subjecting questions of aesthetic theory to empirical inquiry. On one of those occasions a friend showed me a quotation from Aristotle that settled the matter for him. It was heresy when I suggested that we knew more about this problem than Aristotle. Artists are sometimes suspicious of the experimental study of artistic preferences and perhaps with some reason. Sometimes experimental studies are made in aesthetics when the investigator is interested in secondary effects rather than in the aesthetic experience. On the other hand, I have found some artists who are very much interested in such inquiry. A friend who is a portrait painter frequently encouraged experimental studies of this kind at the Art Institute in Chicago. Unfortunately, I have not been able to induce many students of psychology to study experimental aesthetics.

In closing, I should like to comment briefly on the social studies as science. It is unfortunate that the social studies have rather low prestige among the sciences. I believe that this is what we should expect because so far the social studies have not adopted the impartial, objective, and intellectual attitudes of science. Quite generally in these fields the writers argue for social action of some kind, about the right and wrong ways of life, about what is good and what is evil in the opinions of the writers, about the good and the bad names and categories for describing their political friends and enemies. It is the exception when a social scientist studies social phenomena as science to identify the forces at work without name-calling and without injecting his own value judgments into what he is describing. As long as social scientists fail to distinguish between propaganda and science, they will have low prestige among the sciences.

This paper has been concerned with the problems of a subjective metric. Social studies do not need to be quantitative in order to qualify as science. Some of the most important experiments in science deal first of all with the description of basic phenomena in a qualitative way. It usually happens that quantitative methods appear with more intensive study. Here we have considered some exploratory attempts to establish a subjective metric for the measurement of values. I have not succeeded in persuading social science students about the fascinating challenge to develop their field as science. To do so, we must free ourselves from the impulse for social action which has no place here. We should avoid problems in which we have an ax to grind. As citizens we have the privilege and the duty to participate in political elections. But when we work as scientists, we should be aloof from the issues of the moment and the chatter of the market place. Only in scientific detachment and objectivity can we eventually be helpful in developing the social studies as science.

18 THE RATIONAL ORIGIN FOR MEASURING SUBJECTIVE VALUES

L. L. Thurstone and Lyle V. Jones

A method is proposed and empirically demonstrated for extending the law of comparative judgment so as to transform psychological qualities into an additive measurement scale. Application of the method yields results supporting the contention that subjective values can be measured on an additive scale, an equal unit scale with a meaningful zero point.[1]

The Problem

In current scaling methods with the equation of comparative judgment[2] and its variants, the result is a *scale difference* for every pair of stimuli, expressed in terms of an equal unit scale. For a set of n stimuli the subject is presented with each pair of stimuli separately. There are $n(n - 1)/2$ such pairs if no stimulus is presented with its duplicate as a pair. For each such presentation the subject judges which of the pair has more of some attribute x. This attribute may be a property of the stimulus, such as beauty, desirability, or offensiveness. The scale separations of pairs of stimuli are then descriptive of the subjects as well as of the stimuli.

When the scale separations have been determined for all pairs of stimuli, there is no unique zero point. The situation is analogous to that in which we know the differences in elevation between pairs of mountains. Such data give no information about the elevation of any one of the mountains. Numerical values can then be assigned to the stimuli only by setting an arbitrary origin at any one of the stimuli such as the lowest stimulus.

For many investigations this treatment of the scaling problem is ade-

[1] This paper reports research partially supported by the Quartermaster Food and Container Institute for the Armed Forces. The study was initiated jointly by the two authors at the University of Chicago in 1952. Professor Thurstone prepared a draft of a report of the project during the summer of 1955, shortly before his death. While much of the content of that draft has been retained, an earlier method of analysis has been supplanted by that of the present report, which is the responsibility of the second author, who completed the paper in January, 1956, at the University of Chicago. The substantial assistance of Thomas Jeffrey, John Kelton, and John Mellinger of the Psychometric Laboratory, University of North Carolina, is gratefully acknowledged.

[2] See chaps. ii–iii.

quate, but there are other psychological problems where it is desirable to have a rational origin. For example, we might want to say that the subjective value of a certain stimulus is twice that of another stimulus. Such a statement cannot be made unless there exists a rational origin for the scale of subjective values of the stimuli as to the attribute x. This paper describes a method of locating the subjective origin experimentally.

This problem is not new. Horst studied the problem[3] with an ingenious experimental method that will be described with Figure 52. Let the vertical line in that figure represent the affective continuum. The zero point on this continuum represents neutrality or indifference. Any psychological object

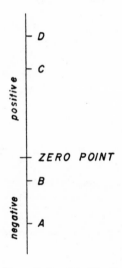

Fig. 52.—Form of stimuli in Horst's study

whose scale value is above this point is one that the average subject in the experimental group considers favorably. Any object below the neutrality point is regarded as unfavorable by the average subject. In order to locate the zero point, Horst listed a number of events that would be generally regarded as disadvantageous (e.g., "spend a night in jail") and other events that would be regarded as desirable (e.g., "go to a good musical comedy"). Then Horst asked his subjects to accept or reject each of a number of questions in the form, "Would you be willing to have the disadvantage B in order to have the advantage C?" If the proportion of subjects who accepted this proposal was over .50, the inference was that the positive affective value of C was greater than the negative affective value of B. In fact, the equation of comparative judgment would give the quantitative difference between the absolute affective values of B and C. But this also determines the location of

[3] P. Horst, "A Method for Determining the Absolute Affective Value of a Series of Stimulus Situations," *Journal of Educational Psychology*, XXIII (1932), 418-40.

the zero point between B and C. In the same manner one can make as many determinations of the zero point as there are combinations of an advantage and a disadvantage. If the zero points so determined are reasonably stable on the scale, their average value can be taken as a rational origin for the subjective scale.

Methodologically this solution is effective, and it serves to demonstrate that a rational origin for the affective continuum can be experimentally located. In practice it has often a limitation in that it is rather awkward to list psychological objects of negative value in some contexts. It would be more convenient in many situations to deal only with objects of positive

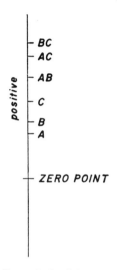

Fig. 53.—Form of stimuli in present study

value. We consider here a variation of the problem in which the zero point will be located with stimuli that are all positive in subjective value.

In Figure 53 are represented only objects of positive affective value. We show the scale locations of three such objects, A, B, and C, and of their combinations AB, AC, and BC. By the combination AB is meant both A and B, and similarly for the other pairs. The subjects are asked to express their preference for each pair of single objects, such as A or B. They are also asked to express their preferences for such choices as AB or C. If a subject has a strong desire for the object C, he might prefer to have C rather than the combination of A and B. The subjects are also asked to express their preferences for such choices as AB or CD.

In analyzing these preference records, each of the single stimuli is assigned a scale value by use of the law of comparative judgment. In addition, each combination such as AB is treated as a separate stimulus, and it is also assigned a scale value. The rational origin is a point on the scale so chosen that the distance from the origin to the combination AB is the sum of the distances to A and to B. Every combination of two stimuli determines in this manner the rational origin. It is then a question of experimental fact whether these zero points are clustered close together or widely scattered. If the experimentally independent determinations of the origin are close together and hence consistent, their average can be taken as the best location of the rational origin. If an internally consistent zero point can be found in experiments of this kind, we shall be able to say that one stimulus is, say, twice as valuable subjectively as some other stimulus. There are a number of interesting implications of such a finding for several of the social sciences.

There is a fundamental assumption in this reasoning which may be stated at the outset. We are assuming that the anticipated satisfaction from ownership of both objects, A and B, is the sum of the anticipated satisfactions from A and from B separately. This is not quite correct, as may be seen by pushing the illustration further. If the recipient already has twenty birthday presents, he is not likely to be so thrilled by the twenty-first present as if that one were the only recognition of the day. However, in setting up these experiments, we are assuming that in dealing with only two presents, the anticipated satisfactions can be regarded as essentially linear for the combinations. Our main object is to locate a rational origin, and for this purpose we shall use combinations of two presents. We need not make the more questionable assumption that the anticipated satisfaction from, say, twenty birthday presents is the sum of the satisfactions that are associated with each of them separately. We shall find that the additive assumption for two stimuli is plausible in terms of experimental findings.

The Experiment

In designing an experiment to test the hypothesis described with Figure 53, it was decided to use five objects that would be appropriate birthday presents for college students who were to be our subjects. In order to describe these objects adequately, each item was illustrated with a picture and a catalogue description. This detailed information was presented on the first page of a schedule to which the subject could refer at will while recording his preferences. It was also decided that the subjects would rather express their preferences by checking pictures than by checking names of the objects. The pictures would probably enable the subjects to keep in mind the nature of the merchandise more easily than the names.

In order to insure differentiation in the scale values of these five items, it seemed desirable that they differ somewhat (but not extremely) in monetary value. It was expected that the actual choices would be determined mainly by individual interests and habits. Nevertheless, extreme differences in price would probably result in extreme proportions of preferences near unity or zero. The scale values would then be unstable and hence less useful in testing the additivity hypothesis of this study. An absurdly extreme comparison like "a new automobile or a new brief case" would result in proportions of preferences at unity. Such a result could not be scaled at all. The five objects seemed to satisfy these preferred conditions.

The verbatim instructions for the schedule were as follows:

Birthday Gift Questionnaire

The purpose of this questionnaire is to investigate preferences for articles which students might receive as birthday gifts. The articles are pictured and described on the following page. Study them carefully before you read further.

[In the actual schedule each of the five following descriptions was accompanied by a halftone illustration.]

Brief case. Rough-grained split leather with disappearing handle. 3-side zipper. Plastic coated fabric lining. Brown color. 16×11 inch size.

Portable 3-speed record player. Plays all record speeds and sizes singly. Full-toned 4×6 inch speaker. Wooden case, covered with scuff-resistant brown artificial leather.

Parker "51" pen and pencil set. Easy-press filler fills quickly and easily. 14-K gold scratch-resistant pen point. Matching propel-repel pencil utilizes 10 to 12 leads on a single filling. Lucite plastic body, satin finish, silver color, metal cap.

Desk lamp. Complete with 18-inch fluorescent bulb. Sturdy steel body with baked-on brown enamel finish. $11\frac{1}{2}$ inches tall, $19\frac{3}{4}$ inches wide.

Webster's International Dictionary. Unabridged, completely up to date. 3,350 pages of large readable print. Comprehensive sections of new words and phrases, biographies, and many other items. 600,000 entries. Bound in buckram.

Assume that you do not possess any of the types of articles pictured here. In the questionnaire are presented choices among various combinations of the articles. For each comparison check the picture of the article or articles you would prefer to own. Consider the articles to be gifts for your own personal use; they may not be sold.

Look at the example comparisons below. [In the schedule three examples were presented and discussed briefly, one illustrating each type of comparison.]

For each comparison on the following pages, check the article or articles you would prefer to own. Remember that your are to judge the articles as if you do not already possess any of them. With some comparisons you may be in doubt, but you should respond anyway.

There are a total of sixty-five preferences to be indicated. You may now turn the page and begin.

In the actual schedules in which the subjects recorded their preferences, there were three types of comparisons. The simplest were of the type "*A* or *B*." Here the subject expressed his preference for the single object *A* or the single object *B*. This type will be referred to as *single-single comparison*. A second type consisted of pairs like "*AB* or *C*." In this case the subject chose between a single item and a double item. This will be called *single-double comparison.* In the third type he selected "*AB* or *CD*." This type will be called *double-double comparison.*

The schedule was built on five objects, which are denoted (*A*) brief case, (*B*) dictionary, (*C*) record player, (*D*) desk lamp, and (*E*) pen and pencil set. There are ten pairs of single objects. That is then also the number of single-single comparisons. In determining the number of single-double comparisons, we note that for each of the ten doublets there are three possible single stimuli. Hence we have a total of thirty single-double comparisons. The number of double-double comparisons is the number of possible pairs of

TABLE 24

PROPORTION OF SUBJECTS WHO PREFERRED STIMULI AT THE LEFT
TO THE STIMULI AT THE TOP-$N = 194$

		\(k \)					\(m \)									
		A	B	C	D	E	AB	AC	AD	AE	BC	BD	BE	CD	CE	DE
	A	50	54	09	32	26	..	..	..	..	04	17	15	02	03	09
	B	46	50	11	28	19	..	06	15	10	..	..	..	04	03	08
i	C	91	89	50	89	72	72	..	77	68	..	73	73	..	..	69
	D	68	72	11	50	32	44	08	..	25	07	..	30	..	09	..
	E	74	81	28	68	50	53	10	33	..	13	49	..	08	..	..
	AB	..	..	28	56	47	50	..	..	..	..	..	..	07	07	24
	AC	..	94	..	92	90	..	50	..	..	..	85	81	..	..	76
	AD	..	85	23	..	67	..	..	50	..	20	..	48	..	08	..
	AE	..	90	32	75	..	..	..	..	50	27	65	..	15	..	..
j	BC	96	..	..	93	87	..	..	80	73	50	..	..	..	..	70
	BD	83	..	27	..	51	..	15	..	35	..	50	..	..	07	..
	BE	85	..	27	70	..	..	19	52	..	..	..	50	17	..	..
	CD	98	96	..	..	92	93	..	..	85	..	..	83	50	..	..
	CE	97	97	..	91	..	93	..	92	..	..	93	..	..	50	..
	DE	91	92	31	..	..	76	24	..	..	30	..	..	..	..	50

NOTE.—Decimal points are omitted in all entries.

the ten doublets without duplication of any of the five objects. Hence we have a total of fifteen double-double comparisons. Listing these three types, we have:

$$
\begin{aligned}
&\text{Single-single comparisons} \ldots\ldots\ldots\ldots\ 10 \\
&\text{Single-double comparisons} \ldots\ldots\ldots\ldots\ 30 \\
&\text{Double-double comparisons} \ldots\ldots\ldots\ 15 \\
&\overline{} \\
&\text{Total} \ldots\ldots\ldots\ldots\ldots\ldots\ldots\ldots\ 55
\end{aligned}
$$

For each subject we have fifty-five choices. Ten additional pairs were included for checks of consistency but are not included in the present analysis. For each of the fifty-five pairs we tabulated the proportion of the subjects who chose each alternative for each pair. There were 194 subjects in the experiment. They were male undergraduate students in the School of Business Administration at the University of North Carolina. In Table 24 appears the proportion of the subjects who chose the stimulus at the left over the stimulus at the top of the table. In each diagonal cell is entered the proportion .50.

Since the discriminal dispersions in the equation of comparative judgment (the standard deviations of preference distributions, one for each stimulus) are different for the three types of comparison, it was necessary to treat these types separately in scaling. For this purpose it is convenient to denote the three types with different subscripts. The plan is shown in Figure 54. The experimentally observed proportions P_{ik} are recorded in the second quadrant of such a table. In every case the first subscript refers to the preferred stimulus, so that P_{ik} is the proportion of subjects who preferred the single stimulus i to the single stimulus k. In this table the subscripts i and k refer to single stimuli, and the subscripts j and m refer to double stimuli. The fifty-five independent proportions are below the main diagonal of the

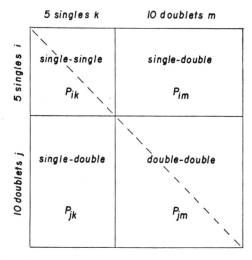

Fig. 54.—Matrix of observed proportions in schematic form

square matrix of Figure 54; their complements appear above the diagonal of the matrix.

The basic data for this study are recorded in Table 24. Inspection of this table shows that it is incomplete. The reason for this situation is that none of the five objects is repeated in the same comparison. For example, there is no entry in Table 24 for a comparison like AB against AC because the item A is common to the two doublets. The scale separation should be the same as that of B and C.

Table 25 shows the normal deviates corresponding to the experimentally observed proportions in Table 24. These are obtained from tables of the normal probability distribution. Because of the restriction to two categories of judgment, Table 25 has a symmetry in that the entries above the principal diagonal are the same as the corresponding entries below that diagonal except for reversal of sign.

TABLE 25

NORMAL DEVIATES x_{gh} CORRESPONDING TO PROPORTIONS IN TABLE 24

			k							m					
	A	B	C	D	E	AB	AC	AD	AE	BC	BD	BE	CD	CE	DE
i															
A	.00	.10	-1.34	-.47	-.64	····	-1.55	-1.04	-1.28	-1.75	.95	-1.04	-2.05	-1.88	-1.34
B	-.10	.00	-1.23	-.58	-.88	.58	-1.41	.74	.47	····	.61	.61	-1.75	-1.88	-1.41
C	-1.34	1.23	.00	1.23	.58	-.15	-1.28	-.44	.67	-1.48	-.03	.52	····	-1.34	.50
D	.47	.58	-1.23	.00	-.47	.08	····	····	····	-1.13	····	····	-1.41	····	····
E	.64	.88	-.58	.47	.00	····	····	····	····	····	····	····	····	····	····
j															
AB	····	····	-.58	.15	-.08	.00	.00	.00	····	····	1.04	.88	····	····	····
AC	····	1.55	.58	1.41	1.28	····	····	····	.00	-.84	.39	.05	-1.48	-1.48	-.71
AD	····	1.04	-.74	····	.44	····	····	.84	.61	-.61	····	····	····	-1.41	.71
AE	····	1.28	-.47	.67	····	····	-1.04	.05	.39	.00	····	····	-1.04	····	1.04
BC	1.75	····	.61	1.48	1.13	····	-.88	-.61	.00	····	.00	.00	····	-1.48	-.52
BD	.95	1.75	.61	····	.03	1.04	.39	····	····	.00	····	.95	.95	····	1.48
BE	1.04	····	····	.52	····	.88	.05	····	····	.00	.95	····	.00	····	.52
CD	2.05	····	····	····	1.41	1.48	····	····	····	····	····	····	····	····	····
CE	1.88	1.88	1.34	1.34	····	1.48	····	····	····	····	····	····	····	.00	····
DE	1.34	1.41	-.50	····	····	.71	-.71	.71	1.04	-.52	1.48	.52	····	····	.00

Discriminal Dispersions of Composite Stimuli

Since this problem is concerned with different dispersions of combinations of stimuli, it will be convenient to have a general formula for them. The equation of comparative judgment, Case 2,[4] takes the general form

$$S_g - S_h = x_{gh}\sigma_{gh}, \tag{1}$$

where $(S_g - S_h)$ is the scale difference between two sets of stimuli, x_{gh} is the normal deviate corresponding to P_{gh}, the proportion of subjects who prefer stimulus set g to stimulus set h, and σ_{gh} is the standard deviation of $(S_g - S_h)$. Equation (1) is based upon an assumption that the reactions or "discriminal processes" of subjects to stimuli may be quantified conceptually, ordered along a particular psychological dimension, say, of preference, and assigned subjective values on an equal unit scale. The distribution of subjective values associated with any stimulus, g, is assumed normal in the subject population, with mean (or modal discriminal process) S_g and standard deviation (or discriminal dispersion) σ_g. The assumptions underlying (1) are subject to empirical verification, by utilization the model to find estimates of the conceptual parameters, by reproducing from those parameters the proportion of subjects in a given sample who chose each stimulus in every stimulus pair, then by testing the goodness of fit of reproduced to observed proportions.

The scale value, S_i, of any *single* stimulus of a stimulus set, may be considered the mean subjective value assigned that stimulus by members of the subject population. The difference between S_i and the subjective value which a single subject a assigns to stimulus i will be called a discriminal deviation.

Let $y_{1a}, y_{2a} \ldots y_{na}$ denote discriminal deviations for the objects in set g, and let $z_{1a}, z_{2a} \ldots z_{ma}$ denote the discriminal deviations for the objects in set h. Then the variance of the difference between the subjective values of the two sets will be

$$\sigma_{gh}^2 = \frac{1}{N} \Sigma \left[(y_{1a} + y_{2a} + \ldots + y_{na}) - (z_{1a} + z_{2a} + \ldots + z_{ma}) \right]^2, \tag{2}$$

where N is the number of subjects. Assuming all of the single objects to have the same variance, we have

$$\sigma_{gh}^2 = n\frac{\Sigma y_{1a}^2}{N} + n(n-1)\frac{\Sigma y_{1a}y_{2a}}{N} + m\frac{\Sigma z_{1a}^2}{N} \\ + m(m-1)\frac{\Sigma z_{1a}z_{2a}}{N} - 2nm\frac{\Sigma y_{1a}z_{1a}}{N}, \tag{3}$$

and, assuming the same correlation between all pairs of single objects,

$$\sigma_{gh}^2 = n\sigma^2 + n(n-1)r\sigma^2 + m\sigma^2 + m(m-1)r\sigma^2 - 2nmr\sigma^2. \tag{4}$$

[4] See chap. iii.

Let us define as the unit of measurement the common discriminal dispersion of single stimuli,

$$\sigma_i = \sigma = 1 \ . \tag{5}$$

Then

$$\sigma_{gh}^2 = n + n(n-1)r + m + m(m-1)r - 2nmr \ , \tag{6}$$

which becomes

$$\sigma_{gh}^2 = (n+m) + r[n(n-1) + m(m-1) - 2nm] \ . \tag{7}$$

Applying this estimation formula to the three cases of this study, we have

(1) when $n = 2$ and $m = 2$,

$$\sigma_{jm}^2 = 4 - 4r \qquad \sigma_{jm} = 2\sqrt{1-r} = u_{22} \text{(double-double)}; \tag{8}$$

(2) when $n = 2$ and $m = 1$,

$$\sigma_{jk}^2 = 3 - 2r \qquad \sigma_{jk} = \sqrt{3-2r} = u_{12} = u_{21} \text{ (single-double)}; \tag{9}$$

(3) when $n = 1$ and $m = 1$,

$$\sigma_{ik}^2 = 2 - 2r \qquad \sigma_{ik} = \sqrt{2}\sqrt{1-r} = u_{11} \text{ (single-single)} \ . \tag{10}$$

Equation (8) is applicable to section (jm) of Table 25, which shows the experimental data for the double-double comparisons. Equation (9) is applicable to section (jk) of the same table, which shows the experimental data for the single-double comparisons. Because of the symmetry of (7) in n and m, the stretching factor $u_{12} = u_{21}$. In other words, the dispersion is the same for $n = 1$, $m = 2$ as it is for $n = 2$, $m = 1$, as was to be expected. Equation (10) applies to section (ik) of Table 25, which shows the experimental results for the single-single comparisons.

From (1), (8), (9), and (10), we can write the equation of comparative judgment corresponding to each of the three sections of Table 25. Then

$$S_i - S_k = x_{ik}u_{11} \qquad \text{(single-single comparison)} ; \tag{11}$$

$$S_j - S_k = x_{jk}u_{12} \qquad \text{(single-double comparison)} ; \tag{12}$$

$$S_j - S_m = x_{jm}u_{22} \qquad \text{(double-double comparison)} \ . \tag{13}$$

It should be noted that the left member of each of these equations denotes the difference between two scale values, and hence it is immaterial where the origin is located. It should also be noted that the scale values are assumed to be independent of their combinations in groups of two. The stretching factors u_{11}, u_{12}, and u_{22} denote the standard deviations in which the normal deviates x are expressed.

Results

By operating appropriately on the sections of Table 25 according to equations (11), (12), and (13), we obtain the matrix of Table 26, where the

TABLE 26
Weighted Normal Deviates, $x_{gh}\sigma_{gh} = S_g - S_h$

	A	B	C	D	E	AB	AC	AD	AE	BC	BD	BE	CD	CE	DE
A	.00	.14	-1.89	-.66	-.90					-3.03	-1.65	-1.80	-3.55	-3.26	-2.32
B	-.14	.00	-1.74	-.82	-1.24		-2.68	-1.80	-2.22				-3.03	-3.26	-2.44
C	1.89	1.74	.00	1.74	.82	1.00		1.28	.81		1.06	1.06			.87
D	.66	.82	-1.74	.00	.66	.26	-2.44		-1.16	-2.56		.90		-2.32	
E	.90	1.24	-.82	-.66	.00	-.14	-2.22	-.76		-1.96	-.05		-2.44		
AB			-1.00	-.26	.14	.00							-2.96	-2.96	-1.42
AC		2.68		2.44	2.22		.00				2.08	1.76			1.42
AD		1.80	-1.28		.76			.00		-1.68		.10		-2.82	
AE		2.22	-.81	1.16					.00	-1.22	.78		-2.08		
BC	3.03			2.56	1.96			1.68	1.22	.00					-1.04
BD	1.65		-1.06		.05		-2.08		-.78		.00			-2.96	
BE	1.80		-1.06	-.90			-1.76	-.10				.00	-1.90		
CD	3.55	3.03			2.44	2.96			2.08			1.90	.00		
CE	3.26	3.26		2.32		2.96		2.82			2.96			.00	
DE	2.32	2.44	-.87			1.42	-1.42			-1.04					.00

TABLE 27

$(\hat{S}_g - \hat{S}_h)$ COMPUTED FROM TABLE 26 BY EQUATION (14)

	A	B	C	D	E	AB	AC	AD	AE	BC	BD	BE	CD	CE	DE	$\sum_{h=1}^{15}(\hat{S}_g-\hat{S}_h)$	$\hat{S}_g$	$\hat{S}_{og}$
A	.00	.03	-2.28	-.58	-1.13	-.73	-3.30	-1.24	-1.78	-3.10	-1.08	-1.53	-3.41	-3.45	-1.99	-25.62	-1.71	.62
B	-.03	.00	-2.44	-.66	-1.00	-.72	-3.19	-1.30	-1.66	-3.36	-1.02	-1.38	-3.55	-3.54	-1.89	-25.74	-1.72	.61
C	2.28	2.44	.00	1.54	1.03	1.35	-.88	.74	.40	-.68	.94	.85	-1.44	-1.48	.04	7.13	.48	2.81
D	.58	.66	-1.54	.00	-.52	-.23	-2.46	-.67	-1.20	-2.50	-.41	-.86	-2.91	-2.58	-1.40	-16.04	-1.07	1.26
E	1.13	1.00	-1.03	.52	.00	.28	-1.96	-.38	-.57	-2.08	-.15	-.46	-2.43	-2.68	-.93	-9.74	-.65	1.68
AB	.73	.72	-1.35	.23	-.28	.00	-2.46	-.25	-.66	-2.29	-.04	-.55	-2.83	-2.66	-.99	-12.68	-.85	1.48
AC	3.30	3.19	.88	2.46	1.96	2.46	.00	1.30	1.01	.17	2.11	1.69	-.24	-.45	1.03	20.87	1.39	3.72
AD	1.24	1.30	-.74	.67	.38	.25	-1.30	.00	-.45	-1.52	.21	-.14	-1.64	-2.37	-.56	-4.67	-.31	2.02
AE	1.78	1.66	-.40	1.20	.57	.66	-1.01	.45	.00	-1.28	.60	.11	-1.66	-1.46	-.11	1.11	.07	2.40
BC	3.10	3.36	.68	2.50	2.08	2.29	-.17	1.52	1.28	.00	1.76	1.49	-.62	-.38	.93	19.82	1.32	3.65
BD	1.08	1.02	-.94	.41	.15	.04	-2.11	-.21	-.60	-1.76	.00	-.16	-2.38	-2.51	-.51	-8.48	-.57	1.76
BE	1.53	1.38	-.85	.86	.46	.55	-1.69	.14	-.11	-1.49	.16	.00	-1.85	-1.87	-.35	-3.13	-.21	2.12
CD	3.41	3.55	1.44	2.91	2.43	2.83	.24	1.64	1.66	.62	2.38	1.85	.00	-.02	1.12	26.10	1.74	4.07
CE	3.45	3.54	1.48	2.58	2.68	2.66	.45	2.37	1.46	.38	2.51	1.87	.02	.00	1.10	26.51	1.77	4.10
DE	1.99	1.89	-.04	1.40	.93	.99	-1.03	.56	.11	-.93	.51	.35	-1.12	-1.10	.00	4.51	.30	2.63

entry in row g and column h is a single estimate of a stimulus difference, $S_g - S_h$. For simplicity, the correlation coefficient r, in equations (8), (9), and (10), was assumed to be zero. The matrix of Table 26 remains incomplete.

A complete matrix of more stable estimates of stimulus differences is generated by computing

$$(\hat{S}_g - \hat{S}_h) = \frac{1}{q} \sum_{\gamma=1}^{q} [(S_g - S_\gamma) - (S_h - S_\gamma)], \qquad (14)$$

defined only for the q columns of Table 26 in which entries appear both in row g and row h; q may have different values for different combinations of g and h.

TABLE 28

ESTIMATES OF THE ADDITIVE
CONSTANT

Stimulus Combination	c
AB	-2.58
AC	-2.62
AD	-2.47
AE	-2.43
BC	-2.56
BD	-2.22
BE	-2.16
CD	-2.33
CE	-1.94
DE	-2.02
$\bar{c}$	-2.33

$$\sigma_c = .23$$

We define an arbitrary origin such that

$$\sum_{h=1}^{15} \hat{S}_h = 0 . \qquad (15)$$

Then

$$\hat{S}_g = \frac{1}{15} \sum_{h=1}^{15} (\hat{S}_g - \hat{S}_h) \qquad (16)$$

yields an estimate of the scale value of each stimulus set, in terms of that origin. The values $\hat{S}_g$ are simply the means of the rows of Table 27.

To locate a rational origin, we solve for the constant in the ten equations of the form

$$(\hat{S}_{AB} - c) = (\hat{S}_A - c) + (\hat{S}_B - c) , \qquad (17)$$

or

$$\hat{S}_{AB} + c = \hat{S}_A + \hat{S}_B . \qquad (18)$$

The ten estimates for c appear in Table 28. Their mean is -2.33, with a standard deviation of .23.

Subtracting the mean estimate of c, -2.33, from each value $\hat{S}_g$ of Table 27 yields the estimated absolute scale value, $\hat{S}_{og}$. In Figure 55 the fifteen scale values are plotted along a single dimension, with reference to the absolute origin. Finally, Figure 56 displays the plot of the ten relationships represented by equation (17), where $\hat{S}_{og} = \hat{S}_g - c$. For confirmation of the additive relationships among scale values, and of the existence of a subjective origin, the ten points in Figure 56 are expected to cluster about a line of unit slope. Considering the simplifying assumptions that have been made, the agreement is reasonably good. The additive character of subjective values is approximately confirmed.

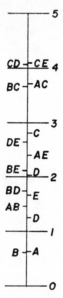

FIG. 55.—Values of $\hat{S}_{og}$, plotted with reference to rational origin

Of incidental interest are the relative sizes of absolute scale values, $\hat{S}_{og}$, for the five single objects. The most preferred object, the record player (C), has a subjective value more than four times as great as the least preferred object, the unabridged dictionary (B). From the scale values we would predict that a typical subject would prefer the record player to the dictionary, the brief case, *and* the desk lamp.

Somewhat surprising is the lack of any systematic relationship between preference for and cost of the stimulus objects. The prices of the five single objects, taken from the retail sales catalogue of 1951 from which the items were selected, are: (A) brief case, 9.95; (B) dictionary, 30.00; (C) record player, 29.95; (D) desk lamp, 7.95; and (E) pen and pencil set, 19.75. Comparison of these prices with the estimates of their absolute subjective values, $\hat{S}_{og}$, Table 27, demonstrates a negligible relationship. The two most costly items, (*B*) dictionary and (*C*) record player, are lowest and highest, respectively, with absolute subjective values of .61 and 2.81. Apparently subjects were guided in their choices neither explicitly nor implicitly in terms of the monetary values of the items.

Implications

This study was designed primarily to test a method of locating a rational origin for a subjective preference scale. In a previous study by Horst a method was found for locating the zero point by using desirable as well as

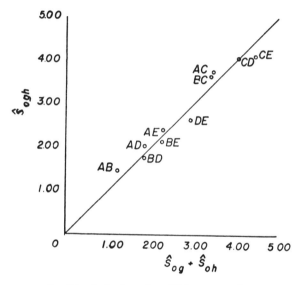

FIG. 56.—A check on the additive assumption

undesirable stimuli, objects, or events. In this study we have found a method of locating the zero point in the subjective preference scale by using only objects that are desirable so that all of them have scale values above the rational zero point. In doing so we have postulated that subjective values can be additive. The subjective value of a combination of two objects has been assumed to be very closely approximated by the sum of the subjective values of the two objects considered singly. We are not assuming that this linearity can be obtained when the composite contains many objects. Furthermore, we recognize that the desirability of a pair of objects is not always the sum of their single desirabilities. A pair of shoes is more than twice as desirable as a right shoe when the left one has been lost. We are assuming that the objects are not dependent in their function or desirability and that one does not substitute for the other. This is, of course, an old and well-known problem.

The problem of locating an origin on the subjective preference continuum may be regarded as of only theoretical interest, but such a judgment is probably in error. There are many interesting aspects of subjective measurement with a rational origin, and we shall indicate a few implications for the social sciences. The additive character of subjective values has been indicated. By locating a rational origin, one legitimately can say that one subjective value is, say, twice that of another. Such comparisons are not possible without a rational origin.

The indifference curves of economic theory are ordinarily regarded as contour lines on a topographic map. The inside contours are regarded as the differences in elevation. Not only can the increments in utility be measured, but it becomes possible to determine the elevation of utility from a rational origin. Combinations of utilities thus become amenable to study, and it should also be possible to study profitably the relations between utility and price. Taking into account the recognized importance of differing discriminal dispersions of stimuli upon prediction of choice,[5] such developments should be of considerable value in market research and consumer preference studies.

In principle it is possible to obtain the appraisal of an experimental population on a group of stimuli, taken separately, and to predict the proportion of that population that would vote for each of several groups of stimuli. The stimuli could be political ideas that could be combined into competing political programs. A survey of all the separate items could enable us to predict the proportion of the population that would vote for one combination rather than some other combination of items. The combinations could be studied in order to find those that are more acceptable than other combinations. The same type of reasoning applies to the study of various social attitudes.

In psychological studies it is of considerable interest to be able to locate a rational origin for the affective continuum of acceptance-rejection or like-dislike. The relations between subjective values as determined from a rational origin and the discriminal dispersions for the prediction of choice should be a fruitful field for further research.

[5] See chap. xiii.

PART **III** ATTITUDE MEASUREMENT

INTRODUCTION

In attempting to adapt and extend the psychophysical methods to interesting stimuli, I found another opportunity when I learned about the work of Floyd Allport in arranging a series of attitude statements to represent gradations from one extreme to the other on some debatable issue. To make such a list with a defensible unit of measurement was then the problem. The paper "Attitudes Can Be Measured" was written after we had done some experimental work with the problem of scaling such material. The paper was criticized by some colleagues in the social studies, but it had some defenders. This paper was the start of a lot of work in the psychometric laboratory on the construction of attitude scales. That subject has developed into a large field, so that it is now a major branch of social psychology.

The second paper in this section describes the scaling of the list of statements that were used by Allport.

The third paper on the study of nationality preferences was an application of paired comparisons and the law of comparative judgment to attitude measurement. As judged by the number of requests for reprints, it is perhaps one of the best-accepted papers that I have written. It was a transition from psychophysics to attitude measurement in our laboratory. Paired comparisons is a far more sensitive method for appraising attitudes than the statement scales, which are always rather crude, but it is not so generally applicable to social issues.

The sixth paper in this section was my presidential address for the Midwestern Psychological Association. It was a review of the problem of attitude measurement and closely related problems. This subject had become quite popular in two or three years.

The seventh and eighth are concerned with experiments in measuring changes in attitudes of school children induced by motion pictures. The Payne Fund studies consisted of about thirty experiments on this problem. In a number of experiments we found a very marked effect on the attitudes of school children from a single motion picture. The most striking effect was found with the film, *The Birth of a Nation*. These studies were described in a lithoprinted report that was available for some years.[1]

The question was frequently discussed whether there was a cumulative effect of several motion pictures on the same issue. Our experiments demonstrated such an effect rather clearly.

---

[1] "The Effects of Motion Pictures on the Social Attitudes of School Children," 69 pages, Document No. 1696, University of Chicago Microfilm Library. The same report was included in *Motion Pictures and the Social Attitudes of Children* (New York: Macmillan Co., 1933).

Another question often discussed was whether a summation effect could be demonstrated for a number of films each of which had only slight propaganda effect. For this purpose we used three films that had only slight effect in changing the attitudes of children as regards the severity or leniency of punishment of criminals. Seven comparable groups at Moosehart were used in this experiment. Different groups, each of about 150 children, saw one film, two films, three films, and no film, respectively. The summation effect on their attitudes was clearly shown.

I used to have the hypothesis that the effect of propaganda films had differential effects, depending on the intelligence and education of the audience, but we did not continue attitude experiments to investigate such problems. The hypothesis was that when propaganda is spread on thick, it might be effective for an unintelligent audience but that it might backfire with a more sophisticated audience. With an educated audience the best propaganda might be a gentle plug inserted in material that was ostensibly concerned with other things, the final result being attained by the summation effect. Events of the last two decades have made me question this hypothesis. It seems that any propaganda can be put over on any audience if it is cleverly planned.

In a small 1929 monograph[2] I described two types of attitude scales (pp. 93–96). These were called the *maximum probability type* and the *increasing probability type*. All of our work was with the first type. Recently there has been interest in the second type of scaling, which lends itself to certain types of attitude problems. The scaling of attitude statements can be accomplished directly from the records of acceptance and rejection for a group of subjects and without the sorting procedure that we used, but, as far as I know, such a scaling procedure has not yet been developed. It can also be done by factor analysis.

When I was working on attitude measurement, I found great interest in the application of attitude scales to all sorts of groups, but I was disappointed in the relative lack of interest in the methodological problems which seemed to be more important for the development of social science. I had only scratched the surface of an important field that justified more fundamental methodological study. In the early thirties we prepared quite a number of attitude scales. When I realized that the psychometric laboratory at the University of Chicago might be swamped with such an enterprise, I decided to stop it. All of the incomplete work on a number of attitude scales was abandoned to make time and room for the development of multiple factor analysis which was already well under way.

[2] L. L. Thurstone and E. J. Chave, *The Measurement of Attitude* (Chicago: University of Chicago Press, 1929).

19 ATTITUDES CAN BE MEASURED

The Possibility of Measuring Attitude

The purpose of this paper[1] is to discuss the problem of measuring attitudes and opinions and to offer a solution for it. The very fact that one offers a solution to a problem so complex as that of measuring differences of opinion or attitude on disputed social issues makes it evident from the start that the solution is more or less restricted in nature and that it applies only under certain assumptions that will, however, be described. In devising a method of measuring attitude, I have tried to get along with the fewest possible restrictions because sometimes one is tempted to disregard so many factors that the original problem disappears. I trust that I shall not be accused of throwing out the baby with its bath.

In promising to measure attitudes, I shall make several common-sense assumptions that will be stated here at the outset so that subsequent discussion may not be fogged by confusion regarding them. If the reader is unwilling to grant these assumptions, than I shall have nothing to offer him. If they are granted, we can proceed with some measuring methods that ought to yield interesting results.

It is necessary to state at the very outset just what we shall here mean by the terms "attitude" and "opinion." This is all the more necessary because the natural first impression about these two concepts is that they are not amenable to measurement in any real sense. It will be conceded at the outset that an attitude is a complex affair which cannot be wholly described by any single numerical index. For the problem of measurement this statement is analogous to the observation that an ordinary table is a complex affair which cannot be wholly described by any single numerical index. So is a man such a complexity which cannot be wholly represented by a single index. Neverthe-

[1] This is one of a series of papers by the staff of the Behavior Research Fund, Illinois Institute for Juvenile Research, Chicago. Series B, No. 110. Reprinted from *American Journal of Sociology*, XXXIII (1928), 529–54.

The original manuscript for this paper has enjoyed a great deal of friendly criticism, some of which turns on matters of terminology and some on the assumptions which are here stated. In order to keep this paper within reasonable length, the description of the detailed psychophysical methods used and the construction of several attitude scales are reserved for separate publication. This paper concerns, then, only an outline of one solution to the problem of measuring attitude.

less, we do not hesitate to say that we measure the table. The context usually implies what it is about the table that we propose to measure. We say without hesitation that we measure a man when we take some anthropometric measurements of him. The context may well imply without explicit declaration what aspect of the man we are measuring, his cephalic index, his height, or weight, or what not. Just in the same sense we shall say here that we are measuring attitudes. We shall state or imply by the context the aspect of people's attitudes that we are measuring. The point is that it is just as legitimate to say that we are measuring attitudes as it is to say that we are measuring tables or men.

The concept "attitude" will be used here to denote the sum total of a man's inclinations and feelings, prejudice or bias, preconceived notions, ideas, fears, threats, and convictions about any specified topic. Thus a man's attitude about pacifism means here all that he feels and thinks about peace and war. It is admittedly a subjective and personal affair.

The concept "opinion" will here mean a verbal expression of attitude. If a man says that we made a mistake in entering the war against Germany, that statement will here be spoken of as an opinion. The term "opnion" will be restricted to verbal expression. But it is an expression of what? It expresses an attitude, supposedly. There should be no difficulty in understanding this use of the two terms. The verbal expression is the *opinion*. Our interpretation of the expressed opinion is that the man's *attitude* is pro-German. An opinion symbolizes an attitude.

Our next point concerns what it is that we want to measure. When a man says that we made a mistake in entering the war with Germany, the thing that interests us is not really the string of words as such or even the immediate meaning of the sentence merely as it stands, but rather the attitude of the speaker, the thoughts and feelings of the man about the United States and the war and Germany. It is the attitude that really interests us. The opinion has interest only in so far as we interpret it as a symbol of attitude. It is therefore something about attitudes that we want to measure. We shall use opinions as the means for measuring attitudes.[2]

There comes to mind the uncertainty of using an opinion as an index of attitude. The man may be a liar. If he is not intentionally misrepresenting his real attitude on a disputed question, he may nevertheless modify the expression of it for reasons of courtesy, especially in those situations in which frank expression of attitude may not be well received. This has led to the

[2] Professor Faris, who has been kind enough to give considerable constructive criticism to the manuscript for this paper, has suggested that we may be measuring opinion but that we are certainly not measuring attitude. It is in part a terminological question which turns on the concept of attitude. If the concept of attitude as here defined is not acceptable, it may be advisable to change the terminology provided that a distinction is retained between (1) the objective index, which is here called the statement or opinion, and (2) the inferred subjective inclination of the person, which is here called the attitude variable.

suggestion that a man's action is a safer index of his attitude than what he says. But his actions may also be distortions of his attitude. A politician extends friendship and hospitality in overt action while hiding an attitude that he expresses more truthfully to an intimate friend. Neither his opinions nor his overt acts constitute in any sense an infallible guide to the subjective inclinations and preferences that constitute his attitude. Therefore we must remain content to use opinions, or other forms of action, merely as indexes of attitude. It must be recognized that there is a discrepancy, some error of measurement, as it were, between the opinion or overt action that we use as an index and the attitude that we infer from such an index.

But this discrepancy between the index and "truth" is universal. When you want to know the temperature of your room, you look at the thermometer and use its reading as an index of temperature just as though there were no error in the index and just as though there were a single temperature reading which is the "correct" one for the room. If it is desired to ascertain the volume of a glass paperweight, the volume is postulated as an attribute of the piece of glass, even though volume is an abstraction. The volume is measured indirectly by noting the dimensions of the glass or by immersing it in water to see how much water it displaces. These two procedures give two indexes which might not agree exactly. In almost every situation involving measurement there is postulated an abstract continuum such as volume or temperature, and the allocation of the thing measured to that continuum is accomplished usually by indirect means through one or more indexes. Truth is inferred only from the relative consistency of the several indexes, since it is never directly known. We are dealing with the same type of situation in attempting to measure attitude. We must postulate an attitude variable which is like practically all other measurable attributes in the nature of an abstract continuum, and we must find one or more indexes which will satisfy us to the extent that they are internally consistent.

In the present study we shall measure the subject's attitude as expressed by the acceptance or rejection of opinions. But we shall not thereby imply that he will necessarily *act* in accordance with the opinions that he has indorsed. Let this limitation be clear. The measurement of attitudes expressed by a man's opinions does not necessarily mean the prediction of what he will do. If his expressed opinions and his actions are inconsistent, that does not concern us now, because we are not setting out to predict overt conduct. We shall assume that it is of interest to know what people *say* that they believe even if their conduct turns out to be inconsistent with their professed opinions. Even if they are intentionally distorting their attitudes, we are measuring at least the attitude which they are trying to make people believe that they have.

We take for granted that people's attitudes are subject to change. When we have measured a man's attitude on any issue such as pacifism, we shall not declare such a measurement to be in any sense an enduring or constitutional constant. His attitude may change, of course, from one day to the next, and it is our task to measure such changes, whether they be due to unknown causes or to the presence of some known persuasive factor such as the reading of a discourse on the issue in question. However, such fluctuations may also be attributed in part to error in the measurements themselves. In order to isolate the errors of the measurement instrument from the actual fluctuation in attitude, we must calculate the standard error of measurement of the scale itself, and this can be accomplished by methods already well known in mental measurement.

We shall assume that an attitude scale is used only in those situations in which one may reasonably expect people to tell the truth about their convictions or opinions. If a denominational school were to submit to its students a scale of attitudes about the church, one should hardly expect intelligent students to tell the truth about their convictions if they deviate from orthodox beliefs. At least, the findings could be challenged if the situation in which attitudes are expressed contains pressure or implied threat bearing directly on the attitude to be measured. Similarly, it would be difficult to discover attitudes on sex liberty by a written questionnaire, because of the well-nigh universal pressure to conceal such attitudes where they deviate from supposed conventions. It is assumed that attitude scales will be used only in those situations that offer a minimum of pressure on the attitude to be measured. Such situations are common enough.

All that we can do with an attitude scale is to measure the attitude actually expressed with the full realization that the subject may be consciously hiding his true attitude or that the social pressure of the situation has made him really believe what he expresses. This is a matter for interpretation. It is something probably worth while to measure an attitude expressed by opinions. It is another problem to interpret in each case the extent to which the subjects have expressed what they really believe. All that we can do is to minimize as far as possible the conditions that prevent our subjects from telling the truth, or else to adjust our interpretations accordingly.

When we discuss opinions, about prohibition for example, we quickly find that these opinions are multidimensional, that they cannot all be represented in a linear continuum. The various opinions cannot be completely described merely as "more" or "less." They scatter in many dimensions, but the very idea of measurement implies a linear continuum of some sort, such as length, price, volume, weight, age. When the idea of measurement is applied to scholastic achievement, for example, it is necessary to force the qualitative variations into a scholastic linear scale of some kind. We judge in a similar way such qualities as mechanical skill, the excellence of handwriting, and the amount of a man's education, as though these traits were strung out along a single scale, although they are of course in reality scattered in many dimensions. As a matter of fact, we get along quite well with the concept of a scale in describing traits even so qualitative as education, social and economic status, or beauty. A scale or linear continuum is implied when we say that a man has more education than another or that a woman is more beautiful than another, even though, if pressed, we admit that perhaps the pair involved in each of the comparisons have little if anything in common. It is clear that the linear continuum which is implied in a "more and less" judgment may be conceptual, that it does not necessarily have the physical existence of a yardstick.

And so it is also with attitudes. We do not hesitate to compare them by the "more and less" type of judgment. We say about a man, for example, that he is more in favor of prohibition than some other, and the judgment conveys its meaning very well with the implication of a linear scale along which people or opinions might be allocated.

The Attitude Variable

The first restriction on the problem of measuring attitudes is to specify an attitude variable and to limit the measurement to that. An example will make this clear. Let us consider the prohibition question, and let us take as the attitude variable the degree of restriction that should be imposed on individual liberty in the consumption of alcohol. This degree of restriction can be thought of as a continuum ranging from complete and absolute freedom or license to equally complete and absolute restriction, and it would of course include neutral and indifferent attitudes.

In collecting samples from which to construct a scale, we might ask a hundred individuals to write out their opinions about prohibition. Among these we might find one which expresses the belief that prohibition has increased the use of tobacco. Surely this is an opinion concerning prohibition, but it would not be at all serviceable for measuring the attitude variable just mentioned. Hence it would be irrelevant. Another man might express the opinion that prohibition has eliminated an important source of government revenue. This is also an opinion concerning prohibition, but it would not belong to the particular attitude variable that we have set out to measure or scale. It is preferable to use an objective and experimental criterion for the elimination of opinions that do not belong on the specified continuum to be measured, and I believe that such a criterion is available.

This restriction on the problem of measuring attitudes is necessary in the very nature of measurement. It is taken for granted in all ordinary measurement, and it must be clear that it applies also to measurement in a field in which the multidimensional characteristics have not yet been so clearly isolated. For example, it would be almost ridiculous to call attention to the fact that a table cannot be measured unless one states or implies what it is about the table that is to be measured: its height, its cost, or beauty or degree of appropriateness or the length of time required to make it. The context usually makes this restriction on measurement. When the notion of measurement is applied to so complex a phenomenon as opinions and attitudes, we must here also restrict ourselves to some specified or implied continuum along which the measurement is to take place.

In specifying the attitude variable, the first requirement is that it should be so stated that one can speak of it in terms of "more" and "less," as, for example, when we compare the attitudes of people by saying that one of them is more pacifistic, more in favor of prohibition, more strongly in favor of capital punishment, or more religious than some other person.

Figure 57 represents an attitude variable, militarism-pacifism, with a neutral zone. A person who usually talks in favor of preparedness, for example, would be represented somewhere to the right of the neutral zone. A person who is more interested in disarmament would be represented somewhere to the left of the neutral zone. It is possible to conceive of a frequency distribution to represent the distribution of attitude in a specified group on the subject of pacifism-militarism.

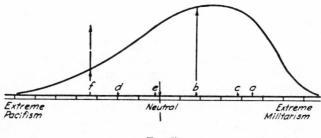

FIG. 57

Consider the ordinate of the frequency distribution at any point on the base line. The point and its immediate vicinity represent for our purpose an attitude, and we want to know relatively how common that degree of feeling for or against pacifism may be in the group that is being studied. It is of secondary interest to know that a particular statement of opinion is indorsed by a certain proportion of that group. It is only to the extent that the opinion is representative of an attitude that it is useful for our purposes. Later we shall consider the possibility that a statement of opinion may be scaled as rather pacifistic and yet be indorsed by a person of very pronounced militaristic sympathies. To the extent that the statement is indorsed or rejected by factors other than the attitude variable that it represents, to that extent the statement is useless for our purposes. We shall also consider an objective criterion for spotting such statements so that they may be eliminated from the scale. In our entire study we shall be dealing, then, with opinions, not primarily because of their cognitive content but rather because they serve as the carriers or symbols of the attitudes of the people who express or indorse these opinions.

There is some ambiguity in using the term "attitude" in the plural. An attitude is represented as a point on the attitude continuum. Consequently, there are an infinite number of attitudes that might be represented along the attitude scale. In practice, however, we do not differentiate so finely. In fact, an attitude, practically speaking, is a certain narrow range or vicinity on the scale. When a frequency distribution is drawn for any continuous variable, such as stature, we classify the variable for descriptive purposes into steps or class intervals. The attitude variable can also be divided into class intervals and the frequency counted in each class interval. When we speak of "an" attitude, we shall mean a point, or a vicinity, on the attitude continuum. Several attitudes will be considered not as a set of discrete entities but as a series of class intervals along the attitude scale.

A Frequency Distribution of Attitudes

The main argument so far has been to show that since in ordinary conversation we readily and understandably describe individuals as more and less pacifistic or more and less militaristic in attitude, we may frankly represent this linearity in the form of a unidimensional scale. This has been done in a diagrammatic way in Figure 57. We shall first describe our objective and then show how a rational unit of measurement may be adopted for the whole scale.

Let the base line of Figure 57 represent a continuous range of attitudes from extreme pacifism on the left to extreme militarism on the right.

If the various steps in such a scale were defined, it is clear that a person's attitude on militarism-pacifism could be represented by a point on that scale. The strength and direction of a particular individual's sympathies might be indicated by the point a, thus showing that he is rather militaristic in his opinions. Another individual might be represented at the point b to show that although he is slightly militaristic in his opinions, he is not so extreme about it as the person who is placed at the point a. A third person might be placed at the point c to show that he is quite militaristic and that the difference between a and c is very slight. A similar interpretation might be extended to any point on the continuous scale from extreme militarism to extreme pacifism, with a neutral or indifference zone between them.

A second characteristic might also be indicated graphically in terms of the scale, namely, the range of opinons that any particular individual is willing to indorse. It is of course not to be expected that every person will find only one single opinon on the whole scale that he is willing to indorse and that he will reject all the others. As a matter of fact, we should probably find ourselves willing to indorse a great many opinions on the scale that cover a certain range of it. It is conceivable, then, that a pacifistically inclined person would be willing to indorse all or most of the opinions in the range d to e and that he would reject as too extremely pacifistic most of the opinions to the left of d and would also reject the whole range of militaristic opinions. His attitude would then be indicated by the average or mean of the range that he indorses, unless he cares to select a particular opinion which most nearly represents his own attitude. The same sort of reasoning may of course be extended to the whole range of the scale, so that we should have at least two, or possibly three, characteristics of each person designated in terms of the scale. These characteristics would be (1) the mean position that he occupies on the scale, (2) the range of opinions that he is willing to accept, and (3) that one opinion which he selects as the one which most nearly represents his own attitude on the issue at stake.

It should also be possible to describe a group of individuals by means of the scale. This type of description has been represented in a diagrammatic way by the frequency outline.

Any ordinate of the curve would represent the number of individuals, or the percentage of the whole group, that indorses the corresponding opinion. For example, the ordinate at b would represent the number of persons in the group who indorse the degree of militarism represented by the point b on the scale. A glance at the frequency curve shows that for the fictitious group of this diagram militaristic opinions are indorsed more frequently than the pacifistic ones. It is clear that the area of this frequency diagram would represent the total number of indorsements given by the group. The diagram can be arranged in several different ways that will be separately discussed. It is sufficient at this moment to realize that, given a valid scale of opinions, it would be possible to compare several different groups in their attitudes on a disputed question.

A second type of group comparison might be made by the range or spread that the frequency surfaces reveal. If one of the groups is represented by a frequency diagram of considerable range or scatter, then that group would be more heterogeneous on the issue at stake than some other group whose frequency diagram of attitudes shows a smaller range or scatter. It goes without saying that the frequent assumption of a normal distribution in educational scale construction has absolutely no application here, because there is no reason whatever to assume that any group of people will be normally distributed in their opinions about anything.

It should be possible, then, to make four types of description by means of a scale of attitudes. These are (1) the average or mean attitude of a particular individual on the issue at stake, (2) the range of opinion that he is willing to accept or tolerate, (3) the relative popularity of each attitude of the scale for a designated group as shown by the frequency distribution for that group, and (4) the degree of homogeneity or heterogeneity in the attitudes of a designated group on the issue as shown by the spread or dispersion of its frequency distribution.

This constitutes our objective. The heart of the problem is in the unit of measurement for the base line, and it is to this aspect of the problem that we may now turn.

A Unit of Measurement for Attitudes

The only way in which we can identify the different attitudes (points on the base line) is to use a set of opinions as landmarks, as it were, for the different parts or steps of the scale. The final scale will then consist of a series of statements of opinion, each of which is allocated to a particular point on the base line. If we start with enough statements, we may be able to select a list of twenty or thirty opinions so chosen that they represent an evenly graduated series of attitudes. The separation between successive statements of opinion would then be uniform, but the scale can be constructed with a series of opinions allocated on the base line even though their base line separations are not uniform. For the purpose of drawing frequency distributions it will be convenient, however, to have the statements so chosen that the steps between them are uniform throughout the whole range of the scale.

Consider the three statements a, c, and d in Figure 57. The statements c and a are placed close together to indicate that they are very similar, while statements c and d are spaced far apart to indicate that they are very different. We should expect two individuals scaled at c and a, respectively, to agree very well in discussing pacifism and militarism. On the other hand, we should expect to be able to tell the difference quite readily between the opinions of a person at d and another person at c. The scale separations of the opinions must agree with our impressions of them.

In order to ascertain how far apart the statements should be on the final scale, we submit them to a group of several hundred people who are asked to arrange the statements in order from the most pacifistic to the most militaristic. We do not ask them for their own opinions. That is another matter entirely. We are now concerned with the construction of a scale with a valid unit of measurement. There may be a hundred statements in the original list, and the several hundred persons are asked merely to arrange the statements in rank order according to the designated attitude variable. It is then possible to ascertain the proportion of the readers who consider statement a to be more militaristic than statement c. If the two statements represent very similar attitudes, we should not expect to find perfect agreement in the rank order of statements a and c. If they are identical in attitude, there will be about 50 per cent of the readers who say that statement a is more militaristic than statement c, while the remaining 50 per cent of the readers will say that statement c is more militaristic than statement a. It is possible to use the proportion of readers or judges who agree about the rank order of any two statements as a basis for actual measurement.

If 90 per cent of the judges or readers say that statement a is more militaristic than statement b ($p_{a>b} = .90$), and if only 60 per cent of the readers say that statement a is more militaristic than statement c ($p_{a>c} = .60$), then clearly the scale separation ($a - c$) is shorter than the scale separation ($a - b$). The psychological scale separation between any two stimuli can be measured in terms of a law of comparative judgment which the writer has recently formulated.[3]

The detailed methods of handling the data will be published in connection with the construction of each particular scale. The practical outcome of this procedure is a series of statements of opinions allocated along the base line of Figure 57. The interpretation of the base line distances is that the apparent difference between any two opinions will be equal to the apparent difference between any other two opinions which are spaced equally far apart on the scale. In other words, the shift in opinion represented by a unit distance on the base line seems to most people the same as the shift in opinion represented by a unit distance at any other part of the scale. Two individuals who are separated by any given distance on the scale *seem* to differ in their attitudes as much as any other two individuals with the same scale separation. In this sense we have a truly rational base line, and the frequency diagrams erected on such a base line are capable of legitimate interpretation as frequency surfaces.

In contrast with such a rational base line or scale is the simpler procedure of merely listing ten to twenty opinions, arranging them in rank order by a few readers, and then merely counting the number of indorsements for each statement. That can, of course, be done provided that the resulting diagram be not interpreted as a frequency distribution of attitude. If so interpreted, the diagram can be made to take any shape we please by merely adding new statements or eliminating some of them, arranging the resulting list in a rough rank order evenly spaced on the base line. Allport's diagrams of opinions[4] are not in any sense frequency distributions. They should be considered as bar diagrams in which are shown the frequency with which each of a number of statements is indorsed. Our principal contribution here is an improvement on Allport's procedure. He is virtually dealing with rank orders, which we are here trying to change into measurement by a rational unit of measurement. Allport's pioneering studies in this field should be read by every investigator of this problem. My own interest in the possibility of measuring attitude by means of opinions was started by Allport's paper, and the present study is primarily a refinement of his statistical methods.

The unit of measurement for the scale of attitudes is the standard deviation of the dispersion projected on the psychophysical scale of attitudes by a statement of opinion, chosen as a standard. It is a matter of indifference which statement is chosen as a standard, since the scales produced by different standard statements will have proportional scale values. This mental unit of measurement is roughly comparable to, but not identical with, the so-called just noticeable difference in psychophysical measurement.

[3] For a more detailed discussion of this law, see chap. iii; for the logic of the psychological *S*-scale, see chap. ii.

[4] Floyd H. Allport and D. A. Hartman, "Measurement and Motivation of Atypical Opinion in a Certain Group," *American Political Science Review*, XIX (1925), 735–60.

A diagram such as Figure 57 can be constructed in either of at least two different ways. The area of the frequency surface may be made to represent the total number of votes or indorsements by a group of people, or the area may be made to represent the total number of individuals in the group studied. Allport's diagrams would be made by the latter principle if they were constructed on a rational base line so that a legitimate area might be measured. Each subject was asked to select that one statement in the list most representative of his own attitude. Hence at least the sum of the ordinates will equal the total number of persons in the group. I have chosen as preferable the procedure of asking each subject to indorse all the statements with which he agrees. Since we have a rational base line, we may make a legitimate interpretation of the area of the surface as the total number of indorsements made by the group. This procedure has the advantage that we may ascertain the range of opinion which is acceptable to each person, a trait which has considerable interest and which cannot be ascertained by asking the subject to indorse only one of the statements in the list. The ordinates of the frequency diagram can be plotted as proportions of the whole group. They will then be interpreted as the probability that the given statement will be indorsed by a member of the group. In other words, the frequency diagram is descriptive of the distribution of attitude in the whole group, and at each point on the base line we want an ordinate to represent the relative popularity of that attitude.

The Construction of an Attitude Scale

At the present time three scales for the measurement of opinion are being constructed by the principles here described.[5] These three scales are planned to measure attitudes on three different variables, namely, pacifism-militarism, prohibition, and attitude toward the church. All three of these scales are being constructed first by a procedure somewhat less laborious than the direct application of the law of comparative judgment, and if consistent results are obtained, the method will be retained for other scales.

The method is as follows. Several groups of people are asked to write out their opinions on the issue in question, and the literature is searched for suitable brief statements that may serve the purposes of the scale. By editing such material, a list of from 100 to 150 statements is prepared expressive of attitudes covering as far as possible all gradations from one end of the scale to the other. It is sometimes necessary to give special attention to the neutral statements. If a random collection of statements of opinion should fail to produce neutral statements, there is some danger that the scale will break

[5] Three attitude scales are now in course of preparation by Mr. E. J. Chave, of the Divinity School, University of Chicago, on attitudes toward the church; by Mrs. Hattie Smith on attitudes about prohibition; and by Mr. Daniel Droba on attitudes about pacifism-militarism. The latter two will be published as Doctor's dissertations.

in two parts. The whole range of attitudes must be fairly well covered, as far as one can tell by preliminary inspection in order to insure that there will be overlapping in the rank orders of different readers throughout the scale.

In making the initial list of statements, several practical criteria are applied in the first editing work. Some of the important criteria are as follows: (1) The statements should be as brief as possible so as not to fatigue the subjects who are asked to read the whole list. (2) The statements should be such that they can be indorsed or rejected in accordance with their agreement or disagreement with the attitude of the reader. Some statements in a random sample will be so phrased that the reader can express no definite indorsement or rejection of them. (3) Every statement should be such that acceptance or rejection of the statement does indicate something regarding the reader's attitude about the issue in question. If, for example, the statement is made that war is an incentive to inventive genius, the acceptance or rejection of it really does not say anything regarding the reader's pacifistic or militaristic tendencies. He may regard the statement as an unquestioned fact and simply indorse it as a fact, in which case his answer has not revealed anything concerning his own attitude on the issue in question. However, only the conspicuous examples of this effect should be eliminated by inspection, because an objective criterion is available for detecting such statements so that their elimination from the scale will be automatic. Personal judgment should be minimized as far as possible in this type of work. (4) Double-barreled statements should be avoided except possibly as examples of neutrality when better neutral statements do not seem to be readily available. Double-barreled statements tend to have a high ambiguity. (5) One must insure that at least a fair majority of the statements really belong on the attitude variable that is to be measured. If a small number of irrelevant statements should be either intentionally or unintentionally left in the series, they will be automatically eliminated by an objective criterion, but the criterion will not be successful unless the majority of the statements are clearly a part of the stipulated variable.

When the original list has been edited with these factors in mind, there will be perhaps 80 to 100 statements to be actually scaled. These statements are then mimeographed on small cards, one statement on each card. Two or three hundred subjects are asked to arrange the statements in eleven piles ranging from opinions most strongly affirmative to those most strongly negative. The detailed instructions will be published with the description of the separate scales. The task is essentially to sort out the small cards into eleven piles so that they *seem* to be fairly evenly spaced or graded. Only the two ends and the middle pile are labeled. The middle pile is indicated for neutral opinions. The reader must decide for each statement which of five subjective degrees of affirmation or five subjective degrees of negation is implied in the statement or whether it is a neutral opinion.

When such sorting has been completed by two or three hundred readers, a diagram like Figure 58 is prepared. We shall discuss it with the scale for pacifism-militarism as an example. On the base line of this diagram are represented the eleven apparently equal steps of the attitude variable. The neutral interval is the interval 5 to 6, the most pacifistic interval from 0 to 1, and the most militaristic interval from 10 to 11. This diagram is fictitious and is drawn to show the principle involved. Curve A is drawn to show the manner in which one of the statements might be classified by the three hundred readers. It is not classified by anyone below the value of 3; half of the readers classify it below the value 6; and all of them classify it below the value 9. The scale value of the statement is that scale value below which just one-half of the readers place it. In other words, the scale value assigned to the statement is so chosen that one-half of the readers consider it more militaristic and one-half of them consider it less militaristic than the scale value assigned. The numerical calculation of the scale value is similar to the calcu-

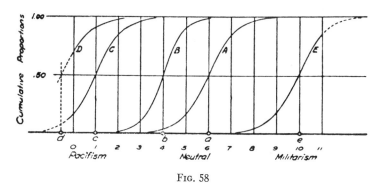

FIG. 58

lation of the limen by the phi-gamma hypothesis in psychophysical measurement.

It will be found that some of the statements toward the ends of the scale do not give complete ogive curves. Thus statement C is incomplete in the fictitious diagram. It behaves as though it needed space beyond the arbitrary limits of the scale in order to be completed. Its scale value may, however, be determined as that scale value at which the phi-gamma curve through the experimental proportions crosses the 50 per cent level, which is at c. Still other statements may be found, such as D, which have scale values beyond the arbitrary range of the scale. These may be assigned scale values by the same process, though less accurately.

The situation is different at the other end of the scale. The statement E has a scale value at e, but owing to the limit of the scale at the point 11, the experimental proportion will be 1.00 at that point. If the scale continued beyond the point 11, the proportions would continue to rise gradually, as indicated by the dotted line. The experimental proportions are all necessarily 1.00 for the scale value 11, and hence these final proportions must be ignored in fitting the phi-gamma curves and in the location of the scale values of the statements.

The Validity of the Scale

The scale must transcend the group measured.—One crucial experimental test must be applied to our method of measuring attitudes before it can be accepted as valid. A measuring instrument must not be seriously affected in its measuring function by the object of measurement. To the extent that its measuring function is so affected, the validity of the instrument is impaired or limited. If a yardstick measured differently because of the fact that it was a rug, a picture, or a piece of paper that was being measured, then to that extent the trustworthiness of that yardstick as a measuring device would be impaired. Within the range of objects for which the measuring instrument is intended, its function must be independent of the object of measurement.

We must ascertain similarly the range of applicability of our method of measuring attitude. It will be noticed that the *construction* and the *application* of a scale for measuring attitude are two different tasks. If the scale is to be regarded as valid, the scale values of the statements should not be affected by the opinions of the people who help to construct it. This may turn out to be a severe test in practice, but the scaling method must stand such a test before it can be accepted as being more than a description of the people who construct the scale. At any rate, to the extent that the present method of scale construction is affected by the opinions of the readers who help to sort out the original statements into a scale, to that extent the validity or universality of the scale may be challenged.

Until experimental evidence may be forthcoming on this point, we shall make the assumption that the scale values of the statements are independent of the attitude distribution of the readers who sort the statements. The assumption is, in other words, that two statements on a prohibition scale will be as easy or as difficult to discriminate for people who are "wet" as for those who are "dry." Given two adjacent statements from such a scale, we assume that the proportion of "wets" who say that statement *a* is wetter than statement *b* will be substantially the same as the corresponding proportion for the same statements obtained from a group of "drys." Restating the assumption in still another way, we are saying that it is just as difficult for a strong militarist as it is for a strong pacifist to tell which of two statements is the more militaristic in attitude. If, say, 85 per cent of the militarists declare statement *A* to be more militaristic than statement *B*, then, according to our assumption, substantially the same proportion of pacifists would make the same judgment. If this assumption is correct, then the scale is an instrument independent of the attitude which it is itself intended to measure.

The experimental test for this assumption consists merely in constructing two scales for the same issue with the same set of statements. One of these scales will be constructed on the returns from several hundred readers of militaristic sympathies and the other scale will be constructed with the same statements on the returns from several hundred pacifists. If the scale values of the statements are practically the same in the two scales, then the validity of the method will be pretty well established.[6] It will still be necessary to use opinion scales with some discretion. Queer results might be obtained with the prohibition scale, for example, if it were presented in a country in which prohibition is not an issue.

An objective criterion of ambiguity.—Inspection of the curves in Figure 58 reveals that some of the statements of the fictitious diagram are more ambiguous than others. The degree of ambiguity in a statement is immediately apparent, and in fact it can be definitely measured. The ambiguity of a statement is the standard deviation of the best-fitting phi-gamma curve through the observed proportions. The steeper the curve, the smaller is the range of the scale over which it was classified by the readers and the clearer and more precise is the statement. The more gentle the slope of the curve, the more ambiguous is the statement. Thus, of the two statements *A* and *B* in the fictitious diagram, the statement *A* is the more ambiguous.

In case it should be found that the phi-gamma function does not well describe the curves of proportions in Figure 58, the degree of ambiguity may be measured without postulating that the proportions follow the phi-gamma function when plotted on the attitude scale. A simple method of measuring ambiguity would then be to determine the scale distance between the scale value at which the curve of proportions has an ordinate of .25 and the scale value at which the same curve has an ordinate of .75. The scale value of the statement itself can also be defined, without assuming the phi-gamma function, as that scale value at which the curve of proportions reaches .50. If no actual proportion is found at that value, the scale value of the statement may be interpolated between the experimental proportions immediately above and below the .50 level. In scaling the statements whose scale values fall outside the ten divisions of the scale, it will be necessary to make some assumption regarding the nature of the curve, and it will probably be found that for most situations the phi-gamma function will constitute a fairly close approximation to truth.

An objective criterion of irrelevance.—Before a selection of statements can be made for the final scale, still another criterion must be applied. It is an objective criterion of irrelevance. Referring again to Figure 57, let us consider two statements that have identical scale values at the point *f*. Suppose, further, that these two statements are submitted to the group of readers represented in the fictitious diagram of Figure 57. It is quite conceivable, and it actually does happen, that one of these statements will be indorsed quite

<hr>

[6] The neutrality point would not necessarily be represented by the same statement for both militarists and pacifists, but the scale separations between all pairs of statements should be practically the same for the two conditions of standardization.

frequently while the other statement is only seldom indorsed in spite of the fact that they are properly scaled as implying the same degree of pacifism or militarism. The conclusion is then inevitable that the indorsement that a reader gives to these statements is determined only partly by the degree of pacifism implied and partly by other implied meanings which may or may not be related to the attitude variable under consideration. Now it is of course necessary to select for the final attitude scale those statements which are indorsed or rejected primarily on account of the degree of pacifism-militarism which is implied in them and to eliminate those statements which are frequently accepted or rejected on account of other more or less subtle and irrelevant meanings.

An objective criterion for accomplishing this elimination automatically and without introducing the personal equation of the investigator is avail-

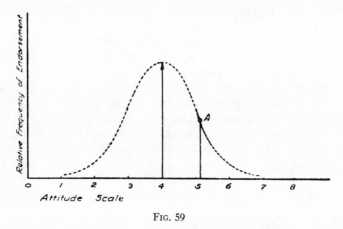

Fig. 59

able. It is essentially as follows: Assume that the whole list of about one hundred statements has been submitted to several hundred readers for actual voting. These need not be the same readers who sorted the statements for the purpose of scaling. Let these readers be asked to mark with a plus sign every statement which they indorse and to reject with a minus sign every statement not to their liking.

If we want to investigate the degree of irrelevance of any particular statement which, for example, might have a scale value of 4.0 in Figure 59, we should first of all determine how many readers indorsed it. We find, for example, that 260 readers indorsed it. Let this total be represented on the diagram as 100 per cent, and erect such an ordinate at the scale value of this statement. We may now ascertain the proportion of these 260 readers who *also* indorsed each other statement. If the readers indorse and reject the statements largely on the basis of the degree of pacifism-militarism implied, then those readers who indorse statements in the vicinity of 4.0 on the scale will not often indorse statements that are very far away from that point on the scale. Very few of them should indorse a statement which is scaled at the point 8.0, for example. If a large proportion of the 260 readers who indorse the basic statement scaled at 4.0 should also indorse a statement scaled at the point 8.0, then we should infer that their voting on these two statements has been influenced by factors other than the degree of pacifism that is implied in the statements. We can represent this type of analysis graphically.

Every one of these other statements will be represented by a point on this diagram. Its x-value will be the scale value of the statement, and its y-value will be the proportion of the 260 readers who indorsed it. Thus, if out of the 260 readers who indorsed the basic statement there were 130 who also indorsed statement No. 14, which has a scale value of, say, 5.0, then statement No. 14 will be represented at the point A on Figure 59.

If the basic statement, the degree of irrelevance of which is represented in Figure 59, is an ideal statement, one which people will accept or reject primarily because of the attitude on pacifism which it portrays, then we should expect the one hundred statements to be represented by as many points hovering more or less about the dotted line of Figure 59. The diagram may of course be more contracted or spread out, but the general appearance of the plot should be that of Figure 59. If, on the other hand, the basic statement has implications that lead to acceptance or rejection quite apart from the degree of pacifism which it conveys, then the proportion of the indorsements of the statements should not be a continuous function of their scale distance from the basic statement. The one hundred points might then scatter widely over the diagram. This inspectional criterion of irrelevance is objective, and it can probably be translated into a more definite algebraic form so as to eliminate entirely the personal equation of the investigator.

Two other objective criteria of irrelevance have been devised. They will be described in connection with the attitude scales now being constructed.

The selection of the statements for the final scale should now be possible. A shorter list of twenty or thirty statements should be selected for actual use. We have described three criteria by which to select the statements for the final scale. These criteria are:

1. The statements in the final scale should be so selected that they constitute as nearly as possible an evenly graduated series of scale values.

2. By the objective criterion of ambiguity it is possible to eliminate those statements which project too great a dispersion on the attitude continuum. The objective measure of ambiguity is the standard deviation of the best-fitting phi-gamma curve as illustrated in Figure 58.

3. By the objective criteria of irrelevance it is possible to eliminate those statements which are accepted or rejected largely by factors other than the degree of the attitude variable which they portray. One of these criteria is illustrated in Figure 59.

Summary of the Scaling Method

The steps in the construction of an attitude scale may be summarized briefly as follows:

1. Specification of the attitude variable to be measured.
2. Collection of a wide variety of opinions relating to the specified attitude variable.
3. Editing this material for a list of about one hundred brief statements of opinion.
4. Sorting the statements into an imaginary scale representing the attitude variable. This should be done by about three hundred readers.
5. Calculation of the scale value of each statement.
6. Elimination of some statements by the criterion of ambiguity.
7. Elimination of some statements by the criteria of irrelevance.
8. Selection of a shorter list of about twenty statements evenly graduated along the scale.

Measurement with an Attitude Scale

The practical application of the present measurement technique consists in presenting the final list of about twenty-five statements of opinion to the group to be studied with the request that they check with plus signs all the statements with which they agree and with minus signs all the statements with which they disagree. The score for each person is the average scale value of all the statements that he has indorsed. In order that the scale be effective toward the extremes, it is advisable that the statements in the scale be extended in both directions considerably beyond the attitudes which will ever be encountered as mean values for individuals. When the score has been determined for each person by the simple summation just indicated, a frequency distribution can be plotted for the attitudes of any specified group.

The reliability of the scale can be ascertained by preparing two parallel forms from the same material and by presenting both forms to the same individuals. The correlation between the two scores obtained for each person in a group will then indicate the reliability of the scale. Since the heterogeneity of the group affects the reliability coefficient, it is necessary to specify the standard deviation of the scores of the group on which the reliability coefficient is determined. The standard error of an individual score can also be calculated by an analogous procedure.

The unit of measurement in the scale when constructed by the procedure here outlined is not the standard discriminal error projected by a single statement on the psychological continuum. Such a unit of measurement can be obtained by the direct application of the law of comparative judgment, but it is considerably more laborious than the method here described. The unit in the present scale is a more arbitrary one, namely, one-tenth of the range on the psychological continuum which covers the span from what the readers regard as extreme affirmation to extreme negation in the particular list of statements with which we start. Of course the scale values can be determined with reliability to fractional parts of this unit. It is hoped that this unit may be shown experimentally to be proportional to a more precise and more universal unit of measurement, such as the standard discriminal error of a single statement of opinion.

It is legitimate to determine a central tendency for the frequency distribution of attitudes in a group. Several groups of individuals may then be compared as regards the means of their respective frequency distributions of attitudes. The differences between the means of several such distributions may be directly compared because of the fact that a rational base line has been established. Such comparisons are not possible when attitudes are ascertained merely by counting the number of indorsements to separate statements whose scale differences have not been measured.

In addition to specifying the mean attitude of each of several groups, it is also possible to measure their relative heterogeneity with regard to the issue in question. Thus it will be possible, by means of our present measurement methods, to discover for example that one group is 1.6 more heterogeneous in its attitudes about prohibition than some other group. The heterogeneity of a group is indicated perhaps best by the standard deviation of the scale values of all the opinions that have been indorsed by the group as a whole rather than by the standard deviation of the distribution of individual mean scores. Perhaps different terms should be adopted for two these types of measurement.

The tolerance which a person reveals on any particular issue is also subject to quantitative measurement. It is the standard deviation of the scale values of the statements that he indorses. The maximum possible tolerance is of course complete indifference, in which all of the statements are indorsed throughout the whole range of the scale.

If it is desired to know which of two forms of appeal is the more effective on any particular issue, this can be determined by using the scale before and after the appeal. The difference between the individual scores, before and after, can be tabulated, and the average shift in attitude following any specified form of appeal can be measured.

The essential characteristic of the present measurement method is the scale of evenly graduated opinions so arranged that equal steps or intervals on the scale *seem* to most people to represent equally noticeable shifts in attitude.

20 THE MEASUREMENT OF OPINION

The present investigation[1] is an attempt to apply psychophysical principles to the measurement of opinion. The provocation for the experiment here reported was the publication by Allport of his novel paper on "Measurement and Motivation of Atypical Opinion in a Certain Group."[2]

Since it is our present purpose to suggest some possibilities and limitations to the problem of opinion measurement and to offer a solution for at least one of its many troublesome features, a brief sketch of Allport's procedure is in place in so far as it directly concerns the present experiment. Allport asked his students to write out their opinions on a number of political issues. We shall limit ourselves to the prohibition question because his scale for that question is more complete than the others. Allport selected thirteen of the opinions to constitute a series or scale. These opinions ranged from extreme "dry" to extreme "wet" with intermediate opinions arranged between the two extremes. He ranked them, in collaboration with several colleagues, in a rank order series in accordance with estimated degree of wetness. In the final series of opinions, each statement is given a serial number.

The following is a list of the thirteen statements, and it will be seen that they shade off from extreme "dry" through intermediate opinions to extreme "wet."

OPINIONS ABOUT PROHIBITION

The present constitutional amendment prohibiting alcoholic liquors and the law interpreting this amendment are both satisfactory: enforcement should be made more severe.

The present amendment and interpretation are satisfactory, but a more uniform enforcement is necessary.

The laws at present are not wholly successful, but they should be upheld since they will be successful after a generation of education and enforcement.

The laws are on the whole acceptable, but minor changes will be found necessary from time to time.

Prohibition is correct in principle and although it cannot be completely enforced, should nevertheless be retained.

[1] This is one of a series of articles prepared by members of the Behavior Research Fund staff of the Illinois Institute for Juvenile Research, Chicago, Series B, No. 106. Reprinted from *Journal of Abnormal and Social Psychology*, XXII (1928), 415–30.

[2] F. H. Allport and D. A. Hartman, *American Political Science Review*, XIX (1925), 735–60.

Though prohibition is good in principle, it cannot be enforced, and therefore is actually doing more harm than good.

It should be left to the separate states to decide whether they wish to permit the open saloon.

The making of wine and beer in the home for strictly private use should be permitted.

Stores, under government control, for the sale of wines and beer not to be consumed on the premises, should be permitted.

It should be left to counties, townships, or cities whether they wish to permit the open saloon.

The sale of light wines and beers should be permitted in licensed cafes and restaurants.

Stores, under government control, for the sale of moderate quantities of any alcoholic liquors should be permitted.

The open saloon system should be universally permitted

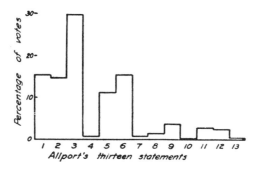

FIG. 60

Each of Allport's students was asked to check that *one* statement which most nearly represented his own opinion about prohibition. A frequency count was made of the indorsements for each of the thirteen statements, and the result is indicated in Figure 60, which is a reproduction of Allport's Figure 4. This figure reminds one of a frequency distribution or a column diagram, but it is quite certain that Allport did not intend that it should be so interpreted because there is really no valid measurement for the base line. The abscissae consist merely of rank orders of the thirteen statements as arranged by Allport and several of his colleagues, and for this reason one can interpret the diagram only in the sense that the height of each column indicates the frequency with which the corresponding statement was indorsed. One cannot assume that the distances on the base line have any interpretation beyond that of rank orders of the statements in the mind of the author. Nor can one assume that the linear separations of the statements on the base line are in any sense proportional to the divergencies of the respective opinions as might, at first sight, be supposed. The linear separation of any two statements on the base line is an entirely fortuitous matter, since it can be altered at will either by a difference of opinion about the rank order of the statements or by inserting new statements in the series or by leaving out some of them. Furthermore, it is not possible to calculate or otherwise assign a central tendency or dispersion of opinion in the group as long as the locations on the base line of the diagram are merely rank orders.

The central purpose of the present study is to solve this problem of constructing a rational method of assigning values for the base line of a scale of opinion. Professor Allport raised this problem with the writer in a recent conversation. One of the first requirements of a solution is that the scale values of the statements of opinion must be as free as possible, and preferably entirely free, from the actual opinions of individuals or groups. If the scale value of one of the statements should be affected by the opinion of any individual person or group, then it would be impossible to compare the opinion distributions of two groups on the same base.

After trying several different schemes in a preliminary way, one was found which seemed feasible. It consists in the application of the same psychophysical principles to the problem of measuring opinion as have been used for gray values, handwriting specimens, and other psychological values. The application is not made without some difficulties, however.

When we decide to represent the distribution of opinion on any given issue in the form of a frequency distribution, it is necessary first to postulate an *opinion variable*. This is the first restriction on the problem. By an opinion variable I mean a variable which is represented by the statements of opinion. For the prohibition question this variable might be the relative degree of restriction of individual liberty which the statements imply. Now it is possible to hold many different opinions concerning prohibition which would not be represented at all on this opinion variable. Thus, for example, a man may hold the opinion that prohibition has increased the use of tobacco. Another man may say that prohibition has removed an important source of government revenue. These are certainly opinions about prohibition, but they do not belong on the particular variable just mentioned because they do not say or imply anything regarding the degree of restriction of individual liberty in the consumption of alcohol. Note that other opinion variables might be adopted for study or scaling which might conceivably include these opinions. It is clearly impossible to think of any sort of scale of opinion on any public issue unless we include only those opinions which naturally fall in a sequence of some sort. At the start we acknowledge, then, a natural restriction in the construction of any scale of opinion, namely, that the scale must be concerned with a specified opinion variable and that many opinions may be expressed, more or less concerned with the issue at stake, which do not belong on the scale.

Ideally the scaling method should be so designed that it will automatically throw out of the scale any statements which do not belong in its natural sequence. Such a test has been devised, but its description will be deferred for separate publication.

The scaling method to be described rests on an assumption which will be stated at the outset. We shall assume that groups of individuals who hold differing opinions about the issue in question, in this case prohibition, are equally able to discriminate between any two statements of opinion. For example, two statements from the scale might be given to several groups that hold differing opinions about prohibition. They might all be asked to decide which of the two statements is the "dryer" in its attitude or implications. The two statements a and b might be such that 70 per cent of one of the groups vote that statement a is the dryer and the remaining 30 per cent that statement b is the dryer. This would give the conclusion that the first statement implies a state of affairs really a little "dryer" than the second statement but that the difference between them is not great enough so that it can be easily distinguished by everybody. The assumption underlying the present scaling method is that the several groups would give about the same returns in their effort to discriminate between the two statements even though the actual opinions about prohibition held by the several groups might vary widely. Stated in another way, the assumption is that two individuals who differ from each other widely in their views about prohibition would find it equally easy, or equally difficult, to say which of two statements is the more in favor of prohibition. This assumption can be experimentally tested, but it has not yet been done.

If this assumption is valid, then the separations between the statements in the scale may be ascertained by psychophysical principles on the common assumption that equally often noticed differences are equal. Theoretically, this assumption is not universally true. The error may be discovered in some experimental situations, but it is probably small in comparison with the gross errors necessarily involved in the study of so fluid an entity as public opinion.

The scaling was conducted as follows. The thirteen statements were mimeographed on small cards, one on each card. The thirteen cards were inclosed in an envelope with a sheet of instructions. The subject was asked to arrange the thirteen cards in serial order beginning with the statement most strongly in favor of prohibition. On this statement he wrote Number 1. The last statement, which he marked 13, was the statement which he considered to be most strongly against prohibition, while the other statements were given intermediate ranks. This sorting of thirteen cards was done by two hundred subjects. For accurate scaling this number should be increased to five or six hundred.

For the purposes of scaling it was necessary to determine for each possible pair of statements the proportion of the two hundred judges who considered one of the statements more strongly in favor of prohibition than the other.

Since the list contained thirteen statements, there were $n(n-1)/2 = 78$ such pairs of statements. This is a rather laborious tabulation, and it increases in magnitude rapidly as the number of statements in the scale increases. The results of this tabulation are given in Table 29.

The reading of the table is explained by the following example: In the first column, the first entry is 177. It means that of the 200 subjects, 177 voted that statement 2 was "wetter" than statement 1. The next entry is 172. It means that of the 200 subjects 172 considered statement 3 "wetter" than statement 1. Similarly, 187 of the 200 subjects thought that statement 4 was "wetter" than statement 1. This column shows the comparisons of statement 1 with each of the others. The second column gives similar comparisons of statement 2 with each of the others, and so on.

TABLE 29

	1	2	3	4	5	6	7	8	9	10	11	12	13
1......		23	28	13	21	1	0	2	0	0	0	2	0
2......	177		52	25	52	3	2	1	0	1	1	2	0
3......	172	148		72	98	5	4	3	4	5	4	4	1
4......	187	175	128		123	4	3	2	2	3	2	2	0
5......	179	148	102	77		3	2	2	2	1	2	2	0
6......	199	197	195	196	197		113	106	99	111	94	95	25
7......	200	198	196	197	198	87		92	84	50	75	82	2
8......	198	199	197	198	198	94	108		56	101	38	49	5
9......	200	200	196	198	198	101	116	144		108	49	53	4
10.....	200	199	195	197	199	89	150	99	92		79	87	1
11.....	200	199	196	198	198	106	125	162	151	121		104	4
12.....	198	198	196	198	198	105	118	151	147	113	96		3
13.....	200	200	199	200	200	175	198	195	196	199	196	197	
Sum	2310	2084	1880	1769	1880	773	939	959	833	813	636	679	45

From Table 29 it is possible to ascertain for any pair of statements the proportion of the whole group of 200 subjects that considered one more "wet" than the other. The summation at the foot of each column shows the total number of votes "wetter than" the statement in that column. Statement 1, which is represented in column 1, is one of the "driest" in the list. Hence, there will be a large count of judgments in which other statements are considered "wetter than" statement 1. Similarly, the last statement in the list, number 13, is probably the "wettest." Therefore there will be relatively few votes "wetter than" it. These summations enable us to arrange the statements in rank order. This has been done in Table 30. It will be seen already in the rank orders that the two hundred judges in this experiment did not agree with Allport's arrangement of his statements in serial order. The most conspicuous disagreement is for his statement 6, which according to the two hundred judges of this study was given a rank of 10. It is clear that if we want to make a graphical representation of the distribution of opinion in a group, it is of very fundamental importance to have the statements arranged in a properly scaled order. Otherwise the appearance of the graphical distribution will be deceptive. Even the two hundred judgments of this experiment should not be considered sufficient to establish the scale with high degree of accuracy. In Table 31 the votes recorded in Table 29 have been reproduced in the form of proportions.

Ideally the votes should be obtained by the method of paired comparison, but that method is prohibitive because of fatigue of the subjects. For this reason I asked the subjects merely to arrange the statements in rank order, and I deduced from the two hundred rank orders the number of times that each statement was considered "wetter" than each other statement.

The scale values of the statements cannot be determined merely by having them arranged in rank order. It is necessary to make use of the actual proportions of judgments for every pair of statements. It is at this point that we may be able to introduce a rational procedure for the construction of a scale.

Let Figure 61 represent the desired scale, and let the opinion variable be

TABLE 30

Total Number of Votes "Wetter than"	Allport's Rank Order	Revised Rank Order
45	13	13
636	11	12
679	12	11
773	6	10
813	10	9
833	9	8
939	7	7
959	8	6
1769	4	5
1880	5	4
1880	3	3
2084	2	2
2310	1	1

TABLE 31

EXPERIMENTAL PROPORTIONS

	1	2	3	4	5	6	7	8	9	10	11	12	13
1	.500	.115	.140	.065	.105	.005	....	.010	....	....	....	.010	....
2	.885	.500	.260	.125	.260	.015	.010	.005	....	.005	.005	.010	....
3	.860	.740	.500	.360	.490	.025	.020	.015	.020	.025	.020	.020	.005
4	.935	.875	.640	.500	.615	.020	.015	.010	.010	.015	.010	.010	....
5	.895	.740	.510	.385	.500	.015	.010	.010	.010	.005	.010	.010	....
6	.995	.985	.975	.980	.985	.500	.565	.530	.495	.555	.470	.475	.125
7	....	.990	.980	.985	.990	.435	.500	.460	.420	.250	.375	.410	.010
8	.990	.995	.985	.990	.990	.470	.540	.500	.280	.505	.190	.245	.025
9	....	....	.980	.990	.990	.505	.580	.720	.500	.540	.245	.265	.020
10	....	.995	.975	.985	.995	.445	.750	.495	.460	.500	.395	.435	.005
11	....	.995	.980	.990	.990	.530	.625	.810	.755	.605	.500	.520	.020
12	.990	.990	.980	.990	.990	.525	.590	.755	.735	.565	.480	.500	.015
13	....	....	.995	....	....	.875	.990	.975	.980	.995	.980	.985	.500

represented for the present merely by the linear extension which is labeled "dry-neutral-wet." It is on this extension that we want to locate the thirteen statements so that we may later erect ordinates over them to show the frequency with which each part of the scale is indorsed by a group. This problem is almost identical, psychophysically, with the problem of scaling handwriting or English composition and the like. There is no origin, datum, or zero point. Psychological scales usually have only an arbitrary origin. We shall arbitrarily designate statement 1, the dryest, as the zero point, and all scale values will be measurements from that statement.

The next step in the construction of the scale is to define a unit of measurement, and this is really the center of the problem. We shall use as our unit of measurement the discriminal dispersion[3] of the statements, and we shall make the assumption that the statements are sufficiently homogeneous so that their respective discriminal dispersions are comparable. This assumption is implied in all psychological scales, including psychological scales of educational products, although I have not seen it explicitly stated. For homo-

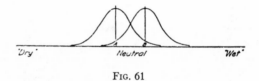

'Dry'   Neutral   'Wet'

FIG. 61

geneous stimuli the following relation can be demonstrated: $d = .953\sigma$ in which d is a stimulus difference which can be discriminated correctly in 75 per cent of the attempts. It is a "just noticeable difference" (j.n.d.) which must be defined in terms of the frequency with which the difference is correctly noticed. The notation σ is the discriminal dispersion or the standard error of observation *for a single stimulus*. It is proportional to the j.n.d. for any specified percentage of correct answers.

The standard error of observation for a single stimulus can never be observed directly. Every objective observation is a comparison of two stimuli or of one stimulus against a group of stimuli as a datum or level. Hence every observation that can be recorded must be in the nature of comparison. For example, the level in the mercury column of a thermometer is compared with the level of the markings, and we have therefore in this simple objective observation *two* observational errors, one for each stimulus member of the judgment. In the present problem we assume that the two qualities or statements are sufficiently homogeneous so that the two observational errors or discriminal dispersions are at least comparable. This will be our unit of measurement on the scale.

Let the curve A in Figure 61 represent the frequency with which state-

[3] For detailed discussion of this concept, see chap. ii.

ment A is perceived at different degrees of "wetness" or "dryness." These frequencies represent the perceptions of statement A by a large group of judges. The scatter would of course be smaller if the curve should represent the same number of repeated observations by a single judge. Let the point A on the base line represent that degree of "wetness-dryness" which is most frequently read into statement A. The standard deviation of this distribution is the discriminal error, σ_A, of A, or we may call it the subjective observational error of A. Let curve B be similarly interpreted. Our assumption, previously stated, is that the statements are sufficiently homogeneous so that their discriminal dispersions may be considered equal or at least comparable.

When the two statements A and B are compared, the apparent difference between the two statements can be represented as a linear distance as long as

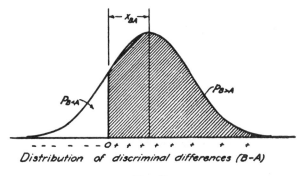

Distribution of discriminal differences (B-A)

Fig. 62

the comparison is explicitly restricted to the assigned opinion variable "wet-neutral-dry." It is probably a safe assumption that the subjective observational errors are uncorrelated. We shall assume, in other words, that the error for stimulus A is independent of the error for stimulus B on each occasion. This assumption is also implied in all educational product scales, although I do not believe that it has ever been stated.[4]

We can imagine a linear separation $(B - A)$ for every comparison. Sometimes this difference will be positive, and occasionally it will be negative. In Figure 62 these differences are represented graphically. The frequencies of observed positive differences, $(B - A) > 0$, are represented to the right of the origin. The observed negative values, $(B - A) < 0$, are shown to the left of the origin. The shaded part of the diagram represents the proportion, $P_{B>A}$, in which B is judged "wetter" than A. The unshaded area represents the proportion, $P_{B<A}$, of judgments in which A is considered to be more "wet" than B. The standard deviation σ_{B-A} of this surface is

$$\sigma_{B-A} = \sqrt{\sigma_B^2 + \sigma_A^2}, \tag{1}$$

[4] See chap. v.

and since σ_A and σ_B are considered to be equal,

$$\sigma_{B-A} = \sigma\sqrt{2}\,. \tag{2}$$

But σ is the unit of measurement for the scale, and hence

$$\sigma_{B-A} = \sqrt{2}\,. \tag{3}$$

The linear separation between the two statements A and B on the final scale should be that degree of perceived difference which is most frequent. In Figure 62 the modal linear separation is the distance x_{BA}. This distance can be expressed in terms of the standard deviation, σ_{B-A}, of the discriminal differences and the observed proportion of judgments, $P_{B>A}$.

Hence

$$S_B - S_A = x_{BA}\sqrt{2}\,, \tag{4}$$

in which S_A and S_B are the two scale values and x_{BA} is the sigma value of the observed proportion of judgments $P_{B>A}$.

Equation (4) enables us to ascertain the scale distance between any two statements. This, of course, does not say anything whatever about indorsements of the statements or their frequency. In fact, the scale values can be ascertained without asking anybody what he himself believes. That is a much simpler problem.

If we should use the above equation directly, we might tabulate the linear separations $(A - B)$, $(A - C)$, $(A - D)$, $(A - E)$, and so on for all comparisons with statement A as a standard. This would yield a scale. We might then do likewise for the comparisons $(B - A)$, $(B - C)$, $(B - D)$, $(B - E)$, and so on for all comparisons with statement B as a standard. This would also yield a scale, and very likely the several scales so constructed would not quite agree. One such scale might be constructed with every one of the thirteen statements in turn as a standard. It is our next problem to determine how these scale values are to be weighted for the construction of a single scale based on all the available stimulus comparisons.

In order to determine the scale distance between any two statements A and B so that all of the available paired comparisons may be taken into account, we might arrange the scale distances as in the following table.

$$(S_C - S_A) - (S_C - S_B) = (S_B - S_A)\,,$$
$$(S_D - S_A) - (S_D - S_B) = (S_B - S_A)\,,$$
$$(S_E - S_A) - (S_E - S_B) = (S_B - S_A)\,,$$
$$(S_F - S_A) - (S_F - S_B) = (S_B - S_A)\,,$$

in which the left-hand members are determined by the observed proportions and by equation (4). We should then have the same numerical value for the scale distance $(S_B - S_A)$ from all of the equations except for the observational errors in the experimentally determined proportions.

Since the standard errors of the numerical values of $(S_B - S_A)$ from the different equations vary, it is necessary to weight these values in determining a final scale distance for $(S_B - S_A)$. In the first equation of the above table we have

$$(S_C - S_A) - (S_C - S_B) = (S_B - S_A) . \tag{5}$$

The standard error of $(S_B - S_A)$ may be written[5]

$$\sigma_{ba} = \sqrt{\sigma_{ca}^2 + \sigma_{cb}^2} , \tag{6}$$

in which

σ_{ba} = standard error of $(S_B - S_A)$,
σ_{ca} = standard error of $(S_C - S_A)$,
σ_{cb} = standard error of $(S_C - S_B)$.

By equation (4), the standard error of $(S_C - S_A)$ is the same as the standard error of x_{CA}, and similarly for other paired comparisons. But[6]

$$\sigma_{ca} = \frac{\sigma_{C-A}}{Z} \sqrt{\frac{p_{CA} \cdot q_{CA}}{N}} , \tag{7}$$

in which

σ_{CA} = standard error of x_{CA},
σ_{C-A} = standard deviation of the distribution of discriminal differences for stimuli C and A,
$\sigma_{C-A} = \sigma\sqrt{2}$ in which σ is the unit of measurement,
Z = ordinate of the probability curve at x_{CA} when area of surface is taken as unity and σ is unity,
N = number of observations,
p_{CA} = proportion of judgments "$C > A$,"
$q_{CA} = 1 - p_{CA}$.

Since in equation (7) the value of $N = 200$ is constant throughout the experiment, and since σ_{C-A} is assumed to be constant, they may be dropped in establishing a weight for the numerical value for each equation in the above table. Hence σ_{ca} will be proportional to

$$\frac{\sqrt{p_{CA} \cdot q_{CA}}}{Z_{CA}} , \tag{8}$$

and, similarly,

$$\sigma_{cb} \text{ is proportional to } \frac{\sqrt{p_{CB} \cdot q_{CB}}}{Z_{CB}} .$$

Substituting in equation (6), we have

$$\sigma_{ba} = \sqrt{\frac{p_{CA} q_{CA}}{Z_{CA}^2} + \frac{p_{CB} \cdot q_{CB}}{Z_{CB}^2}} \tag{9}$$

[5] See Kelley, *Statistical Method*, p. 182.   [6] *Ibid.*, p. 90.

$$W_{BA} = \cfrac{1}{\cfrac{p_{CA} \cdot q_{CA}}{Z^2_{CA}} + \cfrac{p_{CB} \cdot q_{CB}}{Z^2_{CB}}}. \tag{10}$$

If the value of $(S_B - S_A)$ in each of the equations of the above table be given its appropriate weight, as shown by equation (10), the weighted average of the several numerical values of $(S_B - S_A)$ will be the scale distance between the two statements A and B. It should be noted that such an average takes into account the comparison of every one of twelve stimuli with A as a standard and also the comparison of every one of twelve stimuli with B as a standard. It is clear that in a similar manner one may ascertain the weighted average scale distance between B and C, between C and D, and so on.

TABLE 32

	p	q	x	Z	Z^2	pq	pq/Z^2
1.......	.065	.935	1.514102	.126794	.016077	.060775	3.780245
2.......	.125	.875	1.150349	.205853	.042375	.109375	2.581121
3.......	.360	.640	0.358459	.374118	.139964	.230400	1.646138
4.......	.500	.500	0.000000	.398942	.159155	.250000	1.570796
5.......	.385	.615	0.292375	.382250	.146115	.236775	1.620470
6.......	.980	.020	2.053749	.048418	.002344	.019600	8.361775
7.......	.985	.015	2.170090	.037870	.001434	.014775	10.303347
8.......	.990	.010	2.326348	.026652	.000710	.009900	13.943662
9.......	.990	.010	2.326348	.026652	.000710	.009900	13.943662
10.......	.985	.015	2.170090	.037870	.001434	.014775	10.303347
11.......	.990	.010	2.326348	.026652	.000710	.009900	13.943662
12.......	.990	.010	2.326348	.026652	.000710	.009900	13.943662

The procedure could be simplified if there were no holes in a complete table of paired comparisons, but unfortunately this circumstance is unavoidable. A complete table of paired comparisons would show the proportion of judgments $A < B$, $A < C$, $A < D$, $A < E \ldots A < K$. If A, B, C are adjacent stimuli, they will give experimental proportions greater than zero and less than unity. For the judgments $A < E$, $A < F \ldots A < K$, one will obtain either zero or unity because these pairs of stimuli are perhaps so widely divergent on the scale that they are always unanimously discriminated, and no direct scaling is then possible. One can scale such wide separations by parts so that there is a measurable amount of confusion of judgment in each part.

We now proceed to scale the thirteen statements about prohibition by means of equations (4) and (10). The first step is to ascertain the value

$$\frac{pq}{Z^2}$$

for use in equation (10) for each of the entries in Table 31. This has been done for statement 4 in Table 32. The first column in this table shows merely the numerical identification of the statements. Column q is merely the complement of p. Column x shows the sigma value of the given value for p and has been read directly from the Kelley-Wood tables. The item Z was read directly from the same source. The last three columns are self-explanatory. One table like Table 32 was prepared for each of the thirteen statements. It is necessary to carry the calculations to five or six decimals in this instance because of the coarseness of the original scale, which necessitates the use of small values of p and q.

In Table 33 we have the calculation of the scale distance $(S_2 - S_3)$ as an

TABLE 33

	x_2	x_3	d	w	wd
1.	−1.200359	−1.080319	−.120040	.194868	−.023392
2.	0.000000	−0.643345	+.643345	.294164	+.189249
3.					
4.	+1.150349	+0.358459	+.791890	.236560	+.187329
5.	+0.643345	+0.025069	+.618276	.294132	+.181855
6.	+2.170090	+1.959964	+.210126	.057343	+.012049
7.	+2.326348	+2.053749	+.272599	.044832	+.012221
8.	+2.575829	+2.170090	+.405739	.029311	+.011893
9.					
10.	+2.575829	+1.959964	+.615865	.032321	+.019905
11.	+2.575829	+2.053749	+.522080	.031089	+.016231
12.	+2.326348	+2.053749	+.272599	.044832	+.012221
13.					

$$(S_2 - S_3) = \frac{\Sigma wd}{\Sigma w} = +.491929$$

example. The first column shows again merely a numerical identification of each statement. The second column and third column are copied from tables similar to Table 32. Column d is the difference $(x_2 - x_3)$. The next column is the weight w_{23} by equation (10), and the last column is the weighted difference wd.

The scale distance $(S_2 - S_3) = +.492$, which should not be interpreted as accurate beyond the second decimal.

Since there are thirteen statements in the scale, there will be twelve tables like Table 33. If the thirteen statements of Table 30 are arranged in rank order by the total number of votes, we get the twelve comparisons shown in Table 34. Each of the entries in Table 34 was determined by a calculation like that of Table 33. The scale distances between adjacent pairs of statements are shown in Table 34.

From these scale distances between adjacent pairs of statements we obtain the final scale values of Table 35, which constitute our main objective.

The final scale values are shown graphically in Figure 63. Inspection of this figure shows immediately that there are wide ranges in the scale which are not represented by any statements of opinion. Also it appears from the graph that seven of the thirteen statements represent more or less the same attitude, since statements 6, 7, 8, 9, 10, 11, 12 are all scaled within the rather narrow range of .6 of a scale unit.

The final scale takes the appearance of Figure 63, which should be compared with Allport's Figure 4 reproduced here as Figure 60. It is clearly not worth while to attempt a graphical representation of the distribution of opinion except as a bar diagram. The gaps between statements 4 and 8 and between statements 11 and 13 are too great to allow a legitimate frequency distribution to be drawn, and the separation between them is so great that their separation cannot be accurately determined beyond the fact that they are too far apart to make possible a true representation of the distribution of opinion.

In order to construct a scale for the measurement of opinion, it is advisable to start with a rather large number of statements from which a smaller number may be selected for the final scale. These should be so selected that

TABLE 34

Specimens	Scale Separation
S_1-S_2	+ .618872
S_2-S_3	+ .491929
S_3-S_5	− .018756
S_4-S_5	− .294701
S_4-S_8	+1.844339
S_7-S_8	− .050186
S_7-S_9	+ .173674
S_9-S_{10}	+ .058736
S_6-S_{10}	− .032123
S_6-S_{12}	+ .171894
$S_{11}-S_{12}$	− .078929
$S_{11}-S_{13}$	+1.475326

TABLE 35

No.	Scale Value
13	0.000000
11	1.475326
12	1.554255
6	1.726149
10	1.758272
9	1.817008
7	1.990682
8	2.040868
4	3.885207
5	4.179908
3	4.161152
2	4.653081
1	5.271953

they are approximately evenly spaced. When a frequency surface is erected on such a base line, it will be possible to compare it with the corresponding distribution of opinion in another group. With a rational base line as here described it will be possible also to calculate measures of central tendency and of dispersion for each group, but that could not be satisfactorily accomplished with the thirteen statements of Allport on prohibition because of their extremely uneven spacing.

It may be possible to simplify considerably the procedure if, say, one hundred statements were sorted by several hundred subjects into ten piles to represent equal-appearing intervals on a scale. The cumulative frequencies on such a scale might conceivably be treated as a phi-gamma function. The scale values of the statements might then be determined by a procedure

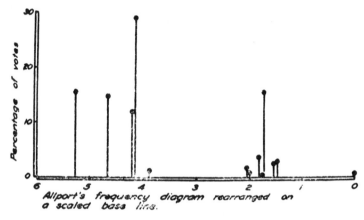

Fig. 63

analogous to the calculation of the limen or 50 per cent point in the usual psychophysical problem. The relative ambiguity of each statement would be measured by the standard deviation of the phi-gamma function for each statement. The final scale would consist of a selection of statements which are as far as possible evenly spaced on the scale and which have the highest possible precision. An experiment to ascertain the validity of such a simplified procedure will shortly be tried. Such a procedure assumes, of course, nothing about the shape of the distribution of opinion in any given group.

The main principle in the measurement of opinion to which the present paper is devoted is the construction of a rational base line for describing the distribution of opinion by which equal intervals on the scale shall represent equally often noticed shifts in opinion or equal-appearing opinion differences. This principle of a rational scale enables one to compare several groups as to distribution, central tendency, and dispersion of opinion on any stated opinion variable, irrespective of the shape of that distribution or the amount and direction of bias in each of the groups.

21 AN EXPERIMENTAL STUDY OF NATIONALITY PREFERENCES

The experiment here reported[1] was designed as a rather severe test of the law of comparative judgment. This psychophysical law states the relation between the psychological separation of the stimuli (the sense distance) and the probability of correct discrimination on any single occasion. The law applies ideally to the situation in which a single observer makes several hundred discriminatory judgments for each possible pair of stimuli in any given stimulus series. The stimuli to which the law refers in its conventional psychophysical setting are the lifted weights, the grey papers, the line lengths, and the rest of the traditional stock in trade of the psychophysicist. The ideal situation above described constitutes Case 1 in the formulation of the law.[2] By a number of assumptions previously described, it is possible to apply the law to those situations in which a *group* of observers are used instead of a single observer and in which each member of the group makes only one discriminatory judgment for each possible pair of stimuli in the stimulus series. We shall here use the simplest form of the law, previously described as Case 5.

We shall also transfer the whole psychophysical reasoning from its traditional stimuli in which the subject responds to the question, "Which of these cylinders is the heavier?" to the question, "Which of these two nationalities would you generally prefer to associate with?" To transfer the application of the law from lifted weights to nationality preferences introduces new factors into the judgments. The nationality preferences are saturated with prejudice and bias, with religious affiliations, and with wide differences in knowledge and familiarity. In addition to these variable factors, the group

[1] This project was started as one of a series of studies carried out under the auspices of the Illinois Institute for Juvenile Research, Series B, No. 122. It was completed as a project of the Local Community Research Committee at the University of Chicago. Reprinted from *Journal of General Psychology*, I (1928), 405–25.

I wish to make special acknowledgment to my research assistant for the Local Community Research Committee, Miss Annette McBroom, who has carried out all of the calculations in this study. Her part in the study has been much more than that of a statistical assistant, for she has made many valuable suggestions regarding the handling of the data. For help in the preparation of the mimeographed forms and in the collection of the original data I wish to acknowledge the effective work of Mr. W. H. Cowley, who was at the time research assistant at the Institute for Juvenile Research.

[2] See chap. iii.

of 239 subjects was also intentionally left as heterogeneous as it was found to be among undergraduates at the University of Chicago. It is clear that with large proportions of Jews, Catholics, Negroes, Protestants, and students whose parents are foreign born, it may be very questionable whether the distribution of attitude toward any one of the twenty nationalities is in any sense normal on the psychological continuum. However, when the calculated proportion of each judgment is compared with the corresponding experimental proportion, the average discrepancy is found to be only .03, which shows rather convincingly that the law of comparative judgment can be used for measuring not only the formal "sense distance" of conventional psychophysics but even so complex a continuum as the degrees of preference of a heterogeneous group of subjects for nationalities and races.

The experiment was performed by asking each of the 239 undergraduates to fill in a mimeographed schedule showing their racial and nationality preferences. The instructions on the schedule were as follows:

An Experimental Study of Racial Attitudes

This is an experimental study of attitudes toward races and nationalities. You are asked merely to underline the one nationality, or race, of each pair that you would rather associate with. For example, the first pair is:

Englishman—South American

If, in general, you prefer to associate with Englishmen rather than with South Americans, underline Englishman. If you prefer, in general, to associate with South Americans, underline South American. If you find it difficult to decide for any pair, simply underline one of them anyway. If two nationalities are about equally well liked, they will have about the same number of underlinings in all of the papers. Be sure to underline one of each pair even if you have to make a sort of guess.

American—Hindu
Englishman—Swede
Japanese—Italian
Hindu—Frenchman
Mexican—American
etc.

The list of pairs was continued so that every one of the twenty-one races or nationalities had been compared with every other one. This required

$$\frac{n(n-1)}{2} = 210$$

judgments which were mimeographed on three letter-sized sheets. The complete list of nationalities and races is given in the tables. In addition to these 210 judgments there were 21 repetitions, making a total of 231 pairs on the mimeographed forms. The purpose of the 21 repetitions was to verify empirically the probable errors of the proportions so that some estimate might be made of the probable error of the resulting scale values, both theoretically and empirically.

The law in the complete form is as follows

$$S_1 - S_2 = x_{12}\sqrt{\sigma_1^2 + \sigma_2^2 - 2 \cdot r_{12} \cdot \sigma_1 \cdot \sigma_2}, \qquad (1)$$

in which

$(S_1 - S_2)$ = sense distance, i.e., the scale distance between the two modal discriminal processes.[3]

x_{12} = the sigma value corresponding to the observed proportion of judgments "R_1 is greater than R_2." R denotes the stimulus. The proportion is designated $P_{1>2}$. The numerical value of x_{12} is positive when $P_{1>2}$ is greater than .50, and it is negative when $P_{1>2}$ is less than .50.

σ_1 and σ_2 = ambiguities (discriminal errors) of the two stimuli, R_1 and R_2.

r_{12} = the correlation between the discriminal deviations involved in the same judgment.

In the present study we have used Case 5, in which the law is applied to a group of observers, each observer giving only one judgment for every stimulus pair. In Case 5 it is also assumed that $r_{12} = 0$ and that the value of σ is unity for every stimulus in the series. With these approximations the law takes the simpler form

$$S_1 - S_2 = x_{12}\sqrt{2} \qquad (2)$$

when σ is chosen as the unit of measurement.

The first results are shown in Table 36. The interpretation of this table may be seen perhaps best by the following direct readings. Of the whole group, 89.8 per cent preferred to associate with Americans rather than with Englishmen; 38.0 per cent preferred to associate with Chinese rather than with Japanese; 37.2 per cent preferred to associate with Russians rather than with Italians. The rest of the table is interpreted in the same manner. These constitute the data on which our measurements will be based.

Our object is to calculate a scale value for each of the 21 nationalities. With these 21 scale values we shall prepare a table of 210 calculated proportions. The discrepancies between these two tables will be the criterion by which to judge the degree to which the law of comparative judgment is applicable to this type of data.

The first step is to ascertain the rank orders of the 21 nationalities. They are obtained by a simple summation of the proportions. These summations are given at the foot of each column in Table 36. The last row gives the absolute rank orders. The rank orders are (1) American, (2) Englishman, (3) Scotchman, and so on.

These rank orders constitute a description of the group of undergraduates,

[3] For the psychophysical terminology here used, see chap. iv.

TABLE 36

EXPERIMENTAL PROPORTIONS

	American	Armenian	Chinese	Englishman	Frenchman	German	Greek	Hindu	Irishman	Italian	Japanese
American		.000	.000	.102	.046	.042	.004	.004	.030	.013	.000
Armenian	1.000		.342	1.000	.983	.912	.545	.270	.975	.782	.481
Chinese	1.000	.658		.992	.954	.950	.675	.447	.987	.882	.620
Englishman	.898	.000	.008		.114	.133	.008	.013	.244	.030	.000
Frenchman	.954	.017	.046	.886		.398	.013	.042	.622	.222	.021
German	.958	.088	.050	.867	.602		.029	.034	.644	.142	.050
Greek	.996	.455	.325	.992	.987	.971		.275	.970	.837	.302
Hundu	.996	.730	.553	.987	.958	.966	.725		.971	.878	.664
Irishman	.970	.025	.013	.756	.378	.356	.030	.029		.063	.054
Italian	.987	.218	.118	.970	.778	.858	.163	.122	.937		.285
Japanese	1.000	.519	.380	1.000	.979	.950	.698	.336	.946	.715	
Jew	.953	.380	.206	.862	.792	.761	.397	.186	.779	.631	.263
Mexican	.992	.621	.336	.992	.987	.975	.660	.399	.983	.916	.536
Negro	.996	.796	.691	.996	.975	.975	.853	.687	.983	.933	.744
Pole	1.000	.428	.291	.975	.983	.886	.452	.208	.954	.808	.360
Russian	.983	.359	.189	.962	.932	.886	.350	.170	.904	.628	.245
Scotchman	.966	.046	.017	.722	.357	.348	.030	.008	.532	.076	.013
Spaniard	.992	.208	.122	.987	.954	.858	.259	.154	.917	.517	.201
South American	.992	.192	.114	.962	.801	.828	.213	.130	.870	.473	.114
Swede	.983	.109	.055	.878	.611	.674	.084	.102	.744	.200	.084
Turk	1.000	.820	.641	.996	.987	.983	.787	.664	.983	.954	.735
Σp	19.616	6.669	4.497	17.884	15.158	14.710	6.975	4.280	15.975	10.700	5.772
Rank order	1	15	18	2	5	6	14	19	4	9	16

TABLE 36—*Continued*

	Jew	Mexican	Negro	Pole	Russian	Scotchman	Spaniard	South American	Swede	Turk	Check Column
American	.047	.008	.004	.000	.017	.034	.008	.008	.017	.000	.384
Armenian	.620	.379	.204	.572	.641	.954	.792	.808	.891	.180	13.331
Chinese	.794	.664	.309	.709	.811	.983	.878	.886	.945	.359	15.503
Englishman	.138	.008	.004	.025	.038	.278	.013	.038	.122	.004	2.116
Frenchman	.208	.013	.025	.017	.068	.643	.046	.199	.389	.013	4.842
German	.239	.025	.025	.114	.114	.652	.142	.172	.326	.017	5.290
Greek	.603	.340	.147	.548	.650	.970	.741	.787	.916	.213	13.025
Hindu	.814	.601	.313	.792	.830	.992	.846	.870	.898	.336	15.720
Irishman	.221	.017	.017	.046	.096	.468	.083	.130	.256	.017	4.025
Italian	.369	.084	.067	.192	.372	.924	.483	.527	.800	.046	9.300
Japanese	.737	.464	.256	.640	.755	.987	.799	.886	.916	.265	14.228
Jew	.....	.282	.090	.489	.487	.809	.610	.586	.753	.149	10.465
Mexican	.718	.....	.282	.720	.739	.992	.903	.823	.941	.254	14.769
Negro	.910	.718	.....	.832	.881	.987	.937	.928	.962	.597	17.381
Pole	.511	.280	.168	.....	.583	.954	.655	.688	.881	.151	12.216
Russian	.513	.261	.119	.417	.....	.921	.669	.580	.799	.090	10.977
Scotchman	.191	.008	.013	.046	.079	.....	.046	.092	.201	.000	3.791
Spaniard	.390	.097	.063	.345	.331	.954	.....	.517	.754	.029	9.649
South American	.414	.177	.072	.312	.420	.908	.483	.....	.765	.042	9.282
Swede	.247	.059	.038	.119	.201	.799	.246	.235	.....	.026	6.494
Turk	.851	.746	.403	.849	.910	1.000	.971	.958	.974	.....	17.212
Σp	9.535	5.231	2.619	7.784	9.023	16.209	10.351	10.718	13.506	2.788	
Rank order	11	17	21	13	12	3	10	8	7	20	

and it would vary from one group to another. In order to use this procedure for any interpretation regarding racial and nationality preferences, it is of course necessary to have a rather homogeneous group. Such a study is now being made with a large group of American-born students with American-born parents, and for several other rather homogeneous groups, similarly defined. Our present object is to test the measurement methods, and it is a better test of our procedure to see how much internal consistency can be obtained with a heterogeneous group.

Some brief description of the group of undergraduates is in order because of the fact that the scale values of the nationalities naturally reflect the makeup of the group of subjects. Table 37 shows the representation of the principal countries among the 249 subjects.

TABLE 37

DESCRIPTION OF EXPERIMENTAL GROUP

Country of Birth	Subject	Father	Father's Father	Father's Mother	Mother	Mother's Father	Mother's Mother
United States	.941	.628	.406	.397	.682	.423	.439
Canada	.017	.046	.013	.021	.038	.025	.021
England	.008	.042	.092	.096	.008	.079	.088
Germany		.059	.159	.138	.063	.151	.142
Ireland		.017	.063	.071	.021	.067	.059
Russia	.021	.100	.100	.092	.075	.088	.088

RELIGION

Jewish.................... .151
Protestant................ .636
Catholic................. .100
None.................... .113

The next step is to prepare a table of corresponding sigma values. This has been done in Table 38. Since the procedure of weighting is awkward in these calculations, we have merely dropped the most unreliable proportions, namely, those above .97 and those below .03. The rest are retained and are given equal weight in the calculations. It will be seen from the results that no serious damage is done by this additional approximation. The sign of each sigma value in Table 38 is positive when its corresponding proportion in Table 36 is above .50, and it is negative when the proportion is less than .50.

Let the scale values of the two nationalities whose scale separation is to be ascertained be designated S_1 and S_2, respectively. Let any other nationality be designated S_k. Then, by (2)

$$S_1 - S_k = x_{1k}\sqrt{2}, \qquad (3)$$

and

$$S_2 - S_k = x_{2k}\sqrt{2}.$$

TABLE 38

SIGMA VALUES CORRESPONDING TO TABLE 36

	American	Armenian	Chinese	Englishman	Frenchman	German	Greek	Hindu	Irishman	Italian	Japanese
American.	0.00			−1.27	−1.68	−1.73	+.11		−1.88	+.78	−.05
Armenian.		0.00	−.41			+1.35	+.45	−.61		+1.19	+.31
Chinese.		+.41	0.00		+1.68	+1.64		−.13		−1.88	
Englishman.	+1.27			0.00		−1.21	−1.11		+.69	−1.07	−1.64
Frenchman.	+1.68	−1.35	−1.68		0.00	−.26		−1.73		+.98	−.52
German.	+1.73	−.11	−1.64	+1.21	+.26	0.00		−1.83		+1.17	+.42
Greek.			−.45	+1.11			0.00	+.60	+1.88	−1.53	−1.61
Hindu.		+.61	+.13		+1.73	+1.83	+.60	0.00			−.57
Irishman.	+1.88	−.78	−1.19	−.69	+.31	−.37	−1.88	−1.17	0.00		
Italian.		+.05	−.31	+1.88	+.77	+1.07	+.98	−.42	+1.53	0.00	
Japanese.		+.31				+1.64	+.52	−.89	+1.61	+.57	0.00
Jew.	+1.67	+.31	+.82	+1.09	+.81	+.71	+.26	−.26	+.77	+.33	−.63
Mexican.		+.83	+.42				+.41	−.49		+1.38	+.09
Negro.		−.18	+.50	+1.77	+1.49	+1.21	+1.05	−.81	+1.68	+1.50	+.66
Pole.		−.36	−.55	+.59	−.37	+1.21	+.12	−.95	+1.30	+.87	−.36
Russian.		−1.68	−.88		+1.68	−.39	+.39		+.08	+.33	+.69
Scotchman.	+1.83	−.81	−1.17	+1.77	−.85	+1.07	−1.88	−1.02	+1.39	−1.43	
Spaniard.		−.87	−1.21	+1.17	+.85	+.95	+.65	−1.13	+1.13	−.04	−.84
South American.		−1.23	−1.60		+.28		−.80	−1.27	+.66	−.07	−1.21
Swede.		+.92	+.36			+.45	−1.38	+.42		−.84	−1.38
Turk.							+.80			+1.68	+.63
	10.06	−4.55	−11.34	10.01	5.98	9.27	−4.40	−11.91	10.14	3.23	−7.39

TABLE 38—Continued

	Jew	Mexican	Negro	Pole	Russian	Scotchman	Spaniard	South American	Swede	Turk	Check Column
American	−1.67					− 1.83	+.81	+.87	+1.23	−.92	−10.06
Armenian	+.31	−.31	−.83	+.18	+.36	+ 1.68	+1.17	+1.21	+1.60	−.36	4.55
Chinese	+.82	+.42	−.50	+.55	+.88			−1.77	−1.17		11.34
Englishman	−1.09				−1.77	.59	−1.68	+.85	−.28		−10.01
Frenchman	−.81				−1.49	.37	−1.07	−.95	−.45		−5.98
German	−.71	−.41	−1.05	−1.21	−1.21	.39	+.65	+.80	−1.38	−.80	9.27
Greek	++.26	+.26	−.49	+.12	+.39	+1.88	+1.02	+1.13	+1.27	−.42	4.40
Hindu	+.89			+.81	+.95		−1.39	−1.13	+.66		11.91
Irishman	−.77			−1.68	−1.30	−.08	−.04	+.07	+.84		−10.14
Italian	+.33	−1.38	−1.50	+.87	−.33	+1.43	+.84	+1.21	+1.38	−1.68	−3.23
Japanese	+.63	−.09	−.66	+.36	+.69		+.28	+.22	+.68	−.63	7.39
Jew	0.00	−.58	−1.34	+.03	+.03	+.87	+1.30	+.93	+1.56	−1.04	1.50
Mexican	+1.34	0.00	−.58	+.58	+.64		+1.53	+1.46	+1.77	+.25	5.86
Negro	++.03	+.58	0.00	+.96	+1.18	+1.68	+.40	+.49	+1.18	+1.03	14.10
Pole	++.03	+.58	−.96	0.00	+.21	+1.41	+.44	+.20	+.84	+1.34	3.16
Russian	−.87	−.64	−1.18	−.21	0.00	0.00	−1.68	−1.33	−.84		2.38
Scotchman	−.28		−1.53	−1.68	−1.41	+1.68	0.00	+.04	+.69	−1.73	−11.06
Spaniard	−.22	−1.30	−1.46	−.40	−.44	+1.33	−.04	0.00	+.72		−1.85
South American	−.68	−.93	−1.77	−.49	−.20	+.84	+.69	−.72	0.00		−3.61
Swede		−1.56	−1.77	−1.18	−.84			+1.73		0.00	−11.74
Turk	+1.04	+.66	−.25	+1.03	+1.34					0.00	10.36
	−1.50	−5.86	−14.10	−3.16	−2.38	11.06	1.85	3.61	11.74	−10.36	0.000

Subtracting,

$$(S_1 - S_2) = \sqrt{2}(x_{1k} - x_{2k}) .$$

Summing for all the nationalities, we have

$$n (S_1 - S_2) = \sqrt{2}\Sigma [x_{ik} - x_{2k}] ,$$

or

$$(S_1 - S_2) = \frac{\sqrt{2}}{n} [\Sigma x_{1k} - \Sigma x_{2k}] . \qquad (4)$$

This enables us to ascertain the scale separation $(S_1 - S_2)$ by making use of all the data. As an example of the application of the summation equation (4), Table 39 has been prepared. The first column is merely a list of the nationalities copied directly from Table 38. The second and third columns are copied directly from the columns "German" and "Swede" in Table 38.

The blank spaces in the second and third columns of Table 39 are transferred from Table 38. The entries in these spaces have been omitted from Table 38 because the proportions on which they are based are too unreliable, being either higher than .97 or lower than .03. In the fourth column of Table 39 are recorded the differences between the paired sigma values.

TABLE 39

CALCULATION OF SCALE VALUES

German (1)
Swede   (2)

	x_{1k}	x_{2k}	$(x_{1k}-x_{2k})$
American	−1.73	....	....
Armenian	1.35	1.23	0.12
Chinese	1.64	1.60	0.04
Englishman	−1.11	−1.17	0.06
Frenchman	−0.26	−0.28	0.02
German	0.00	−0.45	0.45
Greek	....	1.38	....
Hindu	1.83	1.27	0.56
Irishman	−0.37	−0.66	0.29
Italian	1.07	0.84	0.23
Japanese	1.64	1.38	0.26
Jew	0.71	0.68	0.03
Mexican	....	1.56	....
Negro	....	1.77	....
Pole	1.21	1.18	0.03
Russian	1.21	0.84	0.37
Scotchman	−0.39	−0.84	0.45
Spaniard	1.07	0.69	0.38
South American	0.95	0.72	0.23
Swede	0.45	0.00	0.45
Turk	....	....	....
	11.00	7.03	3.97

$$S_1 - S_2 = \frac{\sqrt{2} \cdot (3.97)}{16} = 0.3509$$

Check: $\Sigma(x_{1k} - x_{2k}) = \Sigma x_{1k} - \Sigma x_{2k} = 3.97$

Whenever one of the two sigma values is omitted, the corresponding difference is of course also omitted. The calculation of the scale separation between "German" and "Swede" is based therefore on the remaining sixteen pairs of sigma values, as shown in the fourth column of the table. This fourth column is really inserted primarily for the purpose of a check on the arithmetical work because it is not needed logically for the calculation.

At the foot of Table 39 the substitutions in the summation equation (4) are shown. The arithmetical check on the calculations is also self-explanatory in this case. The scale separation between these two nationalities is 0.3509.

The order in which the scale separations are calculated is given by the absolute rank orders of the twenty-one nationalities shown at the foot of Table 36. The first scale separation to be calculated was "American—Englishman." The second was "Englishman—Scotchman." The successive pairs are chosen from the absolute rank order of Table 36. Consequently there were twenty tables like Table 39 in the present study.

Theoretically, it should be possible to ascertain the scale separation between any two nationalities in the whole list even though they are quite far apart on the scale, but such a procedure would be based on a small number of paired sigma values, many of them dropping out because of low reliability. If two nationalities are widely separated on the scale, there will be so many proportions of 0 and 100 per cent that the scaling cannot be satisfactorily made. A least square solution could be laid out which would take into consideration all of the proportions in the whole of Table 36 with a system of weights, but the solution would be prohibitive. It would require the solution of a set of twenty normal equations with as many unknowns. Such a procedure is not feasible. For that reason the scale separations are determined for pairs of nationalities that are adjacent in absolute rank order.

In Table 40 we have a list of the scale separations of the twenty pairs of nationalities which have been calculated by the procedure shown in Table 39. The next step is to adopt the scale value of one of these nationalities as an origin. The scale value of "American" was chosen as an origin, and, since all other nationalities are preferred less often by our subjects, all of the other scale values are negative. In Table 41 the final scale values have been recorded. They are obtained directly from the scale separations of Table 40 with the scale value of "American" set at zero. It is of course clear that we are here dealing with a scale in which the origin is quite arbitrary. The law of comparative judgment gives the scale separation but says nothing about measurement from any origin.

In Figure 64 the scale values of Table 41 have been represented graphically, but it should be borne in mind that this figure represents merely the distribution of attitude toward these various nationalities in the particular group of this study. If we should want to compare the attitudes of two groups, it would be possible to scale the same list of nationalities for both groups separately and then to correlate the two sets of scale values. A high correlation between the two sets of scale values would show objectively that the two groups have very similar attitudes toward the nationalities in question, while a low correlation would indicate that the two groups are very different in their national preferences. It would, in fact, be rather interesting to make such comparisons for representative groups of students at the universities in different countries, and such a study is now being planned.

If two groups were to be compared in the manner suggested above, it is conceivable that the two scales would differ considerably in the range of scale

TABLE 40

SCALE SEPARATIONS

American—Englishman	1.3413
Englishman—Scotchman	.7549
Scotchman—Irishman	.0859
Irishman—Frenchman	.2830
Frenchman—German	.0919
German—Swede	.3509
Swede—South American	.7336
South American—Italian	.0269
Italian—Spaniard	.1242
Spaniard—Jew	.1281
Jew—Russian	.1803
Russian—Pole	.3175
Pole—Greek	.2047
Greek—Armenian	.0592
Armenian—Japanese	.2572
Japanese—Mexican	.1622
Mexican—Chinese	.2037
Chinese—Hindu	.0474
Hindu—Turk	.4678
Turk—Negro	.0479

values. The present group of subjects has a range of nearly six sigma for the whole list of twenty-one nationalities. Now, if another group should have a range of, say, only three sigma, it would indicate that the latter group is more international in its attitudes, more tolerant of national differences. A wide range of scale values indicates rather strong and rather uniform national preferences. An internationally minded group would give proportions hovering more closely about .50, and hence the scale separations would be, on the whole, smaller than the scale separations for a prejudiced group. We have here a psychophysical tool for making objective the national attitudes of a group. It is conceivable that the method may be of some use in the objective measurement of social attitudes that are usually reported with the prejudice or bias of individual authors and investigators.

With the twenty-one scale values before us in Table 41, we want to ascertain how much internal consistency we may have in such a scale. In order to test for internal consistency, we shall use the scale values as the basis for a set of calculated proportions which may be compared with the experimental proportions from which we started. We return to equation (2). With the scale values known we may calculate the value of x_{12}, and this may be converted into the corresponding proportion by the aid of a probability table. This will be the calculated proportion which is to be compared with the corresponding experimental proportion. An example of the calculations

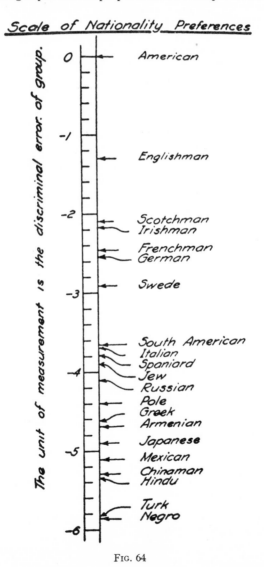

Fig. 64

is shown in Table 42. The first column contains the list of nationalities, as in the previous tables. The second column gives the calculated value of

$$x_{ak} = \frac{S_a - S_k}{\sqrt{2}}$$
$$= .707\ S_a - .707\ S_k\ ,$$

in which

x_{ak} = the sigma value of the calculated proportion of subjects who should prefer nationality "a" rather than nationality "k."

S_a = the scale value for "Swede."

S_k = the scale value of each of the other nationalities in turn. Consequently, the second column in Table 42 will be calculated by the formula

$$x_{ka} = .707 \times 2.9079 - .707\ S_k$$
$$= 2.0559 - .707\ S_k\ .$$

The next column gives the calculated proportion P_c corresponding to the calculated value of x_{ak}. It is obtained directly from the Kelley-Wood tables. Adjacent is the experimental proportion, P_e, obtained from Table 36. The discrepancy between the experimental and the calculated proportions is shown in the last column of Table 42. The average discrepancy for the whole column is calculated at the foot of the table. The last column of the table is

TABLE 41
SCALE VALUES

American	0.0000
Armenian	−4.6824
Chinese	−5.3055
Englishman	−1.3413
Frenchman	−2.4651
German	−2.5570
Greek	−4.6232
Hindu	−5.3529
Irishman	−2.1821
Italian	−3.6684
Japanese	−4.9396
Jew	−3.9207
Mexican	−5.1018
Negro	−5.8686
Pole	−4.4185
Russian	−4.1010
Scotchman	−2.0962
Spaniard	−3.7926
South American	−3.6415
Swede	−2.9079
Turk	−5.8207

inserted partly to enable one to inspect the discrepancy for each pair of nationalities and also for the purpose of arithmetical check on the calculations. The average discrepancy for the twenty nationalities compared with "Swede" is .03, which happens to be the same as the average discrepancy between Tables 36 and 43. The calculations in this study involved twenty-one tables like Table 42, one for each column of Table 36. The average discrepancy of .03 for the twenty comparisons with "Swede" is shown at the

TABLE 42

CALCULATION OF DISCREPANCIES FOR COLUMN "SWEDE" IN TABLE 1

	x_{ak}	P_c	P_e	$P_c - P_e$
American	−2.0559	.020	.017	.003
Armenian	1.2546	.895	.891	.004
Chinese	1.6951	.955	.945	.010
Englishman	−1.1076	.134	.122	.012
Frenchman	−0.3131	.377	.389	−.012
German	−0.2481	.402	.326	.076
Greek	1.2127	.887	.916	−.029
Hindu	1.7286	.958	.898	.060
Irishman	−0.5132	.304	.256	.048
Italian	0.5377	.705	.800	−.095
Japanese	1.4364	.925	.916	.009
Jew	0.7160	.763	.753	.010
Mexican	1.5511	.940	.941	−.001
Negro	2.0932	.982	.962	.020
Pole	1.0680	.857	.881	−.024
Russian	0.8435	.801	.799	.002
Scotchman	−0.5739	.283	.201	.082
Spaniard	0.6255	.734	.754	−.020
South American	0.5186	.698	.765	−.067
Swede	....	....	....	......
Turk	2.0593	.980	.974	.006
	12.5285	13.600	13.506	.094

$$(P_c - P_e) = .094$$

$$|P_c - P_e| = .590$$

$$\text{Average discrepancy} = \left|\frac{P_c - P_e}{n}\right| = \frac{.590}{20} = .030$$

Check for x_{ak}: $nS_a(.707) - \Sigma(.707)S_k = \Sigma(.707 \ S_a - .707 \ S_k) = 12.5285$
Check for $P_c - P_e$: $\Sigma P_c - \Sigma P_e = \Sigma(P_c = P_e) = .094$

foot of the column "Swede" in Table 43. The last row of Table 43 shows the average discrepancy for the twenty comparisons with each nationality.

Inspection of the discrepancies for the different nationalities reveals that the highest discrepancy of .06 occurs for "Jew." Since 15 per cent of the subjects were Jews and since the prejudice against them is common among other members of the group, it is quite probable that the distribution of attitude toward the Jews in this group of subjects deviates considerably from the normal probability curve. It might even be bimodal. Even if the distribution can be represented roughly as bell shaped, its dispersion would probably

TABLE 43

CALCULATED PROPORTIONS

	American	Armenian	Chinese	Englishman	Frenchman	German	Greek	Hindu	Irishman	Italian	Japanese
American		.000	.000	.171	.041	.035	.000	.000	.061	.005	.000
Armenian	1.000		.330	.991	.942	.934	.517	.318	.961	.763	.428
Chinese	1.000	.670		.997	.978	.974	.685	.487	.986	.876	.602
Englishman	.829	.009	.002		.214	.195	.010	.002	.276	.050	.005
Frenchman	.959	.058	.023	.787		.474	.063	.021	.579	.197	.040
German	.964	.067	.026	.805	.526		.072	.024	.605	.216	.046
Greek	1.000	.483	.315	.990	.936	.928		.303	.958	.750	.411
Hindu	1.000	.682	.513	.998	.979	.976	.697		.987	.883	.615
Irishman	.938	.039	.014	.724	.421	.395	.042	.013		.147	.026
Italian	.995	.237	.124	.950	.803	.784	.250	.117	.853		.184
Japanese	1.000	.572	.398	.995	.960	.954	.589	.385	.974	.816	
Jew	.997	.295	.164	.966	.848	.832	.310	.156	.891	.571	.236
Mexican	1.000	.617	.443	.996	.969	.964	.632	.430	.980	.845	.546
Negro	1.000	.799	.655	1.000	.992	.990	.811	.642	.995	.940	.744
Pole	1.000	.426	.265	.975	.916	.906	.442	.254	.943	.702	.356
Russian	.998	.341	.197	.703	.876	.862	.356	.188	.913	.620	.277
Scotchman	.931	.034	.012	.958	.397	.372	.037	.011	.476	.133	.022
Spaniard	.996	.265	.143	.958	.826	.809	.279	.135	.873	.535	.209
South American	.995	.231	.120	.948	.797	.778	.244	.113	.849	.492	.179
Swede	.980	.105	.045	.866	.623	.598	.113	.042	.696	.295	.075
Turk	1.000	.790	.642	1.000	.991	.989	.801	.630	.995	.936	.733
Σp	19.582	6.720	4.431	17.805	15.035	14.749	6.950	4.271	15.851	10.772	5.734
|Pc−Pe|	.012	.025	.020	.026	.040	.035	.032	.027	.031	.044	.028

TABLE 43—*Continued*

	Jew	Mexican	Negro	Pole	Russian	Scotchman	Spaniard	South American	Swede	Turk	Check Column
American	.003	.000	.000	.000	.001	.069	.004	.005	.020	.000	0.415
Armenian	.705	.383	.201	.574	.660	.966	.735	.769	.895	.210	13.282
Chinese	.836	.557	.345	.735	.803	.988	.858	.880	.955	.358	15.570
Englishman	.034	.004	.000	.015	.026	.297	.042	.052	.134	.000	2.196
Frenchman	.152	.031	.008	.084	.124	.603	.174	.203	.377	.009	4.966
German	.167	.036	.010	.094	.138	.628	.191	.222	.402	.011	5.250
Greek	.690	.368	.189	.558	.644	.963	.721	.756	.887	.199	13.049
Hindu	.844	.570	.358	.746	.812	.989	.865	.887	.958	.370	15.729
Irishman	.110	.020	.005	.057	.087	.524	.127	.151	.304	.005	4.149
Italian	.429	.155	.060	.298	.380	.867	.465	.508	.705	.064	9.228
Japanese	.764	.454	.256	.644	.723	.978	.791	.821	.925	.267	14.266
Jew		.202	.084	.363	.449	.901	.536	.578	.763	.090	10.232
Mexican	.798		.294	.685	.760	.983	.823	.849	.940	.306	14.860
Negro	.916	.706		.847	.894	.996	.929	.942	.982	.514	17.294
Pole	.637	.315	.153		.589	.950	.671	.709	.857	.161	12.237
Russian	.551	.240	.106	.411		.922	.586	.627	.801	.112	10.959
Scotchman	.099	.017	.004	.050	.078		.115	.137	.283	.004	3.915
Spaniard	.464	.177	.071	.329	.414	.885		.543	.734	.076	9.721
South American	.422	.151	.058	.291	.373	.863	.457		.698	.062	9.121
Swede	.237	.060	.018	.143	.199	.717	.266	.302		.020	6.400
Turk	.910	.694	.486	.839	.888	.996	.924	.938	.980		17.162
Σp	9.768	5.140	2.706	7.763	9.042	16.085	10.280	10.879	13.600	2.838	210.001
$|P_c - P_e|$	.061	.031	.018	.028	.022	.029	.041	.027	.030	.021	.628

Average discrepancy $= \dfrac{.628}{21} = .0299$

be larger in this group than the dispersion for other nationalities. Either one of these factors would cause a noticeable discrepancy between the experimental and the calculated proportions because our procedure in Case 5 assumes that the distribution of attitude toward each nationality is normal and that the dispersions are the same for all of the nationalities and races.

The average discrepancy between Tables 36 and 43 is shown in the last row of Table 43 to be .0299, or practically 3 per cent. It is very satisfactory considering the fact that the equation that has been used for the scaling contains a number of assumptions that are undoubtedly only roughly approximated by the data.

There were twenty-one repeated pairs in the original mimeographed forms on which the nationality preferences were recorded by the 239 subjects. These repetitions were so arranged that every nationality was represented twice in the twenty-one repeated pairs. The repetitions were scattered at random throughout the lists so that the subject would have slight opportunity to recall his first judgment on a particular pair if he was at all in doubt. The object of these extra or repeated pairs was to ascertain the average error of the original proportions themselves, so that these might be compared with the magnitude of the discrepancies between the experimental and calculated proportions. The average difference between the two proportions of the repeated pairs was .019 or nearly 2 per cent. When this error of the original proportions is compared with the discrepancy between the experimental and calculated proportions, which was .0299, or practically 3 per cent, it is seen that the psychophysical method here described fits the data with surprising accuracy. In fact, the average discrepancy of 2 per cent in the original experimental proportions accounts for a part of the discrepancy between the experimental and the calculated proportions.

Summary

1. The principal object of this study is to show that psychophysical formulations which are made ideally for discriminatory judgments of simple physical stimuli can be applied also to discriminatory judgments involving social values even when these values are loaded with prejudice or bias. The law of comparative judgment in its simplest form, Case 5, is here applied to discriminatory judgments of preference for nationalities and races. The group of 239 subjects was intentionally heterogeneous in that 40 per cent or more of the parents and grandparents were foreign born, 15 per cent were Jews, 64 per cent were Protestants, and 10 per cent were Catholics.

2. The method of paired comparison was used as the experimental procedure. A proportion of judgments of preference was determined for every possible pair of nationalities. On the basis of these experimentally observed proportions the scale value of each nationality or race was calculated by the law of comparative judgment. These are shown graphically in Figure 64.

3. The internal consistency of the calculations is shown by the discrepancies between the experimental and the calculated proportions. The average discrepancy between them was only 3 per cent. The average difference between the repeated proportions in the original form was 2 per cent.

4. The law of comparative judgment can be used for measuring objectively the degree of similarity between two groups as regards their national and racial attitudes, prejudice, or bias. This is accomplished by correlating the scale values of the same list of nationalities for both groups. If the correlation coefficient is high, the two groups are similar in their attitudes toward nationalities and races. If the coefficient is low, they are different in their national and racial preferences.

5. Another application of the law of comparative judgment is in the quantitative measurement of the degree of tolerance of a group for the nationalities in the list. Any measure of the scatter of scale values for the whole list can be used as a quantitative index of the tolerance of the group. When the scatter is wide, the tolerance is low. When the scatter is small, the group is correspondingly more tolerant.

6. The law of comparative judgment can be used to describe objectively the attitudes of a group of subjects toward nationalities and races. The same method can undoubtedly be used also for describing the attitudes of a group toward other social values which are saturated with prejudice and bias. The method is free from the effects of the personal bias of the individual investigator. It is hoped that psychophysical tools may find application not only in the restricted field of sensory discrimination but also in the study of other psychological and social values.

22 THEORY OF ATTITUDE MEASUREMENT

It is the purpose of this paper[1] to describe a new psychophysical method for measuring the psychological or functional similarity of attributes. Its development was motivated primarily for the solution of a particular problem in the measurement of social attitudes and it is in terms of this problem that the new psychophysical method will be described.

Let each of a group of N individuals be labeled as to the presence or absence of each of n attributes. This means that we are dealing with N persons and that each of these persons declares the presence or absence in him of each of the n attributes. It does not matter for our present purposes whether the declarations are made by these people for themselves or by others for them. In our particular problem we are dealing with a list of n statements of opinion, and each person has the option of indorsing or rejecting each of the n opinions. The statement of an opinion is here regarded as a description of an attribute, and the subject merely indicates whether he possesses the attribute. A similar analysis might be made for a series of traits which are supposed to describe people along an extroversion-introversion continuum, an ascendance-submission continuum, and so on. Our primary interest is here in the attitude continuum.

We postulate, for verification, an attitude continuum for the n opinions. Let them describe different attitudes toward the church for purposes of illustration. Some of the opinions reflect attitudes very favorable and loyal to the church; others are neutral or slightly favorable, while still others are slightly or strongly antagonistic to the church. We want an objective procedure for ascertaining whether any particular set of opinions really behaves as a continuum when the indorsements are analyzed.

Let us consider first a pair of opinions, one of which is clearly favorable to the church and the other as clearly antagonistic.

1. I feel the church services give me inspiration and help to live up to my best during the following week.
2. I think the church seeks to impose a lot of worn-out dogmas and medieval superstitions.

Now, on a common-sense basis, we should expect to find that of the people who indorse opinion 1 relatively few will indorse opinion 2. Similarly, those

[1] Reprinted from *Psychological Review*, XXXVI (1929), 222–41.

who indorse 2 will only seldom indorse 1. The following pair of opinions would probably behave differently.

1. I feel the church services give me inspiration and help to live up to my best during the following week.
3. I believe the church is the greatest influence for good government and right living.

If we consider the group of people who indorse 1, we should expect a rather high proportion also indorsing 3 because the two statements are both favorable to the church. The attitudes represented by these two statements may be expected to co-exist in the same person, while 1 and 2 are more or less mutually exclusive.

These facts suggest the possibility of measuring the psychological similarity of opinions in terms of the indorsements. For the two opinions we shall have the three following facts:

$n_{(1)}$ = the total number of individuals in the group N who indorse opinion No. 1.

$n_{(2)}$ = the total number of individuals in the group N who indorse opinion No. 2.

$n_{(12)}$ = the total number of individuals in the group N who indorse both 1 and 2.

Other things being equal, a relatively high value for $n_{(12)}$ means that the two statements are similar. A relatively low value for $n_{(12)}$ means that the two opinions are more or less mutually exclusive.

We shall avoid mere correlational procedures, since it is possible in this case to do better than merely to correlate the attributes. When a problem is so involved that no rational formulation is available, then some quantification is still possible by the calculation of coefficients of correlation or contingency and the like. But such statistical procedures constitute an acknowledgment of failure to rationalize the problem and to establish the functions that underlie the data. We want to measure the separation between the two opinions on the attitude continuum, and we want to test the validity of the assumed continuum by means of its internal consistency. This cannot be done if we had merely a set of correlational coefficients unless we could also know the functional relation between the correlation coefficient and the attitude separation which it signifies. Such a function requires the rationalization of the problem, and this might as well be done, if possible, directly, without using the correlational coefficients as intermediaries.

Before summarizing these indorsement counts into an index of similarity, we shall introduce another attribute of the statement, namely, its reliability. Suppose that there are $N_{(1)}$ individuals in the experimental population whose attitudes toward the church are such that they really should indorse statement 1 if they were conscientious and accurate and if the statement of opinion were a perfect statement of the attitude that it is intended to reflect. Now suppose that as a result of imperfections, obscurities, or irrelevancies in the statement, and inaccuracy or carelessness of the subjects, there are only $n_{(1)}$ indorsements of this statement. Then the reliability of the opinion would be defined by the ratio

$$p_1 = \frac{n_{(1)}}{N_{(1)}}. \tag{1}$$

The notation p_1 means the probability that the statement will be indorsed by a subject who would indorse it if he were accurate and if the statement were a perfect expression of the attitude it is intended to convey. The question naturally arises as to how to ascertain the value of N_1, which could be obtained directly only if the statement were perfect and the subjects absolutely accurate.

We shall consider three methods of determining approximately the reliability of each statement.

1. Let the whole list of opinions be presented twice in random order. If there are fifty opinions in the experimental list, there would be one hundred opinions to be read to the subjects, each opinion being repeated once. Let the indorsement counts for opinion 1 be as follows:

n_1 = total number of subjects who indorse the first presentation of No. 1.

n_1' = total number of subjects who indorse the second presentation of No. 1.

n_{12} = total number of subjects who indorse both presentations of No. 1.

The proportion of those who checked 1 who also checked 2 is

$$p_1 = \frac{n_{12}}{n_1}, \tag{2}$$

and we shall assume that this proportion is the same as the proportion of those whose attitudes are of opinion 1 who actually checked that opinion. In other words,

$$p_1 = \frac{n_1}{N_1}. \tag{1}$$

Similarly, for the second presentation of the same opinion, we have

$$p_1 = \frac{n_{12}}{n_1'} = \frac{n_1'}{N_1}. \tag{3}$$

But we cannot expect the experimental values of n_1 and n_1' to be exactly the same, so we shall use them both for determining the value of p_1 by the product of (2) and (3), so that

$$p_1^2 = \frac{n_{12}^2}{n_1 n_1'},$$

and hence

$$p_1 = \frac{n_{12}}{\sqrt{n_1 n_1'}} \quad \text{(reliability of an opinion) .} \quad (4)$$

2. A second procedure which should give at least roughly comparable results is as follows. Let the entire list of opinions be sorted into any convenient number of groups by the method of equal-appearing intervals. The statements may then be placed in rank order from those that are most antagonistic to the church to those that are most favorable. The detailed procedure for this scaling has been described elsewhere.[2] Then any two adjacent opinions will reflect practically the same attitude, especially if the list is as long as 40 or 50 opinions or more over the whole available range of the attitude continuum.

Let any two adjacent opinions in this rank order series be numbered 1 and 2, respectively. The total number of individuals in the experimental population whose attitudes are represented approximately by the adjacent opinions 1 and 2 may be designated N_{12}. If both of the statements were perfect and if the subjects were absolutely accurate, then we should expect to find n_{12} to be very nearly equal to N_{12}, which is the full number of subjects whose attitudes are that of opinions 1 and 2. Strictly speaking, we are combining here two factors of reliability into one, namely, the reliability of each opinion and the mean conscientiousness of the subjects. The reliability of the statement is the probability that a subject will indorse it if the subject's attitude is that of the opinion. It is a function of such characteristics of the statement as obscurity, subtlety or indirectness of its meaning, or actual ambiguity in its meaning. The reliability of the subject is the probability that he will indorse the opinions that he really should indorse in order truly to represent his attitude. This reliability is a function of such factors as the conscientiousness of the subject and the experimental arrangement. If the subject is asked to read several hundred statements of opinion, he will not read them so carefully as if he is asked to read only a dozen. But we have combined these factors of reliability into a single index, the probability that the statement will be indorsed by the people who should indorse it. If this type of analysis should prove to be fruitful, there will no doubt be further investigations in which these factors of reliability are analyzed separately and explicitly.

Since there are N_{12} individuals who should check opinion 1 and since the actual number who checked this opinion is only n_1, the probability that this statement will be indorsed by those who should indorse it is

$$p_1 = \frac{n_1}{N_{12}}, \quad (5)$$

---

[2] For distinction here made between opinion and attitude, see chap. xix. In this paper is described the construction of an attitude scale by the method of equal-appearing intervals.

and, similarly,

$$p_2 = \frac{n_2}{N_{12}}.\tag{6}$$

These two probabilities are assumed to be practically uncorrelated, so that

$$n_{12} = N_{12}p_1p_2 = \frac{n_1n_2}{N_{12}},\tag{7}$$

or

$$N_{12} = \frac{n_1n_2}{n_{12}},\tag{8}$$

and hence

$$p_1 = \frac{n_{12}}{n_2},\tag{9}$$

and

$$p_2 = \frac{n_{12}}{n_1}.\tag{10}$$

The assumption that the two probabilities of indorsement are uncorrelated is probably incorrect because the subject who is conscientious in reading one of these opinions will of course be likely to be conscientious also in reading the second opinion, and consequently the probability that the two opinions will both be indorsed is not, strictly speaking, the product of the two separate reliabilities. The approximation is perhaps sufficient for our purposes, and it may be hoped that it introduces no violent error.

The above procedure enables us to estimate the reliabilities of the opinions in terms of known data, but this particular method requires that the opinions in the experimental list be first sorted into a rank order series by the method of equal-appearing intervals or into a simple rank order series.

3. A third procedure is really identical with the second above except that instead of obtaining adjacent opinions by submitting the entire series of opinions to a large group for sorting, the experimenter selects adjacent statements by inspection. This is certainly not a safe procedure, and it should be discouraged. A modification that could be acceptable is to select pairs of opinions that are paraphrased forms of the same statement and then apply the logic of the second procedure above. It is by no means certain that these three methods of determining the reliability of a statement will give similar values. It might very well happen that the first procedure described above gives a measure of reliability in terms of factors more restricted than those which enter into the second and third procedures. If such is the case, the first procedure gives values that are too high, while the second and third procedures may give values more appropriate to our purposes.

We now have the following statistical facts about the two opinions whose separation on the attitude continuum is to be ascertained.

n_1 = total number of individuals who indorsed opinion No. 1.
n_2 = total number of individuals who indorsed opinion No. 2.
n_{12} = total number of individuals who indorsed both opinions.

p_1 = reliability of opinion No. 1.

p_2 = reliability of opinion No. 2.

Let one of the opinions have its scale value at S_1 on the attitude continuum of Figure 65. Let there be N_1 persons in the experimental group who should indorse it if they were absolutely accurate and if the statement of opinion were a perfect representation of the attitude it is intended to convey. The actual number of subjects who really do check this opinion is

$$n_1 = N_1 p_1 , \qquad (11)$$

in which p_1 is the reliability of the statement.

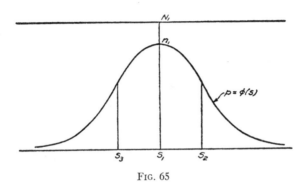

FIG. 65

Now consider another statement whose scale value is at S_2 on the attitude continuum. Since there is a difference $(S_2 - S_1)$ between the attitudes of these two statements, we should not expect all of the n_1 subjects to indorse this second statement. If it were perfect in reliability, then the number of subjects in the group n_1 who also indorse statement 2 will be

$$n_1 \phi = N_1 p_1 \phi , \qquad (12)$$

where ϕ is some value less than unity. Now, it is reasonable to assume that if the two statements are far apart on the scale, then the proportion ϕ of the group n_1 who also indorse the distant statement 2 will be small. This is represented in Figure 65 by the fact that ϕ is a maximum when the separation $(S_2 - S_1)$ is small, while it approaches zero as this separation becomes large. We shall assume that this function is symmetrical about the axis at S_1, so that

$$p_{1(k)} = \phi(S_k - S_1)^2 , \qquad (13)$$

in which $p_{1(k)}$ is the proportion of those who indorse statement 1 who also indorse statement k, while S_k is the scale value of statement k. Our assumption is that $p_{1(k)}$ is a function of the separation $(S_k - S_1)$ but that it is independent of the sign of the separation, which is an arbitrary matter.

We must also take into consideration the fact that statement 2 is probably imperfect as well as statement 1. Let its reliaibity be p_2, and we shall then say that the number of those who check statement 1 who also check statement 2 is

$$n_{12} = n_1\phi p_2 = N_1 p_1 p_2 \phi . \tag{14}$$

The number of those who checked No. 1 who also checked No. 2 is of course the same as the number of those who checked No. 2 and who also checked No. 1. Hence, we may write, by analogy,

$$n_{12} = N_2 p_1 p_2 \phi , \tag{15}$$

or

$$n_{12} = n_1 p_2 \phi , \tag{16}$$

$$n_{12} = n_2 p_1 \phi ,$$

and hence

$$n_{12}^2 = p_1 p_2 n_1 n_2 \phi^2 , \tag{17}$$

or

$$\phi = \frac{n_{12}}{\sqrt{p_1 p_2 n_1 n_2}} . \tag{18}$$

This is the coefficient of similarity of two statements of opinion. When this value is relatively high, the two statements belong close together on the scale, but when ϕ is small, they are far apart.

This formula may be used to determine the reliabilities p_1 and p_2 if the two statements are known to have practically the same scale value. This fact may be known either because of the fact that they are statements of the same idea, one being a paraphrase of the other, or by being scaled by the method of equal-appearing intervals, previously described. Since the coefficient ϕ deviates from unity supposedly only on account of the scale separations, it is in this case unity, the two statements having practically the same scale value. Then

$$1 = \frac{n_{12}}{\sqrt{p_1 p_2 n_1 n_2}} . \tag{19}$$

But

$$N_1 = N_2 ,$$

since both of these symbols represent the same quantity, namely, the number of people in the total group who should indorse both statements at the same scale value if both statements were perfect. Hence

$$N_1 = N_2 = \frac{n_1}{p_1} = \frac{n_2}{p_2} , \tag{20}$$

or

$$n_1 p_2 = p_1 n_2 , \tag{21}$$

and

$$p_2 = \frac{p_1 n_2}{n_1} . \tag{22}$$

Substituting (22) in (19), we have

$$1 = \frac{n_{12}}{\sqrt{p_1 p_2 n_1 n_2}} = \frac{n_{12}}{p_1 n_2} , \tag{23}$$

and hence

$$p_1 = \frac{n_{12}}{n_2} \qquad \text{(for identical or adjacent opinions)} \qquad (24)$$

and, by analogy,

$$p_2 = \frac{n_{12}}{n_1} \qquad \text{(for identical or adjacent opinions)} . \qquad (25)$$

Our next problem concerns the exact formulation of the function

$$\phi_{1k} = f(S_k - S_1) .$$

We shall try first the assumption that it is Gaussian, so that

$$\phi_{12} = \frac{1}{\sqrt{2\pi} \cdot \sigma} \, e^{-(s_1 - s_2)^2/2\sigma^2} . \qquad (26)$$

This means that if a man has indorsed any particular perfect statement No. 1, the probability that he will also indorse another perfect statement No. 2, distant from No. 1 by the scale separation $|S_1 - S_2|$, is assumed to be a Gaussian function of the scale separation. This assumption can be tested empirically by the internal consistency of the scale, but the function can also be studied directly without this assumption by methods that will be left for separate publication. We shall assume for the present experiment that this ϕ-function has a maximum value of unity when the scale separation is zero.

We shall test the index of similarity on a set of ten statements of opinions selected at random from different parts of an attitude scale of 45 such statements. The random set of ten statements is less unwieldy to handle for illustrative purposes than the whole list of 45 in the church scale because the index involves a comparison of each statement with every other statement in the whole list. There will be therefore $10 \cdot 9 \cdot \frac{1}{2} = 45$ comparisons for a set of 10 statements, while there would be $45 \cdot 44 \cdot \frac{1}{2} = 990$ comparisons necessary to handle the whole table of 45 statements.

The ten statements were selected so as to represent several degrees of attitude toward the church, including favorable, unfavorable, and indifferent opinions. Each statement is identified by a code number as follows:

2. I feel the church services give me inspiration and help to live up to my best during the following week.
4. I find the services of the church both restful and inspiring.
6. I believe in what the church teaches but with mental reservations.
11. I believe church membership is almost essential to living life at its best.
15. Sometimes I feel that the church and religion are necessary, and sometimes I doubt it.
32. I believe in sincerity and goodness without any church ceremonies.
34. I think the organized church is an enemy of science and truth.
35. I believe the church is losing ground as education advances.

41. I think the church seeks to impose a lot of worn-out dogmas and medieval superstitions.

43. I like the ceremonies of my church but do not miss them much when I stay away.

In Table 44 we have all the necessary raw data. There are three types of fact here recorded: (1) The total number of individuals who indorsed each of the ten statements. These are found in the diagonal of the table. For example, there were 696 individuals who indorsed statement 4 in the total group of about 1,500 persons who filled in the complete attitude scale. (2) The total number of individuals who indorsed any particular statement and any other particular statement. These data are found in the body of the table. For example, there were 263 individuals who indorsed both statements

TABLE 44

NUMBER OF DOUBLE INDORSEMENTS FOR ALL PAIRS OF OPINIONS

	11	2	4	6	43	15	32	35	41	34
11......	454	334	349	209	60	66	64	85	19	15
2......	334	573	492	263	72	85	81	88	23	15
4......	349	492	696	354	127	163	148	152	26	28
6......	209	263	354	620	152	221	220	225	67	54
43......	60	72	127	152	265	122	116	116	46	33
15......	66	85	163	221	122	407	207	214	72	67
32......	64	81	148	220	116	207	546	315	142	136
35......	85	88	152	225	116	214	315	548	165	166
41......	19	23	26	67	46	72	142	165	224	123
34......	15	15	28	54	33	67	136	166	123	219
p......	.57	.72	.80	.57	.31	.43	.63	.61	.60	.71

6 and 2. (3) The reliability of each of the ten statements. These are found in the last row of the table. They were determined by the second method described above, which was applied to each of the statements in the whole scale of forty-five opinions. For example, the reliability of statement 32 is .63, which means that it was indorsed by 63 per cent of the estimated number of people who should have indorsed it if the statement had been perfect and if the subjects had been perfect in their reading and indorsing.

In Table 45 we have listed the ϕ-values for all the comparisons. This is done by equation (18). The following is an example of the calculation of the ϕ-coefficient for the two statements 4 and 32 with data from Table 44.

$$\phi_{4.32} = \frac{148}{\sqrt{.80 \times .63 \times 696 \times 546}} = .34 .$$

It is seen that the table is symmetrical. The entries along the diagonal are necessarily unity because there is of course no scale separation between a statement and itself. We shall now use these ϕ-values to measure the scale separation between all pairs of statements. This is done by entering an ordinary probability table with the values of ϕ in order to ascertain the deviation from the mean in terms of the standard deviation of the assumed Gaussian function. Each of these deviations will be regarded tentatively as the scale separation between the two statements concerned. When the value of ϕ is small, we shall therefore assign a rather large separation to the two statements. When the value of ϕ is high, near unity, we shall assign a rather small scale separation to the statements. It is more convenient for this prob-

TABLE 45

THE ϕ-COEFFICIENTS OF SIMILARITY FOR ALL PAIRS OF OPINIONS

	11	2	4	6	43	15	32	35	41	34
11.........	1.00	1.02	.92	.69	.41	.31	.21	.29	.10	.07
2.........	1.02	1.00	1.03	.69	.39	.32	.22	.24	.10	.06
4.........	.92	1.03	1.00	.80	.59	.52	.34	.35	.10	.10
6.........	.69	.69	.80	1.00	.89	.89	.63	.65	.31	.23
43.........	.41	.39	.59	.89	1.00	1.02	.69	.70	.44	.29
15.........	.31	.32	.52	.89	1.02	1.00	.85	.89	.47	.41
32.........	.21	.22	.34	.63	.69	.85	1.00	.93	.66	.59
35.........	.29	.24	.35	.65	.70	.89	.93	1.00	.78	.73
41.........	.10	.10	.10	.31	.44	.47	.66	.78	1.00	.85
34.........	.07	.06	.10	.23	.29	.41	.59	.73	.85	1.00

TABLE 46

EXPERIMENTAL SCALE SEPARATIONS BETWEEN ALL PAIRS OF OPINIONS $(S_{top} - S_{side})$

	11	2	4	6	43	15	32	35	41	34
11....	.00	.00	− .41	− .86	−1.34	−1.53	−1.77	−1.57	......	......
2....	.00	.00	.00	− .86	−1.37	−1.51	−1.74	−1.69	......	......
4....	.41	.00	.00	− .67	−1.03	−1.14	−1.47	−1.45	......	......
6....	.86	.86	.67	.00	− .48	− .48	− .96	− .93	−1.53	−1.71
43....	1.34	1.37	1.03	.48	.00	.00	− .86	− .84	−1.28	−1.57
15....	1.53	1.51	1.14	.48	.00	.00	− .57	− .48	−1.23	−1.34
32....	1.77	1.74	1.47	.96	.86	.57	.00	− .38	− .91	−1.03
35....	1.57	1.69	1.45	.93	.84	.48	.38	.00	− .70	− .79
41....	......	......	......	1.53	1.28	1.23	.91	.70	.00	− .57
34....	......	......	......	1.71	1.57	1.34	1.03	.79	.57	.00

lem to use a probability table in which the maximum ordinate is unity than to use a table in which the total area is unity so that the maximum ordinate is .4. It is also more convenient to use a probability table which is entered with the ordinate to ascertain the deviation rather than to use a table which is entered with deviations or proportions to ascertain the ordinates. The latter kind of probability table requires interpolation for this problem. The separation between statements 43 and 6 may be taken as an example. The ϕ-coefficient for these two statements is .89, as shown in Table 45. With this ordinate of the probability curve, the deviation is .48σ, as recorded in Table 46.

The sign of the deviation is determined by the end of the scale which is arbitrarily called positive. In the present case the origin was arbitrarily placed at the opinion least favorable to the church, namely, statement 34. Therefore the statements favorable to the church are arbitrarily called positive with regard to the statements that are unfavorable to the church. It is entirely immaterial for scaling purposes which ends of the sequence of opinions are designated as positive and negative.

The signs in Table 46 are recorded so as to show $(S_{\text{top}} - S_{\text{side}})$. For example, the scale separation $(S_{43} - S_6)$ is found at the intersection of 43 at the top with 6 at the side. It is $-.48\sigma$. Similarly the separation $(S_6 - S_{43})$ is found at the intersection of 6 at the top with 43 at the side. It is $+.48\sigma$. The two halves of the table are symmetrical about the diagonal of zero entries. The ten statements were arranged in Table 44 in order of scale values determined by the method of equal-appearing intervals.[3] All separations as large as $2.\sigma$ or larger were ignored in Table 46 because when the separations become as large as that, their reliabilities become too low to be acceptable. It is entirely arbitrary at what limit we shall drop the separations. They might be extended indefinitely if the observations were weighted, but that is too awkward. In these tables we have recorded separations only as large as $2.\sigma$. There may also be some uncertainty as to how far the Gaussian curve can be used for the function $\phi = f(s)$, and this is another reason for not using scale separations larger than about $2.\sigma$.

We are now ready to determine the average scale separation between successive statements in the present list of ten. It is done as follows:

Let S_1 and S_2 be the scale values of any two statements whose separation is to be measured. Then

$$x_{12} = S_1 - S_2 \qquad (27)$$

is a direct measurement of this separation which is obtained by the index of similarity ϕ_{12}. This index is in turn a function of the raw data n_1, n_2, n_{12}, p_1, p_2, so that

$$\phi_{12} = \frac{n_{12}}{\sqrt{n_1 n_2 p_1 p_2}} = \frac{1}{\sqrt{2\pi}\,\sigma}\, e^{-(S_1 - S_2)^2/2\sigma^2} = \frac{1}{\sqrt{2\pi}\,\sigma}\, e^{-x^2_{12}/2\sigma^2}. \qquad (28)$$

But we also have many indirect measurements of x_{12} which may be shown as follows.

Let S_k be the scale value of any other statement except 1 and 2. Then

$$S_1 - S_k = x_{1k},$$
$$S_2 - S_k = x_{2k},$$

---

[3] A monograph, *The Measurement of Attitude toward the Church* by Thurstone and Chave, (Chicago: University of Chicago Press, 1929). This monograph describes the construction and use of a scale of 45 opinions about the church and the distributions of attitude in several large groups.

so that

$$S_1 - S_2 = x_{1k} - x_{2k} ,\qquad (29)$$

and hence

$$S_1 - S_2 = \frac{1}{n}(\Sigma x_{1k} - \Sigma x_{2k}) .\qquad (30)$$

This equation is more accurate than (27) because it makes use of all the data in Table 44, while equation (27) makes use of only one of the ϕ-coefficients. Applying equation (30) to the data of Table 46 where n is in each of the nine successive comparisons the number of paired values, we obtain the successive scale separations shown in Table 47. We set the origin arbitrarily at state-

TABLE 47

34.	0.0000
	.2757
41.	.2757
	.5629
35.	.8386
	.0800
32.	.9186
	.4010
15.	1.3196
	.1370
43.	1.4566
	.3370
6.	1.7936
	.6113
4.	2.4049
	.2275
2.	2.6324
	.0388
11.	2.6712

ment 34, so that the final scale values from this origin are as shown in Table 47. For example, the final scale separation between opinions 4 and 6 is obtained by equation (30). There are eight paired values for these two opinions in Table 46. The numerical values are as follows:

$$\Sigma x_{4k} = +5.35, \qquad n = 8 ,$$
$$\Sigma x_{6k} = +0.46, \qquad S_4 - S_6 = +0.6113 .$$

Note that the sum Σx_{6k} takes a different value when equation (30) is used to determine the scale separation between opinions 6 and 43 because there are then available ten paired values instead of eight for the interval 4 to 6.

We now want to test the internal consistency of our calculations. On the basis of the final scale values of Table 47 we may construct a table of calculated scale separations. This has been done in Table 48. For example, the scale values of statements 43 and 35 are 1.46 and .84, respectively. Consequently, the calculated scale separation $(S_{43} - S_{35})$ is $+0.62$, as recorded in Table 48, and the separation $(S_{35} - S_{43})$ is the same distance with sign reversed, namely, -0.62, also recorded in the same table. The separations of Table 48 are based entirely on the ten scale values of Table 47.

Now we want to know how closely these calculated scale separations of Table 48, based on the ten scale values, agree with the 45 experimentally independent scale separations of Table 46. The discrepancies between Tables 46 and 48 are listed individually in Table 49. The discrepancies between the

TABLE 48

CALCULATED SCALE SEPARATIONS OF ALL PAIRS OF OPINIONS $(S_{top} - S_{side})$

	11	2	4	6	43	15	32	35	41	34	Σ
11....	.00	−.04	−.27	−.88	−1.21	−1.35	−1.75	−1.83	−2.40	−2.67	−12.40
2....	.04	.00	−.23	−.84	−1.18	−1.31	−1.71	−1.79	−2.36	−2.63	−12.01
4....	.27	.23	.00	−.61	−.95	−1.09	−1.49	−1.57	−2.13	−2.40	−9.74
6....	.88	.84	.61	.00	−.34	−.47	−.88	−.96	−1.52	−1.79	−3.63
43....	1.21	1.18	.95	.34	.00	−.14	−.54	−.62	−1.18	−1.46	−.26
15....	1.35	1.31	1.09	.47	.14	.00	−.40	−.48	−1.04	−1.32	1.12
32....	1.75	1.71	1.49	.88	.54	.40	.00	−.08	−.64	−.92	5.13
35....	1.83	1.79	1.57	.96	.62	.48	.08	.00	−.56	−.84	5.93
41....	2.40	2.36	2.13	1.52	1.18	1.04	.64	.56	.00	−.28	11.55
34....	2.67	2.63	2.40	1.79	1.46	1.32	.92	.84	.28	.00	14.31
Σ.....	12.40	12.01	9.74	3.63	.26	−1.12	−5.13	−5.93	−11.55	−14.31	0.00

TABLE 49

DISCREPANCIES BETWEEN EXPERIMENTAL AND CALCULATED SCALE SEPARATIONS

	11	2	4	6	43	15	32	35	41	34	Σ
11....	.00	.04	−.14	.02	−.13	−.18	−.02	.26	.....	.....	−.15
2....	−.04	.00	.23	−.02	−.19	−.20	−.03	.10	.....	.....	−.15
4....	.14	−.23	.00	−.06	−.08	−.05	.02	.12	.....	.....	−.14
6....	−.02	.02	.06	.00	−.14	−.01	−.08	.03	−.01	.08	−.07
43....	.13	.19	.08	.14	.00	.14	−.32	−.22	−.10	−.11	−.07
15....	.18	.20	.05	.01	−.14	.00	−.17	.00	−.19	−.02	−.08
32....	.02	.03	−.02	.08	.32	.17	.00	−.30	−.27	−.11	−.08
35....	−.26	−.10	−.12	−.03	.22	.00	.30	.00	−.14	.05	−.08
41....	.....	.....	.....	.01	.10	.19	.27	.14	.00	−.29	.42
34....	.....	.....	.....	−.08	.11	.02	.11	−.05	.29	.00	.40
Σ.....	.15	.15	.14	.07	.07	.08	.08	.08	−.42	−.40	.000

$$\text{Average discrepancy} = \frac{\Sigma\,|\,x_e - x_c\,|}{N} = \frac{9.34}{88} = 0.106$$

experimental and the calculated scale separations in Table 49 vary between zero and $.32\sigma$, with a mean discrepancy of only $.106\sigma$. This mean discrepancy is only about $\frac{1}{25}$ or 4 per cent of the range of the scale values, 2.67σ, for the ten statements. Another set of ten statements, also selected at random from the entire list, has been subjected to the same analysis with comparable results.

The question might be raised why we have not used correlational coefficients instead of the ϕ-coefficient here described. Dissimilarity can of course be indicated merely by a correlational index or by contingency methods. Such indexes do not constitute measurement except by a generous interpretation of the word "measurement." We have attempted truly to measure degree of functional dissimilarity of two attributes or reactions. In order to satisfy what seems to be a fundamental requirement of measurement, it is reasonable to expect that if the difference between two entities a and b is, let us say, plus five units, and if the difference between two entities b and c is, let us say, plus three units, then the difference between the two entities a and c should be the sum of these two differences, namely, plus eight units, if all three quantities really measure the same attribute.

This simple requirement is not satisfied by correlational coefficients. If the correlation between a and b is .80 and that of b and c is .40, it does not follow that the correlation between a and c is some additive function of these coefficients. We have postulated a continuum, the attitude scale, and we want to measure separations between points on this continuum so that our measurements are internally consistent, so that $(a - b) + (b - c) = (a - c)$, but such consistency is not found by correlational procedures.

Let it be desired to measure the areas of a lot of circles. Let the diameter of each circle be used as an index of area. It is now possible to arrange the circles in rank order according to area by means of the diameter index. It is also possible to say of two circles that they must have the same areas because their diameters are equal, but these diameter measurements are hardly to be called measurements of areas. Equal increments of the diameter index do not correspond to equal increments of what we set out to measure, namely, area. The unit of measurement of the diameter does not correspond to a constant increment of area. All of this is childishly simple, but the reasoning is the same as regards correlational coefficients. They are not measures of dissimilarity. They are merely numerical indexes of dissimilarity. In fact, correlation coefficients are what one resorts to in the absence of hypothesis and rational formulation. If the problem admits of rational formulation, then that function should be written and tested directly by experiment. If the problem is so complex that it defies analysis, we can still correlate the variables and represent by correlation coefficients the degree of association between them. That is better than nothing, but it is not really measurement by our simple criteria. These considerations have led me to regard correlation coefficients as symbols of defeat. They constitute a challenge to try again and to outgrow the necessity for using them.

My efforts recently in psychological measurement have been to define in every case a continuum, to allocate people, tasks, and other entities to the continuum under investigation, and to check its validity by the simple criteria that have just been described. I believe that such efforts will prove more fruitful for psychological theory than merely to correlate everything with everything else under heaven.

The results of our attempt to construct an attitude continuum are shown graphically in Figure 66, in which the ten opinions are shown with their allocations to the attitude scale. An actual scale for measuring attitude should contain many more opinions, and they should be so selected that they constitute as far as possible an evenly graduated scale. The church scale previously referred to has 45 opinions which have been selected from a list of 130 so as to constitute an evenly graduated scale. Our present purpose has been to show how the *method of similar reactions* enables us to construct

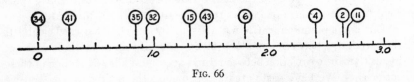

FIG. 66

such a scale from the records of indorsements. It is hoped that the method may also prove useful as an objective test for the validity of other concepts such as extroversion-introversion, ascendance-submission, and the like.

Summary

We have developed a new psychophysical method for measuring the psychological dissimilarity of attributes. This method assumes that if two attributes tend to coexist in the same individual, they are regarded as functionally similar, while if they are more or less mutually exclusive so that they tend not to coexist in the same individual, then they are functionally dissimilar. The degree of similarity is measured in terms of the ϕ-coefficient, which enables us to allocate the attributes along a single continuum and to measure the degree of similarity by scale separations on this continuum or scale. The method may be called a *method of similar attributes* or a *method of similar reactions*.

The ϕ-coefficient enables us to ascertain whether a series of attributes really belongs functionally on the same continuum. This is done by the test of internal consistency, as shown in Table 49. The method has been applied to the record of indorsements of 1,500 people to ten statements of opinion about the church. It has been shown that these opinions can be allocated to a single continuum with measured scale separations. It has been the purpose of this study to make a rational formulation for the association of attributes by which the existence of continuity in a series of attributes may be experimentally established and by which their functional dissimilarities, the scale separations, may be truly measured. For these purposes correlational procedures are inadequate because correlational coefficients are not measurements.

23 A SCALE FOR MEASURING ATTITUDE TOWARD THE MOVIES

The purpose of this paper[1] is to present a scale for measuring attitude toward the movies and to describe the method of its construction. This study was undertaken as one of the projects of the Payne Fund of New York. The research program is directed by Professor W. W. Charters of Ohio State University.

The original collection of opinions about the movies consisted of 258 statements. These opinions, each of which reflects an attitude toward the movies, vary from statements decidedly in favor of the movies through neutral statements to those very much opposed to the movies. They were obtained from literature on the subject, from conversation, and from direct questioning of subjects whose education and experience varied from that of seventh-grade children to that of graduate students in the university.

Each statement was then typewritten on a separate card. As a preliminary method of eliminating the most unsatisfactory and retaining the best statements, as well as to get an approximate idea of the scale values of the statements, the method of equal-appearing intervals[2] was used with a small group of sorters. Twenty-five people who had some understanding of the method being used and who were carefully chosen to make sure that the directions would be thoroughly understood and complied with sorted the cards into eleven piles according to the following instructions:

These cards contain statements about the value of the movies. Please arrange these cards in eleven piles so that those expressing attitudes most strongly in favor of the movies are in pile one, those which are neutral are in pile six, and those which are most strongly against the movies are in the eleventh pile. The intermediate piles should represent equal steps in appreciation or depreciation of the movies.

Do not try to get the same number of cards in each pile. They are not evenly distributed.

The numbers on the cards are code numbers and have nothing to do with the arrangement in piles.

You will find it easier to sort them if you look over a number of the slips, chosen at random, before you begin to sort.

[1] Acknowledgment is made to Miss Ruth Peterson for assistance throughout the entire study and to Miss Marie Thiele for the collection of the original set of statements. Reprinted from *Journal of Educational Research*, XXII (1930), 89–94.

[2] See chap. xix.

The results of these twenty-five sortings were tabulated to show in which piles each statement was placed by the group of sorters. The scale values were then determined graphically. As an example of the method used, one of the graphs is reproduced below.

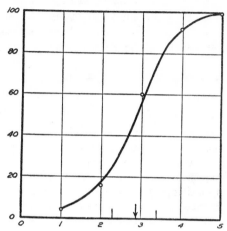

Statement Number 101, "Movies increase one's appreciation of beauty."
$Q_1 = 2.25$
$M = 2.90$
$Q_3 = 3.45$

The figure represents statement Number 101 of the original group which happens to be retained in the final scale as Number 12. The graph shows that all the sorters classified the statement as favorable to the movies. The statement reads "Movies increase one's appreciation of beauty." The curve crosses the 50 per cent level at the value of 2.9. This scale value is such that half the readers classified it as favorable to movies and half of them as less favorable.

The scale value is indicated by the arrowhead on the base line. The lighter lines on either side of the arrowhead indicate the quartile range of values assigned to the statements. The Q-value in this case is 1.20. This is a measure of the ambiguity of the statement.

For the application of a more exact scaling technique 100 statements were chosen from the 258. The choice was based on the following criteria:

(1) A continuity of scale values, i.e., a selection of approximately the same number from each region of the scale.

(2) Selection of statements with small Q-values.

(3) Diction and clearness of the statement itself.

The average Q-value of the statements retained was 1.18, with a range of .40 to 1.90, while the average Q-value of those statements not retained was 1.44, with a range of .50 to 3.25.

Two hundred sets of these one hundred statements were then printed on three by five cards.

The one hundred statements were then arranged in ten envelopes for rank order sortings. The first envelope contained the fifteen statements most strongly in favor of the movies as determined by the preliminary scaling method. The second envelope contained statements 8 to 22, the third envelope 18 to 32, and so on, the tenth envelope containing statements 86 to 100. Thus it is seen that fifty of the one hundred statements were repeated in two envelopes.

The statements in each envelope were in random order, and the envelopes were also put in random order. The ten envelopes of statements were presented to the people who were to sort them with the following directions.

Each envelope in this series contains fifteen cards. On each card is a statement about the movies. Some of these statements are in favor of the movies, and some of them are against the movies. Will you arrange the fifteen statements in each envelope so that the statement which is most in favor of the movies is on top, face up, and the statement which is least in favor of the movies or most strongly against the movies is on the bottom. The cards should all be arranged so that each card is more in favor of the movies than the card under it and less in favor of the movies than the card above it.

In considering each statement ask yourself this question:

"How strongly in favor of the movies is a person who indorses or agrees with this statement?" Try to disregard your own attitude toward the statements.

The identification numbers on the cards have no significance.

Two hundred people sorted the statements by the above directions, putting the fifteen statements in each envelope in rank order.

The results of these sortings were tabulated, and from the tabulations we determined the proportion of times each statement was rated as more strongly in favor of the movies than every other statement. From these proportions the scale separations of the statements in each envelope were determined from the formula[3]

$$b - a = \frac{\Sigma x_{ka} - \Sigma x_{kb}}{n},$$

in which $(b - a)$ is the scale separation between a and b.

x_{ka} is the deviation $(k - a)$ in terms of the standard deviation. It is ascertained from the probability tables by means of the observed proportions $k > a$.

x_{kb} is the deviation $(k - b)$ in terms of the standard deviation.

n is the number of statements minus one.

Since there were overlapping statements in each adjacent pair of envelopes, the scale separations for the whole set of one hundred statements could be calculated. The final scale values of the one hundred statements

[3] See chap. vii, equation (5), p. 74.

ranged from 4.74, the most strongly in favor of the movies, to 0.00, the most strongly against the movies.

The one hundred statements were then divided into ten groups, with a range of .5 scale step in each group. Subsequently, four statements were selected from each group, arriving at a final attitude scale consisting of forty statements approximately evenly spaced on the scale. The complete scale is given below, and the scale value of each statement is shown in parentheses following its serial number. The statements have been arranged in random order.

ATTITUDE TOWARD MOVIES

This is a study of attitudes toward the movies. On the following pages you will find a number of statements expressing different attitudes toward the movies.

√ Put a check mark if you agree with the statement.

✕ Put a cross if you disagree with the statement.

If you simply cannot decide about a statement you may mark it with a question mark.

This is not an examination. There are no right or wrong answers to these statements. This is simply a study of people's attitudes toward the movies. Please indicate your own attitude by a check mark when you agree and by a cross when you disagree.

LIST OF OPINIONS IN THE SCALE

1. (1.5) The movies occupy time that should be spent in more wholesome recreation.
2. (1.3) I am tired of the movies; I have seen too many poor ones.
3. (4.5) The movies are the best civilizing device ever developed.
4. (0.2) Movies are the most important cause of crime.
5. (2.7) Movies are all right but a few of them give the rest a bad name.
6. (2.6) I like to see movies once in a while but they do disappoint you sometimes.
7. (2.9) I think the movies are fairly interesting.
8. (2.7) Movies are just a harmless pastime.
9. (1.7) The movies to me are just a way to kill time.
10. (4.0) The influence of the movies is decidedly for good.
11. (3.9) The movies are good, clean entertainment.
12. (3.9) Movies increase one's appreciation of beauty.
13. (1.7) I'd never miss the movies if we didn't have them.
14. (2.4) Sometimes I feel that the movies are desirable and sometimes I doubt it.
15. (0.0) It is a sin to go to the movies.
16. (4.3) There would be very little progress without the movies.
17. (4.3) The movies are the most vital form of art today.
18. (3.6) A movie is the best entertainment that can be obtained cheaply.
19. (3.4) A movie once in a while is a good thing for everybody.
20. (3.4) The movies are one of the few things I can enjoy by myself.
21. (1.3) Going to the movies is a foolish way to spend your money.
22. (1.1) Moving pictures bore me.

23. (0.6) As they now exist movies are wholly bad for children.
24. (0.6) Such a pernicious influence as the movies is bound to weaken the moral fiber of those who attend.
25. (0.3) As a protest against movies we should pledge ourselves never to attend them.
26. (0.1) The movies are the most important single influence for evil.
27. (4.7) The movies are the most powerful influence for good in American life.
28. (2.3) I would go to the movies more often if I were sure of finding something good.
29. (4.1) If I had my choice of anything I wanted to do, I would go to the movies.
30. (2.2) The pleasure people get from the movies just about balances the harm they do.
31. (2.0) I don't find much that is educational in the current films.
32. (1.9) The information that you obtain from the movies is of little value.
33. (1.0) Movies are a bad habit.
34. (3.3) I like the movies as they are because I go to be entertained, not educated.
35. (3.1) On the whole the movies are pretty decent.
36. (0.8) The movies are undermining respect for authority.
37. (2.7) I like to see other people enjoy the movies whether I enjoy them myself or not.
38. (0.3) The movies are to blame for the prevalence of sex offenses.
39. (4.4) The movie is one of the great educational institutions for common people.
40. (0.8) Young people are learning to smoke, drink, and pet from the movies.

In scoring the attitude scale, we cannot say that one score is better or worse than another; we can only say that one person's attitude toward the movies is more or less favorable than another person's. It is purely arbitrary that attitudes unfavorable to the movies have lower scale values than favorable attitudes.

Any individual's attitude is measured by the average or mean scale value of all the statements he checks. The person who has the larger score is more favorably inclined toward the movies than the person with a lower score.

For the purpose of comparing groups, the distributions of attitude in each group can be plotted, and it can then be said whether and how much one group is more favorable to the movies than another group.

24 THE MEASUREMENT OF SOCIAL ATTITUDES

It is an honor and a privilege for me to have this opportunity of addressing the Midwestern Psychological Association.[1] I wish that I could do justice to the occasion and express my appreciation by an address that is worth listening to. I have selected among the few subjects that are available to me one that may be of fairly general interest while it still involves many theoretical and psychological problems. I shall discuss the measurement of social attitudes. In doing so I shall review the development of the measurement methods that are applicable to attitudes, and I shall also discuss some of the criticisms and questions that have recently been raised about this subject.

Several years ago, when I was teaching conventional psychophysics, it seemed to me that psychophysics was really a very dull subject in spite of the fact that it did offer the satisfaction of clean and quantitative logic. This type of satisfaction is rare in psychological investigation, and consequently psychophysics has stood out as a very dignified topic in psychology in spite of the fact that its intrinsic subject matter has been, on the whole, rather trivial. These depreciative statements about psychophysics can be readily amplified by referring to the conventional publications in this subject. You will then find that one of the elaborate parts of the subject is the determination of limens. There is a great deal of hairsplitting about just how a limen should be determined with the greatest possible precision. In determining a limen, you fit a phi-gamma curve, and then there is more hairsplitting as to whether you should adjust the errors of observation in the proportions or in the stimulus magnitudes. Then you will find the several psychophysical methods compared as to which gives the most reliable limen determination. And then you can find short cuts for these methods by which you can determine somebody's limen very quickly when you are in a hurry for a limen. Now, it seems strange that I have never seen a psychologist who really cared much about any particular person's limen for anything.

I venture the guess that not more than perhaps half a dozen psychologists in this room have ever needed or wanted somebody's limen for anything with a high degree of precision.

Of course we are interested to know the order of magnitude of errors in

[1] Address for the Midwestern Psychological Association, May 9, 1931. Reprinted from *Journal of Abnormal and Social Psychology*, XXVI (1931), 249–69.

visual discrimination as compared with those of various forms of auditory discrimination. Even in a rough pitch discrimination test we are determining a limen in a sense, but these problems never involve any profundities of curve-fitting for the limen of an individual subject. Why then does psychophysics bother so much about methods, and short cuts for these methods, which are never used on individual subjects except when an individual serves as a specimen for some type of situation in which the methods must be adapted to the conditions of each problem anyway? This bothered me also in teaching the subject, and I came to share the distrust of my students in the significance of the whole subject.

One way in which to retain the satisfactions that can be found in the logic of this subject is to change its content. We have tried this, and it has seemed to some of us that psychophysics thereby takes on an entirely new aspect. Instead of asking a person which of two cylinders is the heavier, we might as well ask him something interesting, such as, "Which of these two nationalities do you in general prefer to associate with?" or, "Which of these two offenses do you consider to be in general the more serious?" or, "Which of these two pictures or colored designs do you like better?" Questions of this sort of discrimination might be multiplied indefinitely, and if they could be handled with some sort of psychophysical logic, it is clear that we should have here the possibilities of objective description of more psychological significance than the sensory limen.

The first objection that I encountered is that the very term "psychophysics" should be strictly limited to the field of sensory discrimination. I find justification for extending the use of psychophysics even to questions that are interesting by referring to Titchener. He says: "Fechner was chiefly interested in the intensive aspect of mental processes, and among mental processes in sensation. His example has led other inquirers to give a disproportionate amount of attention to the laws of sensation intensity." It is unfortunate that Mr. Titchener did not happen to ask his students to judge the relative merits of handwriting specimens or of English compositions or to make social judgments because then I am sure that we should now have the permission to use psychophysical methods in a wide variety of problems.

Furthermore, if instead of printing our questions on a piece of paper, we should rig up an elaborate automatic contraption for exposing these questions, running the said contraption by an electric motor and spreading plenty of kymographs and telegraph keys and speech keys and time markers all around the room, then I am sure that our studies would qualify as experimental psychology. But since we ask the subject to indicate his response with a pencil instead of by a telegraph key, our investigations have been outside the pale of experimental psychology.

When the constant method is used in its complete form so that every stimulus serves in turn as a standard, then it becomes the method of paired comparison. There was no quantitative logic for handling the method of paired comparison so as to obtain measurement which satisfied the criterion of internal consistency. This difficulty was overcome by finding an equation that satisfied this criterion. It has been referred to as the law of comparative judgment. With this rational equation and the method of paired comparison we have made several studies involving social stimuli and in which the subjects were asked to express various kinds of judgments other than mere comparison of physical magnitudes.

In one of these experiments a list of twenty nationalities was presented to several hundred students.[2] The nationalities were arranged in pairs so that every nationality was paired with every other one in the list. The students were asked to underline one nationality of each pair to indicate which of the two nationalities they would rather associate with. The returns were tabulated in the form "proportion of the subjects who prefer nationality A to nationality B." With these experimental proportions and by the law of comparative judgment, the scale separation was calculated for each pair. By means of these data it was possible to construct a linear scale of attitude to which each nationality was allocated. At the top of the list is the American, next come other English-speaking countries, and at the bottom of the list are nationalities or races other than our own. This order is what one should expect, but the scale values could not be predicted.

In general the scaling is accomplished on the principle that if the group of subjects very generally prefers A to B, then the proportion of the subjects who vote for A will be high, perhaps close to unity.[3] If, on the other hand, the two nationalities are about equally well liked by the group, then there will be about as many subjects who vote for A as there are subjects who vote for B. Hence, the proportion above described will be close to .50, and the two nationalities will have zero separation; that is, they will have the same scale value.

In an experiment of this sort the criterion of internal consistency consists in the discovery that by assigning one scale value to each of the nationalities, we can reconstruct all of the experimentally independent proportions. With twenty nationalities in the list we have twenty scale values, and these must be sufficient to lock the 190 experimentally independent proportions within the known probable errors of the given proportions.

One of the criticisms of this procedure has been that the entries in the list are not true nationalities. For example, in the list occur such entries as Jew, Negro, South American. It is not necessary to restrict ourselves to accepted anthropological classifications in these experiments. We are measuring the degree of affect for or against the social objects listed. This is legitimate even if some of the classifications are races rather than nationalities or religions or groups of nationalities. For example, it is conceivable that some of the students disliked South Americans in general without knowing much about them and without stopping to debate whether these South Americans whom

[2] See chap. xxi.　　　　　　　　　　　　　　[3] See chap. iii.

they disliked were one or twenty nationalities. The category is a conversational one which lends itself to the expression of affect, and it therefore serves
our purposes even if the psychological or affective category does not fit the
accepted anthropological or political classifications. There is, of course,
nothing to prevent the use of other classifications so long as the categories
lend themselves to the expression of the likes and dislikes of people generally.

Another criticism that has been offered against experiments of this type
is that it would make a difference if the question were worded differently.
For example, in the form here described the question was "Which of these
two nationalities or races would you rather associate with?" Now, so runs
the objection, what would happen if the question were "Which would you
rather have as a fellow student?" "Which would you rather have for a neigh-
bor?" "Which would you rather have your sister marry?" and "Which
would you rather do business with?"[4] Fortunately, this question could be
answered by an experiment. Fifteen hundred blanks were used in which
there were three hundred blanks with each of the five questions. These were
arranged in random order so that it was a matter of chance which of the five
forms was given to each of the fifteen hundred subjects in the experiment.
When the blanks had been filled in, they were sorted out into five piles according to the question on the blank. The twenty nationalities were then
allocated to a scale separately for each of the five questions. The twenty
nationalities were found to be in the same rank order in the scales which
were constructed on the basis of the five questions. This proves that the scale
value of a nationality is determined primarily not by the detailed form of the
question but rather by the general degree of like or dislike of the subjects
for each nationality. This general like or dislike is what we have called the
potential action toward the object or attitude.

On the other hand, if the question had been "Which nationality would you
rather have as a servant?" it is quite conceivable that the scale values might
have been different, because such a question is not calculated to bring out the
attitude of the subject toward the nationality with regard to social equality.
If the question asked which of the nationalities is the more intelligent, which
is physically superior, which is more emotional, which is the taller, it is
quite certain that the scale values would have been different.

The generalization of the last experiment might be made by noting that
a subject could be halfway through the blank, responding by underlining
one of each pair, and still not remember what the question was that he was
answering by his underlining. This means merely that the subject gets a set
of checking preferences without recalling the cognitive detail of the question.
The question has then served its usefulness by giving the subject a set of
expressing his attitudes rather than some intellectual judgment about the

[4] Frederick R. Eggan, "An Experimental Study of Attitude toward Races and Nationalities" (Master's thesis, University of Chicago, 1928).

nationalities in question. The scale value of each nationality measures the affective value of the nationality for the group of subjects.

It is obvious that the scale value of each nationality in these experiments is a description of the group of subjects as much as it is a description of the nationalities. If the same experiment were repeated with Italian students or with Russian students, the scale values of the nationalities would undoubtedly be radically different.

This suggests the possibility of measuring cultural similarities or dissimilarities. Suppose that these paired comparison schedules were filled in by university students in ten different countries. The scale value of each of the twenty nationalities would be calculated separately for each of the ten countries. We could then calculate the correlation coefficient for the scale values of the twenty nationalities in two countries, for example, the German and the French students. If the correlation coefficient were high, it would indicate a similarity in the nationality preferences of the two groups of students. If the correlation were low, it would measure dissimilarity of the two groups of students as to their national preferences. If country C is very much hated by A and liked by B, then that difference would be measurable by the difference in the scale value for nationality C in the scales for groups A and B. In this way, international affiliations and antipathies might be described in a quantitative manner. Of course, differences might appear in different occupational groups and in different regions of the same country.

Suppose that one group of subjects likes all of the twenty nationalities about equally well. Then the twenty nationalities would have the same scale value. Suppose that another group of subjects has very decided likes and dislikes among the twenty nationalities. Some of the nationalities would then have high scale values, while others would have conspicuously low scale values. In other words, the spread in scale values would be much greater for the second group than for the first group. The intolerance of a group is measured by the spread in scale values. In this manner it would be possible to measure the tolerance of different countries for other countries. These measurements of international tolerance might conceivably have considerable social interest.

Some of our experiments have been set up so as to measure the effect of social stimuli on the international attitudes of high school children. We have worked with a number of motion picture films as stimuli.[5] In Genoa, Illinois, the film *Four Sons* was shown in the local theater, and 131 children in grades 7 to 12 inclusive were given free tickets. Several days before the performance they were asked to fill in a paired comparison schedule of nationality preferences. The Germans were included in this list. The morning after the performance the children again filled in the same schedule. It was

[5] See chaps. xxiii, xxv–xxvi, and L. L. Thurstone, "The Effect of a Motion Picture Film on Children's Attitudes toward the Germans," *Journal of Educational Psychology*, XXIII (1932), 241–46.

assumed that the attitudes of the children did not change toward the twenty nationalities during the course of a week or ten days between the two schedules except for the possible effect of the film on their attitude toward Germans. The film made the children much more friendly toward Germans. This experiment and others of the same general type demonstrate that the effect of a single social stimulus on the international attitudes of the subjects can be measured.

The same general technique has been used for measuring attitude toward crimes.[6] In such experiments a list of crimes was arranged in the same paired forms, and the subjects were asked to indicate for each pair which of the two crimes they considered to be the more serious. In this manner it was found in one town that the attitudes of children toward gambling were considerably affected by seeing the picture *Street of Chance*. The film had the effect of making the children regard gambling as a more serious offense after seeing the picture. These experiments with motion pictures have been effectively conducted by Miss Ruth Peterson.

The question has been raised as to the degree of permanence of these effects. In order to answer this question we have repeated the schedules of comparison in several towns after an interval of four to five months. The attitudes have returned about half-way toward their original values in four months, but these effects vary, of course, with the film used and the frequency of other social stimuli. In one town the effect lasted without diminution for five months.

When a series of social stimuli has been allocated to an affective continuum by the method of paired comparison, we have the scale separations, but we do not have a rational origin for the affective continuum. This is a problem for which Mr. Horst has found a very ingenious solution. It is of some psychological interest to locate a series of stimuli to an affective continuum in such a manner that the measurements refer to a datum of affective neutrality. The solution by Mr. Horst consists in asking a group of subjects to compare one stimulus A which is likely to be favorably regarded with another stimulus B which is likely to be considered unfavorable. The subject is asked this question, "Would you be willing to endure the disadvantage B in order to have the advantage A?" The proportion of subjects who are willing to accept B in order to have A locates the affective origin between the two stimuli. The same procedure can of course be extended to a whole series of stimuli so that the location of an affective datum in the series can be tested by the criterion of internal consistency.

Another method of measuring attitude is to use a statement scale.[7] This consists in a series of opinions which are submitted to the subject for indorse-

---

[6] See chap. xxvi.

[7] L. L. Thurstone and E. J. Chave, *The Measurement of Attitude* (Chicago: University of Chicago Press, 1929).

ment or rejection. These statements or opinions have been so selected that they constitute an evenly graduated series and so that a scale value can be given to each opinion. If the opinions A, B, C, D are four successive opinions in such an evenly graduated scale about prohibition, for example, then the following conditions would be satisfied. If one person indorses opinion A and another person indorses opinion B, then a group of observers should find some difficulty in saying which of the two opinions is more favorable to prohibition. Let us suppose that three-fourths of the observers would say that opinion A is more favorable to prohibition than opinion B. Then this degree of difficulty in judging which of them is the more favorable to prohibition constitutes a measure of the separation between the two statements of opinion on the attitude scale. Now, if opinion C is so chosen that three-fourths of the observers say that B is more favorable to prohibition than C, then the scale separation between A and B is the same as the separation between B and C. In this manner a series of statements is selected from a large number so that the apparent increment in attitude from one statement to the next is the same for the whole series.

With a scale value assigned to each statement or opinion, it is of course easy to calculate the median scale value of all the statements that any given individual has indorsed. This median scale value is the score of that person on the attitude scale. The meaning of these scores can be illustrated further as follows. Suppose that three individuals, X, Y, Z, have attitude scores on prohibition which are equally spaced. Then the difference or increment in attitude between X and Y would seem to be the same as the difference in attitude between Y and Z. In other words, it would be just as difficult to discriminate between X and Y as to which is the more favorable to prohibition as it is difficult to discriminate between Y and Z. This is the basis for the construction of the attitude scales. The psychophysical experimental methods by which the attitude scales are constructed so as to satisfy these requirements are beyond the scope of this paper.

The statement scale enables one to make several types of measurement of which the following are examples.

The attitude of an individual subject can be measured by means of a statement scale. The paired comparison procedure enables us to compare groups of subjects, but the statement scale procedure is preferable for measuring the attitudes of individual subjects. The range of statements that the individual indorses gives some indication of his tolerance. It is possible to plot a frequency distribution of the attitudes of a group of people toward labor unions, for example. This distribution has a central tendency or average, and it has a measurable dispersion. Two groups of people may then be found to have the same average score on a disputed issue, but one of the two groups may be more heterogeneous than the other. The degree of heterogeneity in attitude of a group of people is directly measured by the standard deviation of the frequency distribution of their attitude scores. This is an important aspect of group comparisons which can be reduced easily to measurement in terms of the dispersion of the scores.

In two small towns, West Chicago and Geneva, Illinois, an experiment was arranged so that a film favorable to the Chinese was shown in one town and a film unfavorable to the Chinese was shown in the other town.[8] The two films were *Welcome Danger*, which is thought to be unfriendly to the Chinese and which has been so criticized by the Chinese themselves, and *Son of the Gods*, which is generally thought to be friendly in its interpretation of Chinese culture. The films were shown in the local theaters, and the children were given free tickets to the performances. In each town the children were asked to fill in a statement scale about the Chinese several days before seeing the film and also the morning after seeing it. The results show a very decided shift in favor of the Chinese in Geneva, where *Son of the Gods* was shown. In West Chicago there was a small opposite effect where the children saw the film *Welcome Danger*. The effect of a single social stimulus, such as a motion picture film, on the international attitudes of school children can be described by the statement scale as well as by the paired comparison method.

The statement scale is constructed by asking a group of one hundred judges to sort out a list of opinions into a series of eleven successive piles to represent attitudes from one extreme to the other. The question was raised early in our experiments whether the attitudes of the judges themselves would influence the final scale values of the statements in the scale. For this reason Mr. Hinckley set up an experiment with a scale for measuring attitude toward the Negro. He had 114 statements about the Negro. At one extreme were the opinions that the Negro is the equal of the white man and should have equal social privileges. At the other extreme were the opinions that the Negro is inferior to the white man and should not have the same social privileges. Three groups of judges were used, namely, one group of white college students friendly toward the Negro, one group of white college students who thought the Negro was definitely inferior, and one group of educated Negroes. The whole list of 114 statements was scaled separately for the three groups of judges. The result was that the three scales so constructed were practically identical, thus proving that the attitudes of the judges have no serious effect on the measuring function of the statement scale.

It is possible to apply the statement scale method to the measurement of social trend. This will be illustrated in terms of attitude toward the Germans and the French. A collection of quotations from newspaper editorials has been made by Mr. Russell. His quotations cover the twenty year period 1910–30. A group of judges sorted the editorial quotations into a series of eleven piles ranging from No. 1, expressing extreme admiration for the Germans, to No. 11, expressing extreme contempt for them. The scale value

[8] See chap. xxv.

of each quotation was calculated. Then the average scale value of all the quotations from the year 1910 was determined. It is the mean attitude toward the Germans for that year. The average scale value of all the quotations from year 1911 was determined, and it is the mean attitude toward the Germans for that year. In this manner the mean attitude toward the Germans was represented quantitatively, so that this social trend for a period of twenty years could be inspected in a single graph.

For this particular issue the curve shows the expected depression in the average scale value for the Germans during the years of the war and a corresponding rise in average scale value for the French during the same period. Of course the curves so plotted represent only the attitudes of the editorials of one large newspaper. Mr. Russell is now making this type of inquiry for four newspapers, namely, the *New York Times*, the *World*, the *Chicago Daily News*, and the *Chicago Tribune*. The curves for these four newspapers are similar. They all show a return of attitudes toward the prewar values with interesting deviations that correspond to popularly discussed issues at various times. The newspapers also show some differences in the rapidity with which their editorials return toward prewar attitudes for Germany. We have here the possibility of measuring the changes in attitudes as represented in the press during past times even though the attitude scales were not available for these periods. It will be interesting to study by these quantitative methods the rapidity with which international attitudes have changed before and after each of the recent modern wars by analyzing the foreign press for a few years before and after each war. It will also be of interest to correlate these rates of change with other social facts such as facility of communication, similarity of language and culture, and the like. Perhaps this will be a psychophysical contribution to the methods of history.

Many of the criticisms and questions that have appeared about attitude measurement concern the nature of the fundamental concepts involved and the logic by which the measurements are made. I shall consider a few of these questions briefly.

One of the most frequent questions is that a score on an attitude scale, let us say the scale of attitude toward God, does not truly describe the person's attitude. There are so many complex factors involved in a person's attitude on any social issue that it cannot be adequately described by a simple number such as a score on some sort of test or scale. This is quite true, but it is also equally true of all measurement.

The measurement of any object or entity describes only one attribute of the object measured. This is a universal characteristic of all measurement. When the height of a table is measured, the whole table has not been described but only that attribute which was measured. Similarly, in the measurement of attitudes, only one characteristic of the attitude is described by a measurement of it.

Further, only those characteristics of an object can be measured which can be described in terms of "more" or "less." Examples of such description are: one object is longer than another, one object is hotter than another, one is heavier than another, one person is more intelligent than another, more educated than another, more strongly favorable to prohibition, more religious, more strongly favorable to birth control than another person. These are all traits by which two objects or two persons may be compared in terms of "more" or "less."

Only those characteristics can be described by measurement which can be thought of as linear magnitudes. In this context, linear magnitudes are weight, length, volume, temperature, amount of education, intelligence, and strength of feeling favorable to an object. Another way of saying the same thing is to note that the measurement of an object is, in effect, to allocate the object to a point on an abstract continuum. If the continuum is weight, then individuals may be allocated to an abstract continuum of weight, one direction of which represents small weight while the opposite direction represents large weight. Each person might be allocated to a point on this continuum with any suitable scale which requires some point at which counting begins, called the origin, and some unit of measurement in terms of which the counting is done.

The linear continuum which is implied in all measurement is always an abstraction. For example, when several people are described as to their weight, each person is in effect allocated to a point on an abstract continuum of weight. All measurement implies the reduction or restatement of the attribute measured to an abstract linear form. There is a popular fallacy that a unit of measurement is a thing—such as a piece of yardstick. This is not so. A unit of measurement is always a *process* of some kind which can be repeated without modification in the different parts of the measurement continuum.

Not all of the characteristics which are conversationally described in terms of "more" or "less" can actually be measured. But any characteristic which lends itself to such description has the possibility of being reduced to measurement.

We admit that an attitude is a complex affair which cannot be wholly described by any single numerical index. For the problem of measurement this statement is analogous to the observation that an ordinary table is a complex affair which cannot be wholly described by any single numerical index. So is a man such a complexity which cannot be wholly represented by a single index. Nevertheless we do not hestiate to say that we measure the table. The context usually implies what it is about the table that we propose to measure. We say without hesitation that we measure a man when we take some anthropometric measurement of him. The context may well imply without explicit declaration what aspect of the man we are measuring, his cephalic index, his height or weight or blood pressure or what not. Just in the same sense we shall say here that we are measuring attitudes. We shall state or imply by the context the aspect of people's attitudes that we are measuring. The point is that it is just as legitimate to say that we are measuring attitudes as it is to say that we are measuring tables or men.

Whenever a common word is adopted for scientific use, it nearly always suffers some restriction in its connotation in favor of greater precision of meaning. This has happened in many sciences, so that it is by no means peculiar to psychological terms. Consider, for example, such words as elasticity, momentum, force, which are after all common ordinary words, but as they are used by the physicist they are very much restricted and more precise while still retaining the essential ordinary idea. So it is in psychology with terms like sensation, perception, illusion, meaning, idea, and concept. Now when we turn scientific logic and experimental psychophysical procedures to the subject of attitudes, we find it necessary to restrict here also the rather loose conversational meaning of this term in order to make it at all suitable for scientific discourse.

Our present definition of the term may be briefly stated as follows: *Attitude is the affect for or against a psychological object.* Affect in its primitive form is described as appetition or aversion. Appetition is the positive form of affect, which in more sophisticated situations appears as liking the psychological object, defending it, favoring it in various ways. Aversion is the negative form of affect, which is described as hating the psychological object, disliking it, destroying it, or otherwise reacting against it. Attitude is here used to describe *potential action* toward the object with regard only to the question whether the potential action will be favorable or unfavorable toward the object. For example, if we say that a man's attitude toward prohibition is negative, we mean that his potential actions about prohibition may be expected to be against it, barring compromises in particular cases. When we say that a man's attitude toward prohibition is negative, we have merely indicated the affective direction of his potential action toward the object. We have not said anything about the particular detailed manner in which he might act. In this sense the term attitude is an abstraction in that it cannot be described without inserting the cognitive details that are irrelevant, but this is also true of many of the simplest concepts in daily use.

The affect about an object may be of strong intensity, or it may be weak. The positive and negative affect therefore constitutes a linear continuum with a neutral point or zone and two opposite directions, one positive and the other negative. Measurement along this affective continuum is of a discriminatory character with the discriminal error as a unit of measurement.

Against this restricted definition of attitude as the affective character of potential action about a psychological object there have been raised several questions. It has been pointed out that the emotional experiences of the past constitute an integral part of a man's attitude. If we should use the term in that inclusive manner, we should say that a man's attitude toward religion consists in part of his childhood experience with Sunday schools. The man

might then say that his attitude toward religion is that he went to church
when he was a child. I should prefer to say that such a fact is really not a
part of his attitude toward religion but that it may help to *explain* how he
got that way. It is quite conceivable that two men may have the same degree
or intensity of affect favorable toward a psychological object and that their
attitudes would be described in this sense as identical but that they arrived
at their similar attitudes by entirely different routes. It is even possible that
their factual associations about the psychological object might be entirely
different and that their overt actions would take quite different forms which
have one thing in common, namely, that they are about equally favorable
toward the object.

In these discussions the term psychological object has its customary
meaning. It may refer to a physical object, or it may refer to an idea, a plan
of action, a form of conduct, an ideal, a moral principle, a slogan, or a symbol. In fact, it may refer to any idea about which the subject may express
positive or negative affect.

There comes to mind the uncertainty of using an opinion as an index of
attitude. The man may be a liar. If he is not intentionally misrepresenting
his real attitude on a disputed question, he may nevertheless modify the expression of it for reasons of courtesy, especially in those situations in which
frank expression of attitude may not be well received. This has led to the
suggestion that a man's action is a safer index of his attitude than what he
says. But his actions may also be distortions of his attitude. A politician
extends friendship and hospitality in overt action toward a Negro while
hiding an attitude that he expresses more truthfully to an intimate friend.
Neither his opinions nor his overt act constitutes in any sense an infallible
guide to the subjective inclinations and preferences that constitute his attitude. Therefore we must remain content to use opinions or other forms of
action merely as indexes of attitude. It must be recognized that there is a
discrepancy, some error of measurement as it were, between the opinion or
overt action that we use as an index and the attitude that we infer from such
an index.

But this discrepancy between the index and "truth" is universal. When
you want to know the temperature of your room, you look at the thermometer and use its reading as an index of temperature just as though there
were a single temperature reading which is the "correct" one for the room.
If it is desired to ascertain the volume of a glass paperweight, the volume
is postulated as an attribute of the piece of glass, even though volume is an
abstraction. The volume is measured indirectly by noting the dimensions
of the glass or by immersing it in water to see how much water it displaces.
These two procedures give two indexes which may not agree exactly. In
every situation involving measurement there is postulated an abstract
continuum such as volume or temperature, and the allocation of the thing
measured to that continuum is accomplished by indirect means through one

or more indexes. Truth consists only in the relative consistency of the several indexes, since it is never directly known. We are dealing with the same type of situation in attempting to measure attitude. We postulate an attitude variable which is like practically all other measurable attributes in the nature of an abstract continuum, and we must find one or more indexes which will satisfy us to the extent that they are internally consistent. Only to the extent that different indexes are consistent can we be justified in postulating the attitude as a trait, for a trait is never directly measured.

If we should find that what a man says has absolutely no relation to what he does, then such inconsistency would constitute a serious limitation on the legitimacy of the abstraction of attitude. However, when we actually carry out such comparisons, we do find that the correlation is positive between verbally expressed attitudes and overt action. The correlation is not perfect, but it is certainly positive. Discrepancies will arise, as when a subject expresses himself as favorable to prohibition although he himself violates it. But if the correlation is tabulated for a large group of people, it is found that the attitude scores for those who vote for prohibition are markedly different from those who vote against it, and a similar positive correlation is found between attitude scores and overt action about drinking. The reason for limiting ourselves to verbal expressions of attitude is that they can be evaluated with more certainty, and they are much more available than a list of overt acts. This type of correlation between attitude and overt action was the subject of a recent study by Mr. Stouffer.

In order to deal with overt actions as expressive of attitudes in a feasible manner Mr. Rosander has prepared lists of situations with alternative overt acts. He asks the question, "In the following situations, which of the given alternatives are you most likely *to do?*" Then follows description of a situation with a number of alternative overt acts. For example, in a situation scale on the Negro occurs the following:

The congregation of the church you attend has always been white. One Sunday morning a Negro attends the services.
   a. You do nothing about it.
   b. You complain to the minister.
   c. You welcome the Negro to the church.
   d. You shake hands with him and ask him to come again.
   e. You sound out opinion to find how many want to keep out Negroes.
   f. You tell the fellow he had better move along.
   g. You ask the minister to tell him that he is not wanted.
   h. You tell the fellow he had better leave before you throw him out.
   i. You defend the Negro against some who complain of his presence.
   j. You give the Negro friendly warning that perhaps he had better not come back.

The various overt responses are to be scaled in a manner analogous to the procedure for the statements of opinion. It is quite probable that these two types of scale, the opinion scale and the situation scale, will be highly correlated.

We take for granted that people's attitudes are subject to change. When we have measured a man's attitude on any issue such as pacifism, we shall not declare such a measurement to be in any sense an enduring or constitutional constant. His attitude may change, of course, from one day to the next, and it is our task to measure such changes, whether they be due to unknown causes or to the presence of some known persuasive factor, such as the reading of a discourse on the issue in question. However, such fluctuations may also be attributed in part to error in the measurements themselves. In order to isolate the errors of the measurement instrument from actual fluctuations in attitude, we must calculate the standard error of measurement of the scale itself, and this can be accomplished by methods already well known in mental measurement.

We shall assume that an attitude scale is used only in those situations in which one may reasonably expect people to tell the truth about their convictions or opinions. If a denominational school were to submit to its students a scale of attitude about the church, one might find that some students would hesitate to make known their convictions if they deviate from the orthodox beliefs of their school. At least, the findings could be challenged if the situation in which attitudes were expressed contained pressure or implied threat bearing directly on the attitude to be measured. Similarly, it is difficult to discover attitudes on sex liberty by a written questionnaire, because of the well-nigh universal pressure to conceal such attitudes when they deviate from supposed conventions. It is assumed that attitude scales will be used primarily in those situations that offer a minimum of pressure on the attitude to be measured. Such situations are common enough.

However, it is sometimes of considerable interest to inquire what the distribution of attitude may be in a group which is known to be influenced by social pressure or taboo. If, for example, a group of college students are asked to express their attitude on the subject of sex liberty, the results might indicate conformity with conventional standards. Such a result might be interpreted to mean that the students agree with conventional ideals in regard to sex liberty, or the results might be challenged as reflecting only the social taboo against deviations from the conventional standards. If, on the other hand, the results should be a distribution of unconventional attitudes, the interpretation would be more conclusive in that the expressed attitude appears in spite of the known taboo. It goes without saying that the distribution of attitude on any social issue and with any particular group must be interpreted in terms of the known factors that may influence judgment.

The question has been raised whether the concept of attitude as here used and as measured by an attitude scale is not hypothetical rather than "real." It is just as hypothetical as the concept of intelligence, which is measured by what it supposedly does. But these concepts are hypothetical in the same sense that the concepts force, momentum, volume, are hypothetical in physical science. No one has ever seen or touched a force or a momentum or a volume. They are measured by what they supposedly do. The legitimacy of these abstractions can be tested only in the consistency by which they operate in experience. Not infrequently these hypothetical entities are discarded either, first, because they lead to inconsistencies in experience or, second, because they have to be multiplied in number so that they become as numerous as the effects that they are intended to explain or facilitate in analysis. As long as biologists insisted on the definition of instincts in terms of overt acts, they found that the instincts had to be as numerous as the overt acts to be accounted for, and then the instinct abstraction lost its usefulness. The instincts probably could be defined more successfully in terms of the other end of the psychological act. The concept of intelligence is a useful though hypothetical entity. It is postulated that intelligence is that which is dynamically common to a large group of overt acts. The degree of this hypothetical power which we call intelligence is estimated in terms of overt performances, and the term is successful to the extent that different forms of adaptive overt performance are positively correlated. The greater confidence with which we handle such a hypothetical entity as force is completely contained in the higher degree of consistency with which the hypothetical force is measured in different forms of its expression. We are here dealing with a similar hypothetical entity, attitude toward a social or psychological object. It is part of the convenience of language to speak of a force as though it were the "cause" of the movement of a particle, and just so we speak of intelligence as the cause of conduct that is regarded as particularly adaptive, and we speak of attitude as the cause of that conduct which is favorable or unfavorable toward a psychological object.

The consistency by which the term "attitude" may be established as useful is to be found in the indorsements of different opinions. Consider these two opinions about the church: "I find the services of the church both restful and inspiring," and "I think the church is a divine institution." One of these statements concerns the effect of the church service on the individual subject. The other expresses a belief in the divine character of the church. Considered objectively and logically, there should be no necessary correspondence between these two statements. They are declarations about totally different things, objectively regarded. But among all the people who indorse the first statement there will be a large proportion who also indorse the second statement. That which these two objectively entirely different statements have in common is the postulated favorable affect of the subject toward the psychological object, the church. To the extent that such consistencies in indorsements can be found, we are justified in postulating a common core and in naming it.

An example of the opposite kind may serve better to illustrate the justification for postulating the common factor of attitude. Consider the statement, "Going to church will not do anyone any harm." You find by actually trying it that the pious people indorse this statement. They can hardly do otherwise. On the other hand, some of the hard-boiled atheists also indorse it if they don't think that churchgoing is going to be specially harmful. Here you have people from both ends of the affective continuum indorsing the same statement. If all of our opinions behaved that way upon statistical analysis, we would have no attitude scales, and we would not even be able to postulate the attitude continuum. But fortunately most of the opinions that we now write behave much better than that one did. This criterion we have called the criterion of irrelevance.

Perhaps the nature of the underlying concept of attitude can be finally best illustrated by an extreme example that I have found useful on several occasions. Suppose that you would all be given a list of statements about communism with the request that you check those statements that you think are true, and suppose that you were in a sufficiently docile mood to undertake the task. Some of the statements are very frankly favorable to communism, some are even extreme, others straddle the question with neutral assertions, others are derogatory, and some are bitter denunciations of the communists. Now I shall venture the guess that the large majority of this audience would register strong denunciation of communism. Since these statements have been scaled on an affect continuum, I could plot the frequency distribution of your attitudes toward communism, and it would probably be strongly skewed with a mode at the anti-end of the scale. Here you would have given me a clear indication that you react against this social object or symbol that has been placed before you.

But now suppose that I should turn on you with the request that you all write out a statement of what it is that you have been talking about, just what these doctrines are that you have so universally denounced. I should then not be at all surprised if some of you would have difficulty in telling me just what the doctrines of communism are toward which you have reacted so strongly. Those of you who would venture to write such statements would undoubtedly differ widely in what you say that you have expressed yourself about. Now the important point for the purpose of attitude measurement is that your vagueness in supplying cognitive detail does not in the least invalidate your expression of attitude. Even though you might differ in your detailed description of the communism symbol, you might all agree that it is bad, that those who subscribe to such a symbol should be sent to jail, and that such doctrines should be kept out of the country. We have here a clear registration of affective value, a strong negative affective valuation of a symbol, and that is all that we are trying to find when we measure social attitudes. Of course, it would be socially interesting and perhaps important that we should get together on what it is that we feel so strongly about, but for the purposes of attitude measurement we have done our task when the positive or negative affect has been recorded in terms of the discriminal dispersion as a unit of measurement.

I must make it clear that in discussing these various issues, such as religion, communism, birth control, municipal ownership, race prejudice, pacifism, and so on, I am not advancing any doctrines whatever. I have personal convictions on some of these issues, and so does everybody else, but in these studies we are concerned merely with the description of the degree of affect for or against various social symbols by psychophysical methods. In giving each person a positive or negative score on a disputed social issue, we do not say anything whatever as to whether his attitude is good or bad, whether his attitude should be censured or encouraged. That is a matter of interpretation in each issue, and it is not the scientific problem with which we are concerned.

In closing, I shall mention only one other question that has appeared on several occasions. It has been suggested that the attitude scales might be used in order to eliminate undesirable students from colleges and universities. They might be given an attitude scale on patriotism or on religion or on something else that is supposed to tell whether a person is desirable or not from any particular point of view. In the first place, you would immediately make liars of many applicants who differ with you in their political or religious convictions on the issue in question. We have not yet combined the attitude scales with the lie detector, although such experiments are contemplated. But even if it were possible to ascertain the political and religious attitudes of people under conditions which would detect when they are lying, it would be a vicious policy for any educational institution to adopt.

It has been proposed that attitude scales might be used to determine whether a course of instruction in social science has had the desired effect. To be sure, one of the important results of social science instruction is change in social attitude. But to make the passing of a course contingent on taking the so-called right attitude on any particular social issue would be preposterous. I am unalterably opposed to any such policy for judging progress in social science courses.

I have reviewed some of our attempts to extend the experimental methods and the logic of psychophysics beyond the field of sensory discrimination to which it has been limited by psychological tradition. It has been stated by economists and by other social scientists that affect cannot be measured, and some of the fundamental theory of social science has been written with this explicit reservation. Our studies have shown that affect can be measured. In extending the methods of psychophysics to the measurement of affect, we seem to see the possibility of a wide field of application by which it will be possible to apply the methods of quantitative scientific thinking to the study of feeling and emotion, to aesthetics, and to social phenomena.

25 THE MEASUREMENT OF CHANGE IN SOCIAL ATTITUDE

The experiment to be described in this paper[1] was set up in order to ascertain whether the effect of a single motion picture on the social attitudes of school children could be measured by an attitude scale in the statement form. The plan was, in brief, to let the school children of one town see a film favorable to Chinese culture, and in a second town the school children were shown a film that has been criticized as unfriendly to the Chinese. Before and after seeing the film in their respective towns, the children filled in a statement scale about the Chinese. The results show that the attitudes of the children were changed in opposite directions in the two towns, thus demonstrating the effect of the films as well as verifying the methods used.

TABLE 50

Town in Illinois	Motion Picture Given	Theater	Size of Town (1920 Census)	Size of School	No. in Exp. Group	Grades	Date of First Scale	Date of Motion Picture	Date of Second Scale
Geneva.......	*Son of the Gods*	Fargo	2803	230	182	9–12	5/19	5/26	5/27
West Chicago.	*Welcome Danger*	School	2594	225	172	9–12	5/19	5/26	5/27

The two towns selected for the experiments were Geneva, Illinois, and West Chicago, Illinois. The relevant facts about these two towns are given in Table 50. The film *Son of the Gods* has been considered rather friendly in its interpretation of Chinese culture. It was shown in Geneva, Illinois. One week before and the day after seeing this picture, the children filled in a statement scale about the Chinese. This attitude scale was constructed by the method of equal-appearing intervals. The scale value of each statement is recorded for each opinion in the list. It was constructed by the pooled judgments of

[1] Reprinted from *Journal of Social Psychology*, II (1931), 230–35. This is one of a series of experimental studies on the effect of motion pictures on the social attitudes of children. These studies were made possible by a grant from the Payne Fund. The author wishes to acknowledge the assistance of Professor W. W. Charters of Ohio State University, Mr. C. C. Byerly, School Superintendent at West Chicago, and Mr. H. M. Coultrap, School Superintendent at Geneva, Illinois. Miss Ruth C. Peterson conducted the experiments. We wish to acknowledge the assistance of the First National Picture Distributing Corporation, Mr. Paul Polka of Maywood, and Mr. Rubens of Balaban and Katz in making special arrangements about the film *Son of the Gods*, and of Paramount Famous Lasky Corporation in the arrangements for the film *Welcome Danger*.

thirty subjects. Since the detailed methods of constructing an attitude scale have been described elsewhere,[2] they will not be repeated here.

In Figure 67 we have the frequency distribution of attitudes of these children to the Chinese as determined on May 19, 1930, before they saw the picture. The picture was shown in the local theater by special arrangement on May 26, 1930. On the morning after seeing the picture, the children again

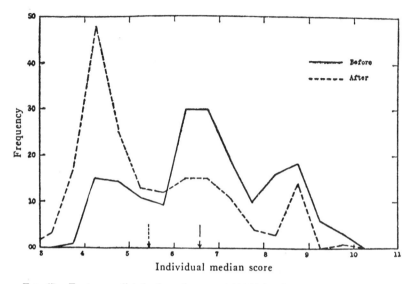

Fig. 67.—Frequency distribution of scores of 182 high school children in Geneva, Illinois, on a scale of attitude toward the Chinese before and after seeing the film *Son of the Gods*.

filled in the statement scale about the Chinese. They had been told previously that the scale was to be filled in twice several days apart. In Figure 67 we have shown also the frequency distribution of their attitudes toward the Chinese after seeing the film. The shift in attitude as a result of the picture is striking. The picture evidently made the children more friendly toward the Chinese. The statistical facts about the two frequency distributions are as follows:

Number of children...................... 182
Mean attitude score (before).............. 6.63
Mean attitude score (after)............... 5.45
Standard deviation of scores (before)........ 1.46
Standard deviation of scores (after)......... 1.54
Correlation between the two sets of scores.... + .57
Ratio of the difference to the probable error of
the difference.......................... 16.98

[2] L. L. Thurstone and E. J. Chave, *The Measurement of Attitude* (Chicago: University of Chicago Press, 1929).

We are undoubtedly justified in concluding that the film *Son of the Gods* has the effect of making the children more friendly toward the Chinese. It is of some interest to establish that the effect of a single film on the social attitudes of children can be measured by a statement scale.

It is more difficult to find films that are antagonistic to foreign nationalities than to find films that are, on the whole, friendly toward foreign cultures. The film *Welcome Danger* has been criticized by the Chinese for its unfriendly manner of dealing with the Chinese, and it was therefore selected for this experiment. The film was shown in West Chicago. One week before and the day after seeing the picture, the children filled in the same scale about the

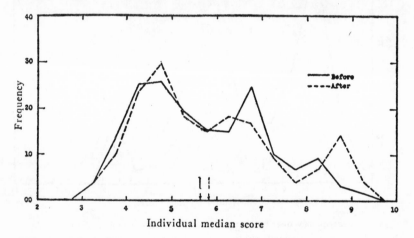

FIG. 68.—Frequency distribution of scores of 172 high school children in West Chicago, Illinois, on a scale of attitude toward the Chinese before and after seeing the film *Welcome Danger*.

Chinese that was used in Geneva. The two frequency distributions, before and after, are shown in Figure 68. Here there is evident a slight shift in the opposite direction. The statistical facts about the two frequency distributions are as follows:

Number of children......................	172
Mean attitude (before)....................	5.66
Mean attitude (after).....................	5.81
Standard deviation (before)...............	1.42
Standard deviation (after).................	1.56
Correlation between two sets of attitude scores	+ .58
Ratio of the difference to the probable error of the difference...........................	2.22

It is evident that the film *Welcome Danger* made the children somewhat more unfriendly toward the Chinese, although the effect of this film against the Chinese was by no means so marked as the effect of the previous film favorable to the Chinese. It would be interesting to compare the relative ease of moving an audience in the favorable and in the unfavorable directions about a foreign country or race. Unfortunately, that cannot be done experimentally unless the appeal of the two stimuli can be equated by criteria other than their measured effect on the audience.

The present experiments show that a single film has a measurable effect on the international attitudes of school children and that these effects can be measured by a statement scale.

The statement scale about the Chinese contained the following instructions and opinions. The scale value is recorded for each opinion in the following list. The attitude score is the median scale value of all the opinions indorsed by the subject. The scale values are not printed on the blanks given to the subjects.

This is a study of attitudes toward the Chinese. On the other side of this page you will find a number of statements expressing different attitudes toward the Chinese.

√ Put a check mark if you agree with the statement.

✕ Put a cross if you disagree with the statement.

Try to indicate either agreement or disagreement for each statement. If you simply cannot decide about a statement you may mark it with a question mark.

This is not an examination. There are no right or wrong answers to these statements. This is simply a study of people's attitudes toward the Chinese. Please indicate your own convictions by a check mark when you agree and by a cross when you disagree.

√ Put a check mark if you agree with the statement.

✕ Put a cross if you disagree with the statement.

Scale Value	
6.5	1. I have no particular love nor hate for the Chinese.
10.1	2. I dislike the Chinese more every time I see one.
4.7	3. The Chinese are pretty decent.
7.2	4. Some Chinese traits are admirable but on the whole I don't like them.
0.5	5. The Chinese are superior to all other races.
8.7	6. The Chinese as part of the yellow race are inferior to the white race.
3.5	7. I like the Chinese.
2.8	8. The more I know about the Chinese the better I like them.
11.0	9. The Chinese are aptly described by the term "yellow devils."
1.8	10. The high class Chinese are superior to us.
5.2	11. The Chinese are different but not inferior.
11.5	12. I hate the Chinese.
4.1	13. Chinese parents are unusually devoted to their children.
7.7	14. Although I respect some of their qualities, I could never consider a Chinese as my friend.
1.2	15. I would rather live in China than any other place in the world.
9.7	16. There are no refined nor cultured Chinese.
6.0	17. The Chinese are no better and no worse than any other people.

8.4   18. I think Chinese should be kept out of the United States.

2.2   19. I consider it a privilege to associate with Chinese people.

10.6   20. The Chinese are inferior in every way.

9.4   21. I don't see how anyone could ever like the Chinese.

3.0   22. Chinese have a very high sense of honor.

8.6   23. I have no desire to know any Chinese.

1.4   24. Chinese people have a refinement and depth of feeling that you don't find anywhere else.

9.8   25. There is nothing about the Chinese that I like or admire.

3.9   26. I'd like to know more Chinese people.

26 INFLUENCE OF MOTION PICTURES ON CHILDREN'S ATTITUDES

This is one of a series[1] of studies to ascertain whether the effect of motion pictures on school children can be measured and whether the effects of different kinds of pictures can be predicted. The present report concerns two experiments with the films *Street of Chance* and *Hide Out*. The plan of each experiment was to ask the children to fill in certain schedules intended to reveal their attitudes on the issue which seemed to be involved in the film. These schedules were filled in by the children before and after seeing the film. If the film had any effect on social attitudes, it might be revealed by changes in the scores on the schedules filled in before and after seeing the film. Such effects have been found to be measurable for several films.

The film *Street of Chance* describes the life of a gambler in such a way that the children might conceivably be affected in their attitudes toward gambling. By special arrangement this film was shown in the Strand Theater in Mendota, Illinois, on May 22, 1929. Mendota is a town of about 4,000 population. There were 240 children in the experimental group in grades 9 to 12, inclusive. A paired comparison schedule of crimes was presented to the children on May 15, 1929, before seeing the film, and also on May 23, 1929, after seeing the film. The second filling-in of the schedule was done on the morning after seeing the film. The children were given free tickets to the local theater where the film was shown in an afternoon performance. This was done in order to give as much as possible of the natural setting for the effectiveness of the picture as ordinarily seen by the children.

The paired comparison schedule had the following instructions:

[1] Reprinted from *Journal of Social Psychology*, II (1931), 291–305. This is one of a series of experimental studies on the effect of motion pictures on the social attitudes of children. These studies were made possible by a grant from the Payne Fund. I wish to acknowledge the assistance of Professor W. W. Charters of Ohio State University, Mr. M. E. Steele, Superintendent of Schools, Mendota, Illinois, and Mr. O. V. Shaffer, Superintendent of Schools, Princeton, Illinois. I am especially indebted to Miss Ruth Peterson for her effective planning and managing of these experiments.

For the experiment at Mendota, Illinois, acknowledgment is also made to the Paramount Famous Lasky Corporation and to Mr. A. M. Robertson of the Strand Theater. In Princeton, Illinois, we had the assistance of the Universal Film Exchanges, Incorporated, and of Mr. Jerome Reith of the Apollo Theater.

A Study of Attitude toward Crime

Write your name here..

Boy or girl...Age..Grade.........................

This is a study of attitudes toward crime. You are asked to underline the one crime of each pair that you think should be punished most severely. For example, the first pair is:

speeder—pickpocket

If, in general, you think a speeder should be punished more severely than a pick-pocket, underline speeder. If you think a pickpocket should be punished more severely than a speeder, underline pickpocket. If you find it difficult to decide for any pair be sure to underline one of them, even if you have to guess.

speeder—pickpocket	bank robber—gambler
gambler—bootlegger	pickpocket—drunkard
drunkard—beggar	quack doctor—bootlegger
gangster—tramp	beggar—gangster

Then followed seventy-eight comparisons of the type indicated above. There were thirteen crimes in the list, and every crime was paired with every other. The children were told that they would be asked to fill in these schedules twice, so that they would not be surprised when asked to do it a second time. The schedules were filled in during school hours, and the picture was shown in the local theater. Nothing was explicitly said about any connection between these two events, but there is no guaranty that some of the children may not have suspected that there was an association between them. The ideal procedure is to separate these events so that the subjects do not think of any association between the picture to which they are given free admission and the attitude schedules which they fill in during school hours.

In Table 51 we have a summary of the raw data for the schedules that were filled in before seeing the picture, and in Table 52 we have a similar table for the schedules that were filled in after seeing the picture. Table 51 shows, for every pair of offenses, the proportion of the children who thought that the offense listed at the top of the table was more serious than the offense listed at the side of the table. If the proportion $P_{a>b}$ is very high, say .90, the interpretation is, of course, that the children thought generally that offense a is much more serious than b and that a should be the more heavily punished.

With these data it was possible to calculate the scale value of each of the thirteen offenses by the law of comparative judgment.[2] The simplest form of this law was used for these calculations, namely, Case 5, so that

$$S_a - S_k = x_{ak} \sqrt{2} , \tag{1}$$

[2] See chaps. ii–iv, vii, xix, xxi.

in which S_a and S_k are scale values and x_{ak} is the deviation from the mean of the probability surface in terms of its standard deviation which corresponds to the observed proportion of children who said that a was more serious than k. In the same manner we may write the equation for the two stimuli b and k in the form

$$S_b - S_k = x_{bk} \sqrt{2} \ . \tag{2}$$

Subtracting (2) from (1), we have

$$S_a - S_b = \sqrt{2}\,[x_{ak} - x_{bk}]\ . \tag{3}$$

Writing this equation in summation form so as to involve all comparisons with the stimuli a and b, we have

$$n\,(S_a - S_b) = \sqrt{2}\,[\Sigma x_{ak} - \Sigma x_{bk}]\ , \tag{4}$$

TABLE 51

PROPORTION OF SCHOOL CHILDREN IN MENDOTA, ILLINOIS, WHO SAID THAT THE OFFENSE AT THE TOP OF THE TABLE IS MORE SERIOUS THAN THE OFFENSE AT THE SIDE OF THE TABLE*

		b.r. 1	gam. 2	p.p. 3	dr. 4	q.d. 5	b.l. 6	beg. 7	gang. 8	tr. 9	sp. 10	p.t. 11	ki. 12	sm. 13
Bank robber....	1	.....	.07	.08	.05	.27	.29	.01	.50	.00	.06	.02	.73	.21
Gambler......	2	.93	.....	.71	.52	.76	.92	.07	.92	.05	.41	.49	.90	.81
Pickpocket....	3	.92	.29	.....	.25	.67	.75	.02	.86	.02	.39	.42	.87	.68
Drunkard......	4	.95	.48	.75	.....	.81	.95	.01	.92	.03	.37	.62	.91	.87
Quack doctor...	5	.73	.24	.33	.19	.....	.49	.02	.70	.02	.12	.22	.64	.55
Bootlegger.....	6	.71	.08	.25	.05	.51	.....	.00	.79	.01	.09	.26	.68	.50
Beggar........	7	.99	.93	.98	.99	.98	1.00	.....	.96	.42	.86	.96	1.00	.99
Gangster......	8	.50	.08	.14	.08	.30	.21	.04	.....	.02	.08	.08	.36	.31
Tramp........	9	1.00	.95	.98	.97	.98	.99	.58	.98	.....	.91	.97	.99	1.00
Speeder.......	10	.94	.59	.61	.63	.88	.91	.14	.92	.09	.....	.58	.90	.92
Petty thief.....	11	.98	.51	.58	.38	.78	.74	.04	.92	.03	.42	.....		.78
Kidnaper.....	12	.27	.10	.13	.09	.36	.32	.00	.64	.01	.10		.....	.27
Smuggler......	13	.79	.19	.32	.13	.45	.50	.01	.69	.00	.08	.22	.73	.....

* For example, 48 per cent of the children said that it is more serious to be a gambler than to be a drunkard. These records were made on May 15, 1929, *before* seeing the film *Street of Chance*.

TABLE 52

PROPORTION OF SCHOOL CHILDREN IN MENDOTA, ILLINOIS, WHO SAID THAT THE OFFENSE AT THE TOP OF THE TABLE IS MORE SERIOUS THAN THE OFFENSE AT THE SIDE OF THE TABLE*

	b.r.	gam.	p.p.	d.r.	q.d.	b.l.	beg.	gang.	tr.	sp.	p.t.	ki.	sm.
Bank robber..........	.....	.21	.07	.05	.33	.30	.02	.50	.00	.06	.03	.62	.27
Gambler.............	.79	.....	.49	.30	.64	.69	.05	.82	.04	.27	.36	.73	.69
Pickpocket..........	.93	.51	.....	.30	.72	.70	.03	.87	.02	.32	.38	.84	.70
Drunkard...........	.95	.70	.70	.....	.84	.87	.06	.89	.04	.33	.53	.92	.84
Quack doctor........	.67	.36	.28	.16	.....	.50	.02	.68	.01	.11	.19	.65	.54
Bootlegger..........	.70	.31	.30	.13	.50	.....	.02	.73	.02	.10	.24	.70	.51
Beggar.............	.98	.95	.97	.94	.98	.98	.....	.99	.36	.79	.94	.98	.98
Gangster............	.50	.18	.13	.11	.32	.27	.01	.....	.01	.06	.11	.38	.34
Tramp..............	1.00	.96	.98	.96	.99	.98	.64	.99	.....	.87	.95	.99	.98
Speeder............	.94	.73	.68	.67	.89	.90	.21	.94	.13	.....	.64	.92	.89
Petty thief..........	.97	.64	.62	.47	.81	.76	.06	.89	.05	.36	.....		.76
Kidnaper	.38	.27	.16	.08	.35	.30	.02	.62	.01	.08		.....	.36
Smuggler...........	.73	.31	.30	.16	.46	.49	.02	.66	.02	.11	.24	.64	.....

* For example, 70 per cent of the children said that it is more serious to be a gambler than to be a drunkard. These records were made on May 23, 1929, *after* seeing the film *Street of Chance*.

from which it follows that

$$S_a - S_b = \frac{\sqrt{2}}{n} \left[\Sigma x_{ak} - \Sigma x_{bk} \right] . \tag{5}$$

This is the equation used for calculating the scale separation between the two stimuli a and b, and similar forms were used for the calculation of all other scale separations. The numerical values of Σx_{ka} and of Σx_{bk} were obtained from the tabulated proportions in Tables 51 and 52. Since the details of these calculations have been previously described, they will not be repeated here.[3]

The first column of Table 53 gives the names of the offenses in the list. The second and third columns give the scale values before and after seeing the film *Street of Chance*. In Figure 69 we have plotted the scale values "after" against the scale values "before." A linear plot is immediately apparent, with a conspicuous exception for the scale value of gambler which

TABLE 53

SCALE VALUES

Crime	Before	After	After (Adjusted)
Gangster...........	.000	.000	.045
Bank robber........	.006	−.069	−.028
Kidnaper...........	.078	.036	.082
Bootlegger.........	.430	.445	.512
Smuggler...........	.518	.423	.489
Quack doctor.......	.563	.429	.495
Pickpocket.........	1.097	.994	1.089
Petty thief.........	1.358	1.268	1.376
Gambler...........	1.536	.867	.955
Drunkard..........	1.610	1.344	1.456
Speeder...........	1.702	1.607	1.732
Beggar............	2.775	2.626	2.801
Tramp.............	2.965	2.866	3.053

was evidently rated as much more serious, relative to the other offenses, after seeing the film. Low scale values represent the more serious offenses. The variations in the "before" and "after" scale values for each of the other offenses show very slight changes, which may be interpreted as due to slight chance errors in the experimental proportions.

The shift in the scale value for "gambler" cannot be so interpreted. The film quite evidently had the effect of making the children regard gambling as a much more serious offense than they did before seeing the film. The same effect is shown graphically in another manner in Figure 70. Before this figure could be drawn, it was necessary to adjust the scale values to a common unit. The adjustment was made on the "after" scale values. The nature of the adjustment can be explained as follows.

Imagine that the subjects were asked to fill in these paired comparison schedules one hundred times. No matter how much interest they have in the task or in the issue involved, they would get bored with the performance until their underlinings would finally become so indifferent as to be almost a

[3] See chaps. iii, xxi.

chance matter. They would, nevertheless, still regard certain offenses as more serious than certain other offenses, but their indifference to filling in the schedules would obscure the affective values of the stimuli. It will be noticed that the slope of the linear plot in Figure 69 is not unity. The spread of the scale values on the second occasion is slightly smaller than the spread of scale values on the first filling-in of the schedules. In fact, the slope of the line in Figure 69 is .95, as determined by the method of averages. This deviation of the slope below unity is a measure of a slight degree of indifference to the task on the second occasion as compared with the first. The discriminal error was slightly larger, and the scale separations in terms of the discriminal error, therefore, seem to be slightly smaller on the second occasion. The adjustment of the second set of scale values is made by assuming that the average true scale value remained unaltered by the film and by the filling-in of the schedules. A stretching factor of .95 was introduced into the second set of scale values so that the two sets would be directly comparable, and these two sets of scale values are shown graphically in Figure 70.

If Figure 70 were drawn without this adjustment for the slight enlargement of the discriminal error, the second set of scale values would have a spread slightly smaller than the first. In the present instance the scale value

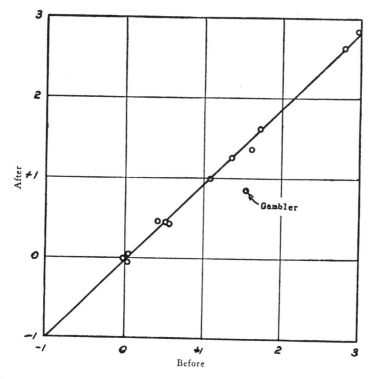

Fig. 69.—Seriousness of crimes as judged by 240 school children in Mendota, Illinois, before and after seeing the film *Street of Chance.*

of "gambler" made such a large jump that the comparison with special regard to this one offense would be practically unaffected by the adjustment.
However, theoretically, the adjustment should be made in order to take account of the fact that the discriminal error is increased by a slight amount of
indifference or boredom with the repetition of the task of filling in the
schedule.[4]

In Figure 70 we have the two sets of scale values placed in proximity for

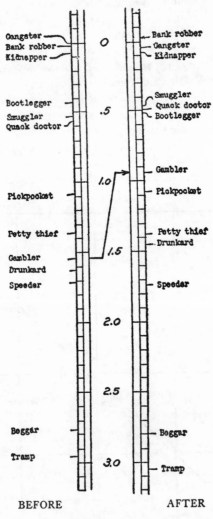

BEFORE   AFTER

FIG. 70.—Seriousness of crimes as judged by 240 school children in Mendota, Illinois,
before and after seeing the film *Street of Chance*.

[4] This stretching factor constitutes, in effect, a measurement of boredom. This psychophysical principle may have many applications in psychological investigation.

direct comparison. It can readily be seen that the scale values do not change markedly, except for "gambler," which was regarded to be a much more serious offense after seeing the film than it was before the performance. The film *Street of Chance* was selected for this experiment because it was thought that it might even make the children more lenient toward gambling, owing to interest in the gambler who was the principal figure in the film. The results of the experiment show clearly that such was not the case. The film had the opposite effect, namely, to make the children regard gambling as more serious than they did before. It is also quite likely that the concept of gambling was altered in the minds of these children. It is not unlikely that many of these children were unfamiliar with high-powered gambling and that the film caused a shift in the cognitive aspects of the concept of gambling as well as in the affective aspects. On the whole, the film may be said to have a socially approved effect on the children because they became more severe in their judgment of gambling even though a gambler was an interesting principal figure in the film.

Another experiment was carried out at Princeton, Illinois, with the film *Hide Out*. This experiment was planned in the same manner as the previous one. The film was shown in the Apollo Theater in Princeton, Illinois, on May 26, 1929. This town also has a population of about 4,000. The film was seen by 254 school children in grades 9 to 12, inclusive. The schedules were filled in during school hours on May 19, 1929, before seeing the film and again on May 27, 1929, the morning after seeing the film. This film was a second choice for the experiment, since it was found that our first-choice film for this experiment had already been shown in this town. The experiment was completed, although we were not satisfied with the film for our present experimental purposes. It involved bootlegging, and we decided to measure attitude toward bootlegging in two ways. The paired comparison schedule of offenses was given to the children before and after seeing the film. "Bootlegger" is included in the list of thirteen offenses, and it was thought that attitudes of the children toward bootlegging might be affected by the film. We also gave this group of children a statement scale about prohibition. The instructions for this statement scale about prohibition were as follows:

A STUDY OF ATTITUDE TOWARD PROHIBITION

Write your name here..

Boy or girl..............................Age..............................Grade..................

This is a study of attitude toward Prohibition. On the other side of this page you will find a number of statements expressing different attitudes toward Prohibition.

√ Put a check mark if you agree with the statement.

✕ Put a cross if you disagree with the statement.

Try to indicate either agreement or disagreement for each statement. If you simply cannot decide about a statement, you may mark it with a question mark.

This is not an examination. There are no right or wrong answers to these statements. This is simply a study of people's attitudes toward Prohibition. Please indicate your own convictions by a check mark when you agree and by a cross when you disagree.

Before each statement in the following list we have recorded its scale value. These scale values were, of course, omitted from the printed schedules that the children filled in. The scale values were used in determining the attitude score of each child toward prohibition. The detailed methods of constructing these scales have also been previously described so that they need not be repeated here.[5]

√ Put a check mark if you agree with the statement.

X Put a cross if you disagree with the statement.

Scale
Values

5.5   1. It is absolutely immaterial whether we have prohibition or not.

8.6   2. The Eighteenth Amendment should be repealed and local option adopted.

6.4   3. Prohibition should come as the result of education, not legislation.

0.8   4. The entire state and national resources should be mobilized for prohibition enforcement.

8.2   5. Liquor should be sold by licensed liquor dealers in restricted amounts.

0.4   6. Prohibition should be retained at all costs.

9.3   7. Prohibition is undesirable because it drives the liquor traffic underground rather than eliminates it.

1.4   8. Possession of intoxicating liquor in any form should subject individuals to punishment.

9.2   9. Prohibition should be a matter to be decided by the individual, and not by the government.

3.5   10. The present prohibition laws are necessary for the good of the United States.

7.5   11. Manufacture of wines and beer in the home should be permitted.

10.4   12. The open saloon system should be universally permitted.

6.9   13. Prohibition is not desirable now because there is not a sufficiently large majority in favor of it to make enforcement effective.

5.6   14. Both good and bad results have come from the Eighteenth Amendment.

10.2   15. Prohibition has been tried and has proved a miserable failure.

3.7   16. While the Eighteenth Amendment is a part of the constitution it should be observed.

7.0   17. Prohibition is good in principle but it is doing more harm than good because it cannot be enforced.

10.2   18. The Eighteenth Amendment should be repealed.

[5] See chap. iii.

2.5   19. Prohibition prevents many accidents and should, therefore, be enforced.

4.6   20. It must be admitted that the Eighteenth Amendment is a restriction of personal liberty, but it has benefitted many people.

3.2   21. The national government should increase its appropriation for prohibition enforcement.

4.4   22. Although not completely satisfactory, the present prohibition is preferable to no prohibition.

3.3   23. The restriction of personal liberty under prohibition is entirely justified by the benefits.

4.5   24. The experiment of prohibition may prove to have some value and may, therefore, be worth trying.

7.8   25. Prohibition is an infringement upon personal liberty.

2.4   26. The effect of prohibition on the national life of America is more than constructive.

2.3   27. The present prohibition laws are satisfactory and their enforcement should be more severe.

1.8   28. Since the liquor traffic is a curse to the human family it must be dealt with by law.

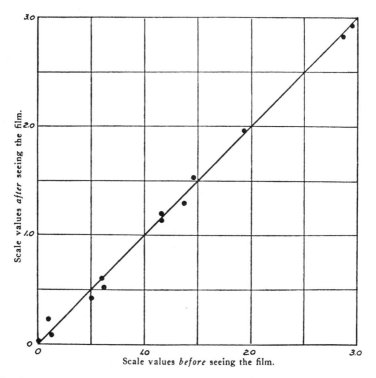

Fig. 71.—Scale of values of 13 crimes by paired comparison for 254 school children in Princeton, Illinois, on prohibition before and after seeing the film *Hide Out*.

These statements were adapted from a Doctor's thesis by Mrs. Hattie Smith.[6]

In Figure 71 we have plotted the "after" scale values of the thirteen offenses against the "before" values. The diagram shows a linear plot with no conspicuous deviations, and hence we conclude that the affective judgments about these offenses were not affected by this film. The slight variations are due merely to chance fluctuations in the experimental proportions. In Figure 72 we have plotted the frequency distributions of scores on the statement scale of attitude toward prohibition before and after seeing the film. The two means are indicated on the base lines of the distributions. This diagram reveals also no significant change in the attitudes of these children toward

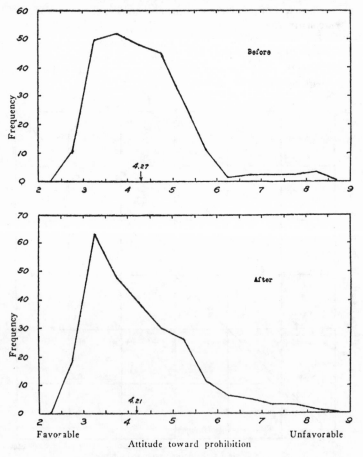

FIG. 72.—Frequency distribution of attitudes of 254 school children in Princeton, Illinois, on prohibition before and after seeing the film *Hide Out*.

[6] H. N. Smith, "The Construction and Application of a Scale for Measuring Attitudes about Prohibition" (Doctor's thesis, University of Chicago).

prohibition as a result of seeing the film *Hide Out*. There was a slight change in the mean scores slightly more favorable toward prohibition after seeing the film than before seeing it, but we do not regard this change to be large enough to be attributed to the film with any degree of certainty. Our conclusion is, therefore, that the film *Hide Out* did not have any measurable effect on the attitudes of the children toward bootlegging or toward prohibition.

These two experiments illustrate the application of two methods of measuring affect, namely, the paired comparison procedure and the statement scale procedure. In other experiments both of these procedures have demonstrated measurable effects of motion-picture films on the social attitudes of school children. In one of the films here discussed, namely, *Street of Chance*, a conspicuous effect of the film was demonstrated. The film made the children more severe in their judgment of gambling than they were before seeing the film. It seems to be evident from these experiments and from others of a similar type that motion pictures can be used to affect the social attitudes of school children and that these effects can be objectively measured.

27 COMMENT

In response to the request of the editors[1] I am glad to write a few comments on the interesting paper by Nettler and Golding on attitude-scale validation. The authors have a worth while idea in proposing what they call the "known-group method of validation." It is certainly plausible to check an attitude scale by comparing attitude scales with the previously known attitudes of the subjects. I shall add only a few minor comments on several points related to this paper.

It might be in order to call attention to the nature of the theoretical problem on which E. D. Hinckley[2] wrote his Doctor's dissertation and to which the authors refer. At the time when Hinckley made his study, the criticism had been made that an attitude scale was determined largely by the attitudes of the people who happened to be selected for sorting the statements. To investigate this problem, Hinckley submitted the same material to three groups of people whose median attitudes could be assumed to be different. They were. The three separate scales so constructed were linearly related with displacement in the means in the expected directions. Since the object of an attitude scale is to obtain a metric which enables us to describe the dispersion of attitude in a group as a frequency distribution, the three scales that Hinckley constructed from three different groups of subjects give the same frequency distribution. The arbitrary origin for the scale was shown to have no effect on the shape of the distribution. The nature of this problem should be understood by students of attitude measurement theory.

It has been a long time since I wrote a paper entitled "Attitudes Can Be Measured."[3] On the question of definition I recall my own experience at the time of my first paper on the possibility of measuring attitudes. When I first decided to extend the psychophysical methods in this field, I defined attitude as the intensity of positive or negative affect for or against a psychological object. A psychological object is any symbol, person, phrase, slogan, or idea toward which people can differ as regards positive or negative affect. It is entirely irrelevant whether the symbol has the same cognitive meaning to all

[1] Reprinted from *American Journal of Sociology*, LII (1946), 39–40.

[2] "The Influence of Individual Opinion on Construction of an Attitude Scale," *Journal of Social Psychology*, III (1932), 283–96.

[3] Chap. xix.

the subjects or whether the object even exists at all. If the psychological object x is some symbol that people argue about as to indorsement or rejection, it is legitimate to study this psychological phenomenon even if it can be shown that the symbol has different meanings to different people. There was a storm of protest against my definition of attitude, and my old friend Professor Faris· joined in the criticism, which was to the effect that the unmeasured residual was somehow the important thing. At one time I even wrote a definition of attitude according to which it was merely the sum total of everything that a man feels and thinks about a psychological object, or words to that effect. I did not have the courage of my conviction in sticking to the original definition. I tried to avoid controversy when it would have been better to ignore it.

Another form of criticism which may still be current was to the effect that an attitude score is supposedly invalid because two people might have the same score in attitude toward some psychological object x in spite of the fact that they have totally different backgrounds and different motivations. This confusion in thinking is not uncommon in the social studies. If we applied the same logic in other situations, we should say, for example, that it is incorrect to describe two men as having the same stature because one of them might be fat while the other is thin. The fact that two individuals have the same score in an attribute is, of course, no guaranty that the antecedents or other related variables are also identical. Much argument about social phenomena is just about at this level.

Perhaps the most commonly debated question in this domain is that of validation of an attitude scale by relating it to overt conduct. It seems to be rather generally assumed that the validity of an attitude scale, with its verbal statements, must be determined by its agreement with overt conduct. This is a mistaken notion. A man may find it expedient to act in a manner which is not indicative of how he feels. In other situations he may find it expedient to make statements which are inconsistent with his preferences. If there is inconsistency between what a man says about x and what he does about x, which shall we take as indicative of his attitude? Perhaps neither. In such a case I should prefer to find out what he says to his best friends when he is not in danger of being quoted. To me, attitude means primarily how a man feels about any designated psychological object. In practical life he may find it expedient to deviate from his own attitude in his public statements or in his actions. What he says and what he does may both be inconsistent with his feelings about x. In giving an attitude scale, one must make the same kind of interpretation as in any other experimental procedure in which there is always a possibility of some systematic or constant error.

In using attitude scales, one must always beware of the social pressures that may induce the subjects to hide their true feelings. As between verbal statements and overt actions, it is probably easier to arrange situations where a man may reveal his attitudes verbally. In dealing with controversial issues about which there is a good deal of pressure, we must depend largely on the skill of the examiner in arranging situations in which people will reveal their attitudes with the least possible distortion. It is a serious error to assume that a man's attitudes are clearly indicated by what he says, merely because that agrees with what he does. Both might be wrong.

There are two lines of experimental development which have not yet been adequately explored in attitude studies. One of the major problems in the construction of an attitude scale is to insure that it is unidimensional. That is a simple factor problem. When I worked on attitude measurement I had not begun to develop multiple factor analysis. The factorial methods should enable us to determine the dimensionality of attitudes in any particular domain and to select for each scale only those statements which belong closely to a single objective dimension.

Another procedure is to use paired comparisons. We found these to be more sensitive than the attitude scales in our studies of the effect of motion pictures on the attitudes of high school children. I refer to the thirty experiments which we carried out under a Payne Fund research grant some fifteen years ago or more. They were never published except in lithoprinted reports. The paired-comparison method should be more often used, but it can also be put in easily manageable equivalent forms such as the psychophysical method of successive intervals.

The authors of this paper refer to criticisms by R. K. Merton[4] about the additive nature of the scores. In the monograph by E. J. Chave and myself[5] there were described two types of attitude scales which depend on the nature of the issue. In one of these the indorsements can be expected to cover the range up to a score point, whereas in the other type the individual indorsements may be expected only at or near the score point. This depends on the nature of the issue.

[4] "Facts and Factitiousness in Ethnic Opinionaires," *American Sociological Review*, V (1940), 13–28.

[5] *The Measurement of Attitude* (Chicago: University of Chicago Press, 1929).